Political
Obligation
and Civil
Disobedience:
Readings

Political Obligation and Civil Disobedience: Readings

edited by

MICHAEL P. SMITH
Boston University

and

KENNETH L. DEUTSCH
The Pennsylvania State University

THOMAS Y. CROWELL COMPANY/NEW YORK
ESTABLISHED 1834

To Our Families

To Our Families

Preface

"Man is born free; and everywhere he is in chains." Jean Jacques Rousseau made this observation two centuries ago, but his words take on renewed significance in our age of crisis. The moral problem of the conditions under which one individual or group should be subject to the power of another is one of the central questions in the history of political thought. This question also forms the basis of such contemporary issues as black power, conscientious objection, war resistance, problems of bureaucratic control of individual choices, and the decline of autonomy in an increasingly technological age.

Precisely because our political order is in a period of crisis, renewed interest in the issue of obligation and resistance is a natural result. Presently, this problem is being given attention in specialized courses and seminars in Political Science, History, and Philosophy. In addition, many core courses in American Politics are requiring students to be familiar with this crucial issue of contemporary political theory. Finally, the "educated public" seeks some understanding of this moral and political problem. The objective of our book is to talk across this wide range of reader interests, without talking down to any of them. Our criteria for the selection of readings are philosophical coherence and lucidity of presentation, so that, hopefully, we may clarify the complex dimensions of the problem of political obligation and civil disobedience.

Therefore, the book presents the various schools of political philosophy which have dealt with this problem. Each school is examined to determine those grounds on which the exercise of political power is justified. The spectrum ranges from the individualistic anarchism of Thoreau to the absolute obedience required by some of the extreme organicists.

The central concern of our book is the moral evaluation of political power. The selected essays and readings deal with various criteria for justifying political controls by subjecting them to scrutiny concerning their sources, their limits, and their ends or purposes. We are also concerned with the *method* by which each school of political thought attempts to *justify* its normative position, that is to say, with the types of reasons and the kinds of thinking (e.g., intuitionism vs. empiricism) used to justify a value position on the question of political obligation. Contemporary arguments about obligation and resistance often fail to delineate the grounds for various positions and their logical and epistemological foundations. This book begins with the premise that no theory of political obligation or civil disobedience can be valid unless the kind of thinking underlying it is sound and reliable. When we examine the conflicting philosophies, this central question of *metaethics* is considered, both in our opening essay and in our remarks preceding each philosophical school.

After having analyzed representative philosophers from six different schools of thought, the third part of the book focuses on the contemporary debate within American democratic theory about questions of civil disobedience in a pluralist democracy. Each of the selections in this part addresses itself to the problem of political order, disobedience and violence in a democratic society.

The final section of the book deals with several contemporary applications of the problem of obligation and disobedience. Such issues as black power and protest, "New Left" resistance in the United States, and alternative responses to bureaucratic control, have been selected to highlight the moral crisis of obligation in our contemporary age of anxiety, estrangement and anomie.

Several persons deserve mention for their direct and indirect contributions to the development of this book. We owe an initial intellectual debt to Felix Oppenheim and Guenter Lewy of the University of Massachusetts, for first calling our attention to some of the problems in political theory dealt with throughout this work. We also wish to thank Herbert J. Addison, Herman Makler, Catherine Wilson, and Kenneth L. Culver of Thomas Y. Crowell, for their editorial advice and assistance during the various stages of manuscript preparation. Our able research assistants Mark A. Pfeiffer, Ann Warren, and Leo Blackburn provided invaluable aid in organizing the various chores necessary to bring the book to fruition. Finally, Professor Smith would like to express his gratitude to the Department of Government at Dartmouth College for generously providing time and support while this manuscript was in preparation and to his former colleagues at Dartmouth, who acted as sounding boards for many of the ideas developed herein. Professor Deutsch wishes to thank Dean William C. Havard of the Virginia Polytechnic Institute for consistently encouraging him to treat normative political theory as a key dimension in the development of a genuine "science of politics."

September, 1971   M.P.S.
                                                       K.L.D.

Contents

III. Civil Disobedience and Democracy 235

IV. Contemporary Applications 311

Political Obligation and Civil Disobedience: Readings

I/The Study of Political Obligation and Civil Disobedience

1/ Perspectives on Obligation and Disobedience

MICHAEL P. SMITH AND KENNETH L. DEUTSCH

INTRODUCTION

Philosophers and social critics throughout much of recorded history have continued to ask one basic question: Why should I accept a situation in which the relations between me and some other individual or group restrict my liberty? "Why should I obey the government?" is a question that has been much more frequently raised throughout the history of political philosophy than "Under what conditions may I disobey my government?" The distinction is a central one. It is a matter of burden of proof. The former question starts from an individualistic bias and assumes that in some sense the individual is above the state. The latter assumes that man is so much a social and political animal and owes such a debt of nurturance and growth to civil society and the state that the burden of proof must rest upon him. The diverse positions people assume in answering these questions constitute their attempts to explain, justify, or condemn *political obligation* or *resistance*.

What are political obligation and resistance? What political and philosophical forms have they taken? How can either be justified? Theories of political obligation ask the question, To whom should the individual ultimately be obligated—to his individual conscience or moral code, to his family or other secondary associations such as his church, or to the social collectivity frequently termed the state? *Political obligation* thus may be defined as the individual's duty or responsibility toward the law, political authority, and civil society.

The second major concept discussed in this book is *civil disobedience*. In this study, civil disobedience will designate the individual acts that fulfill *all* of the following five conditions: [1]

(1) The individual action is *illegal*—i.e., it breaks a law.
(2) It does so *publicly* rather than privately or covertly;

SOURCE: This article is published for the first time in this volume.
[1] For stipulative definitions similar in some but not all respects to this definition, see Hugo Bedau, "On Civil Disobedience," *Journal of Philosophy* (October, 1961); and Carl Cohen, "Essence and Ethics of Civil Disobedience," *The Nation* (March 16, 1964).

(3) To draw public attention to an act, situation, law, or condition perceived by the disobedient to be unjust, illegitimate, or both;

(4) To protest the perceived injustice with a view to changing it for the better;

(5) And with a willingness to suffer the political consequences of the act of defiance.

Some scholars also argue that civil disobedience must be "civil" in another sense: nonviolent. However, a few writers feel that some acts involved in protesting racism or certain acts of sabotage, if they are organized as *selective* violence to *property* but not to *persons,* constitute symbolic objection to the "capitalist system" or some other perceived source of injustice and also fall under the rubric "civil disobedience." But this latter debate will not be resolved here. Clearly not all grounds for civil disobedience are grounds for the resort to violence in an act of *rebellion,* but very likely all grounds that can justify the latter also legitimate the former. Since the subject of this book is the nature, scope, and limits of political obligation and since among the classical responses to perceived tyranny are included violent revolution and even tyrannicide, selective violent actions (e.g., sabotage, looting, and burning) consciously and deliberately conceived as *political* acts are classified as one among an array of possible forms of *political resistance.*

The *forms* of political resistance, therefore, may be taken to include, in ascending order: legal political dissent; civil disobedience (as defined in points 1 through 5 above); confrontationist protest activities, employing the *threat* of violence to bring about rapid social change by generating apprehension over confrontation tactics; selective acts of violence against property, often undertaken to give credibility to threats of wider violence (e.g., SDS-Weatherman tactics); and, finally, violent revolution and political assassination, the most extreme and irreversible forms of political resistance.

The problem of political obligation and resistance is a very ancient one. The classical Greeks were among the first to concern themselves with the justification of political life. Their conception of "balance," right proportion, or harmony played a leading role in their search for something permanent underlying the apparently random flux of sense phenomena. In politics their inquiry took the form of a quest for an immutable law, expressing itself in the customs and ordinances of various peoples and nations. Such a law of "nature" or "rational" law was appealed to as early as the fifth century B.C. as a standard by which to judge the validity of the actions of both subjects and temporal rulers.

A classical case of conflict between this supposedly unwritten, immutable law of "nature," considered to be divine, and a positive royal decree is found in Sophocles' tragedy *Antigone*. Compelled by a "higher" law, the heroine feels obliged in conscience to violate the king's ordinance, though she is well aware she will incur severe punishment. She rejects the king's argument that any act of civil disobedience will invite civil disorder. Thus, for Sophocles, political authority and obedience are *limited* and the justification for this limitation is predicated on the notion of a "higher law," a source of obligation greater than that of the state.

The classical Greeks were to bequeath to Western political tradition still a second answer to the question of political obligation. In Plato's *Crito*, Socrates, depicted as unjustly imprisoned and condemned to death, defends the authority of the law even against the admonition of cherished friends who urge him to violate it and seek safety in escape. Why does Socrates defend the authority of the law he thinks has acted unjustly? If indeed the law is "unjust" and Socrates' freedom is threatened by the law, why not escape? To Socrates and many future theorists and critics, the social collectivity is deemed to be higher in honor and value than any isolated individual. The individual owes a threefold debt to the lawmakers of his city-state, "first because in disobeying [them] he is disobeying his parents; secondly because [they] are the authors of his education; thirdly because he has made an agreement with [them] that he will duly obey [their] commands."

For Socrates, a citizen must be allowed to fully argue his case and attempt to persuade the law-making body to adopt his viewpoint. Yet, if he chooses to argue rather than to leave his city, and if he should fail, nothing remains for him but to accept his fate. He owes an irreparable debt to the community and is bound to it by agreement, a tacit contract. A citizen may be allowed to leave his country if he disagrees with its laws. But if he chooses to stay and reap the benefits of citizenship, he is morally obliged to be loyal and to accept the consequences of his disagreement with any particular law. In sum, for Socrates the individual owes his nurturance and moral education to his society and has contractually promised to obey its laws.

The two classical answers to the question "Why should I obey the state?" offer us two levels of analysis of the moral problem. The first is at the level of *political ethics*. Political ethics "determines and recommends the adoption of certain general principles or rules or standards of conduct." [2] Political ethics asks, "How should men live, or,

---

[2] Felix E. Oppenheim, *Moral Principles in Political Philosophy* (New York: Random House, 1968), p. 8. For the central distinction between *ethical* and *meta-ethical* thinking that underlies the subsequent sections of this essay and the structure of the entire book, we are deeply grateful to Professor Oppenheim. We are also indebted to Robert N. Beck, *Perspectives in Social Philosophy*, (New York: Holt, Rinehart and Winston, 1967).

given a particular situation, should one obey or disobey the law?" The second level of analysis, the level of *political metaethics*, asks the prior question: "Can one justify, and if so, *how* can one justify an ethical position concerning loyalty or disobedience to the actions of the state?"

Most of the conflicting schools of political ethics claim, or at very least assume, that the civil disobedience or strict obedience that they prescribe can be supported by reference to some higher-order standard of goodness (e.g., "self evident" individual natural rights in John Locke).

It is therefore essential to ask by what *method* each philosophical school decides between competing standards of "goodness," between conflicting conceptions of "justice." That is to say, how do we *know* that a political value is "good" and therefore a suitable standard for justifying political obligation or civil disobedience? How do we know, for instance, that communal living is a more appropriate route to "self-actualization" than is the creativity of Henry David Thoreau's recluse? How do we know that the pursuit of the greatest pleasure for the greatest number is a better goal than, say, following one's duty as perceived by one's conscience, even if, on balance, this act produces pain and suffering? How do we discover *which* laws, regimes, and persons are the embodiment of "injustice" and hence ought to be resisted? Do we know *intuitively*—that is to say, immediately, through a sixth sense, a special insight into moral goodness? Or do we know *naturally*, through a teleological understanding of the essential ends or purposes of man and society, which purposes are being fulfilled or violated? Do we know *dialectically*, by gaining a "scientific" insight into the conflict of opposites in history and the ultimate resolution of those conflicts? Or is their *no* cognitive way by which we can discover intersubjective standards of good or right conduct? Do we live in a Sartrean existential theater of the absurd, surrounded by a purposeless and often hostile environment, where our only duty is to choose, consciously, to live according to the dictates of our own personal moral code? All these questions are questions not of ethics but of *metaethics*—and in deciding which school or combination of schools of political obligation makes most sense to him, the individual is also obliged to assess the viability of conflicting underlying metaethical assumptions. Therefore, a central objective of this book is to make the reader aware of *both* levels of analysis: the justification of different principles of political obligation as well as the distinctions between conflicting principles themselves.

THE ETHICS AND METAETHICS OF POLITICAL OBLIGATION AND DISOBEDIENCE

In order to clarify the philosophically relevant positions concerning political obligation and political resistance, the positions are divided into six schools of political ethics: (1) Ethical Naturalism, (2) Organicism, (3) Contractualism and Consent, (4) Utilitarian Individualism, (5) Philosophical Anarchism, and (6) Existentialism. Each school of thought advances an important principle of political ethics vis-à-vis political obligation and civil disobedience within the context of its metaethical assumptions. Thus, in turn, the metaethical assumptions of selected representatives of each school will be examined. This will enable the reader to evaluate for himself the relative political, metaethical, and historical merit of the six philosophies of political ethics.

The Ethical Naturalists [3]

The Ethical Naturalists argue that man has a clearly defined human nature that is part of divine creation or an ordered pattern in nature. The cosmos includes a *law* of nature or "natural law." The natural law is said to prescribe "the good" for man and society. In the view of the Ethical Naturalists, precepts of natural law are not arbitrarily constituted by any group but, rather, are "discovered" by human reason or intuition embedded in the nature of man. This makes the natural law *objective* or independent of particular circumstances and interests, and *universal*, in that it applies to all men in all places. Just as there are universal and objective principles of individual morality for the Ethical Naturalists, so there are objective or natural principles of the social good. Justice "resides" in the very structure of things and of man. Because there is a single definition of man, so can there be but a single definition of justice for all men. Law must be in conformity with these objective principles of morality; it must embody "right reason" to oblige man in conscience. The good state is that state whose laws and activities reflect the law of nature. If the state contravenes the natural law, an individual is morally obliged to disobey. This justification for civil disobedience has had such historical advocates as Sophocles, Thomas Aquinas, and Martin Luther King, Jr. There is a common thread in the Ethical Naturalist positions, namely, that man is morally obliged to obey "just" authority, because the

---

[3] The reader should distinguish our use of the term "naturalist" from its use by some philosophers to designate those who advocate a metaphysics of materialism or pantheism.

state, when ordered by natural law and the social good, serves as the vehicle for the fulfillment of man's nature. Likewise, the state is *limited* by these objective, natural standards since men are obliged to obey *only* "just" authority. If an individual violates the common good by breaking a "just law," the state properly has the right to punish, even to restrain, the offender, so as to maintain order. However, if a ruler contravenes these objective precepts, he *loses* his title of legitimacy and his laws become "unjust." They no longer oblige in conscience.

The Organicists

The Organicists regard the state or community as a higher entity than the individual. The state is a system of law and order that represents the higher self. The individual has a moral obligation to fulfill his "true" or inner self, his "soul" (Hegel's "Reason"), divorced from worldly materialism. His highest fulfillment is to *transcend* his base self, to be free to do only what he *ought* to do rather than what he *wants* to do. Like Platonic idealists, the Organicists hold that the presence of laws and state constraints "forces man to be free" from his base appetites. In obeying the laws of the state, which are designed to promote the virtuous life, man liberates his "rational" self from matter. He fulfills his "true" self.

The relations that the totality of individual "selves" form is an *organism,* the state, in which the sum of the parts cannot be identified with the whole. The whole becomes greater than its parts. The individual becomes subordinated to this "higher self" as represented by the state. The individual, thus, has a moral duty to this "higher self," which is a being superior to the individuals who compose it. Many political theorists and spokesmen for political regimes have argued some form of Organicism. These men range from Rousseau, Hegel, and T. H. Green to Mussolini and Hitler. Their political positions have ranged from direct democracy to hierarchical authoritarianism.

The Social Contract Theory

The contractual theory of the origin of the state is as old as Plato. Its fullest development came in the seventeenth and eighteenth centuries, in the writings of Thomas Hobbes and of John Locke. It is clear that a contract is an agreement, sometimes called a "covenant," between at least two parties. The contracting parties in a "social contract" may be, first, the people and the government; second, individuals with other individuals; or, third, both. The contract doctrine is a kind of analogy drawn from human experience to provide a basis for understanding political obligation. In effect, it says that the kind of relationship established between two private parties in a contract has its analog in the relationships we have as individuals to the government. The contract theory, for example, is certainly one way of stating that the relationship between governed and government is not asymmetrical. That is to say, there may be instances when one of the two parties fails to conform to its agreement. Even the absolutist Hobbes releases the individual from obligation to the state if the "sovereign" is unable to provide order and security. Locke does likewise when the state contravenes the "natural rights" of the individual to life, liberty, and estates.

Utilitarian Individualism

Utilitarians reject the notion of transcendental values. They reject any attempt to deify the state. Jeremy Bentham, the foremost exponent of this school, believed that man did and should serve only two masters: pleasure and pain. Men instinctively obey these "natural" impulses. Whether or not human acts can be labeled good or bad depends for the Utilitarians entirely on the *consequences* to which the acts lead. Thus, Bentham proposed the ethical criterion of *utility*, or usefulness, as a standard by which behavior could be justified. Acts that produce a preponderance of pleasure for human beings he called "good." Acts that reduce pleasure or heighten pain he called "bad."

The Utilitarian view of law and the state is a pragmatic justification of political obligation. The individual is obligated to the state as long as the state provides on balance the means and the goods for the satisfaction of the pleasure principle. In Bentham's terminology, the state must be ordered in such a way as to preserve the greatest happiness for the greatest number. Law is simply a political expression of the combined desires of the people. The law should represent the collective total of individual pleasures. To the extent that it does so, it is sovereign.

Yet those who are charged with upholding or applying the law should be restrained by considerations of expediency and utility. If the state should fail to preserve the greatest happiness for the greatest number, the individual retains the *right* to resist, but it is his *duty* to resist only if he is thoroughly convinced that reform or revolution will bring greater benefits (or material pleasures) to man than those provided by the established power structure. For the Utilitarians, only a theory of knowledge that is *empirical* and a method of reasoning that is inductive can be of value to the individual in his relation to the state. Truth and value can be defined only in pragmatic terms, and, therefore, political obedience or resistance must be judged by their *results* in increasing pleasure and avoiding pain.

Philosophical Anarchism

Philosophical Anarchism is not a new position in political discourse; the Chinese philosopher Lao-tzu in the sixth century B.C. espoused an antistatist position. During the Middle Ages, the more revolutionary interpretations of the Monastic Franciscans had close affinities to Anarchism. More recent examples include Richard Godwin, Leo Tolstoy, and Max Stirner. Today, some segments of the New Left once again have offered the Anarchist ("without rule") thesis.

The popular stereotype portrays the Anarchist as a wild-eyed nihilist bent on creating confusion and disorder in order to cripple and topple the existing social order. This picture fails to do justice to the Anarchist critique of civil society that places the individual on a plane of *almost* complete sovereignty. It is true that some Anarchists categorically deny the right of any government to exercise power, but most Philosophical Anarchists simply oppose government based on force or coercion. Most Anarchists assume that human nature is inherently good. They argue that men possess a fundamental sense of decency, which impels them to cooperate voluntarily in programs that are reasonable. The Anarchists believe that organized systems of power pervert or inhibit the basically noble human impulses.

A prominent American literary figure of the nineteenth century, Henry David Thoreau, exemplifies the Anarchist crusade against organized authority. Invoking the doctrine of *individual nullification,* he preached and practiced a program of civil disobedience. It was his conviction that individual conscience stood above all law and government and that the individual had a *personal obligation* to disobey any rule or statute that his conscience could not affirm. Thoreau contended that an individual standing for what he considered right was more worthy than the largest of majorities standing for the wrong. He, therefore, upheld the Jeffersonian maxim that the best government is one that governs least.

In essence, most Anarchists share the conviction that moral obligation derives from a principle of "conscience" that transcends the sphere of political power relationships in worldly affairs. Morality is not established by political authority and does not necessarily reside in human law. Morality can never be achieved by force. In the final analysis, what is "good" and "right" is not validated by the political power of any given state; the ultimate measure of "justice" is individual knowledge and conscience. Philosophical Anarchists view the state not as some kind of organism but, rather, as a machine for coercion. Whoever wields this coerceive machine is likely to be corrupted by power. When the state has disappeared, Anarchists foresee the end of coercion, mechanization, and uniformity.

Existentialism: The Problem of Choice

Existentialism is a comparatively new school of thought within the Western tradition. Such philosophers as Soren Kierkegaard, Jean-Paul Sartre, and Albert Camus have been concerned with the loss of individuality as the result of mass culture and technology and with the consequent alienation of the human person from himself as well as from his associates and productions. The loss of meaning in life through the division of the human spirit is the existentialist's abiding concern especially because of the persistent experience of despair within his social and political life.

The Existentialists proffer an important philosophical alternative to some of the other schools discussed above. This attitude is directed toward human existence. Previous philosophies discussed man in terms of some essential human nature derived from reason (e.g., Naturalists) or pure forms (e.g., Organicists). The existentialist is in opposition to such traditional conceptualism. He believes that *what* man is can be determined only from *how* he acts. That is to say, man's essence can be found only in his *concrete existence*. Therefore, Existentialists take into account the whole fabric of human endeavor. In effect, each individual must create his own essence, or character, throughout his lifetime by his free choice of interests and actions, whether they be based on "reason," "emotion," "basic drives," or some combination of the three. Thus existence *precedes* essence since the latter is not completed until life with its endless series of choices is terminated by death.

Albert Camus, the French literary figure and Nobel prize winner, analyzes the possibility of *rebellion* as the basis for an analysis of man's social existence. To Camus, rebellion against constituted authority is basic to man; it removes the individual from his solitary condition. If a man makes a decision to rebel, it is because he has made the decision that human society *has* some value; he is released from despair. Rebellion is not nihilistic. The rebel asks for reasons for living. He fights to preserve his very integrity. Rebellion is, in effect, the secular will not to surrender.

Nonetheless, for Camus, there must be limitations to rebellion. The violent rebel may destroy *life* in the attempt to translate his own notion of absolute justice into material political terms. Rebellion without limitation often means slavery. The rebel must recognize limits. Some element of realism is necessary to every political ethic, even an ethic of rebellion. The potential rebel must keep in mind that without some order, when rebellion is viewed as the *sole* value, there are duties but no rights. Without some pattern for ordering duties, rights, and obligations, the possibility of realizing the rebel's values is denied. Rebellion, prudence, and obligation are, for Camus, in a state of tension and also tragically interrelated. They are conditions for and limitations of each other.

It is the view of the authors that each of the schools of political obligation and civil disobedience discussed in this book brings to the reader's attention some aspect of human relationships that are politically salient and warrant consideration when any person develops his own normative position on this basic issue of political philosophy. For example, the Ethical Naturalists warn the individual not to consider the law of the state as absolute with no moral criterion for evaluation. The contract theorists uphold the notion that, to be binding, authority must rest on the consent of the governed. The Organicists stress the value of human interdependence within the community. The Utilitarian argues that the state must meet some human *needs*, and it is better conceived of as a means rather than an end in itself. The Anarchists decry the steady concentration of political power and criticize the tendency to standardize and level out. In its place they proffer the creativeness of the free individual. Finally, Existentialists dramatize the alienation prevalent in contemporary postindustrial society and warn of the need for man to choose in order to escape despair. It is not claimed that these philosophies are of equal merit. It is argued that each position must be given serious consideration if one is to attempt to take into account most of the central concerns of human life when he develops an ethical position on the issue of obligation and resistance.

However, the individual choice of *which* values concerning this issue are most acceptable must also be based on defensible metaethical foundations. This is doubly important because philosophers whose ethical positions on the question of political obligation are poles apart may share the *same* metaethical perspective. Both Locke and Rousseau, for example, are metaethical *intuitionists*. Both believe that their political ethics can be intersubjectively justified by reference to certain immediately obvious, self-evident, intuitively comprehensible principles. Thus Locke defends his doctrine of "natural rights" and limited government on the metaethical appeal to intuitive moral reason that "teaches all men who will but consult it" that the principle of equal natural rights is "evident in itself." Rousseau's metaethical appeal is also to a special inner moral faculty, accessible to all men, "written in the depths of [man's] heart by conscience and reason."

A central difficulty with relying on intuitionist metaethics as a basis for a theory of political ethics is well brought out by the following illustration. Normative concepts such as Rousseau's community, "general will," and belief in self-realization in a civil society with no conflicting private loyalties sharply contrast with Locke's individualism, majority rule, and concept of self-realization through the pursuit of private interests and the acquisition of private property. Similarly, Rousseau claims that the individual has an obligation even unto death to obey the commands of the "general will" qua "general will" that are intended to fully civilize him. In contrast, Locke countenances the right of revolution by a majority if what he regards as basic natural rights to life, liberty, and estates, collectively termed "property," are violated by the constituted authority. Despite these striking normative contrasts on the question of the purposes of the state and the political obligation owed the state, both Locke and Rousseau attempt to morally justify their positions by laying claim to the intuitive obviousness of their conflicting cherished values.

Ethical Naturalists and Utilitarians share the belief that the "true" nature of man and society or the correct standards of justice can be objectively (i.e., intersubjectively) demonstrated through use of "reason" and distinguished from "false" ends and standards. They differ, however, with respect to the *process* or *method* by which the rational faculty arrives at its conclusions and obtains certain knowledge of good or right conduct. In brief, the metaethical theories that underlie the Ethical Naturalist school of political obligation may be *intuitionistic*, as in the case of the immediate apprehension of final ends or "right reason" in Aquinas. Or they may hold that through *natural reason* and reflection *alone* (e.g., Aristotelian teleology) or with the help of religious *faith* (e.g., Martin Luther King, Jr.) man can acquire a certain cognitive knowledge of the ends and purposes "natural" to man and his world. By implication he can also acquire reliable knowledge of "unnatural" and therefore bad conditions, laws, and societies. For Bentham and the Utilitarians, the extent to which a society is fulfilling man's "nature" by maximizing pleasure and minimizing pain can be determined by reason aided by *empirical* methods. The hedonistic principle itself is justified by an appeal to a descriptive definition of the ethical term *happiness* in terms of the descriptive term *pleasure*. Thus Utilitarian ethics becomes the empirical science of measuring the pleasurable and painful aspects of human life.

The implications of the various schools of metaethics underlying Ethical Naturalism and Utilitarianism are clear. If man can acquire certain knowledge of right moral principles either through some basic "sixth sense" or by reason, reflection, or calculation of man's "natural needs whether biological, social or spiritual," [4] and if these principles, once discovered, *contradict* the positive laws of his society, his moral

---

[4] Mulford Q. Sibley, "On Political Obligation and Civil Disobedience," *Journal of the Minnesota Academy of Science*, XXXIII (1965), 68.

and political obligation is clearly to *resist* those laws, publicly to point out the discrepancy between justice and reality, to obey his "well formed" conscience. In brief, the citizen's duty to obey the laws turns on the degree to which they express man's basic human nature, whether intuitively, scripturally, scientifically, or teleologically discovered.

Interestingly, Ethical Naturalist theorists of political obligation have had disagreements among themselves at *both* the ethical and the metaethical level; that is to say, they have disagreed as to *what* "nature" is telling them and as to *how* they 'have arrived at their moral judgments. For example, at the ethical level, Martin Luther King, Jr., appeals to natural law to support his conclusion that segregation is inimical to the development of the human personality and that *all* instances of conflict between the individual conscience and the laws of the state should be resolved in favor of the former. In contrast, other Ethical Naturalists such as Aristotle and Aquinas have argued respectively that "natural slavery" is justified and that only *extreme* cases of perceived political injustice can justify disobedience because man needs *order* to develop his personality and because acts of resistance or rebellion may produce disproportionate "scandal" and "disorder." At the metaethical level, as pointed out above, Ethical Naturalists may claim to arrive at their certain knowledge of man's "natural" ends either through an intuitive process of "rational insight" (Aquinas), natural reason aided by religious insight (King), or natural reason alone (Aristotle).

Some of the political philosophers discussed in this book (e.g., David Hume, Thomas Hobbes, and Jean-Paul Sartre) have assumed a *noncognitivist* metaethical position. Noncognitivists believe that basic ethical principles, including principles of political obligation, *cannot* be shown to be objectively true or false. Ethical principles are *expressive* of subjective preferences or attitudes and, unlike factual judgments, possess no "cognitive status." Thus, according to the noncognitivist school, two individuals may agree on all the facts of a case in question and yet one may uphold and the other oppose the ethical principles of civil disobedience or the right of resistance.

For example, according to Hobbes, man calls that which is the object of his *appetite* good, "there being . . . [no] common rule of good and evil, to be taken from the nature of the objects themselves." From this metaethical and psychological assumption of subjective egoism is derived the need for civil society, absolute civil order, and almost unlimited political obligation—to free man from the state of nature where, in Hobbes's words, "his private appetite is the measure of good and evil." Thus, irreconcilable moral conflicts may be settled only by authoritative positive legal pronouncements. Except for the ultimate right of self-preservation, which no man can relinquish, Hobbes refused to countenance any disobedience to positive laws, no matter how unjust the individual might subjectively judge them to be.

Yet, starting from noncognitivist assumptions, it might likewise be argued that since no objective standard of morality can be found intuitively or in human nature, no person or group has the right to impose its particular standards of morality on the community or world at large and only the laws that in some way embody or represent all relevant value perspectives deserve obedience.

Finally, a modern Existentialist noncognitivist like Sartre might argue that given the absurdity and finality of the external environment, man cannot transcend his situation but must *create* his own values by making personal choices in the immediate present. The only moral and political obligation recognized by the Sartrean existentialists is to live the *authentic* life, to choose one's own values— whether these dictate stoic passivity or political rebellion. Sartrean existential man is allowed no appeal to higher authority, intuitive insight, or scientific proof to bolster his position. Nothing can relieve man of personal responsibility for making his own decisions. His only obligation is to have the courage of his convictions, whatever the consequences, wherever his convictions carry him.

The inclusion of the metaethical dimension in the study of political obligation is necessary as a tool of analysis. It provides the individual with an understanding of the *bases* used by both government and citizen to justify their ethical positions in contemporary political discourse generally and on the problem of political obligation in particular. Which values respecting this problem are most acceptable must be based upon defensible metaethical as well as ethical foundations if an individual is to convince his fellow citizen of the rectitude of his position.

THE VIETNAM WAR: A CASE STUDY
IN THE CONFLICT OF MORAL PRINCIPLES

Major political and moral issues such as the Vietnam War can serve to highlight the problem of the justification of obligation or resistance within a particular political system. Representative philosophers from the six schools discussed above, utilizing their ethical and metaethical positions, could face the moral question of the Vietnam War in the following way:

ISSUES IN THE VIETNAM WAR	PHILOSOPHICAL CRITIQUE
1. The executive has exceeded his prerogatives.	1. Contract Theorists: Presidential conduct of the war has abridged legislative rights and violated the Constitution.
2. Intervention in a civil war.	2. Organicists: One social body has no right to intervene in the domestic problems of another.
3. Authoritarian practices of the Thieu regime.	3. Philosophical Anarchists: Not only is all war coercive generally, but this war especially contributes to greater repression *within* South Vietnam.
4. Over forty thousand Americans are dead. Are the issues or goals advanced by the government worth the cost?	4. (a) Utilitarians: Too many American families are suffering domestic pain. The goals cannot return these dead, and more deaths are not worth the military investment. (b) Philosophical Anarchists: Individual conscience should decry any situation that results in such a great loss of human life.
5. Morality of the means. Consider the history of napalming, civilian bombings, and the My Lai incident.	5. (a) Ethical Naturalists: These methods are so brutal as to violate standards of natural law and human dignity. (b) Existentialists: Soldiers and bureaucrats who follow blindly the orders of their superiors are in a state of despair. Human choice is abridged by such a condition.
6. No real threat to our national interest (security or welfare) is at stake.	6. Utilitarians: If the war does not enhance our security or general happiness, why continue such a charade?
7. Vacillation of our stated goals. Are we to protect freedom, self-determination, or our own national interests?	7. Ethical Naturalists: Our goals or purposes must be in accord with immutable standards of morality. Such vacillation of our purposes weakens our moral position in justifying a policy because it lacks a clearly articulated "just cause."

ISSUES IN THE VIETNAM WAR

PHILOSOPHICAL CRITIQUE

8. Consider the costs in domestic unrest, in political priorities, in national character, and in international prestige.

8. (a) Utilitarians: This policy is creating for the participants more present pain than could ever be matched by future pleasure.
(b) Organicists: The social fabric is being destroyed and our communal consensus has attenuated.

9. Increasing militarization of our domestic society and the creation of a "garrison state" is, and may continue to be, the result of the policy.

9. (a) Existentialists: Such militarization will create greater isolation, bureaucratization, and dehumanization than has existed. This, in turn, may lead to a more submissive citizen, perhaps an automaton who will eschew the need for human choice.
(b) Philosophical Anarchists: Such militarization enhances the prospects for greater domestic control, which will delimit individual or group spontaneity.

Some might, of course, wish to discuss possible moral justifications for the Vietnam War in terms of utility or individual moral duty. What is necessary for the reader to consider is the importance and scope of the problem of moral justification in any vital issue of contemporary political discourse.

POLITICAL OBLIGATION IN A PLURALIST DEMOCRACY

It is alleged by some philosophers and political commentators that, in a "democratic" polity, political obligation has a special merit and that civil disobedience has a particular demerit. For example, the British ethical and political philosopher Thomas Hill Green has stated:

Supposing then the individual to have decided that some command of a "political superior" is not for the common good, how ought he to act in regard to it? In a country like ours, with a popular government and settled methods of enacting and repealing laws, the answer of common

sense is simple and sufficient. He should do all he can by legal methods to get the command cancelled, but till it is cancelled he should
conform to it.[5]

Like Green, such contemporary critics as Justice Abe Fortas have
stated that part of being a good citizen in a democracy requires the
citizen to adhere to the principles of democratic authority. Citizens
should obey that authority when decisions are made by elected representatives and ultimately by majority vote, in conformity with recognized procedural rules. In this view the citizen's obedience to decisions is required as long as there are (a) free discussion, (b) further
scheduled votes, and (c) the potential to form new majorities. A good
citizen in a continuing democracy will not withhold obedience to a
decision democratically arrived at. If he does withhold his obedience,
he does not act as a good democrat.[6]

Other social critics have pointed to the wide discrepancy between
democratic theory and existing political practices in a procedural democracy. They have shown that there exists a basic inequality in political resources. This is especially acute because of unequal wealth
and unequal access to the media of communications. The process required to change laws is cumbersome, formalistic, and slow in an age
of rapid technological change. The Supreme Court in our own system
is likewise often slow and too limited in time and jurisdiction to deal
with the masses of cases involving administrative decisions. Therefore, civil disobedience might be justified to focus public attention on
social and moral problems by public acts of defiance, which can capture access to the media through symbolic protest activity such as
draft-card burnings.

Both Fortas and his many critics, however, assume that once the
channels of communication are open to all, once the courts and the
legislature can be made more responsive through heightened efficiency or concern with the articulated issues, and once political resources are made more equitable, then democratic man must still be
obliged to obey all laws "democratically" arrived at.

Moreover, both of these positions tend to view *government* as the
primary, if not the sole, source of social tyranny. This perspective
overlooks the possibility that powerful and well-organized social and
economic groups can become as tyrannical as any governmental elite.
It also overlooks the very real difficulty of persuading majority opinion to accept an unpopular position. In so doing, this perspective

---

[5] Thomas Hill Green, *Lectures on Principles of Political Obligation* (London:
Longmans, Green, 1960), p. 111.
[6] For a powerful criticism of this position, see Rex Martin, "Civil Disobedience,"
Ethics (January 1970), 123–139.

overlooks a possible *justification* for state action in cases where the government seeks to regulate unbridled group conflict or even to *protect* individual civil liberties from abuse by powerful "private governments" or by majority tyranny.

Advocates of "democratic pluralism" actually tend to lionize the role of the *group* in political life. They argue that a shared group responsibility for making political decisions operates to bolster the individual's sense of political efficacy by simplifying his alternatives, narrowing the range of his interests, and providing him with advice, information, and a sense of belonging or community. By this reasoning, if the individual feels personally effective and secure as a result of his group memberships, he will be less likely to seek psychological gratifications through quiescent obedience to political authority.

To what extent does the practice of democratic pluralism live up to the abstract model of pluralist theorists? Thus far, the study of political obligation has led to the restatement of a classic dilemma. If the individual abandons political liberty and self-direction for the sake of personal security, authoritarian government is the likely result. If he exercises his self-will and his liberty to the fullest, he may opt for anarchy.

But democratic pluralism in practice poses still a third possibility. It forces the individual to face a trilemma: If the pluralist democrat exercises his freedom *in moderation* he may become a slave to majority opinion, either in society at large or *within* his group; i.e., the social groups that lighten the individual's burden may *shape* as well as reflect individual preferences. Moreover, it is always possible for *dominant* social groups in a political democracy to employ the mystique of majoritarianism to justify the imposition of their mores on society at large; and it is always possible for *any* social group whose membership are not unanimous in their preferences to tyrannize over a minority of *its* members.

It is quite clear that in practice democratic pluralism has failed to live up to the promise of pluralist theory. In at least three senses, pluralism fails to come to grips adequately with the problem of political tyranny. First, the mystique of majoritarianism has often been used to justify the enthronement of standards of conventional wisdom in determining the informal ground rules for "legitimate" political participation. As several recent critics of pluralism have pointed out, there is no guarantee that all major groups in a pluralist society will succeed in gaining political access and legitimacy. And the cards are quite often stacked against groups lacking the resources to organize effectively and against groups seeking to articulate grievances of a psychological or "utopian" nature that fall outside the traditional economic dimension of interest-group liberalism. Members of such groups, continually frustrated in their aspirations, are certainly unlikely to gain a sense of efficacy and control from group membership. Indeed, alienation or a persecution complex is the more likely by-product of continuously closed access.

A second major shortcoming of pluralism in practice is that, in a pluralist democracy, societywide tyrannical majorities are often displaced by dominant majorities *within* societal groups. What is to be done with the 49 per cent of the members of a group or organization who disagree with the policy preferences or the vision of the good society articulated by the group's leaders or by a majority of its members? Or, for that matter, what is to be done with a majority of a group's members when inadequate mechanisms exist even to secure the "representativeness" of the group leadership?

Finally, it is clear that the sheer size and geographical dispersal of many groups in contemporary America contradict the ethic of "belonging," mutual support, and solidarity mentioned earlier as possible sources of relief from the agonizing burden of political obligation and disobedience. To what extent and by what means can the dues-paying local member of even the national Chamber of Commerce organization experience a sense of efficacy and control over the economic policies of the national government? To what extent do the mechanisms used by the national leaders of his organization resemble the techniques, say, of Fyodor Dostoevsky's Grand Inquisitor? (Viz., "Today people are more than ever persuaded that they are completely free, yet they have brought their freedom to us and laid it humbly at our feet.") Stated differently, to what extent does the relinquishment of active citizenship, of the individual participatory ethos, for the sake of political success defined in terms of "earthly bread," manifest Dostoevsky's classical tension between individual political liberty and material happiness?

In the final analysis, then, pluralism in practice leaves many questions unanswered. It solves the paradox of freedom for some groups but not for others. It actually expands the danger of majority tyranny by opening up the possibility of many coercive majorities *within* social groups. It loses sight of "public interest" goals and produces remote, impersonal interest-group bureaucracies. Finally, it is one dimensional; that is to say, it defines political success solely in terms of maximizing the material well-being of group members and typically organizes individuals around their *productive* roles.

In conclusion, no completely satisfactory answer to the trilemma of freedom and obligation has been found. Nonetheless, at least the range of alternative consequences facing the individual in his relationship to society and the state has been more clearly delineated. Perhaps attempts to reduce the perennial problem of political obligation to a single formula cannot succeed. But the purpose of political philosophy in moments of social crisis is to call our attention to criteria that in present circumstances are forgotten, overlooked, or denied yet must be acknowledged if any of the values associated with justice, liberty, or community are to be realized. Each school of political philosophy has tried to clarify some politically salient aspect of human relationships that, as the occasion requires, one may need to recognize and defend—be it the consent of the governed, human interdependence, social utility, or individual dignity.

The individual's obligation to consider questions of obedience and resistance is not relinquished by the fact that he is a citizen of a "democratic" political system. Perhaps, with the range of choices more clearly in mind, the individual is as prepared as he can ever become to face up to the paradoxes of political freedom and obligation.

2 / On Political Obligation and Civil Disobedience

MULFORD Q. SIBLEY

The United States, during the past five years, has given birth to new versions of very old issues in dramatizing such central questions as the bases of political obligation and the legitimacy or illegitimacy of civil disobedience. In Birmingham, while in prison, Martin Luther King wrote his *Letter from Birmingham Jail* in which he restated the justification for deliberate disobedience of law; and in Berkeley, California, a similar problem was posed during the autumn of 1964 by leaders of the greatest student revolt of the present generation. At the same time, public officials seek to restate the duty to obey law, apparently without qualification. Thus, the late President Kennedy, in 1962, maintained that Americans were not free to choose the laws they should obey (N.Y. *Times*, 1962:22); and Senator Goldwater, in the campaign of 1964, denounced those who, in his judgment, were condoning both direct action in general and civil disobedience in particular (N.Y. *Times*, 1964:12). Recent articles, moreover, have given a certain popularity to the issue (Bedau, 1961; Cohen, 1964; Frankel, 1964); and dry questions that a few years ago

SOURCE: *Journal of the Minnesota Academy of Science*, XXXIII, 1 (1965), 67–72. Reprinted by permission of the author and the publisher.

seemed to be appropriate only for desiccated professors of political philosophy have suddenly taken on new life.

There is, of course, a long tradition that may cast considerable light on the current discussion of political obligation and civil disobedience. This paper proposes to re-examine certain aspects of that tradition, to relate them to the contemporary debate, and to vindicate both the right and the obligation of civil disobedience.

Three points are developed. First, the long-standing disquietude about the claims of the State to our obedience is examined. We seek to illustrate this by reference to certain classical statements of St. Augustine, and to adapt these statements to the uncertainties of others and to the language of our own day. Secondly, we remind ourselves of the various doctrines that, in light of the disquietude, have been advanced to provide a basis for political obligation. Noting the merits and weaknesses of each, it is argued that no one of them furnishes an adequate foundation for political obligation. Thirdly, building upon the fact of uneasiness and such insights as are provided by the several accounts of obligation, the attempt is made to restate a basis for obligation and to develop criteria for judging when civil disobedience is legitimate.

THE DISQUIETUDE ABOUT LEGITIMACY

The anxiety concerning legitimacy may be illustrated if we recall the dilemmas confronted by St. Augustine, the fifth-century Church Father, who sought to evaluate all political systems in terms of their justice. On the one hand, he conceived of a city of God, whose members are destined for salvation, who are pure in heart, and who are members of the heavenly city. On the other side are those condemned to spiritual death, who have turned away from God, and whose destiny is presumably hell. The cities or states of human history stand between the city of God and the city of the damned, since any given historical society will be composed of both the saved and the condemned. Out of this commingling of heavenly and nonheavenly citizens arises political authority to provide a kind of uneasy peace pending the coming of the end of history, the date of which no man knows and which may be imminent or remote in time.

What puzzles Augustine—and presumably all those exercised about the issue of political obligation—is whether any distinction can be made between and among the types of political authority he has known or about which he has read. Are all of equal value and equally entitled to obedience? Or are some legitimate and others illegitimate? If so, how do we distinguish between the legitimate and the illegitimate? In Augustine's thinking, political authority did not exist in Eden but is the result of the necessity for coercion that accompanies the Fall of Man. Can distinctions be made between and among historical societies, so that one feels a greater sense of obligation to some than to others—always keeping in mind that all grow out of wickedness?

Augustine tried out two alternative answers (Bk. II, Ch. 21; Bk. IV, Ch. 4; Bk. XIX, Ch. 21, 23, and 24). His first point of departure was Cicero's statement that a people is a multitude of men associated together by a common acknowledgment of right and a community of interests. Augustine interpreted "right" to mean "true justice." And true justice includes not only giving to each man his due and to society what belongs to it, but also genuine worship of the one true God. Taking these requirements together, he concluded that there had been in reality no just society in history. Yet without justice, he asked, what is any kingdom but a great robbery? *Remota justitia quid regna nisi magna latrocinia?* From this point of view, no historic political society has satisfied the Augustinian criterion of legitimacy and, inferentially, our obligation to all such societies reaches the vanishing point.

But he tended to withdraw in horror from what seems to be the logic of his position and he asked whether there may not be a more reasonable or, perhaps, usable definition of a people. He found the clue to his second conception in the fact that while all historic political societies have been little better than "robberies," it is equally true that even robber bands have at least one of the characteristics of Cicero's *populus:* They are associations of men united by the objects of their love and with rules for the distribution of spoils. Although they may not be just in terms of their ends, they do and must provide a certain ordering—if only to carry out robbery efficiently and to distribute the spoils according to regular rules—and order is valuable regardless of its goals. At least, it is better than disorder. Or, as a modern scholar has put it, there is "law" even among the "outlaws" (Merriam, 1934: Ch. III). Every robber band, Augustine suggested, is a little kingdom and, contrariwise, every kingdom is an enlarged robber band. Both provide a measure of order and, perhaps, this is about all we can expect in this world of fallen men. The implication of this view would seem to be that every well established power structure, since it at least establishes order, has a certain claim on our obedience. By contrast with his true justice test of legitimacy, Augustine's second-level definition would seem to open the way to a well nigh unqualified notion of obligation. And, indeed, he seemed to suggest precisely this: The only ground for disobedience is presumably a specific Scriptural command (Deane, 1963:147, 89, 90).

Nor is St. Augustine the only great thinker to give evidence of a profound uncertainty over the degree of legitimacy present in political societies. Although St. Thomas Aquinas seemed to think that even relatively bad governments may be implicitly seeking good ends, he appeared to imply the very mixed character of all political rule and he envisioned occasions on which men may have to consider disobedience. Luther was bothered by the contrast between the maxims of the Sermon on the Mount, on the one hand, and the apparent imperatives of statecraft, on the other. Rousseau appeared to think that most historic political authority has been—at least in considerable measure—simply a disguise for illegitimate ends. As for the Marxist tradition, it is Augustinian in its despair about any possibility of congruence between "justice" and historic states, but hopeful in its belief that the historic process itself will provide a "solution" by wiping out all class-biased (and therefore unjust) organizations, thus opening the way for a true morality.

Obviously, the disquietude expressed by many thinkers has a foundation in our actual experience. Governments that exist presumably to promote peace actually encourage war on a large scale (Cook, 1962). Rulers established to help guarantee freedom tend to destroy it. Governing classes placed in control of the state machinery by an originally democratic process become oligarchies and thus restrict or destroy the process.

Under circumstances of this kind, can one wonder at Augustine's despair or be surprised by his tendency to state, in effect, that any kind of order must be obeyed, since it is at least an order? Can we escape his seeming conclusion that in effect all political societies are, relative to true justice, at about the same level, and that it is hopeless to differentiate between and among them with any certainty?

LEGITIMACY AND OBLIGATION

Despite this ubiquitous disquietude about the possibility of distinguishing political societies from one another, the tradition of political philosophy has obviously made some attempt to do so.

The Naturalist View

Perhaps the most persistent effort to construct a theory of political obligation has been that of what we might call the naturalists. Although there are many rather diverse views included under this designation, they have in common the notion that man's true ends can be rationally determined, can be separated from false ends, and can furnish a foundation for natural law whose precepts will provide grounds for distinguishing between legitimate and illegitimate rule. By this account, man is a political animal whose ends are naturally fulfilled only within a political society. That system of rule is binding, then, which conforms in its main outlines to the precepts of Nature conceived as a rationally discovered system of ends or goals. Beginning with such presumably self-evident propositions as that we should seek the good and avoid the evil, the naturalists then ask what the good for man may be held to be. Their answer turns on an examination of his natural needs, whether biological, social, or spiritual. From these needs they deduce such principles as that order is essential; that government is necessary for order; that legitimate government is that that enhances achievement of goals natural to man and discourages ends that are unnatural. The individual's obligation to obey positive law turns on the degree to which it expresses natural law, or at least does not contradict it.

One difficulty with natural law conceptions in differentiating between legitimate and illegitimate systems of rule is that the distinction between natural and unnatural ends is not easy to determine. What is natural tends to be a function of the culture, and objective standards, where they may be held to exist, are ambiguous at best. Is the government of the United States legitimate, for example? The present Constitution was adopted by procedures that violated the law of the land at the time. Is not the admonition to act according to positive law a principle of natural law? Why, under natural law principles, am I obliged to obey the Constitution? Some naturalists might say that because it has existed for a long time and has been generally obeyed, "prescription" makes the government established under it legitimate, hence obligatory. But does this imply that anything old— e.g., the institution of war—carries with it the odor of moral sanctity simply because of that fact? This is simply one example of the many questions on which naturalist views seem to cast a light that is uncertain at best.

Contract

According to another position, contract provides the basis for obligation. Although many versions of the contract theory have existed— among them those of Hobbes, Locke, Rousseau, for example—they have in common the notion that each of us has made an agreement with his fellows to obey a government—either under certain specified conditions and limitations (as with Locke) or without qualification.

The objections to contract theories are numerous. When did members of the present generation contract with one another to obey the rules of a document drawn up in 1787? When did the British agree to obey the government of William the Conqueror—that "bastard" leading an "armed banditti," as Tom Paine used to call him—after 1066? Even if we maintain that a given generation agrees to submit itself to political rule, why is this alleged contract binding on future generations who have made no such specific agreement? Nor does the doctrine of an implicit consent stated by such thinkers as Socrates (in Plato's *Crito*) and Locke meet the issue, for by the time I have reached the age of discretion, I have been so conditioned by the culture and language of a nation that my decision to remain in that nation is hardly a free one.

Yet another important question is whether we should regard the keeping of promises—a central value imperative under contract theories—as the supreme value. To be sure, the principle that promises should be fulfilled is an important one, but it would seem doubtful that it ought to take precedence over all other considerations in making up one's mind about what is right at a given moment; and if one accept this notion, promises should be only one factor in making a decision on what is right. My promise can never be interpreted as one committing me to obey under all circumstances and regardless of my sense of right at a particular time.

Utility

Some have asserted that obligation might be based on utility. If the government promotes more pleasure than pain, said the nineteenth-century utilitarians, and assuming that pleasure is equivalent to "good" and pain to "evil," then I am obliged to obey, since it is to my interest to do so. The great merit of a utilitarian view is that it attempts to make less vague such often rationalizing formulae as "vital interests" and "general welfare." On the other hand, it is obvious that even a utilitarian scheme must begin with propositions not derived from utility; and since "obligation" tends to be identified with "interest," the problem of obligation, as Carritt has pointed out (Carritt, 1935), is really evaded or ignored.

Organicism

Organicist positions have something in common with naturalist statements but need not put their viewpoint in terms of a natural law. In the tradition stemming from Rousseau and Hegel, and embracing, to some extent, such thinkers as Green, the general will of the moral community binds me because it is the true or real will of myself. Thus I am obliged to obey because I have a moral duty to transcend the limitations of my "empirical" self and to release the "true self" that is struggling to be born—a self, purged of egoism, that understands that only obedience to the general will can make for moral progress. My empirical self, which operates in terms of self-interest, can be transcended only by being constantly reminded through the law of the unselfish being that is constantly at war with it. Out of this conflict arises the distinction between mere "interest" and "obligation." The former means unlimited freedom to express my present self, the latter the freedom to do what I ought in terms of my rational self.

There are many difficulties with the organicist position; among them is the problem of discovering the identity of the true self. This problem is similar to the question confronted by the naturalist when he attempts to find out the meaning of right reason or the ends of Nature. Does the law of every historical state, for example—no matter what its contents may be—automatically identify my true self? The historical state notoriously reflects compromise and clashing economic interests. In what sense, then, can it be said to speak for my true or moral self?

Evaluation of Views

The upshot of all this is that all traditional accounts of the basis of political obligation are inadequate in one or more respects. At the same time, if we do not push them too far, each of them gives us an insight into the complexity of treating obligation, and each, moreover, points up one aspect of the problem. Naturalist views surely reflect an important desideratum for any doctrine of legitimacy—a nonarbitrary, nonconventional set of standards by which we can judge political authority. Contract positions dramatize the notion that authority to be binding must repose on consent as well as embody the morally defensible statements stressed by the naturalist. Utilitarian views warn us against taking refuge in such unsatisfactory and vague expressions as "national interest" or "national honor." Finally, organicist ideas rightly stress the social and political dimensions of what we call "personality" and, therefore, the unreality of completely discrete "individuals."

An adequate theory of obligation will have to take account of both the strengths and the weaknesses embodied in the several traditional views.

Disquietude, Obligation, and Civil Disobedience

Having now suggested the anxiety about political society and having summarized important attempts to provide an adequate foundation for political obligation, I turn, in this last section, to (a) a restatement of the issue of political obligation that will take account of both Augustine's dilemma and the weaknesses and strengths in the several analyses of obligation, and (b) a justification, under certain circumscribed conditions, of civil disobedience.

Restatement of the Issue

A theory of obligation requires, first, a delineation of what a fully legitimate authority would be; second, a similar sketch of an ideal illegitimate ruler; and third, judgment of all historical authorities by standards arising out of our standards of legitimacy and illegitimacy. Our obligation is greatest to those alleged authorities that endeavor by their actions to approximate legitimacy, and least to those that appear to forget the criteria of moral licitness.

From the viewpoint of this paper—and of an important tradition in Western political thought—a completely legitimate authority is one that exists in a society that has reconciled our consciousness of individuality with our feeling of belonging to others. In such a society —envisioned in greater or lesser degree by such thinkers as St. Thomas Aquinas, Rousseau, Marx, Engels, and Lenin—each person would be free and spontaneous and yet would be associated with his fellows for collective endeavors. The order demanded when men mingle with one another would not find itself in tension with personalities that have ends beyond the social order.

In a perfectly legitimate society, it would seem, the coordinating machinery of the society, so necessary when men become specialized in their tasks, would primarily administer "things," as the Marxist communist version would have it. Direct coercion of men, and particularly the utilization of physical force, would vanish. Law would become, in Emerson's pregnant words, a mere "memorandum"; and once individual personalities read the words of the memorandum, they would see immediately the legitimacy of its prescriptions. Law "making" itself would be the end result of a consensus-gathering process, with formal voting reduced to the vanishing point. The pull of special economic interests would have been abolished through common ownership and administration of resources, and distribution in accordance with need (a need that each self-disciplined individual would determine). Taxation as we know it today would have vanished, since collective necessities would be supplied from the total product before individual distribution could take place. Armies would, of course, be no more. Complete freedom of expression would obtain.

Under conditions of this kind, in other words, authority would, so to speak, be fully authoritative and would carry its own "power." *Vera justitia*—true justice—would obtain.

If, now, one were to imagine an ideal illegitimate system of political relations, one need only spell out the reverse of the picture of legitimacy. The coordinating machinery of society would manipulate men for its own ends in such a way that they would not even be aware of their own exploitation. If perchance they resisted, force without stint would be applied, sometimes without even the pretense of using forms of law. Law and principles of morality would be determined completely by the ruling classes, any distinction between right and might being eliminated. Threats of various kinds would keep the population cowed and submissive. Law would be imposed with no explanation of the reasons supporting it. Armies would, of course, play an important role, one road to political power being success in military intimidation. Spontaneity would be discouraged in every way, even in the realms of sport and recreation.

This dichotomization between legitimate and illegitimate is obviously based on a particular view of what the conception of humanity implies by way of social ordering, and in this respect the notion of legitimacy is directly connected with those perspectives that earlier were termed naturalist—in the sense that legitimacy implies a situation in which man's true nature has been fulfilled. But there are also elements of the contractual, insofar as consent becomes a fully developed and genuine ingredient in political relations. Utilitarian ideas are relevant, too, at least to the degree that authority would necessarily have to appeal to judgments about consequences and would have to define objectives in concrete terms. Finally, organicist conceptions are mirrored in the overcoming of the alienation of men from their fellows.

Just as Augustine's first definition of a commonwealth emphasized the fact that no historical society is fully legitimate, so does my formulation maintain the highly mixed and morally ambiguous character of all past and present regimes. Every political system is partly robbery and piracy and yet it is also, in terms of Augustine's second definition, some kind of order that we deem valuable. At best, any given historical scheme can be justified only relatively and our obligation is only a relative or conditional one.

What criteria can we discover for distinguishing between relatively legitimate and relatively illegitimate regimes?

We might see an answer, first, in terms of the procedures whereby decisions are reached and, second, in relation to the substance of the decisions themselves.

With respect to procedures, any claimed authority that closes avenues to the enhancement of its legitimacy would seem to be attacking the principle of authority at its roots. Thus any quasi-authority that cuts off criticisms, reduces freedom of expression, or deliberately withholds information is undermining the basic foundations in that it is denying the means for nonviolent change in the direction of greater legitimacy. Other procedural values are scarcely less important, and for the same reason: among these are reasonably nonarbitrary procedures in criminal and civil courts and the absence of too wide a discretion in the sphere allocated to the executive. In general, any serious denial of the rule of law subjects a regime to the charge of too great a degree of illegitimacy.

If the framework allows change and progress in the direction of full authority, then the substance of many decisions can be tolerated, if not fully approved, on grounds either that they are ethically neutral or that, given the actual conditions obtaining, they may be relatively justified. Thus, under conditions of perfect legitimacy, physical coercion would disappear. Within the relativities of history, however, some coercion under certain specific circumstances might be regarded as supportable.

But some decisions would seem to be ruled out in a virtually absolute sense. Thus the deliberate and premeditated taking of life under the guise of "authority" would appear to be beyond the pale. This prohibition of deliberate killing might be said to derive from the notion that a central function of authority is to enhance life and not to destroy it. In particular circumstances, to be sure, we might well be uncertain as to what constitutes deliberate and premeditated taking of life as against accidental or unintended killing; but surely capital punishment and war would be ruled out, at a minimum.

Then, too, a high substantive priority would be a property system that assures a livelihood for all, even though distribution of economic power might be far from the norms of pure legitimacy. The property question assumes high-order priority because of its close relation to the objective of enhancing life.

These, then, are among the most significant of the procedural and substantive values, the denial of which by the quasi-authorities of history would seem to reduce political obligation to the vanishing point and open the way for morally legitimate civil disobedience. Having stretched out ideal-type legitimacy and illegitimacy and their adaptation to the relativities of history, the principles under which civil disobedience may be justified can now be spelled out.

Justification of Civil Disobedience

Those who would support civil disobedience, we suggest, must act with a sense of responsibility, give the benefit of the doubt to the law, be fairly certain that basic norms of procedure and substance have been violated, disobey overtly rather than covertly, act nonviolently, and recognize that the individual himself, rather than a group, has the right and obligation to decide when civil disobedience is required.

RESPONSIBILITY. By responsibility is meant that the purpose and possible consequences of the proposed civil disobedience must be carefully weighed before the decision is made. Thus mere impulse must be ruled out as incompatible with rational human action.

BENEFIT OF THE DOUBT. Fully admitting that any given legal and political system is a mixture of the aspiration for legitimacy and an attack on legitimacy, the benefit of any doubt, it would seem, should be given to the existing law or decree. This is because we can share with Augustine the view that the value of order—any kind of order, or, in other terms, any system of mutual expectations—is so great that unless the system can be shown to be gravely deficient in its moral underpinnings, it must be assumed to have a certain claim, however bastardized.

NORMS OF PROCEDURE AND SUBSTANCE VIOLATED. In deciding whether the presumption of obligation to obey is to be overthrown, reference should be made to the notion of legitimacy suggested earlier, both in its ideal-typical form and in its adaptation to the exigencies and relativities of the historical situation. First of all, one should give primary weight to procedures and to the notion of rank ordering of values in the procedural framework. A system of rule that disregards the basic norms of even relative authority is contradicting its implicit purpose, which is, let us repeat, a more solidly based authority from the moral point of view. Similarly, to the extent that the basic substance of decisions contradicts the ends for which quasi-authorities are established, to that degree does claimed authority cease to be morally obligatory, even in a relative sense.

Thus when alleged authority silences a man through intimidation, takes a life in war, kills a person under the guise of punishment, or deprives human beings of livelihoods through an inadequate property system, it thereby undermines its own authority and correspondingly weakens its claims on my obedience. After a certain point has been reached, if I do obey, it will be because of sheer expediency and not by virtue of a sense of obligation.

It was considerations of this kind that led Martin Luther King, in

1963, to violate court orders forbidding him to protest segregation (King, 1963:7); that impelled students at the University of California to occupy buildings in violation of law; and that often send the conscientious objector to jail for refusing to register under the conscription law.

OVERT, NOT COVERT DISOBEDIENCE. It is precisely because the civilly disobedient take seriously their political obligation that they feel impelled to violate the law deliberately and overtly. They make public announcement of it, accept responsibility, and stand ready to suffer the consequences in terms of a penalty. They disobey because they value law and deem the rule they are violating to be either no law (the natural law view) or bad law (the positivist position). Although they recognize that no alleged law can be fully authoritative in the mixed world characteristic of history, they insist that it must meet certain minimum requirements lest it destroy its very *raison d'être*. They thus vindicate the *principle* of law in the very act of violating a particular command.

NON-VIOLENCE. The disobedience must be not only overt but also nonviolent. One cannot consistently protest against the undermining of authority by the historical state and, at the same time, utilize violence in the process. For violence runs counter to the idea of moral authority, it denigrates human personality, and, in effect, it subverts the foundations of the order to which I am appealing as a civilly disobedient person. Thus violent revolution tends to be self-defeating, destroying the foundations of moral order while it claims to be seeking a more nearly legitimate authority. When violence is used to secure revolutionary change, it is as illegitimate and therefore as unauthoritative as the violence of a war waged by the quasi-authorities of history.

DECISION BY THE INDIVIDUAL. In deciding whether to be disobedient, the individual in the end must be guided by his own conscience.

Some thinkers, to be sure, are dissatisfied with conclusions of this kind, protesting that the individual cannot and must not determine when he should and should not obey. Typical of these critics is Dr. Will Herberg, who wrote:

> Every man has his conscience; and if the individual conscience is absolutized (that is, divinized), and made the final judge of laws to be obeyed or disobeyed, nothing but anarchy and the dissolution of the very fabric of government would result (*National Review,* 1964, p. 580).

In response to such objections, we might well remind ourselves that "conscience" originally meant "joint knowledge" and that in considerable measure it still has this connotation. One's conscience about a particular matter is developed within a social context, is nourished by constant testing against the views of others, is not the product of mere impulse, and is animated by a sense of responsibility both to humanity and to oneself. Both naturalist and organicist views would stress this conception; and some versions even of contractualist and utilitarian positions would not dissent. In other words, the conscience cannot be regarded as the vain subjective ghost of some mythical discrete individual.

We might also ask who *should* make the decision, if not the individual person. Where would Dr. Herberg turn? To the church? But which church? And how can we assume that the church is a better judge of matters of right and wrong than the individual? To the state? But would the historical state *ever* advise us to break its laws? And how can we differentiate the state from Augustine's band of robbers without appealing to an authority beyond the state? Would Dr. Herberg have recognized Hitler's state as authoritative? If not, whose judgment, if not his own, would he have accepted?

There would seem to be no alternative to the individual conscience. Informed and carefully examined, it must be the final judge of civil disobedience, as of other matters. Even if it be in error, it must still be followed, as St. Thomas Aquinas has so persuasively argued (*Summa*, First Part of II, Q. IX, Art. 5; *Quodlibet*, 27).

As for the charge of anarchy, it has been the burden of this paper to maintain that any legal or political system is far safer in the hands of those who obey or disobey law on conscientious grounds—and with a more or less conscious doctrine of obligation in the background—than it is in the custody of those who either obey or disobey law without thought and without criticism. An historical order reposing on conscience may have elements of durability; but one bottomed on unreflective obedience and impulsive disobedience can be swept away by whim and happenstance. Possible civil disobedience is the price we pay for an order resting, in part at least, on awareness that all historical regimes are in some degree illegitimate and may have to be resisted. But this price is far less than the moral and social charge assessed when we assume that all alleged law must be automatically obeyed; for automatic obedience implies automatons in the guise of men—a denial of the aspiration for autonomy and moral authority, which is the most distinctive quality of humanity.

In our day particularly, with its large-scale manipulation of human beings, the civilly disobedient may not only vindicate their own personal integrity but also render a genuine social service. They vividly remind us that all power tends to corrupt; that shock techniques are needed to recall so-called democracies to their own principles; that elites often become both stupid and immoral; and, to recur to St. Augustine, that only a relatively thin line may separate the ruler claiming political authority from the pirate chief.

REFERENCES

AQUINAS, ST. THOMAS. *Quodlibet.*

AQUINAS, ST. THOMAS. *Summa Theologica.*

AUGUSTINE, ST. *The City of God.*

BEDAU, HUGO A. 1961. On Civil Disobedience. *Jour. of Phil.,* LVIII: 21.

CARRITT, E. F. 1935. *Morals and Politics.* London, Oxford University Press.

COHEN, C. 1964. Essence and Ethics of Civil Disobedience. *The Nation,* March 18.

COOK, F., 1962. *The Warfare State.* New York, Macmillan.

DEANE, HERBERT A. 1963. *The Political and Social Ideas of St. Augustine.* New York, Columbia University Press.

EMERSON, R. W. *Politics.*

FRANKEL, C. 1964. Is It Ever Right to Break the Law? *N.Y. Times Mag.,* Jan. 12, pp. 17, 36, 39, 41.

GREEN, THOMAS HILL. *Principles of Political Obligation.*

HERBERG, WILL. 1964. A Religious 'Right' to Violate the Law? *National Review,* 16:12, pp. 579–580.

HOBBES, THOMAS. *Leviathan.*

KING, MARTIN L. 1964. *Why We Can't Wait.* New York, Signet, New American Library.

LOCKE, JOHN. *Second Treatise of Civil Government.*

MERRIAM, C. 1934. *Political Power.* New York, Whittlesey House, McGraw-Hill.

National Review, July 14, 1964.

New York Times, Oct. 1, 1964; Sept. 4, 1964.

PLATO, *Crito.*

ROUSSEAU, JEAN JACQUES. *The Social Contract.*

II/Conflicting Philosophies

NATURALISM

I think we all have moral obligations to obey
just laws. On the other hand, I think that we
have moral obligations to disobey unjust laws
because non-cooperation with evil is just as
much a moral obligation as cooperation with
good.

—MARTIN LUTHER KING, JR.

Ethical Naturalists believe that
law, to oblige in conscience, must conform to objective principles of
morality "discovered" by human reason, a logical and intuitive faculty embedded in the nature of man. For Ethical Naturalists, obedience to law and constituted authority is limited. If statutory law de-
viates from "natural law" precepts, the individual has the right, and
sometimes even the duty, to resist and disobey. The central difficulties found in this ethical school occur (a) when men of good will attempt to come into agreement, in *operational* terms, on precisely
which abstract moral standards are natural law precepts and (b)
when two such precepts come into conflict with one another in concrete situations.

In our essay "Law, Order, and Civil Disobedience," we analyze
Thomas Aquinas' teleological naturalism in terms of his theory of the
natural ends or purposes of the state and his emphasis on the obligation of the political regime to help the members of the political community achieve their ultimate purpose in life, spiritual fulfillment.
The essay offers a detailed examination of Aquinas' several evalua-
tive standards by which to judge the morality of acts of civil
disobedience—all of which are grounded in the essentially Aristotelian prudential concept of *proportion* or *balance* between ends and
means.

A contemporary restatement of the classical natural law position is
poignantly expressed by Martin Luther King, Jr., in his "Letter from
Birmingham Jail." Dr. King, confronting a group of clergymen who
desire the preservation of social order above all else, argues that transcendent "higher law" moral standards are superior to the positive
laws of any state and that all rational men are capable of compre-
hending such transcendent standards. Thus, the laws of any sovereign
state must be congruent with the higher law if they are to bind in
conscience. For King, racial segregation laws were inimical to natural

37

morality, and therefore were unjust and did not require obedience. Indeed, they required "noncooperation," which entailed nonviolent civil disobedience.

The General Board of the National Council of Churches, in its policy statement "Religious Obedience and Civil Disobedience," affirms the position of the early Christian martyrs that "We must obey God rather than man." A Christian is obligated to follow his conscience or "right reason" in resisting human injustice. Nonetheless, the statement argues that if civil disobedience is to conform to Christian values, it must be a deliberate, public, and peaceable act and the disobedient must be prepared to accept the consequences of his actions.

3 / Law, Order, and Civil Disobedience

MICHAEL P. SMITH AND KENNETH L. DEUTSCH

Civil disobedience is a persistent theme in twentieth-century political thought. The right to resist unjust authority has been invoked by numerous spokesmen who perceive their governments as either illegitimate or authoritarian or as both. These perceptions have stimulated many contemporary critics of the Vietnam War and black militants to inquire into the conditions that might justify civil disobedience.

In the face of these developments, few contemporary political theorists have examined the relevance of Thomas Aquinas' theory of political obligation to the perennial question of man's relationship to the state. Those who have dealt with the Thomist political philosophy have chosen to focus on problems such as natural law, popular sovereignty, or the medieval theory of kingship rather than on the particular question of civil disobedience. This essay will examine the aspects of Aquinas' political philosophy that comprise a comprehensive theory of political obligation and resistance and will attempt to analyze the relevance of his theory to individuals and groups living in contemporary pluralist societies such as our own.

SOURCE: This article is published for the first time in this volume.

THE INDIVIDUAL IN SOCIETY:
THE NEED FOR A STATE

For Thomas Aquinas, the whole process of social life is encompassed in a single natural and divine harmony that ultimately ends in salvation. The secular world governed by "reason" is essential for the realization of man's ultimate end. However, unlike earlier and more conservative Neoplatonic philosophers, Aquinas' justification of the secular world is not solely instrumental. That is to say, as "man is naturally a social and political animal," he cannot live without society. He is a social being precisely because he is not self-sufficing; he cannot fulfill *in vacuo* the human moral choice needed to attain his "proper" end as a rational creature (salvation). He needs the help and guidance of others to accomplish this objective.

Aquinas further argues that "the fellowship of society being . . . natural and necessary to man, it follows with equal necessity that there must be some principle of government within society." The governing of society, in turn, presupposes some principle of authority. Since the "aim" of social life is to inculcate virtue and morality, it is the task of the constituted authority in the state to further a virtuous and ethical life that will help in the attainment of "real beatitude." For Aquinas, the state is not an end in itself (as in Aristotle), nor a remedy for sin (as in Augustine). Rather, the state serves as an instrument for promoting virtue for a transcendent end that is not realizable within the confines of the secular state.

In Aquinas' terminology, for a society to be "natural" is for it to be a part of the divine plan. The divine pattern of authority puts the ruler in a very prominent yet responsible position. The duty of the temporal authority is to ensure *peace* because it is only in a peaceful society that individuals can pursue virtue. The elevation of *peace* and *order* to the first objectives of government results from Aquinas' concern about the need for social harmony, if individuals are to achieve "virtue."

THE RULE OF LAW
IN SOCIETY AND THE STATE

It is precisely because of his normative commitment to social harmony that Aquinas' concept of law is developed. If one is to understand his approach to political obligation, one must first understand his theory of law. Law in its broadest sense, for Aquinas, is a rule of action that is dependent on "reason." Because life in the state is only a preparation for a greater afterlife, individuals in the state should be guided by rules and regulations that are in conformity with "eternal reason." The ruler, to be legitimate, has to administer law, which should be perfectly harmonious with the divine plan.

Aquinas divided law into four hierarchically interrelated categories:

ETERNAL LAW. For Aquinas, divine reason and wisdom comprise an eternal law—a law governing the whole of creation; a law not made but eternally existing, and therefore, unknowable to man in its entirety, yet the source of all "true" law on earth. Ultimately, right and wrong in the practical field of man's actions depend on whether or not these actions conform to eternal law.

NATURAL LAW. The Thomistic man's "rational" nature allows him to *share* in the eternal reason. This human participation in divine reason, this practical reflection in man of divine intuition, is what Aquinas calls "natural law." Through it, man is provided with *objective, changeless, universal* rules or principles of action. In its fundamental precept, natural law commands man to "do good" and "avoid evil," or, in teleological terms, to be himself and rationally to follow his natural *inclinations,* in order to reach his natural *end,* the beatific vision, which is complete happiness.

HUMAN POSITIVE LAW. Legislation is defined by Aquinas as "a rational ordering of things which concern the common good, promulgated by whoever is charged with the care of the community." Positive law issued by the legislator when "derived from" natural law is binding in conscience. Positive law is just only if and when it conforms to natural law. For Aquinas, law of the state that counters a principle or violates a precept of natural law is not "law" at all. It loses its legitimacy, for no human law can validly exist without justice; and justice consists in conformity to the rule of "right reason."

DIVINE POSITIVE LAW. In Thomistic terminology, divine positive law is a derivation of eternal law, which proceeds from God as a kind of anthropomorphic legislator. It supplements the limitations of human reason and consists of rules made known to man by divine inspiration at different periods in history. These rules are contained in the Scriptures.

Aquinas' justification for both political obligation and civil disobedience is inextricably related to his concept of the binding character of human law. Not unlike Hobbes, Aquinas views human law as a matter of social and psychological necessity. In his words, there are "indeed some young men readily inclined to a life of virtue . . . for such, paternal guidance and advice are sufficient. But there are others, of evil disposition . . . these it is necessary to *restrain* from wrongdoing by *force* and by *fear*. When they are thus prevented from doing evil, a quiet life is assured to the rest of the community; and they are themselves drawn eventually, by force of *habit* to do voluntarily what once they did only out of fear, and so to practice virtue."

Aquinas contends that the binding power of human law is derived from three properties: its objective, its author, and its content. Laws can be considered just when they are directed to promote the general welfare (objective), when the law enacted does not exceed the assigned powers of the enactor (author), and when the burdens that the laws impose are distributed so as to promote the common welfare (content).

Aquinas argues that laws may be "unjust" and therefore not morally binding in two circumstances. First, "When they are detrimental to human welfare" (i.e., when they violate the above norms). However, the standard for civil disobedience in this case is *prudential* rather than unlimited. Aquinas believed that the right to disobey laws that are harmful to human welfare might be *abrogated* if "scandal" or "disturbance" might result from the act of civil disobedience. In Aquinas' exact words, "Such laws do not bind in conscience . . . except perhaps in order to avoid scandal or disturbance, for which a man should even yield his right." It would appear that if forced to choose between the dangers of anarchy or an unjust political regime, Aquinas would opt for the latter.

In contrast, when laws are contrary to divine goodness, as in the case of laws commanding idolatry, "Such laws may under *no* circumstances be obeyed." Hence, Aquinas' first condition permitting disobedience to human positive law is essentially the *unconditional duty* to disobey "unjust laws," which conflict with divine reason and the *conditional right* to disobey unjust laws that either inequitably distribute burdens or benefits or that exceed the powers of the enactor —provided a balanced judgment has been made on the degree of "disturbance" likely to result from disobedience.

In order to comprehend the full scope of Aquinas' theory of civil disobedience, we must go beyond this conscientious right or duty to disobey "unjust laws" and consider his conception of just and unjust *governmental forms.*

RULERSHIP AND THE BASES
OF LEGITIMATE AUTHORITY

For Aquinas, the governmental authority must guide the community toward the attainment of "higher" ends. This means that it should be an embodiment of Christian virtues. There are three virtuous forms of rulership in Aquinas' theory: monarchy, oligarchy, and democracy. The monarch leads not only by wise decree but also by love, dignity, and moral example. Aquinas contends further that the monarch must be a superior moral being, indeed a sort of symbolic embodiment of the moral aspirations of the society. This means that the king has a dual function. He is responsible for the good administration of the state. He also should rule in such a way as to create conditions for the fulfillment of human perfection. Thus, in exercising his twofold but mutually related powers, the king's powers are limited by his *responsibilities.*

Moreover, kingship, or "just rule by one," is the ideally best form of government for Aquinas because the "common good" can be promoted most effectively when there is *unity* or *order* in the community and because "that which itself is a unity can more easily produce unity." Monarchy is also preferable because even a corrupt monarch is still likely to preserve *peace,* and peace is the essential prerequisite for human perfectibility. Aquinas' early analysis of monarchy as the best governmental form seems to contradict his later praise of the *mixed* constitution in the *Summa.* In the latter, Aquinas foreshadows modern trends in democratic theory when he argues that peace and right order in the community are best promoted when *all* in some respect *participate* in the government.

> This is the best form of constitution which results from a judicious admixture of the kingdom, in that there is one person at the head of it; of *aristocracy* in that many participate in the government according to virtue; of *democracy* or popular rule in that rulers may be elected from the people and the whole population has the right of electing its rulers.

Contemporary scholars see no inconsistency in Aquinas with respect to this point. Étienne Gilson explains Aquinas' position in terms of the distinction between society and the state.

> We are to understand by this that the best form of government is that which places the *social body* under the direction of one man, but not that the best form of government is one in which the direction of

the *state* is in the hands of one man. The prince or king can only insure the common good of people when he is dependent upon them. He must, therefore, appeal for the collaboration of all social forces useful to the common good if he is to direct and unite them.

Similarly, C. N. R. McCoy explains the mixed form as the "tempered" or *best possible* form of monarchy, which Aquinas believed to be a necessary safeguard to prevent degeneration into tyranny, the worst governmental form.

Aquinas' texts that most directly relate to the question of the *bases* of legitimate authority also seem contradictory upon first examination. For instance, in an early writing Aquinas states: "Authority derives always, from a formal point of view, from God (and it is this which produces the duty of obedience)." However, there is a human element involved in Aquinas' treatment of legitimate authority in the *Summa:* "all law is directed to the common well-being of men, and for this reason *alone* does it obtain the power and validity of law: so to the extent that it falls short of this effect it has no power of obligation."

In effect, although the power of the ruler is beyond the *legal* control of the people, his *moral* responsibility to observe the law remains in full effect. To Aquinas, rulership is in the nature of a *trust.* The ruler *can* exercise unlimited political power, but he only does so *legitimately* by acting as the agent and representative of the community.

In summary, in his concern for the prevention of royal abuses and the establishment of guarantees against arbitrary rule, Aquinas proposes a kind of elective monarchy to give the people an opportunity to choose the best candidate and to place, if needed, new restrictions on his power. He advises a *tempering* of royal power by blending it with aristocratic and democratic elements. Let one command, stated Aquinas, but *let many participate* in the government according to their abilities. And let it not be forgotten, he adds, that all may be elected to power and that the right to elect the rulers is the right of the people.

TYRANNY: THE BREAKDOWN
OF LEGITIMATE AUTHORITY

Aquinas stresses that the legitimate ruler is "just" power according to "law." But this law must be in conformity with the natural law. The tyrant is one who seeks his own private interests and controls by *force* instead of ruling with justice. Tyranny is the *perversion* of rulership. A king is only a king insofar as he is just. The duty of the just ruler is to establish the welfare of the community. The well-being of the state is based on peace, moral enhancement, and a sufficient distribution of material goods. Since tyranny does not fulfill these three values, to overthrow such government is not, strictly speaking, sedition. To be sure, the tyrant himself is much *more* guilty of sedition by spreading discord and strife among his subjects.

Tyranny, the corruption of kingship, is the worst form of government. "When government is unjustly exercised by one man who seeks personal profit from his position instead of the good of the community subject to him, such a ruler is called a tyrant." Moreover, since a unitary power lacking internal friction is more efficient, the tyrant is more efficiently evil.

Because Aquinas feared the corruption of unified rulership, he defined a number of conditions whereby the ruler could lose his claim to *legitimacy*. The monarch might lose claim to obedience either because of the *way* in which his authority has been *obtained* or because of the way he has *used* that authority. Usurping power by violence or simony (graft) constitutes *procedural* defect that prevents the establishment of just authority, "for whosoever possesses himself of power by violence does not truly become lord or master. Therefore, it is permissible, when occasion offers, for a *person* to *reject* such authority."

There are also two ways in which a defect may arise due to substantive misuse of power. First, the matter ordered by an authority may be contrary to the ultimate *objective* for which that authority was constituted. When translated from Thomistic jargon, this means that a government established to promote economic well-being may order genocide. In this case, it is not a right but, rather, a *duty* to resist. Second, those in authority may command acts that exceed the *competence* of their authority (e.g., a ruler who demands undue payment). In this circumstance, obedience is left to the discretion of the subjects.

Given this set of criteria developed in the early *Commentary on the Sentences* (1253–1255), Aquinas seems to be condoning a *personal* right of resistance to tyranny. Also in the *Sentences,* Aquinas seems to advocate tyrannicide as a method of dealing with the usurper:

> With regard to the fifth objection, it must be noted that Cicero was speaking of a case where a person had possessed himself of power through violence, either against the will of his subjects or by compelling their consent, and where there was no possibility of appeal to a higher authority who could pass judgment on such action. In such a case, *one who liberates his country by killing a tyrant is to be praised and rewarded.* [The italics are the authors'.]

No such notion of self-help is present in Aquinas' treatment of tyranny in the later *On Princely Government* (ca. 1266). The language

in the later work indicates that tyranny must be excessive before resistance is necessary. If tyranny does become repressive, individual
tyrannicide is still not possible. In Aquinas' words, "it has been
argued that it would be an act of virtue for the powerful citizens to
kill the tyrant, even exposing themselves to the peril of death for the
liberation of the community. . . . *But this does not agree with Apostolic teaching.*" The remedy against tyranny outlined in *On Princely
Government* lies not in the private judgment of *individuals* but in the
hands of *public authority.* What, then, are the recourses against the
tyrant? Aquinas contends that if the community *elects* the ruler, it
would not be contrary to justice for it to *depose* the king or to curb
his power. To be sure, the tyrant leaves himself open to the loss of
fealty by failing to discharge the duties of his office as governor of the
community. If, however, the right to appoint the king belongs to some
superior authority, then the remedy against tyranny must be sought
from it: A contemporary example of appeal to higher authority might
be the parliamentary vote of no confidence in the British political system. Finally, when there is no hope of human aid through public authority, the last recourse is to pray for "divine intervention," which
Aquinas believed could turn the cruel heart to gentleness.

What, then, is to be done? Must the individual wait for divine intervention when faced with a tyrant like Hitler? Or may he kill the
tyrant? Some of the historical analysts who have tried to grapple with
this problem have assumed *a priori* that Aquinas' more "mature"
thought is his most "representative" thought. For example, Martin
Grabmann argues:

> In his search for truth, Thomas corrected, supplemented or retracted
> his own earlier views whenever new matter or deeper knowledge
> proved them to be inadequate or erroneous.

Working from this premise, Grabmann grants absolutely no significance to the statement in the *Commentary on the Sentences* that
seems to condone individual tyrannicide.

Similarly, R. W. and A. J. Carlyle, while not altogether ignoring
the statement in the *Commentary on the Sentences,* nevertheless
argue that it is "clear that this was not the mature judgment of St.
Thomas." They indicate that Aquinas intended to deal with the matter further in *On Princely Government* but never completed the work.

Yet it can be argued with equal logic that the early position, written and taught before Aristotle was translated from the Greek, was
more truly representative of Aquinas' own thinking. In this work,
after all, he was not faced with the task of reconciling Aristotle with
Christianity. Some evidence for this point of view is reflected in

Thomas Gilby's argument that "as [Aquinas'] Aristotelianism grew, so the need for state action was more firmly emphasized."

It is possible to raise an added consideration by drawing a parallel between individual tyrannicide and capital punishment. Although Aquinas felt that the taking of someone's life was the gravest of all breaches, he nonetheless did justify the death penalty. In so doing, he reasoned that it might become necessary to cut off a member of society if that member's corruption became a clear menace to the body politic. However, this deed could be done only by regularly constituted authority and not by private persons.

Finally, one might consider the view of Cardinal Cajetan, a prominent sixteenth-century scholastic philosopher. Cajetan centers his interpretation of Aquinas' position on tyrannicide on certain passages from the *Summa* that discuss the culpability of the person who kills a sinner.

In the *Summa*, Aquinas directs himself to the question of whether it is lawful for a private individual to kill a man who has sinned. He cites Augustine's contention that an individual who kills an evildoer without sanction of public authority is guilty of *murder*, since the individual has dared to usurp a power not conferred upon him by God. He concludes that "it is lawful to kill an evildoer insofar as it is directed to the welfare of the whole community, so that it belongs to him *alone* who has charge of the common good and is entrusted to persons of rank having *public authority*: wherefore *they alone*, and not private individuals, can lawfully put evildoers to death."

Nevertheless, in reply to the objection that it is lawful for the private individual to kill the sinner, since Moses so commanded, Aquinas seems to foreshadow Martin Luther's concept of the "divine avenger":

> The person by whose authority a thing is done really does the thing. . . . Wherefore those who, at the Lord's command, slew their neighbors and friends, would seem not to have done this themselves, but rather He by whose authority they acted thus: just as a soldier slays the foe by authority of his sovereign and the executioner slays the robber by the authority of the judge.

By juxtaposing these two statements, Cajetan concluded that Aquinas entertained a twofold moral standard with respect to individual tyrannicide, accepting it as a legitimate means of removing the usurper but rejecting it as a method of redress against the legitimate ruler who rules tyrannically. The only other possible support for the Cajetan position is suggested in the previously cited passage from the *Commentary on the Sentences* where Aquinas argues that those who *usurp* power by violence or simony (graft) "[do] not truly become lord or master. Therefore, it is permissible when occasion offers for a *person* to *reject* such authority."

Although the Cajetan position begins in textual documentation, the particular passages from the *Summa* that are the cornerstone of his interpretation remain imprecise, at best, and weaken his position by entrusting "revenge" to persons in public authority, at worst. Moreover, to use Aquinas' argument in the *Sentences* to support the Cajetan hypothesis would require the tortured use of the term "reject" to mean "kill." "To reject" could encompass an entire array of acts of resistance, such as political protest, nonviolent civil disobedience, and voluntary political exile, rather than merely signifying tyrannicide. In sum, Cajetan, like his counterparts, leaves the question of Aquinas and tyrannicide basically unresolved.

Civil Order and the Right of Resistance

Aquinas puts an awesome moral obligation on any ruler's shoulders. As he states, "if ordinary men are praised for helping the needy, settling disputes, rescuing one who is oppressed, how much more, then does he deserve praise of men and reward of God who gladdens a whole country with peace, restrains the violent, preserves the righteousness and orders the actions of men by his laws and precepts. The greatness of kingly virtue becomes further apparent from another fact; that is from a king's singular likeness to God since a king does in his kingdom what God does in the universe." It is because of these obligations heaped upon legitimate rulers that tyrants are held to be guilty not only for their own sins but also for the sins they encourage in their subjects. But, let us first examine Aquinas' penchant for order.

There is no *unconditional* right to revolution in Aquinas. Aquinas' chief objection to revolution is that it is an act of *disorder*. As such, it conflicts with his fundamental conception of society as part of the ordered pattern of the universe. For Aquinas, revolution is a form of change so fraught with violence and uncertainty that the community often suffers greater harm from the attendant disruptions than it would were the existing regime allowed to remain in power. For Aquinas, there can be no justice without order. Violent revolutions destroy the stability upon which orderly human relationships must be founded. To be sure, Aquinas is no friend of tyranny and he realizes that tyrannical government may oppress the human spirit. Between the evils of tyranny and violent disorder, Aquinas seems, on balance, however, to opt for the former. One of the reasons he counsels against revolution is that he believes its aftermath may result in more severe tyranny than was experienced before. To Aquinas, harmony is the first prerequisite of society. The aftermath of revolution is chaos. In a state of chaos, where custom has been abrogated and authority destroyed, it is impossible for an individual to develop his potentialities, and thereby reach his final end, which is the attainment of union with God. Civil order, in short, for Aquinas, is the precondition for civilized existence.

There are, however, certain situations under which rebellion can be justified when it is the means for accomplishing a "legitimate revolution." The theory behind a legitimate or justified revolution is that the ruler loses his right to rule by his repressive behavior and that sovereignty then reverts to the people. Consequently, a legitimate revolution is not directed against a rightful ruler. Citizens have the right of revolution only when the ruler has *lost* his right to rule. The conditions for a justified revolution are set down not as absolute requirements but as prudential norms, because historical contingencies are too diverse:

(1) The government has become *habitually* tyrannical, with no prospect of a change for the better within a reasonable time.

(2) All legal and peaceful means to recall the ruler to a sense of duty (true kingship) have been exhausted.

(3) There is a reasonable probability the justified revolution will be successful.

(4) The revolutionaries do not comprise a movement of only a single faction, one social class, or one geographical district but have the backing of the people as a whole.

TOWARD AN EVALUATION OF AQUINAS' THEORY OF OBLIGATION AND RESISTANCE: CONTRIBUTIONS, LIMITATIONS, AND APPLICATIONS

Clearly it has been shown that in Aquinas' normative theory of political obligation there is not only a right to disobey an unjust power, but sometimes there is even a duty to resist such a power. As D'Entreves puts it: "His teaching on the subject can . . . be said to bear witness to that transformation of the Christian doctrine of obedience into a doctrine exactly opposed to the theory of passive obedience held by older [such as Augustine] and later [such as Luther and Calvin] Christian political thinkers."

Aquinas has made a lasting contribution to the normative problem

of the individual in the state. The whole tenor of his political speculation is based on the premise that state power is of a *limited* nature
and subject to legal restraint. The unyielding insistence that he
placed on the subordination of human law to a "natural and divine
law" better prepared the state for the later institutionalization of limited or constitutional government.

Aquinas was no organicist. He did not assume that man is so much
a social animal and owes such a debt of nuturance to civil society
that he is morally subservient to that society. He qualified the assertion of individual subordination to the "common good" by distinguishing the political community as a unity of order and harmony
rather than a strictly *organic* unity. The passage in which the importance of this distinction to the theory of political obligation is underlined appears in the *Commentary on the Nicomachean Ethics:* "But it
must be noted that this unity, a unity which is the political community . . . is only a unity of order and not an unconditional unity.
Consequently the parts which form it can have a sphere of action
which is distinct from that of the whole."

This statement clarifies the function of the individual in society. As
D'Entreves has said, "the role of the individual is neither minimized
nor denied; it is simply enhanced and brought as it were upon a
higher plane. The integration of the individual in the whole must be
conceived as an enlargement and an enrichment of his personality,
not as a degradation to the mere function of a part without a value of
its own."

Nonetheless, in Aquinas, the concept of political authority per se
was probably heightened by gaining a degree of independence from
its Augustinian derivation as a remedy for sin. Still, the Augustinian
theory taught the duty of passive obedience, the willful acceptance of
suffering from tyrants, and obeisance to *de facto* rule. In Aquinas, the
definite *checks* of legitimacy in the acquisition of rule, the general
welfare standard, the supremacy of law, and the right and even duty
to resist repression are present.

When attempting to evaluate Aquinas, one is faced with very clear
metaphysical assumptions. He showed basic confidence in the orderli-
ness and purposefulness of the universe; it has a system-like quality.
It is this faith in order and purpose that is the center of his system.
The experience of wrestling with Aquinas' system is "like an attempt
to master a vast hydraulic network with all sorts of buttons and levers marked God, Nature, Law, Justice, The Good, The Common
Good, Reason, Happiness, and First Principles. Press one button and
the others move out; pull out one lever and the others retract." Aquinas' system should make social scientists like David Easton and Talcott Parsons jealous and envious.

The very basis of Aquinas' *normative* theory of political obligation seems to rest on his *metaethical* assumptions about the discoverability of "natural law" precepts. He offers natural law as dispassionate reason. But Aquinas, in reality, offers not primarily the guidance of reason (inductive and deductive logic) but the reassurance of a common *intuitive* spirit when apprehending the natural law. However, men often disagree as to what their intuitive spirit is telling them about the "natural law." Both John Locke and Aquinas, for example, are intuitionists. Both believe that their ultimate principles of political ethics can be intersubjectively justified by reference to certain immediately obvious, intuitively comprehensible natural principles. Yet in ethical and practical terms, Locke was less of a monarchist and more of a revolutionary than the prudential Aquinas. Moreover, what is considered "natural" in Monte Cassino, Italy, in 1200 or in Lockean England is not always considered "natural" in America, in 1972. To cite a more pointed contemporary example, President Nixon's definition of "natural" justice is not even remotely similar to the antiwar movement's intuitive understanding of the nature of political morality. Aquinas' normative political theory thus becomes rather dogmatic in approach. Since this approach starts with a "firm assurance that one's own system of moral beliefs is the only correct system, one may then brand all other systems as erroneous."

As a product of his time, Aquinas' blending of conflicting metaethical assumptions about the discoverability of precepts for just action has caused much consternation to contemporary scholars seeking objective justification for civil disobedience. Aquinas sees no inconsistency between faith and reason. He utilizes the term "reason" in a particular sense that resembles more closely the intuitive spirit we call faith than it does the positive rules of logic and empirical evidence that modern students of politics term reason. For Aquinas, "right reason" and faith thus become tautological.

Thomistic moral certitude and metaethical justification are based on an uncritical acceptance of divine revelation and a certitude about "the nature of things" as disclosed by his carefully circumscribed metaphysics. If political theory and political obligation are dependent on some larger intuitive understanding of the universe, the "correct" normative political theory can only be derived from "correct" metaphysical assumptions about man in the universe. When conceived in this light, conflicting justifications for civil disobedience can become competing absolutist ideologies. The inevitable conflict of political ideals in a pluralist society then tends to become a Manichean struggle between good and evil.

REFERENCES

All of the quotations from Aquinas' writings used in this essay were drawn from a limited number of specialized passages from Aquinas' enormous corpus of writings, and, hence, extensive footnoting in the text of the chapter was avoided. The three principal primary sources include *On Princely Government,* Book I, Chap. 1–3, 5–6, 9, 14–15; *Commentary on the Sentences of Peter Lombard,* Dist. 44, Qu. 2; and *Summa Theologica,* Part I, II, Qu. 90–97, 105, and Part II, II, Qu. 42, 58, 64.

Several secondary sources were closely consulted in the preparation of this essay. Sources mentioned or quoted in the text of the chapter were: R. W. and A. J. Carlyle, *A History of Medieval Political Theory* (New York: Barnes and Noble, 1928); A. P. D'Entreves, ed., *Aquinas: Selected Political Writings* (Oxford: Basil Blackwell, 1948), Introduction; D'Entreves, *The Medieval Contribution to Political Thought* (London: Oxford University Press, 1939); Thomas H. Gilby, *The Political Thought of Thomas Aquinas* (Chicago: University of Chicago Press, 1958); Étienne Gilson, *The Christian Philosophy of St. Thomas Aquinas* (New York: Random House, 1956); Martin Grabmann, *Thomas Aquinas: His Personality and Thought* (New York: Russell and Russell, 1963); George Kateb, *Political Theory: Its Nature and Uses* (New York: St. Martin's Press, 1968); and C. N. R. McCoy, *The Structure of Political Thought* (New York: McGraw-Hill, 1963). The discussion of "legitimate revolution" follows the contemporary neo-Thomist position elaborated by Austin Fagothey, *Right and Reason* (St. Louis: Mosby, 1963). Other helpful sources were Henri Grenier, *Thomistic Philosophy* (Charlottetown, Canada: St. Dunstan's University, 1949); Christian Bay, "Civil Disobedience," *Encyclopedia of the Social Sciences,* pp. 473–487; Andrew Hacker, *Political Theory* (New York: Macmillan, 1961); and Lee Cameron McDonald, *Western Political Theory* (New York: Harcourt, Brace and World, 1968).

4 / Letter from Birmingham Jail*

MARTIN LUTHER KING, JR.

April 16, 1963

MY DEAR FELLOW CLERGYMEN:

While confined here in the Birmingham city jail, I came across your recent statement calling my present activities "unwise and untimely." Seldom do I pause to answer criticism of my work and ideas. If I sought to answer all the criticisms that cross my desk, my secretaries would have little time for anything other than such correspondence in the course of the day, and I would have no time for constructive work. But since I feel that you are men of genuine good will and that your criticisms are sincerely set forth, I want to try to answer your statement in what I hope will be patient and reasonable terms.

I think I should indicate why I am here in Birmingham, since you have been influenced by the view which argues against "outsiders coming in." I have the honor of serving as president of the Southern Christian Leadership Conference, an organization operating in every southern state, with headquarters in Atlanta, Georgia. We have some eighty-five affiliated organizations across the South, and one of them is the Alabama Christian Movement for Human Rights. Frequently we share staff, educational and financial resources with our affiliates. Several months ago the affiliate here in Birmingham asked us to be on call to engage in a nonviolent direct-action program if such were deemed necessary. We readily consented, and when the hour came

---

* AUTHOR'S NOTE: This response to a published statement by eight fellow clergymen from Alabama (Bishop C. C. J. Carpenter, Bishop Joseph A. Durick, Rabbi Hilton L. Grafman, Bishop Paul Hardin, Bishop Holan B. Harmon, the Reverend George M. Murray, the Reverend Edward V. Ramage, and the Reverend Earl Stallings) was composed under somewhat constricting circumstances. Begun on the margins of the newspaper in which the statement appeared while I was in jail, the letter was continued on scraps of writing paper supplied by a friendly Negro trusty, and concluded on a pad my attorneys were eventually permitted to leave me. Although the text remains in substance unaltered, I have indulged in the author's prerogative of polishing it for publication.

SOURCE: *Why We Can't Wait* (New York: Harper & Row, Publishers, Inc., 1963). Copyright © 1963 by Martin Luther King, Jr. Reprinted by permission of the publisher.

we lived up to our promise. So I, along with several members of my staff, am here because I was invited here. I am here because I have organizational ties here.

But more basically, I am in Birmingham because injustice is here. Just as the prophets of the eighth century B.C. left their villages and carried their "thus saith the Lord" far beyond the boundaries of their home towns, and just as the Apostle Paul left his village of Tarsus and carried the gospel of Jesus Christ to the far corners of the Greco-Roman world, so am I compelled to carry the gospel of freedom beyond my own home town. Like Paul, I must constantly respond to the Macedonian call for aid.

Moreover, I am cognizant of the interrelatedness of all communities and states. I cannot sit idly by in Atlanta and not be concerned about what happens in Birmingham. Injustice anywhere is a threat to justice everywhere. We are caught in an inescapable network of mutuality, tied in a single garment of destiny. Whatever affects one directly, affects all indirectly. Never again can we afford to live with the narrow, provincial "outside agitator" idea. Anyone who lives inside the United States can never be considered an outsider anywhere within its bounds.

You deplore the demonstrations taking place in Birmingham. But your statement, I am sorry to say, fails to express a similar concern for the conditions that brought about the demonstrations. I am sure that none of you would want to rest content with the superficial kind of social analysis that deals merely with effects and does not grapple with underlying causes. It is unfortunate that demonstrations are taking place in Birmingham, but it is even more unfortunate that the city's white power structure left the Negro community with no alternative.

In any nonviolent campaign there are four basic steps: collection of the facts to determine whether injustices exist; negotiation; self-purification; and direct action. We have gone through all these steps in Birmingham. There can be no gainsaying the fact that racial injustice engulfs this community. Birmingham is probably the most thoroughly segregated city in the United States. Its ugly record of brutality is widely known. Negroes have experienced grossly unjust treatment in the courts. There have been more unsolved bombings of Negro homes and churches in Birmingham than in any other city in the nation. These are the hard, brutal facts of the case. On the basis of these conditions, Negro leaders sought to negotiate with the city fathers. But the latter consistently refused to engage in good-faith negotiation.

Then, last September, came the opportunity to talk with leaders of Birmingham's economic community. In the course of the negotiations, certain promises were made by the merchants—for example, to remove the stores' humiliating racial signs. On the basis of these promises, the Reverend Fred Shuttlesworth and the leaders of the Alabama Christian Movement for Human Rights agreed to a moratorium on all demonstrations. As the weeks and months went by, we realized that we were the victims of a broken promise. A few signs, briefly removed, returned; the others remained.

As in so many past experiences, our hopes had been blasted, and the shadow of deep disappointment settled upon us. We had no alternative except to prepare for direct action, whereby we would present our very bodies as a means of laying our case before the conscience of the local and the national community. Mindful of the difficulties involved, we decided to undertake a process of self-purification. We began a series of workshops on nonviolence, and we repeatedly asked ourselves: "Are you able to accept blows without retaliating?" "Are you able to endure the ordeal of jail?" We decided to schedule our direct-action program for the Easter season, realizing that except for Christmas, this is the main shopping period of the year. Knowing that a strong economic-withdrawal program would be the by-product of direct action, we felt that this would be the best time to bring pressure to bear on the merchants for the needed change.

Then it occurred to us that Birmingham's mayoralty election was coming up in March, and we speedily decided to postpone action until after election day. When we discovered that the Commissioner of Public Safety, Eugene "Bull" Connor, had piled up enough votes to be in the run-off, we decided again to postpone action until the day after the run-off so that the demonstrations could not be used to cloud the issues. Like many others, we waited to see Mr. Connor defeated, and to this end we endured postponement after postponement. Having aided in this community need, we felt that our direct-action program could be delayed no longer.

You may well ask: "Why direct action? Why sit-ins, marches and so forth? Isn't negotiation a better path?" You are quite right in calling for negotiation. Indeed, this is the very purpose of direct action. Nonviolent direct action seeks to create such a crisis and foster such a tension that a community which has constantly refused to negotiate is forced to confront the issue. It seeks so to dramatize the issue that it can no longer be ignored. My citing the creation of tension as part of the work of the nonviolent-resister may sound rather shocking. But I must confess that I am not afraid of the word "tension." I have earnestly opposed violent tension, but there is a type of constructive, nonviolent tension which is necessary for growth. Just as Socrates felt that it was necessary to create a tension in the mind so that individuals could rise from the bondage of myths and half-truths to the unfettered realm of creative analysis and objective appraisal, so must we see the need for nonviolent gadflies to create the kind of tension in society that will help men rise from the dark depths of prejudice and racism to the majestic heights of understanding and brotherhood.

The purpose of our direct-action program is to create a situation so crisis-packed that it will inevitably open the door to negotiation. I therefore concur with you in your call for negotiation. Too long has our beloved Southland been bogged down in a tragic effort to live in monologue rather than dialogue.

One of the basic points in your statement is that the action that I and my associates have taken in Birmingham is untimely. Some have asked: "Why didn't you give the new city administration time to act?" The only answer that I can give to this query is that the new Birmingham administration must be prodded about as much as the outgoing one, before it will act. We are sadly mistaken if we feel that the election of Albert Boutwell as mayor will bring the millennium to Birmingham. While Mr. Boutwell is a much more gentle person than Mr. Connor, they are both segregationists, dedicated to maintenance of the status quo. I have hope that Mr. Boutwell will be reasonable enough to see the futility of massive resistance to desegregation. But he will not see this without pressure from devotees of civil rights. My friends, I must say to you that we have not made a single gain in civil rights without determined legal and nonviolent pressure. Lamentably, it is an historical fact that privileged groups seldom give up their privileges voluntarily. Individuals may see the moral light and voluntarily give up their unjust posture; but, as Reinhold Niebuhr has reminded us, groups tend to be more immoral than individuals.

We know through painful experience that freedom is never voluntarily given by the oppressor; it must be demanded by the oppressed. Frankly, I have yet to engage in a direct-action campaign that was "well timed" in the view of those who have not suffered unduly from the disease of segregation. For years now I have heard the word "Wait!" It rings in the ear of every Negro with piercing familiarity. This "Wait" has almost always meant "Never." We must come to see, with one of our distinguished jurists, that "justice too long delayed is justice denied."

We have waited for more than 340 years for our constitutional and God-given rights. The nations of Asia and Africa are moving with jet-like speed toward gaining political independence, but we still creep at horse-and-buggy pace toward gaining a cup of coffee at a lunch counter. Perhaps it is easy for those who have never felt the stinging darts of segregation to say, "Wait." But when you have seen vicious mobs lynch your mothers and fathers at will and drown your sisters and brothers at whim; when you have seen hate-filled policemen curse, kick and even kill your black brothers and sisters; when you see the vast majority of your twenty million Negro brothers smothering in an airtight cage of poverty in the midst of an affluent society; when you suddenly find your tongue twisted and your speech stammering as you seek to explain to your six-year-old daughter why she can't go to the public amusement park that has just been advertised on television, and see tears welling up in her eyes when she is told that Funtown is closed to colored children, and see ominous clouds of inferiority beginning to form in her little mental sky, and see her beginning to distort her personality by developing an unconscious bitterness toward white people; when you have to concoct an answer for a five-year-old son who is asking: "Daddy, why do white people treat colored people so mean?"; when you take a cross-country drive and find it necessary to sleep night after night in the uncomfortable corners of your automobile because no motel will accept you; when you are humiliated day in and day out by nagging signs reading "white" and "colored"; when your first name becomes "nigger," your middle name becomes "boy" (however old you are) and your last name becomes "John," and your wife and mother are never given the respected title "Mrs."; when you are harried by day and haunted by night by the fact that you are a Negro, living constantly at tiptoe stance, never quite knowing what to expect next, and are plagued with inner fears and outer resentments; when you are forever fighting a degenerating sense of "nobodiness"—then you will understand why we find it difficult to wait. There comes a time when the cup of endurance runs over, and men are no longer willing to be plunged into the abyss of despair. I hope, sirs, you can understand our legitimate and unavoidable impatience.

You express a great deal of anxiety over our willingness to break laws. This is certainly a legitimate concern. Since we so diligently urge people to obey the Supreme Court's decision of 1954 outlawing segregation in the public schools, at first glance it may seem rather paradoxical for us consciously to break laws. One may well ask: "How can you advocate breaking some laws and obeying others?" The answer lies in the fact that there are two types of laws: just and unjust. I would be the first to advocate obeying just laws. One has not only a legal but a moral responsibility to obey just laws. Conversely, one has a moral responsibility to disobey unjust laws. I would agree with St. Augustine that "an unjust law is no law at all."

Now, what is the difference between the two? How does one determine whether a law is just or unjust? A just law is a man-made code that squares with the moral law or the law of God. An unjust law is a code that is out of harmony with the moral law. To put it in the terms of St. Thomas Aquinas: An unjust law is a human law that is not rooted in eternal law and natural law. Any law that uplifts human personality is just. Any law that degrades human personality is unjust. All segregation statutes are unjust because segregation distorts the soul and damages the personality. It gives the segregator a false sense of superiority and the segregated a false sense of inferiority. Segregation, to use the terminology of the Jewish philosopher Martin Buber, substitutes an "I–it" relationship for an "I–thou" relationship and ends up relegating persons to the status of things. Hence segregation is not only politically, economically and sociologically unsound, it is morally wrong and sinful. Paul Tillich has said that sin is separation. Is not segregation an existential expression of man's tragic separation, his awful estrangement, his terrible sinfulness? Thus it is that I can urge men to obey the 1954 decision of the Supreme Court, for it is morally right; and I can urge them to disobey segregation ordinances, for they are morally wrong.

Let us consider a more concrete example of just and unjust laws. An unjust law is a code that a numerical or power majority group compels a minority group to obey but does not make binding on itself. This is *difference* made legal. By the same token, a just law is a code that a majority compels a minority to follow and that it is willing to follow itself. This is *sameness* made legal.

Let me give another explanation. A law is unjust if it is inflicted on a minority that, as a result of being denied the right to vote, had no part in enacting or devising the law. Who can say that the legislature of Alabama which set up that state's segregation laws was democratically elected? Throughout Alabama all sorts of devious methods are used to prevent Negroes from becoming registered voters, and there are some counties in which, even though Negroes constitute a majority of the population, not a single Negro is registered. Can any law enacted under such circumstances be considered democratically structured?

Sometimes a law is just on its face and unjust in its application. For instance, I have been arrested on a charge of parading without a permit. Now, there is nothing wrong in having an ordinance which requires a permit for a parade. But such an ordinance becomes unjust when it is used to maintain segregation and to deny citizens the First-Amendment privilege of peaceful assembly and protest.

I hope you are able to see the distinction I am trying to point out. In no sense do I advocate evading or defying the law, as would the rabid segregationist. That would lead to anarchy. One who breaks an unjust law must do so openly, lovingly, and with a willingness to accept the penalty. I submit that an individual who breaks a law that conscience tells him is unjust, and who willingly accepts the penalty of imprisonment in order to arouse the conscience of the community over its injustice, is in reality expressing the highest respect for law.

Of course, there is nothing new about this kind of civil disobedience. It was evidenced sublimely in the refusal of Shadrach, Meshach and Abednego to obey the laws of Nebuchadnezzar, on the ground that a higher moral law was at stake. It was practiced superbly by the early Christians, who were willing to face hungry lions and the excruciating pain of chopping blocks rather than submit to certain unjust laws of the Roman Empire. To a degree, academic freedom is a reality today because Socrates practiced civil disobedience. In our own nation, the Boston Tea Party represented a massive act of civil disobedience.

We should never forget that everything Adolf Hitler did in Germany was "legal" and everything the Hungarian freedom fighters did in Hungary was "illegal." It was "illegal" to aid and comfort a Jew in Hitler's Germany. Even so, I am sure that, had I lived in Germany at the time, I would have aided and comforted my Jewish brothers. If today I lived in a Communist country where certain principles dear to the Christian faith are suppressed, I would openly advocate disobeying that country's antireligious laws.

I must make two honest confessions to you, my Christian and Jewish brothers. First, I must confess that over the past few years I have been gravely disappointed with the white moderate. I have almost reached the regrettable conclusion that the Negro's great stumbling block in his stride toward freedom is not the White Citizen's Counciler or the Ku Klux Klanner, but the white moderate, who is more devoted to "order" than to justice; who prefers a negative peace which is the absence of tension to a positive peace which is the presence of justice; who constantly says: "I agree with you in the goal you seek, but I cannot agree with your methods of direct action"; who paternalistically believes he can set the timetable for another man's freedom; who lives by a mythical concept of time and who constantly advises the Negro to wait for a "more convenient season." Shallow understanding from people of good will is more frustrating than absolute misunderstanding from people of ill will. Lukewarm acceptance is much more bewildering than outright rejection.

I had hoped that the white moderate would understand that law and order exist for the purpose of establishing justice and that when they fail in this purpose they become the dangerously structured dams that block the flow of social progress. I had hoped that the white moderate would understand that the present tension in the South is a necessary phase of the transition from an obnoxious negative peace, in which the Negro passively accepted his unjust plight, to a substantive and positive peace, in which all men will respect the dignity and worth of human personality. Actually, we who engage in nonviolent direct action are not the creators of tension. We merely bring to the surface the hidden tension that is already alive. We bring it out in the open, where it can be seen and dealt with. Like a boil that can never be cured so long as it is covered up but must be opened with all its ugliness to the natural medicines of air and light, injustice must be exposed, with all the tension its exposure creates, to the light of human conscience and the air of national opinion before it can be cured.

In your statement you assert that our actions, even though peaceful, must be condemned because they precipitate violence. But is this a logical assertion? Isn't this like condemning a robbed man because his possession of money precipitated the evil act of robbery? Isn't this like condemning Socrates because his unswerving commitment to truth and his philosophical inquiries precipitated the act by the misguided populace in which they made him drink hemlock? Isn't this like condemning Jesus because his unique God-consciousness and never-ceasing devotion to God's will precipitated the evil act of crucifixion? We must come to see that, as the federal courts have consistently affirmed, it is wrong to urge an individual to cease his efforts to gain his basic constitutional rights because the quest may precipitate violence. Society must protect the robbed and punish the robber.

I had also hoped that the white moderate would reject the myth concerning time in relation to the struggle for freedom. I have just received a letter from a white brother in Texas. He writes: "All Christians know that the colored people will receive equal rights eventually, but it is possible that you are in too great a religious hurry. It has taken Christianity almost two thousand years to accomplish what it has. The teachings of Christ take time to come to earth." Such an attitude stems from a tragic misconception of time, from the strangely irrational notion that there is something in the very flow of time that will inevitably cure all ills. Actually, time itself is neutral; it can be used either destructively or constructively. More and more I feel that the people of ill will have used time much more effectively than have the people of good will. We will have to repent in this generation not merely for the hateful words and actions of the bad people but for the appalling silence of the good people. Human progress never rolls in on wheels of inevitability; it comes through the tireless efforts of men willing to be co-workers with God, and without this hard work, time itself becomes an ally of the forces of social stagnation. We must use time creatively, in the knowledge that the time is always ripe to do right. Now is the time to make real the promise of democracy and transform our pending national elegy into a creative psalm of brotherhood. Now is the time to lift our national policy from the quicksand of racial injustice to the solid rock of human dignity.

You speak of our activity in Birmingham as extreme. At first I was rather disappointed that fellow clergymen would see my nonviolent efforts as those of an extremist. I began thinking about the fact that I stand in the middle of two opposing forces in the Negro community. One is a force of complacency, made up in part of Negroes who, as a result of long years of oppression, are so drained of self-respect and a sense of "somebodiness" that they have adjusted to segregation; and in part of a few middle-class Negroes who, because of a degree of academic and economic security and because in some ways they profit by segregation, have become insensitive to the problems of the masses. The other force is one of bitterness and hatred, and it comes perilously close to advocating violence. It is expressed in the various black nationalist groups that are springing up across the nation, the largest and best-known being Elijah Muhammad's Muslim movement. Nourished by the Negro's frustration over the continued existence of racial discrimination, this movement is made up of people who have lost faith in America, who have absolutely repudiated Christianity, and who have concluded that the white man is an incorrigible "devil."

I have tried to stand between these two forces, saying that we need emulate neither the "do-nothingism" of the complacent nor the hatred and despair of the black nationalist. For there is the more excellent way of love and nonviolent protest. I am grateful to God that, through the influence of the Negro church, the way of nonviolence became an integral part of our struggle.

If this philosophy had not emerged, by now many streets of the South would, I am convinced, be flowing with blood. And I am further convinced that if our white brothers dismiss as "rabble-rousers" and "outside agitators" those of us who employ nonviolent direct action and if they refuse to support our nonviolent efforts, millions of Negroes will, out of frustration and despair, seek solace and security in black-nationalist ideologies—a development that would inevitably lead to a frightening racial nightmare.

Oppressed people cannot remain oppressed forever. The yearning for freedom eventually manifests itself, and that is what has happened to the American Negro. Something within has reminded him of his birthright of freedom, and something without has reminded him that it can be gained. Consciously or unconsciously, he has been caught up by the *Zeitgeist,* and with his black brothers of Africa and his brown and yellow brothers of Asia, South America and the Caribbean, the United States Negro is moving with a sense of great urgency toward the promised land of racial justice. If one recognizes this vital urge that has engulfed the Negro community, one should readily understand why public demonstrations are taking place. The Negro has many pent-up resentments and latent frustrations, and he must release them. So let him march; let him make prayer pilgrimages to the city hall; let him go on freedom rides—and try to understand why he must do so. If his repressed emotions are not released in nonviolent ways, they will seek expression through violence; this is not a threat but a fact of history. So I have not said to my people: "Get rid of your discontent." Rather, I have tried to say that this normal and healthy discontent can be channeled into the creative outlet of nonviolent direct action. And now this approach is being termed extremist.

But though I was initially disappointed at being categorized as an extremist, as I continued to think about the matter I gradually gained a measure of satisfaction from the label. Was not Jesus an extremist of love: "Love your enemies, bless them that curse you, do good to them that hate you, and pray for them which despitefully use you, and persecute you." Was not Amos an extremist for justice: "Let justice roll down like waters and righteousness like an ever-flowing stream." Was not Paul an extremist for the Christian gospel: "I bear in my body the marks of the Lord Jesus." Was not Martin Luther an extremist: "Here I stand; I cannot do otherwise, so help me God." And John Bunyan: "I will stay in jail to the end of my days before I make a butchery of my conscience." And Abraham Lincoln: "This nation cannot survive half slave and half free." And Thomas Jefferson: "We hold these truths to be self-evident, that all men are created equal. . . ." So the question is not whether we will be extremists, but what kind of extremists we will be. Will we be extremists for hate or for love? Will we be extremists for the preservation of injustice or for the extension of justice? In that dramatic scene on Calvary's hill three men were crucified. We must never forget that all three were crucified for the same crime—the crime of extremism. Two were extremists for immorality, and thus fell below their environment. The other, Jesus Christ, was an extremist for love, truth and goodness, and thereby rose above his environment. Perhaps the South, the nation and the world are in dire need of creative extremists.

I had hoped that the white moderate would see this need. Perhaps I was too optimistic; perhaps I expected too much. I suppose I should have realized that few members of the oppressor race can understand the deep groans and passionate yearnings of the oppressed race, and still fewer have the vision to see that injustice must be rooted out by strong, persistent and determined action. I am thankful, however, that some of the white brothers in the South have grasped the meaning of this social revolution and committed themselves to it. They are still all too few in quantity, but they are big in quality. Some—such as Ralph McGill, Lillian Smith, Harry Golden, James McBride Dabbs, Ann Braden and Sarah Patton Boyle—have written about our strug-

gle in eloquent and prophetic terms. Others have marched with us
down nameless streets of the South. They have languished in filthy,
roach-infested jails, suffering the abuse and brutality of policemen
who view them as "dirty nigger-lovers." Unlike so many of their moderate brothers and sisters, they have recognized the urgency of the
moment and sensed the need for powerful "action" antidotes to combat the disease of segregation.

Let me take note of my other major disappointment. I have been so
greatly disappointed with the white church and its leadership. Of
course, there are some notable exceptions. I am not unmindful of the
fact that each of you has taken some significant stands on this issue. I
commend you, Reverend Stallings, for your Christian stand on this
past Sunday, in welcoming Negroes to your worship service on a non-
segregated basis. I commend the Catholic leaders of this state for in-
tegrating Spring Hill College several years ago.

But despite these notable exceptions, I must honestly reiterate that
I have been disappointed with the church. I do not say this as one of
those negative critics who can always find something wrong with the
church. I say this as a minister of the gospel, who loves the church;
who was nurtured in its bosom; who has been sustained by its spiritual blessings and who will remain true to it as long as the cord of
life shall lengthen.

When I was suddenly catapulted into the leadership of the bus protest in Montgomery, Alabama, a few years ago, I felt we would be
supported by the white church. I felt that the white ministers, priests
and rabbis of the South would be among our strongest allies. Instead,
some have been outright opponents, refusing to understand the freedom movement and misrepresenting its leaders; all too many others
have been more cautious than courageous and have remained silent
behind the anesthetizing security of stained-glass windows.

In spite of my shattered dreams, I came to Birmingham with the
hope that the white religious leadership of this community would see
the justice of our cause and, with deep moral concern, would serve as
the channel through which our just grievances could reach the power
structure. I had hoped that each of you would understand. But again
I have been disappointed.

I have heard numerous southern religious leaders admonish their
worshipers to comply with a desegregation decision because it is the
law, but I have longed to hear white ministers declare: "Follow this
decree because integration is morally right and because the Negro is
your brother." In the midst of blatant injustices inflicted upon the
Negro, I have watched white churchmen stand on the sideline and
mouth pious irrelevancies and sanctimonious trivialities. In the midst
of a mighty struggle to rid our nation of racial and economic injustice, I have heard many ministers say: "Those are social issues, with

which the gospel has no real concern." And I have watched many churches commit themselves to a completely otherworldly religion which makes a strange, un-Biblical distinction between body and soul, between the sacred and the secular.

I have traveled the length and breadth of Alabama, Mississippi and all the other southern states. On sweltering summer days and crisp autumn mornings I have looked at the South's beautiful churches with their lofty spires pointing heavenward. I have beheld the impressive outlines of her massive religious-education buildings. Over and over I have found myself asking: "What kind of people worship here? Who is their God? Where were their voices when the lips of Governor Barnett dripped with words of interposition and nullification? Where were they when Governor Wallace gave a clarion call for defiance and hatred? Where were their voices of support when bruised and weary Negro men and women decided to rise from the dark dungeons of complacency to the bright hills of creative protest?"

Yes, these questions are still in my mind. In deep disappointment I have wept over the laxity of the church. But be assured that my tears have been tears of love. There can be no deep disappointment where there is not deep love. Yes, I love the church. How could I do otherwise? I am in the rather unique position of being the son, the grandson and the great-grandson of preachers. Yes, I see the church as the body of Christ. But, oh! How we have blemished and scarred that body through social neglect and through fear of being nonconformists.

There was a time when the church was very powerful—in the time when the early Christians rejoiced at being deemed worthy to suffer for what they believed. In those days the church was not merely a thermometer that recorded the ideas and principles of popular opinion; it was a thermostat that transformed the mores of society. Whenever the early Christians entered a town, the people in power became disturbed and immediately sought to convict the Christians for being "disturbers of the peace" and "outside agitators." But the Christians pressed on, in the conviction that they were "a colony of heaven," called to obey God rather than man. Small in number, they were big in commitment. They were too God-intoxicated to be "astronomically intimidated." By their effort and example they brought an end to such ancient evils as infanticide and gladiatorial contests.

Things are different now. So often the contemporary church is a weak, ineffectual voice with an uncertain sound. So often it is an archdefender of the status quo. Far from being disturbed by the presence of the church, the power structure of the average community is consoled by the church's silent—and often even vocal—sanction of things as they are.

But the judgment of God is upon the church as never before. If today's church does not recapture the sacrificial spirit of the early church, it will lose its authenticity, forfeit the loyalty of millions, and be dismissed as an irrelevant social club with no meaning for the twentieth century. Every day I meet young people whose disappointment with the church has turned into outright disgust.

Perhaps I have once again been too optimistic. Is organized religion too inextricably bound to the status quo to save our nation and the world? Perhaps I must turn my faith to the inner spiritual church, the church within the church, as the true *ekklesia* and the hope of the world. But again I am thankful to God that some noble souls from the ranks of organized religion have broken loose from the paralyzing chains of conformity and joined us as active partners in the struggle for freedom. They have left their secure congregations and walked the streets of Albany, Georgia, with us. They have gone down the highways of the South on tortuous rides for freedom. Yes, they have gone to jail with us. Some have been dismissed from their churches, have lost the support of their bishops and fellow ministers. But they have acted in the faith that right defeated is stronger than evil triumphant. Their witness has been the spiritual salt that has preserved the true meaning of the gospel in these troubled times. They have carved a tunnel of hope through the dark mountain of disappointment.

I hope the church as a whole will meet the challenge of this decisive hour. But even if the church does not come to the aid of justice, I have no despair about the future. I have no fear about the outcome of our struggle in Birmingham, even if our motives are at present misunderstood. We will reach the goal of freedom in Birmingham and all over the nation, because the goal of America is freedom. Abused and scorned though we may be, our destiny is tied up with America's destiny. Before the Pilgrims landed at Plymouth, we were here. Before the pen of Jefferson etched the majestic words of the Declaration of Independence across the pages of history, we were here. For more than two centuries our forebears labored in this country without wages; they made cotton king; they built the homes of their masters while suffering gross injustice and shameful humiliation—and yet out of a bottomless vitality they continued to thrive and develop. If the inexpressible cruelties of slavery could not stop us, the opposition we now face will surely fail. We will win our freedom because the sacred heritage of our nation and the eternal will of God are embodied in our echoing demands.

Before closing I feel impelled to mention one other point in your statement that has troubled me profoundly. You warmly commended the Birmingham police force for keeping "order" and "preventing violence." I doubt that you would have so warmly commended the police force if you had seen its dogs sinking their teeth into unarmed, nonviolent Negroes. I doubt that you would so quickly commend the policemen if you were to observe their ugly and inhumane treatment of Negroes here in the city jail; if you were to watch them push and curse old Negro women and young Negro girls; if you were to see them slap and kick old Negro men and young boys; if you were to observe them, as they did on two occasions, refuse to give us food because we wanted to sing our grace together. I cannot join you in your praise of the Birmingham police department.

It is true that the police have exercised a degree of discipline in handling the demonstrators. In this sense they have conducted themselves rather "nonviolently" in public. But for what purpose? To preserve the evil system of segregation. Over the past few years I have consistently preached that nonviolence demands that the means we use must be as pure as the ends we seek. I have tried to make clear that it is wrong to use immoral means to attain moral ends. But now I must affirm that it is just as wrong, or perhaps even more so, to use moral means to preserve immoral ends. Perhaps Mr. Connor and his policemen have been rather nonviolent in public, as was Chief Pritchett in Albany, Georgia, but they have used the moral means of nonviolence to maintain the immoral end of racial injustice. As T. S. Eliot has said: "The last temptation is the greatest treason: To do the right deed for the wrong reason."

I wish you had commended the Negro sit-inners and demonstrators of Birmingham for their sublime courage, their willingness to suffer and their amazing discipline in the midst of great provocation. One day the South will recognize its real heroes. They will be the James Merediths, with the noble sense of purpose that enables them to face jeering and hostile mobs, and with the agonizing loneliness that characterizes the life of the pioneer. They will be old, oppressed, battered Negro women, symbolized in a seventy-two-year-old woman in Montgomery, Alabama, who rose up with a sense of dignity and with her people decided not to ride segregated buses, and who responded with ungrammatical profundity to one who inquired about her weariness: "My feets is tired, but my soul is at rest." They will be the young high school and college students, the young ministers of the gospel and a host of their elders, courageously and nonviolently sitting in at lunch counters and willingly going to jail for conscience' sake. One day the South will know that when these disinherited children of God sat down at lunch counters, they were in reality standing up for what is best in the American dream and for the most sacred values in our Judaeo-Christian heritage, thereby bringing our nation back to those great wells of democracy which were dug deep by the founding fathers in their formulation of the Constitution and the Declaration of Independence.

Never before have I written so long a letter. I'm afraid it is much too long to take your precious time. I can assure you that it would have been much shorter if I had been writing from a comfortable desk, but what else can one do when he is alone in a narrow jail cell, other than write long letters, think long thoughts and pray long prayers?

If I have said anything in this letter that overstates the truth and indicates an unreasonable impatience, I beg you to forgive me. If I have said anything that understates the truth and indicates my having a patience that allows me to settle for anything less than brotherhood, I beg God to forgive me.

I hope this letter finds you strong in the faith. I also hope that circumstances will soon make it possible for me to meet each of you, not as an integrationist or a civil-rights leader but as a fellow clergyman and a Christian brother. Let us all hope that the dark clouds of racial prejudice will soon pass away and the deep fog of misunderstanding will be lifted from our fear-drenched communities, and in some not too distant tomorrow the radiant stars of love and brotherhood will shine over our great nation with all their scintillating beauty.

Yours for the cause of Peace and Brotherhood,

MARTIN LUTHER KING, JR.

5 / Religious Obedience and Civil Disobedience: A Policy Statement of the National Council of the Churches of Christ in the United States of America

ADOPTED BY THE GENERAL BOARD JUNE 7, 1968

I. MAN ACTS POLITICALLY

Men are political creatures; they are seldom politically inert. Usually they act for their own political advantage or aggrandizement. Sometimes they act for the sake of principle or for the benefit of others,

SOURCE: Policy statement of the General Board of the National Council of the Churches of Christ, New York, New York.

even to their own disadvantage. Often they act with mixed motives and effects. When they fail to act at all, they yield the ground to others, and thus share responsibility for the political outcome.

God calls men to act within and upon the structures of their time for the serving of their fellow men. When they obey this calling, they are acting politically. Since most men act politically most of the time (if only by default), their religious obedience does not add a new kind of *action* so much as a new *direction*. Instead of acting politically for personal or partisan advantage, the man who seeks to obey God's calling tests all his actions by their effect on the whole commonwealth, particularly upon the disadvantaged, who are the special object of divine compassion.

He does not choose whether to act politically or not to act politically so much as whether to act obediently or not to act obediently to God's calling. Once a man's (political) course is set toward the serving of his fellow men and away from serving his own advantage at the expense of his fellow men, the mode or level of his (political) action will be determined by tactical and ethical considerations arising from his circumstance.

II. THE RANGE OF MAN'S ACTION BASED ON CONSCIENCE

The range of possible action is broad, and men seeking to obey God's will have chosen various modes of action at various times:

A. ABSTENTION. Some Christians believe that they should not attempt, either individually or corporately or both, to influence the political structures of their time. (Their abstention, however, is not without effect—sometimes crucial effect—upon political events.)

B. ACTION WITHIN THE EXISTING STRUCTURES OF CIVIL LAW AND GOVERNMENT. This is the most common mode of obedient action, particularly in modern democracies, for those citizens who share in determining the structures. It includes the kinds of action protected by the First Amendment of the U.S. Constitution—freedom of speech, freedom of press, freedom of assembly and petition (including orderly picketing)—which are thereby incorporated in the existing structures.

C. PEACEABLE, PUBLIC ACTION IN OPPOSITION TO A PARTICULAR LAW OR POLICY. When citizens support a democratic system of government in general, but oppose a particular law or policy they consider unjust, they sometimes resort to systematic civil disobedience of that law. (Even in a representative democracy there is often a lag between the frontiers of Christian conscience and some laws passed by the legislature, as in the case of laws upholding discrimination and segregation which after a century were acknowledged to be contrary to both Christian principles and the Constitution of the nation.)

D. Action in Resistance to a Particular Law or Policy. Political action which is *covert* (such as the Underground Railroad by which Quakers and others spirited escaped slaves to Canada) or *violent* is an option beyond the range of civil disobedience, though still directed against a limited target of felt injustice rather than against the existing structure as a whole.

E. Action in Revolution Against an Entire System of Government. Covert and violent action designed to overthrow the existing system of government altogether is *revolution* rather than *resistance,* and men seeking to obey the will of God have sometimes resorted to it for reasons such as those stated in the American *Declaration of Independence,* a historic manifesto of revolution.

We recognize that when justice cannot be secured either through action within the existing structures or through civil disobedience, an increasing number of Christians may feel called to seek justice through resistance or revolution. Therefore, a study should be made of the alternatives of resistance and revolution in the light of Christian principles and experience.

III. "WE MUST OBEY GOD RATHER THAN MAN"

In the Western tradition which shaped the American political system, it is generally agreed that the function of government is to secure justice, peace and freedom for its citizens, and to maintain order, not as an end in itself, but as a condition necessary for the existence of justice, peace and freedom. Christians find this tradition generally compatible with their understanding of the divinely-ordained function of the state.

When, however, a particular government fails to provide justice, peace or freedom, it is not maintaining true order, and Christians should remain faithful to their understanding of what order ought to be, even at the cost of disobeying that government. In such circumstances, it is the government which has become insubordinate to God's order, and not those who disobey that government. Rather, they show their genuine respect for rightful "governing authority" by criticizing, resisting or opposing the current misusers of that authority.

Although Christians recognize the importance of order for human society, in every period of history there has been a Christian witness against giving absolute or unquestioning obedience to any civil authority. The first allegiance of Christians is to God, and when earthly rulers command what is contrary to the will of God, Christians reply as did Peter and John, "We must obey God rather than men." (Acts 5:29) Whatever the penalty for disobedience to human law, it has not deterred some Christian martyrs in every age from pointing by their death beyond man's order to God's order.

IV. CONSCIENCE: ONE AND MANY

At no time, however, have Christians been unanimous in agreeing how or when they should "obey God rather than men." The essential problem is to determine when the state represents God's instrument of order and when it represents man's tyranny. The decision is a fateful one, and Christians have taken it only with reluctance.

Individual conscience, though more sensitive than the aggregate of men, is often eccentric, obsessive or obtuse, and needs the correction that can come from sympathetic encounter with the consciences of others. Both individual and group can benefit by supportive confrontation within the religious community: the individual may become aware of countervailing facts and factors, and the community may find its equanimity disturbed by the anguish of the individual.

Since the warning of the need for change comes to and through individual conscience, the community should safeguard its expression, however strident or abrasive it may seem. A more acute problem is posed for the community when the protesting conscience progresses from dialogue to demonstration, from conversation to civil disobedience. Then the community is inclined to chide the dissenter with having gone too far, with having somehow exceeded the bounds of conduct permissible to Christians. Yet the briefest reflection on history will remind us that this judgment is not accurate. Some of the most venerated Christian saints and sages have spent part of their lives in prison or have been banished or executed for defying the civil authorities of their time, and this was not a reproach to them but a sign of their obedience to God.

V. WITNESS: WORDS AND DEEDS

Civil law in the United States distinguishes between speech and action. Acts which violate the law can be punished, but speech cannot unless it poses a "clear and present danger" to public safety. This distinction in law and jurisprudence has proved to be a valuable safeguard of the rights to free communication of ideas. Christian theology, however, does not recognize such a dichotomy between the witness of word and deed, for the former without the latter is "hypocrisy." The Christian who is impelled to speak against an unjust law is not necessarily excused from action because of civil interdiction. He is responsible before God for his deeds as well as his words, and cannot yield that responsibility to anyone, even to the magistrate.

VI. CIVIL DISOBEDIENCE:
ITS ROLE AND OPERATION

Civil disobedience is used in this statement to mean deliberate, peaceable violation of a law deemed to be unjust, in obedience to conscience or a higher law, and with recognition of the state's legal authority to punish the violator.

A. CIVIL DISOBEDIENCE IS *deliberate*. It is consciously willed and intended, based on deep conviction, and entered into with full awareness of the consequences, after the failure of less disruptive alternatives. Violation of law through ignorance or inadvertence is not civil disobedience.

B. CIVIL DISOBEDIENCE IS *public*. There is no effort to conceal it from the authorities; on the contrary, they are often given advance notice of intended acts of civil disobedience. Even when such advance notice is not given, one result of civil disobedience frequently is to focus public awareness on injustice by overt acts of disobedience.

C. CIVIL DISOBEDIENCE IS *peaceable*. It seeks to minimize the harm done to others through willingness to suffer hurt rather than to inflict it. A criminal action, for instance, is one by which the perpetrator harms the commonwealth for his own advantage, whereas in civil disobedience the perpetrator seeks to benefit the commonwealth at his own risk and disadvantage.

D. Civil disobedience is *violation of a law deemed to be unjust* in obedience to conscience or a higher law. It is usually entered into by those who feel they have no choice but to disobey—as Luther put it, "Here I stand, God help me. *I can do no other.*" The authority appealed to beyond civil statutes may be conscience, God's commandments, the moral law, natural law, the good of mankind or some other norm of conscience for which one is willing, even compelled, to risk offending civil authorities and public opinion.

E. Civil disobedience entails *recognition of the state's legal authority to punish those who violate the law.* In a society in which the man who seeks to obey God can honor and subordinate himself to the civil order as a whole, and is compelled by conscience to disobey only one law or group of laws, he will recognize the state's power to punish violators of the law, including himself. If the government or the civil order as a whole is so corrupt or demonic that to criticize any aspect of it is to court death as an enemy of the regime (as was the case in Hitler's Germany), then the Christian may reluctantly conclude that he cannot willingly recognize or submit to the state's power to punish at all, in which case he is engaged, not in civil disobedience, but in civil resistance or revolution [with which this statement does not attempt to deal].

The foregoing is a description of the form of civil disobedience exemplified by Henry David Thoreau, Leo Tolstoy, Mohandas Gandhi, and Martin Luther King, Jr. So understood, it is a limited and moderate mode of political action, and we call upon Christians and other men of good will to recognize it as a valid instrument for those who seek justice, constant with both Christian tradition and the American political and legal heritage.

VII. RESPONSE OF THE CHURCH TO CIVIL DISOBEDIENCE

The Christian Church owes to its members who undertake civil disobedience the following measures of support:

Pastoral and material care of the individual and his family;

Exploration and testing of the individual's views within the Christian community;

Interpretation of the moral legitimacy of the individual's position, even if the majority of the Church does not agree with him;

Protection of his legal rights, including the right to counsel;

Pursuit of judicial review or amendment of unjust statutes;

Enactment of laws more nearly conformable to moral principles.

81 FOR,   6 AGAINST,   15 ABSTENTIONS

CONTRACT AND CONSENT

> The obligation of subjects to the Sovereign, is
> understood to last as long, no longer, than the
> power by which he is able to protect them.
>
> —THOMAS HOBBES, *Leviathan*

> And when the body of the people, or any sin-
> gle man is deprived of their [natural] right
> . . . then they have liberty to appeal to
> heaven, whenever they judge the cause of suf-
> ficient moment.
>
> —JOHN LOCKE, *Second Treatise*

In her brilliant article "Obligation
and Consent," the second part of which is reprinted here, Hanna Pitkin focuses attention on such questions as: Under what circumstances
are political revolutions justified? Whom are we obliged to obey?
Why should some rule and some be ruled? Why are we obliged to
obey even "legitimate" authority? Mrs. Pitkin critically examines the
history of consent theory in order to assess the value of social contract theorists in answering these basic questions of political obligation.

The late E. F. Carritt's classical analysis of Hobbes's theory of obligation is a succinct statement of the implications of Hobbes's theory
of psychological egoism and insecurity. Self-interested men prefer
tyranny to anarchy. They obey laws out of fear that other rapacious
men, of "equal . . . intent and capacity to injure," pose a greater
threat than does the Leviathan state. All men gain from a general loss
of liberty, because at least their lives are protected. Man is thus willing to obey *all* dictates of the Leviathan that he has created by a covenant or contract to relinquish all sovereignty to the State. But if the
state should lose its capacity to protect the life of all, through war or
other causes of weakness, the heretofore total obligation to obey positive law is revoked. The principle of self-defense is Hobbes's only justification for civil disobedience.

" 'The Consent of the Governed' in Two Traditions of Political
Thought," by Fred H. Willhoite, Jr., discusses several different usages
of the concept of "consent" in political discourse, such as "continuing
consent," "formative consent," and "consensus." These usages are
shown to be quite distinctly treated in the intuitionistic rationalist

tradition of Locke, which treats "reason" as a special faculty that provides man with "moral insight," and in the voluntaristic tradition of
Hobbes, which treats reason only as logic or cunning in the service of
man's passion and his will.

6 / Obligation and Consent—Part II

HANNA PITKIN

A reexamination of even the most
venerable traditional problems of political theory can sometimes
yield surprisingly new and relevant results.[1] The problem of political
obligation, for example, and its most popular "solution," based on
consent, turn out on reexamination to be rather different from what
we have come to assume about them. The problem of political obligation resolves itself into at least four mutually related but partially
independent questions:

1. The limits of obligation ("*When* are you obligated to obey, and
   when not?")
2. The locus of sovereignty ("*Whom* are you obligated to obey?")
3. The difference between legitimate authority and mere coercion ("Is
   there *really* any difference; are you ever *really* obligated?")
4. The justification of obligation ("*Why* are you ever obligated to obey
   even a legitimate authority?")

And the consent theory of obligation, as exemplified in Locke's *Second Treatise* and Joseph Tussman's *Obligation and the Body Politic*,
turns out to yield a new formulation—perhaps a new interpretation
of consent theory, perhaps an alternative to it—that might be labeled either the doctrine of the "nature of the government" or the
doctrine of "hypothetical consent." [2]

It teaches that your obligation depends not on any actual act of

SOURCE: *The American Political Science Review*, LX (March 1966), 39–52. Reprinted by permission of the author and publisher.

[1] This and part of the following paragraph are intended to summarize the argument of "Obligation and Consent—I," *American Political Science Review*, LIX
(December 1965), 990–999.

[2] John Locke, *Second Treatise of Civil Government;* Joseph Tussman, *Obligation
and the Body Politic* (New York: Oxford, 1960).

consenting, past or present, by yourself or your fellow-citizens, but on the character of the government. If it is a good, just government doing what a government should, then you must obey it; if it is a tyrannical, unjust government trying to do what no government may, then you have no such obligation. Or to put it another way, your obligation depends not on whether you have consented but on whether the government is such that you *ought* to consent to it, whether its actions are in accord with the authority a hypothetical group of rational men in a hypothetical state of nature would have (had) to give to any government they were founding. Having shown how this formulation emerges from Locke's and Tussman's ideas, I want now to defend it as a valid response to what troubles us about political obligation, and as a response more consonant than most with the moral realities of human decisions about obedience and resistance. At the same time the discussion should also demonstrate how many different or even conflicting things that one might want to call "consent" continue to be relevant—a fact which may help to explain the tenacity of traditional consent theory in the face of its manifest difficulties. Such a defense and demonstration, with detailed attention to such decisions, are difficult; the discussion from here on will be more speculative, and will raise more questions than it answers.

THE THEORY APPLIED

Our new doctrine seems most obviously satisfactory as a response to question three, concerning the difference between legitimate authority and mere coercion. For it teaches that legitimate authority is precisely that which *ought* to be obeyed, to which one ought to consent, which deserves obedience and consent, to which rational men considering all relevant facts and issues would consent, to which consent can be justified. Anything or anyone else who tries to command us is then merely coercing, and is not entitled to our obedience. This answer to the question is essentially what Wittgenstein calls a "point of grammar"; it reminds us of the way concepts like "authority," "legitimacy," "law" are related in our language (and therefore in our world) to concepts like "consent" and "obedience." [3] To call something a legitimate authority is normally to imply that it ought to be obeyed. You cannot, without further rather elaborate explanation, maintain simultaneously *both* that this government has legitimate authority over you *and* that you have no obligation to obey it. Thus if

[3] Ludwig Wittgenstein, *Philosophical Investigations* (New York: Macmillan, 1953). See also Stanley Louis Cavell, "The Claim to Rationality" (Unpublished Ph.D. dissertation, Harvard University, 1961), esp. Chapter I.

you say that you consent to it (recognize it as an authority), that statement itself is normally a recognition of the obligation to obey, at least at the moment it is uttered. Part of what "authority" means is that those subject to it are obligated to obey. As an answer to question three, then, this doctrine tells us (something about) what legitimate authority *is* by reminding us of something about what "legitimate authority" *means*. But of course that is not yet to provide criteria for telling apart the two species—legitimate authority and mere coercion—when you encounter them in reality.

Thus, insofar as our *real* need is for a practical way of deciding whether to obey or resist this government right now, or which of two rival authorities to follow, our new theory seems less adequate. Its response to our question three does not seem immediately helpful with questions one and two; and surely those are of the most concern to real people confronted with decisions about action. It just does not seem very helpful to tell a man considering resistance to authority: you must obey if the government is such that you ought to obey. But neither is traditional consent theory very helpful to this man; indeed, one of its weaknesses has always been this matter of detailed application. Perhaps it is even a mistake to assume that a theory of political obligation is supposed to tell a man directly what to do in particular cases.[4]

One might argue, however, that such a theory should at least tell him what sorts of considerations are relevant to his decision, direct his attention and tell him where to look.[5] And in that regard, I suggest that traditional consent theory is defective, for it directs such a man's attention to the wrong place. It teaches him to look at himself (for his own consent) or at the people around him (for theirs), rather than at the merits of the government. Where it demands obedience, consent theory does so on the grounds that he or the majority have consented; where it justifies resistance, it does so on the grounds that consent was never given or has been exceeded. Thus the man who must choose is directed to the question: have I (we) consented to this? The new doctrine formulated in this essay seems at least to have the virtue of pointing such a man in the right direction. For it tells him: look to the nature of the government—its characteristics, structure, activities, functioning. This is not much of a guide, but it is a

---

[4] See, for example, Margaret Macdonald, "The Language of Political Theory," in A. Flew, ed., *Logic and Language: First Series* (Oxford: Basil Blackwell, 1960), pp. 167–186.

[5] This suggestion is advanced, against Miss Macdonald's argument, in S. I. Benn and R. S. Peters, *Social Principles and the Democratic State* (London: George Allen & Unwin, 1959), pp. 299–301.

beginning much more usefully related to what men need to think about when they make such choices.

Let us consider seriously what sorts of things people really think about when they confront a genuine decision about obedience and resistance, and what sorts of things they ought to think about. But anyone who undertakes to do that is immediately overwhelmed by the complexity and multiplicity of what seems relevant, and by the many different imaginable cases. We need to consider a list of specific cases at least as diverse as these:

> Socrates, as presented in the *Crito* and the *Apology*.
> An ordinary criminal.
> An American student engaging in civil disobedience.
> A Mississippi Negro who decides to join a revolutionary group.
> A South African Negro who decides to join a revolutionary group.
> A minor official in Nazi Germany, who continues to carry out his functions.

Even a brief review of such cases teaches at least this much: the occasions for contemplating and possibly engaging in disobedience are extremely varied; and a great many kinds of non-obedience are available, from flight through crime to attempted revolution.[6] Some forms of non-obedience are violent, others not; some are personal and others organized; some are isolated actions and others a systematic program of action; some are directed against a particular law or decree and others against an entire system of government. To a person confronted with a real decision about resistance or obedience, it makes an enormous difference what kind of action is contemplated. Circumstances that may justify escape or isolated refusal to obey a particular law may not suffice to justify revolution; indeed, some forms of resistance (like civil disobedience) may even be provided for within a political system.

Next, we may notice that all of our examples are, or could reasonably be, people in conflict. Socrates may never have been in doubt as to what he would do, but his friends certainly disagreed with him at first; and he cast his own argument in the form of a confrontation between the desire "to play truant" and the admonitions of the laws. All of our examples (with the exception of the criminal?) might have good, serious reasons for resistance. None of them ought to feel entirely free to pursue those reasons without first weighing them against something else—his *prima facie* obligation to obey. One might say: all these men ought to feel a certain tie to their governments, their societies, in the sense in which Socrates feels such a tie,

[6] Something like this point is suggested by Tussman, *op. cit.*, p. 43.

but some of them might nevertheless be justified in disobeying or resisting. That he does not sufficiently feel such a tie, that he has no (good) reason, no justification for disobedience, is precisely what makes the case of an "ordinary" criminal different from the rest. This is at least in accord with the formula offered by our new theory: normally law, authority, government are to be obeyed and resistance requires justification. You are not morally free to resist as a matter of whim.

The real person confronted by a problematic situation about obedience needs to know that, but he obviously needs to know much more. He needs to know much more specifically when resistance is justified and what might count as a justification. Does he learn this by thinking about his own past consent or that of his fellow-citizens, as traditional consent theory would suggest? Or does he learn it by assessing the nature and quality of the government?

Our cases of potential disobedience show an interesting division in this respect. Three of them—the student and the two Negroes—seem quite unlikely to think much about their own past consent—when and whether they consented, how often and how seriously, expressly or tacitly, and so on. What they are likely to think about is the "outrageous" conduct and "oppressive, unjust" structure of the government, and of the possible consequences of resistance. The criminal (since we have defined him as "ordinary") is not likely to think about either obligations to obey or justifications for his action. The Nazi might well cite his consent to the Fuehrer, his oath of office, pledges of absolute obedience, and so on, as a justification for continued obedience despite "certain unpleasant government measures that perhaps ought not to have been taken." And Socrates is passionately aware of his ties to the Athenian laws, the gratitude he owes them for past favors, the power of his past consent to them.

Thus both Socrates and the Nazi do seem to look to past consent rather than to the nature of the government. But the significance of this fact has yet to be assessed; for on closer examination, each of their cases reveals an important weakness in traditional consent theory. From the case of the Nazi we can learn that even express consent may not be enough; and from that of Socrates, the difficulties of applying past consent as a guide to action.

It might be tempting to say that of our six cases, only Socrates is truly moral, for only he thinks about his obligations and commitments to the laws. But the example of the Nazi saves us from this simplistic response, by showing that sometimes past promises and oaths are not enough to determine present obligations. Sometimes a man who cites even an express oath to obedience, is being not admirable but hypocritical, refusing to recognize where his real duty lies. We would not want to say that past oaths and promises count for nothing, that they can be ignored at will. We all feel the power of the argument that you ought to be consistent, that it isn't fair to pick up your marbles and go home just because it's your turn to lose under the rules you have accepted so far. But that is partly because such a partisan assessment of the rules is likely to be biased. If you can in fact show that the rules are really unfair, then any time is a good time to change them. Again, normally rules and authorities are to be obeyed; when occasions for questioning this obligation arise, what is ultimately needed is an assessment of the rules or authorities. Mere reference to your "going along with them" in the past is not enough.

No doubt if a man had no political obligation he could acquire one by a promise or contract. But that by no means proves that political obligation can be acquired *only* by promise or contract; it may be that a quite independent political obligation is sometimes reinforced by an oath to obey, at other times (partly) countered by a promise to resist. A personal past commitment to obey need not settle the matter.

Indeed, the case of the Nazi calls attention to something traditional consent theory seems to have overlooked: the duty to resist. There are times in human history when men are not merely free(d) from an obligation to obey, but positively obligated to oppose the powers that be. The authors of the Declaration of Independence recognized this, despite their heavy reliance on Locke; for they saw resistance to tyranny not merely as man's right but as his duty. Locke, and traditional consent theory in general, make no provision for such a duty, nor can it be easily accommodated within their framework. There is provision in Locke's system for majority resistance to a tyrannical government, and a duty to follow such a majority. But *individual* resistance has a highly ambiguous status at best, and is certainly *not* a duty.[7] For if political obligation arises from contract, the violation or overstepping of this contract leaves each individual free to do as he likes with regard to the tyranny. True, the individual is still then bound by natural law; but natural law does not command the punishment of offenders, it only permits it. And amending the Lockeian system on this score would obviously require fundamental changes in its individualistic presuppositions.

Similarly, traditional consent theory teaches that at times of civil war or successful revolution, when an old authority structure collapses, each individual is free to place his consent anew wherever he wishes and thinks best for himself. If he thinks it fit to follow a highway robber then, he is free to do so. But when we contemplate real cases, would we not rather want to maintain that even in chaos there

[7] Locke, *op. cit.*, pars. 121, 149, 168, 203–4, 208–9, 211–12, 220, 232, 240–3.

is responsibility, that even then the individual has some obligation to think of others as well as himself, the welfare of society or mankind as well as his own?

It seems that insufficient attention has been given to the failure of traditional consent theory to provide for any obligation to resist, or any obligation to choose responsibly when new authorities must be chosen. Indeed, divine right, prescription and utilitarianism can accommodate such obligations far more easily than a contract theory can. As for the "nature of the government" or "hypothetical consent" doctrine developed in this essay, it too would presumably require amendment on this score. An enlarged version might hold: your obligation is to obey what deserves obedience and consent, and to resist what deserves resistance and rejection (leaving the important possibility that many persons or agencies deserve neither obedience nor resistance). But it is not obvious to me whether the obligation to resist tyranny should be construed as a part of political obligation at all, or as an occasional alternative to it. The question seems related to that of whether revolution is a special part of political life or a breakdown of the political.

THE CASE OF SOCRATES

Though the Nazi may continue to obey on the grounds that he has sworn to do so, we may find that he thereby fails to perform his true obligations. Why, then, does Socrates' position—equally founded on past personal consent—strike us as so exemplary and moral? I would suggest that the distinguishing thing about Socrates' situation is this: he can find no fault with the Athenian laws, nor even with the Athenian way of administering them. Only his own particular conviction and sentence are (almost fortuitously) unjust. And his dialogue with the laws is essentially a way of expressing or establishing this fact. Socrates' past consent is not so much compelling in its own right, as it is a way of expressing and reinforcing his present judgment that there is nothing basically wrong with the system, no justification for resistance. What amazes us about him is not this judgment, nor the refusal to accept a single case of injustice as a justification for disobedience. These are relatively ordinary positions to take. What amazes us about him is that he construes disobedience so widely, to include even flight; and that he is willing to perform his obligation down to the minutest detail, even at the cost of his life.[8]

[8] Plato, *Crito*, 50: "are you not going by an act of yours to overturn us—the laws, and the whole state, as far as in you lies?" B. Jowett translation (New York: Random House, 1937).

The suggestion is, then, that Socrates' focus on his past acceptance of the laws and his gratitude to them is in fact an evaluation of the Athenian government (or the expression of such an evaluation). We need to recall that this same moral Socrates refused to carry out an "authoritative" order given him in the time of the Thirty Tyrants, because it was unjust, and would apparently have refused to carry out injustice voted by a democratic majority as well.[9] In those earlier situations, one may suppose, what Socrates thought about was the injustice of what he had been ordered to do, and of those who issued the order, not his own (tacit?) consent to them.

To this line of argument a traditional consent theorist might respond: Socrates looks to his own past consent in order to find and determine its limits, in order to see whether this new governmental action does not exceed what he had consented to. But if we take that seriously as a model of what the moral man must do when he contemplates resistance, we set him an extremely difficult task. How is Socrates to know *to what* he has consented, particularly if his consent has been tacit? Surely it is not enough to say that he has consented only to those precise things the government did in the past, so that any new or unprecedented action is automatically *ultra vires*. But if not that, then to what does one give tacit consent? Is it to the particular people then in authority, or to the authority of the office they hold, or to the laws that define and limit that office, or to the body that makes those laws, or to the Constitution that lays down rules and procedures for the making of laws, or to the principles behind that Constitution, or to the fellow-members of the society, or even to all of mankind? In particular cases, these various foci of loyalty may come into conflict; then knowing that one has consented to them all at a time when they were in agreement is no help for deciding what to do.

In short, though two of our examples do look to their own past consent in deciding what to do, one of them thereby fails to perform his true obligation, and the other seems to be using the language of consent to express a favorable assessment of the government. Furthermore, we have noted at least two disadvantages of personal consent as a criterion: the difficulty of knowing *to what* you have consented (especially if consent was tacit), and the fact that even an express oath to obey may sometimes be outweighed by an obligation to resist.

Besides an individual's personal consent, traditional consent theory offers as an alternative criterion the "consent of the governed," the consent of all, or a majority of one's fellow-citizens. Of such consent, too, we would have to say that it cannot simply be dismissed as irrel-

---

[9] Plato, *Apology*, 32.

evant. Even our Negro in Mississippi or South Africa might think about how widely shared his grievances are. But again, the consent or dissent of the majority cannot by itself be decisive for defining your obligation. Majorities are sometimes wrong, and have been known to do evil. Resistance might be justified in Athens under the Thirty Tyrants or in Nazi Germany despite the majority.

But majority consent does enter the argument at another level, in a way quite different from the relevance of personal consent. Majority consent may be relevant as a *way* of assessing, as *evidence about* the nature of the government, given that the nature of the government bears on political obligation. In fact, a variety of considerations each of which we might want to call "consent of the governed" can be used in the process of evaluating a government. They may come into conflict with each other, and their relative weight and importance will be a matter of one's political values, of what kind of government he thinks desirable or even tolerable.

It is useful to distinguish here between the "procedural" criteria yielded by the consent of the governed for assessing a government, and the "substantive" ones. Procedural criteria are those which concern the institutional structure and political functioning of the government, the way in which it makes decisions and takes actions. To assess its nature, we want to know about the way a government functions in relation to the governed—whether it is responsive to them or forces its policies on them. Thus we look for machinery for the expression of popular desires; we look for the degree of popular participation in or control over decisions, for channels for the redress of grievances, for access to power. At the same time we look also for signs of repression, of propaganda, of coercion. We look, of course, not merely at the institutions defined on paper, but at their actual functioning in the largest social sense. Denial of suffrage to Negroes in South Africa is very different from denial of suffrage to women in Switzerland (and theorists would do well to think about why this is so). But roughly speaking, a government is likely to seem to us deserving if it is open to the governed, reprehensible if it rules them against their will. This general criterion may well be expressed by some formula like "the consent of the governed"; but that formula must not be taken too simply, and that criterion must not be regarded as our only one.

Besides this vague cluster of procedural criteria, we have in addition substantive ones. We may look also at the substance of what the government does—whether it pursues good, benevolent, justifiable policies. A government that systematically harms its subjects, whether out of misguided good intentions or simply for the selfish gain of the rulers, is to that extent illegitimate—even if the subjects do not know it, even if they "consent" to being abused. But even here "the consent of the governed" is *relevant* as important evidence, for one of the main ways we estimate whether people are being well treated is by whether they seem to like what they get. Only we may sometimes need to consider other evidence as well; the consent or dissent of the governed need not be decisive as to the goodness or justness of a government's policies.

It is the relationship between at least these two kinds of criteria that is likely to determine our assessment of a government, whether it deserves support or opposition. Thus we may all agree that a government pursuing very bad policies and forcing them on its subjects, so that it is obviously doing great harm to them and other countries, and doing so despite their attempts at protest and without their consent —such a government clearly is the occasion for resistance. Conversely, if we find a government that truly has the consent of its subjects although they have wide sources of information and true opportunities to dissent and criticize, and if that government pursues only the most praiseworthy policies, then few of us would urge revolution or resistance to it. The problematic cases are, of course, the ones in between, where procedure and substance are partly good, partly bad, and you need to make evaluations and decisions. Here it begins to be a matter of your metapolitics—how you think of men and societies, what positions you are willing to take and defend, and take responsibility for.

Suppose, for example, that a government is procedurally open, with genuine channels for controlling policy from below, but it engages in vicious policies. Then, one might want to say, the citizen is not free to engage in revolution; he has channels available and it is his duty to use them, to change the policy. But what if he tries to do so, and fails because the majority continues to approve of the wickedness? What if he is a member of a permanent minority group, being systematically abused and exploited by an eager, consenting majority? Then the seemingly open channels of consent are not truly open to him. Might there not come a point when violent minority resistance of some sort is justified?

Or suppose that a government is benevolent, so no one can criticize its actions, but in procedure it is simply autocratic and dictatorial. Is revolution justified against a benevolent dictatorship? This might be the case, for example, if men need political participation in order to be really well, in order to reach their full human potential. Then bad procedure would itself become a substantive grievance.

The theoretical complications possible here are legion, but at least this much seems clear: evaluating a government in order to decide whether it deserves obedience or resistance, requires attention both to the way it works and to what it does. In both cases something like consent is relevant; it may be a formula for expressing some rather complex requirements concerning opportunities for dissent and participation, or it may be evidence of good policies. Thus even if we adhere to the doctrine of hypothetical consent or the nature of government, majority consent may still be relevant in a subordinate capacity for assessing a government, for working out more detailed answers to our questions one and two about consent, the specific practical "when" and "whom" of obedience. But here "the consent of the governed" is not one simple thing, decisive for obligation; rather, it is relevant in a number of different, potentially conflicting ways.

And all of these ways put together differ, in turn, not merely from personal consent, but also from the doctrine of hypothetical consent developed in this essay.[10] That legitimate authority is such that one ought to consent to it, is a precept built into English grammar, into the meanings of these terms. That a legitimate government is one which has the consent of (a majority of) the governed—is procedurally responsive to them or looks after their interests, or both—is one particular position about what kind of government is desirable for men. More accurately, it is a cluster of positions, depending on the relative weight given to procedural and substantive criteria. Though these positions are very widely shared today, and though they were shared by almost all traditional consent theorists, they are not the only conceivable positions on this subject. Someone might undertake to argue, for example, that a government is legitimate only to the extent that it fosters high culture, or to the extent that it promotes the evolution of a master race. That would be to reject majority consent as any sort of criterion for assessing a government. But the doctrine of hypothetical consent holds even for someone taking such an unorthodox position; even for him, a legitimate government would be the one that deserves consent, to which everyone ought to consent. Both the philosophical weakness and the historical persistence and strength of traditional consent theory rest in its failure to distinguish these very different arguments.

Finally, even if we succeed in evaluating a government, that does not seem fully to settle how we must behave toward it. One final, important consideration seems relevant: the action taken must be appropriate. To the diversity of ways in which one can obey or support, resist or overthrow a government, there correspond a diversity of conditions when the various actions may be appropriate or justified. The fact that some action is justified, that some abuse has taken place, does not mean that just any action will do. A man mistreated

[10] For the latter distinction, compare Benn and Peters, *op. cit.*, pp. 329–331.

by his superior may kick his dog. We can understand, and perhaps even sympathize, but surely the action is not justified. Not just any violation of law will qualify as civil disobedience or attempted revolution. This observation is presumably related to the traditional assertion of consent theorists, that it is necessary to "exhaust the remedies" available, to suffer "a long train of abuses" before violent resistance is justified. Where other actions are appropriate, revolution may not be called for.

Thus it begins to seem that a decision about obedience and resistance ought to be measured not merely against the character of the government, but against all the relevant social circumstances—what alternatives one can envision, and what consequences resistance is likely to have. Revolution would not seem justified, for example, if one had no hope of its being followed by an improvement in conditions. If it would simply substitute one tyranny for another, or if it would annihilate the human race through the resulting violence, then it does not seem justified.[11]

But a doctrine that casts its net so wide, making all social circumstances at least potentially relevant, that sees both an obligation to obey and an obligation to resist, and that stresses so much the individual burden of decision, seems very close to the social utilitarianism examined in the first half of this essay. It seems to say, with the social utilitarian, you are obligated to obey when that is best on the

---

[11] One difficulty of this discussion is that it seems to make human decisions look excessively rational. Are any abstract principles of this kind really relevant to what real people think about when they must decide? Is a man on the point of rebellion or revolution not much more likely to be moved by strong emotion— by an overwhelming anger or sense of outrage?

But I would like to suggest that the human capacity for outrage is, as it were, the emotional correlate to rational moral principles. It is our inner, helpless response to a violation of principles of right and wrong, as we sense them, perhaps quite inarticulately. Outrage (unlike mere anger) is an emotion of principle. I take it that this is what Albert Camus means when he insists that "the act of rebellion is not, essentially, an egoistic act," even though it can "of course" have "egoistic motives." *The Rebel* (New York: Vintage, 1956), p. 16. The rebel, the man who acts from a sense of outrage, says not merely "I don't want to put up with this," but "No man ought to have to put up with this." And by feeling "no man ought . . ." he acts, in a sense, on principle. Compare Tussman, *op. cit.*, pp. 78–79.

Of course a man's feeling that his situation is outrageous is one thing; whether the situation is in fact outrageous is another. A three-year-old may feel outraged at not being allowed to drink the detergent. We may sympathize with his feelings, but cannot condone the resulting violence. Not every feeling of outrage is a valid assessment of the world; but then, not every rational judgment that the limits of contractual obligation have been exceeded is valid either. No doubt rational judgments are more likely to be right; that is one advantage of rationality.

whole for society (all of mankind?), and obligated to resist when *that* is best on the whole. But that formula, and social utilitarianism, seem to neglect again the obligatory nature of law and authority in normal circumstances, the *prima facie* obligation to obey. Being subject to law, government, authority means precisely an obligation (normally) to do what *they* say is best, rather than judge the welfare of society for yourself and act on your private judgment. Yet there are times when you must resist in the name of something very like the welfare of society. Whether these two positions are compatible remains somehow problematic; but before we can make a final stab at the matter, we must finish applying our new doctrine to our four questions about political obligation.

JUSTIFYING POLITICAL OBLIGATION

We come now to question four, the matter of justification: "why are you ever obligated to obey even legitimate authority?" Here again our "nature of the government" doctrine does not at first seem a very useful answer. For it can only say: because of the nature of the government, because the government is such that you ought to obey it and consent to it, because a rational man would do so. But that answer is not likely to still the question. For someone genuinely puzzled about obligation in this (philosophical) way is likely to persist: "how does that 'ought' bind me, *why* must I do what a rational man would do, what if I don't *want* to be rational?"

But the reader may have noticed by now that all of the theories and versions of theories we have considered are subject to this same difficulty to some extent. Some seem better designed to cope with it than others; yet we can always push the question further back: why must I do what God commands, why must I do what history teaches, why must I do what is best for me personally, why must I do what I have promised? Even traditional consent theory is liable to this difficulty; and it is remarkable that despite Hume's early criticism, we continue to believe in consent theory while ignoring this problem. For Hume had already told the consent theorist:

> You find yourself embarrassed when it is asked, *Why we are bound to keep our word?* Nor can you give any answer but what would, immediately, without any circuit, have accounted for our obligation to allegiance.[12]

The obligation to keep one's word is no more "natural" and self-evident and indubitable than political obligation itself; though either

[12] David Hume, "Of the Original Contract," in Sir Ernest Barker, ed., *The Social Contract* (New York: Oxford, 1960), p. 161.

may sometimes reinforce the other, neither can give the other absolute justification. The two obligations are essentially separate and equal in status.[13] Why, then, does the traditional consent theorist, so doubtful about the validity of political obligation, take the obligation of keeping contracts as obvious? Why, if he imagines a state of nature, is it always stripped of political authority but inevitably equipped with a natural law that dictates the keeping of one's word? Hume uses these questions as a rhetorical device to attack consent theory, but they can also be taken seriously as a way of learning something more about the consent theorist.

For a theorist does not choose his beliefs and his doubts. The traditional consent theorist simply finds himself in doubt about (the justification of, or limits of, or validity of) political obligation; it just seems obvious to him that there is a problem about it. And he simply is not in doubt about promises or contracts; it just seems obvious to him that they oblige.

At one level one can argue that both the consent theorist's doubt and his assumption spring from the peculiar picture of man and society he seems to hold. If your picture of man in the abstract is of a man fully grown, complete with his own private needs, interests, feelings, desires, beliefs and values, and if you therefore never think about how he grew up and became the particular person he became, then he may well seem to you an ineluctably *separate* unit, his ties to other individuals may seem mysterious or illusory and will require explanation. Given man as such a separate, self-contained unit, it does indeed seem strange that he might have obligations not of his own choosing, perhaps even without being aware of them, or even against his will. Furthermore, self-assumed obligations may then strike you as a way of overcoming this separateness. For it is easy to confuse the fact that promises and contracts are self-assumed, with the idea that the *obligation to keep* them is self-assumed as well. That is, the person who makes a promise seems to recognize and commit himself to the institution of promises; the person who makes a contract seems to acknowledge thereby the binding character of contracts, so that a later refusal to accept them as binding strikes one as a kind of self-contradiction. But of course this is a confusion. The

[13] This assertion is not about the relative claims that the two obligations—political obedience and promise-keeping—have on us, where they come into conflict. It seems obvious to me that no single, binding principle could be found to govern such a question. There are occasions when a vitally important promise is clearly a more important obligation than obedience to some minor law; on the other hand, the keeping of a minor promise is no excuse whatsoever for treason. But the assertion that the two obligations are separate and equal is not meant to bear on this question. It is meant only to say: there is no reason to suppose that promising is more "natural" or basic than obeying authority, and hence no reason to derive the latter from the former.

making of particular promises or contracts presupposes the social institution of promising or contracts, and the obligation to keep promises cannot itself be founded on a promise.

In truth, there is something profoundly wrong with the consent theorist's picture of man. Every free, separate, adult, consenting
individual was first shaped and molded by his parents and (as we
say) society. It is only as a result of their influence that he becomes
the particular person he does become, with his particular interests,
values, desires, language and obligations. The only thing truly separate about us is our bodies; our selves are manifestly social. But
surely even the consent theorist knows this, so the problem becomes
why he nevertheless holds, or is held captive by, a different and peculiar picture. Could that picture be not so much the cause as the by-
product of his philosophical doubt?

After all, consent theorists are not the only ones troubled about political obligation. Political theorists of other persuasions have also
been led, or have led themselves sometimes to ask "why are you ever
obligated to obey even legitimate authority?" But if none of the theories of political obligation is able to deal adequately with that question, it must be quite peculiar, not nearly as straightforward as it
looks. Perhaps it is a question that cannot be fully answered in the
ordinary way. But what sort of question is that; and if it cannot be
answered, how should it be treated? Tussman rejects it as a symptom
of "moral disorder"; I would suggest instead that it is a symptom of
philosophical disorder, the product of a philosophical paradox. If so,
it will not disappear—the theorist will not stop being bothered by it
—unless we can show how and why it arises, why anyone should so
much as suppose that political obligation in general needs (or can
have) a general justification. But that would require a discussion of
the nature of philosophical puzzlement far beyond the scope of this
essay.

What can be done here is something much more limited and less
effective. Having suggested that the status of political obligation and
of the obligation to keep promises is essentially the same—that neither is more "natural" than or can serve as an absolute justification
for the other—we can approach our question four about political obligation by first pursuing a parallel question about promises. For in
the area of promises some extremely useful work has been done in
philosophy in recent years—work which can be applied to the problem of political obligation.[14]

---

[14] See particularly J. L. Austin, *Philosophical Papers* (Oxford: Clarendon, 1961),
chs. 3, 6 and 10; John Rawls, "Two Concepts of Rules," *Philosophical Review*,
LXIV (January, 1955), 3–32; and S. L. Cavell, "Must We Mean What We
Say?" in V. C. Chappell, *Ordinary Language* (Englewood Cliffs, N.J.: Prentice-Hall, 1964), esp. pp. 94–101.

Philosophers have sometimes asked a question like our question four about promises: "why are you (ever) obligated to keep (any of) your promises (whatsoever); why do promises oblige?" This question, too, can be answered in terms of divine commandment or utilitarian consequences, social or individual; and here, too, the answers are less than satisfactory. "God commands you to keep your word" is no answer to the nonbeliever, nor to someone heretical enough to demand proof of God's will. The utilitarian response tends to dissolve the obligation altogether, so that your duty is always to do what produces the best results, quite apart from whether you have made any promises on the subject. And, of course, a consent argument is out of the question here ("you have promised to keep your promises"?).

What has been suggested by philosophers is this: "promise" is not just a word. Promising is a social practice, something we *do*, something children have to learn *how* to do. It has rules, penalties, roles and moves almost in the way that games have them. Children do not learn what a promise is by having one pointed out to them; they learn gradually about what it means to "make a promise," "keep (or break) a promise," "be unable to promise but certainly intend to try," "have said something which, in circumstances, amounted to a promise," and so on. Promising is not just producing certain sounds ("I promise"), for a phonograph might make those sounds, or a man rehearsing a play, or a philosopher explaining the practice, yet none of these would actually be promising. Promising, rather, is taking on an obligation. That is, "to promise" does not mean "to make certain sounds," but rather "to take on an obligation."

Now, of course, we do not always do what we have promised. Sometimes we act contrary to our obligations, and sometimes we are wholly or partly excused from performing what we had promised. If for example, keeping a promise would frustrate the purpose for which it was made, or would lead to great evil, or has become impossible, we may be excused from performing. So about any particular promise we have made it may sometimes be relevant to ask: am I still obligated to perform or not? That is, normally, in principle promises oblige; a promise is a certain kind of obligation. But sometimes, under certain circumstances, there is reason to question or withdraw or cancel that obligation in a particular case. In such circumstances we weigh the alternatives, the possible consequences of performance and failure to perform. But our obligations, including that of the promise, continue to be among the factors that must be weighed in the decision. The obligation of a promise does not simply disappear when there is occasion to question it; it only is sometimes outweighed.

But philosophers are sometimes led to wonder *categorically*, about *all* promises: do they oblige; what are the reasons pro and con; why am I ever obligated to keep any promise? And here, of course, there are no *particular* circumstances to weigh in the balance; the question is abstract and hypothetical. What sort of answer is possible to this question? First, that this is what a promise *is*, what "promise" means. A promise is a self-assumed obligation. If you *assume* an obligation and have not yet performed it, nor been excused from it, then you *have* an obligation; in much the same way as someone who puts on a coat, has a coat on.[15] To ask why promises oblige is to ask why (self-assumed) obligations oblige. And to the question why obligations oblige the only possible answer would seem to be that this is what the words mean.

Beyond this one can only paraphrase Wittgenstein: there are a hundred reasons; there is no reason. There is no absolute, deductive answer to the question "why does any promise ever oblige?" beyond calling attention to the meaning of the words. There is no absolute, indubitable principle from which the obligation can be deduced. It is, to be sure, related to any number of other principles, obligations and values; but the relationship is more like a network (or patchwork) than like a hierarchical pyramid. It is simply a mistake to suppose that there might be such an absolute principle, such a deductive proof. We have no right to expect one. (Why, then, does the philosopher expect one; why can we ourselves be led to share his expectation when we are in a "philosophical mood"?)

John Rawls has pointed out that utilitarianism will not do as a criterion for the keeping of particular promises—as a standard for *when* promises oblige.[16] To say "keep your promises only when that maximizes pleasure and minimizes pain" is to miss precisely the *obligatory* nature of a promise; having once promised you are not free to decide what to do merely on utilitarian grounds. But, Rawls says, utilitarian considerations *are* relevant at a different level of argument, for assessing the social practice of promising. For we can ask "must we (should we) have an institution like promising and promise-keeping at all?" And here utilitarian reasons seem relevant; we may try to justify the social practice by its useful consequences.

Stanley Cavell has argued that this implies a degree of freedom of choice on our parts which we do not in fact have.[17] To evaluate the practice of promising pro and con, we would have to envision alternatives. And how shall we envision a society which knows no obligation to keep one's word? (For it is not, of course, the particular English locution "I promise" that is being assessed, but the practice of assuming obligations and holding people to their word.) We seem to have no choice about the pros and cons of such an institution. It is

---

[15] Compare Cavell, "Must We Mean What We Say?" *op. cit.*, pp. 96, 99.
[16] *Op. cit.*, Part II.   [17] "The Claim to Rationality," Chapter VIII.

not socially useful; it is indispensable to the very concept of society and human life.

But even if we could and did evaluate as Rawls suggests, and "decide" that the institution of promising is on balance socially useful, even this would not provide an absolute justification for the keeping of particular promises. For what are we to answer the man who says: "granted that we must have the practice of promising, and granted promising means taking on an obligation; still, why am *I* obliged to keep my promise? Why can't *I* be an exception?" To him we can only say, that is how obligation and promises work. Of course you *can* refuse to keep your promise, but then you are failing to perform an obligation.

Now the same line of reasoning can be applied to the question "why does even a legitimate government, a valid law, a genuine authority ever obligate me to obey?" As with promises, and as our new doctrine about political obligation suggests, we may say that this is what "legitimate government," "valid law," "genuine authority" *mean.* It is part of the concept, the meaning of "authority" that those subject to it are required to obey, that it has a right to command. It is part of the concept, the meaning of "law," that those to whom it is applicable are obligated to obey it. As with promises, so with authority, government and law: there is a *prima facie* obligation involved in each, and normally you must perform it. Normally a man is not free to decide on utilitarian grounds whether or not he will do a certain thing, if that thing happens to be against the law or required by law; he is not free to make a decision on his own the way he would be free where the law is silent. The existence of the law on this subject normally constitutes an obligation, just as having promised normally constitutes an obligation, so that one is not free to decide what to do just as if no promise had been made. (This is not, of course, to say that everything claiming to be law is law, that everyone claiming to have authority has it, that every statement alleged to be a promise is in fact one. It says only: *if* something is a promise, law, obligation, *then* normally it obliges.) This kind of response to question four is obviously almost the same as the one our doctrine of hypothetical consent yielded to question three: government and authority are concepts grammatically related to obligation and obedience. A legitimate government is one that you ought to obey and ought to consent to because that is what the words mean. But as before, this answer is likely to seem purely formal, and empty. It will not satisfy someone genuinely puzzled about the justification of political obligation.

But as with promises, all that one can say beyond calling attention to the meanings of the words, is that no absolute, deductive justification exists or is necessary. There are no absolute first principles from which this obligation could be derived. It is related to all kinds of other obligations in all kinds of ways, to be sure, but the relationship is not hierarchical and deductive. In particular, as we have seen, the obligatory nature of promises is no more or no less absolute and indubitable than the obligation to obey laws. Again, following Rawls' suggestion, one might attempt a utilitarian assessment of such institutions or practices as law, government and authority. And here, I suppose, there may be somewhat more room for discussion than with promises. For it is not at all obvious that government and law are indispensable to human social life. But can we conceive society without any such thing as authority? One function of the idea of the state of nature in classical consent theories does seem to be a kind of indirect demonstration of the utilitarian advantages of having governments and laws. If such things did not exist, Locke seems to argue, we would have to invent them.[18]

But as with promises, even a recognition of the necessity or utilitarian advantages of such things as authority, law and government is no absolute answer to the man who is questioning his particular obligation to obey, who wants to be an exception. There is no such absolute answer, and can be none. Nothing we say is absolutely beyond question. Again, you *can* disobey but in the absence of excuses or justifications you violate an obligation when you do so.

The parallel between promises and authority as obligations is not perfect. For one thing, promises are explicitly taken on oneself; political obligation (I have argued) need not be. Furthermore, promises are normally made to particular persons, whereas political obligation is sometimes confounded by our question two, by the problem of rival authorities. We have noted the difficulty of determining to whom or what consent is given: particular officials, their positions, the laws, the Constitution, the people of the society. This means, among other things, that political obligation is open to a kind of challenge not normally relevant to promises. We saw that, following Rawls, both promises and political obligation can be challenged at two very different levels: sometimes we may claim to be excused from performing in a particular case (for instance because of conflicting obligations or overwhelming difficulties). And sometimes we may want to challenge and assess the whole institution with the obligations it defines. But in

---

[18] It is significant, in this respect, that consent theorists so often speak of contracts or covenants, rather than simple promises or oaths. For of course the idea of a contract or covenant implies that you get something in return for the obligation you take on, and in a way at least suggests the informal additional ties of gratitude. But there are other differences as well, a contract being more formal and usually more explicit than a promise.

addition, political obligation can be challenged also on a third level. Sometimes we may refuse to obey neither because our particular case is exceptional, nor because we question such obligation categorically, but because the one who is claiming authority over us does not in fact have it. We may resist a government that has become tyrannical not as a special, personal exception, and not because we are against government, but because *this* government no longer deserves obedience. Such a challenge is made on principle, *in accord* (as it were) with the "rules" of political obligation.

But the differences between promises and political obligation do not affect the point to be made here. That point concerns our question four, the search for a justification for having to obey (or having to keep a promise); and it is essentially twofold. First, we have said, "authority," "law," and "government" are grammatically, conceptually related to obligation, as is "promise." And beyond this, the quest for some "higher," absolute, deductive justification is misguided. Insofar, then, as the grammatical point does not seem to still the question, does not get at what someone philosophically puzzled wants to ask, what is needed is not a better justification, but an account of why the philosopher is driven to ask the question in the first place.

THE DUALITY OF OBLIGATION

As Locke suggests in his preface, the consent theorist's purpose is a dual one. He wants both to show that men are sometimes justified in making revolutions, and to show that men are normally bound to obey governments and laws. And this is, indeed, what must be shown, since both these things are in fact true. The fact is that on one hand men are in some sense above or outside the institutions of their society, its laws, its government. They can measure and judge these institutions. Though they have not themselves made them they can change them; and sometimes even violent change may be justified. On the other hand, men are also part of and subject to their society, bound by its norms and authorities. Not every attempt at revolution is justified.

To say that men are both superior to their government and subject to it is to express a paradox. Because it seems so paradoxical, the traditional social contract theorists saw it instead as a temporal sequence: *first* men were free and could make a commonwealth, *then* they became bound by it (within the limits of a contract). We have seen some of the difficulties that result. Finding an accurate and unparadoxical way to express this paradoxical truth seems to me the most interesting problem connected with political obligation, but it is important to notice that this problem is not confined to political obligation. We are both superior to and subject to *all* our obligations, and *that* is what requires an accounting. Discussing it will reveal one final, rather subtle way in which obligation both is and is not a matter of consent—but all obligation, not just the obligation to obey.

We are familiar enough from ethics with the view of a number of philosophers (notably Kant) that an action is not fully moral unless the actor knows what he is doing and does it for the right reasons. An action done for selfish motives but accidentally producing some charitable result is not (really, fully) a charitable action. A moral action is one taken *because* it is right, on principle. On analogy we might want to say that a man cannot (really, fully) obey an order unless he recognizes that it is an order, that the man issuing it has authority over him. He cannot (really, fully) obey a law or a government unless he recognizes it as valid law or legitimate government; only then will what he does (really, fully) *be* obeying. If I "order" a leaf to fall from a tree, and the leaf immediately does so, it is not obeying my order; if I silently and secretly "order" my neighbor to mow his lawn and he does so, he is not (really, fully) obeying my order. Even if he hears and understands what I am saying, he is not (really, fully) obeying me unless he recognizes what I say as an order, considers me as having authority to order him about, and mows the lawn *because* of my order.

Consequently, the capacity for this kind of awareness and intention is a precondition for being fully obligated. This is why leaves cannot be obligated (except in storybooks) where they are anthropomorphized, and children cannot fully do so. It may be right to punish or reward a child, but the child is not yet fully a moral agent capable of recognizing and therefore of having obligations.

It is not difficult to regard this kind of awareness and intention as a form of consenting to one's obligation. If (really, fully) obeying an order presupposes the recognition of it as an order and of the man who issues it as having authority, then surely that recognition resembles a kind of (perhaps tacit) consent to his authority. And then it becomes easy to take a final further step, and say you are not (really, fully) obligated unless you recognize, acknowledge, accept, acquiesce in, consent to that obligation. Such a line of reasoning undoubtedly has heightened the appeal of consent theory for a number of writers, and it clearly is the main basis for Tussman's stress on consent. He chooses agreement rather than force or habit as the nature of political association precisely because,

'I have a duty to . . .' seems to follow from 'I have agreed to' in a way that it does not follow from 'I am forced to' or 'I am in the habit of.' This is sometimes expressed as the view that obligations are, or even must be voluntarily assumed.[19]

But even if one accepts these transitions and concludes that obligation in the full moral sense always requires consent, it by no means follows that obligation consists *only* of this inner awareness and intent. For that would imply that anyone failing or refusing to consent for any reason whatsoever is thereby excused from the obligation in question, does not have that obligation, cannot meaningfully be blamed or criticized for failing to perform it.[20] But no major ethical theorist, least of all Kant, would be willing to accept that consequence, any more than Tussman is willing to let the morally unaware clods in society disobey laws whenever they please.

It is necessary to recognize that obligation has not one, but two fundamental aspects—the inner, "awareness" aspect stressed by Tussman, and an outer aspect having to do with the way others see what we do, how it looks objectively. These two aspects of obligation may be seen as corresponding to two familiar strains in ethical theory: the teleological, concerned with the consequences of action, and the deontological, concerned with its motives.[21] The former deals primarily in the outer, shared world of facts and events, and takes as fundamental the concept of the *good;* the latter deals primarily in the inner, personal world of thoughts and feelings, and takes as fundamental the concept of *right.* I would suggest, following Cavell, that both are a necessary part of any valid account of morality and obligation, that neither can be ignored outright in assessing action.

Those moral philosophers who have stressed the deontological side of moral appraisal have been concerned particularly with the matter of giving praise: a person does not deserve full credit for an act of charity, of courage, of obedience, unless his intentions were charitable, courageous, obedient. He should not get full credit for an action that merely looks charitable "from the outside," if his own perception of what he was doing was quite otherwise. To a lesser extent this is also true of blame: you are responsible for the damage you do, no matter how good your intentions were, but good intentions may be a *partial* excuse. Those philosophers who have stressed the teleological orientation of moral appraisal have been more concerned with blame or responsibility, but most particularly with duty. Your duty is not merely to intend good behavior, but to behave well; the performance and its results are what define your duty.

But in a way this dichotomization—deontology for praise, teleology

---

[19] *Op. cit.,* p. 8.   [20] Benn and Peters, *op. cit.,* p. 322.
[21] This and the next three paragraphs lean heavily on Cavell, "The Claim to Rationality," p. 323 and all of Part II.

for duty—misses the point. For the real difficulty is in determining *what* action has been performed, what actually was done. It is naming the action (correctly) that is the problem: was it, should we call it, an act of charity, an act of obedience, considering what took place, considering his intentions? Having put it that way, one wants to say that the two modes of assessment are always both relevant, but not equally relevant to all actions. To the assessment of certain actions, inner intention is much more relevant; to the assessment of others, outer events will seem decisive. Lying is more a matter of inner intent, deceiving more a matter of outward results. Moreover it may be that, in a broader sense, whole categories of action vary in this respect. It may be, for example, that inner awareness is categorically more relevant in face-to-face, personal relationships than in public, political conduct. We do care more about motive and intention in assessing personal relationships and actions—love, anger and forgiveness—than in assessing political actions in the public realm.

If this is so, it deserves more attention than it has received from political theorists. No doubt it has something to do with the fact that in personal morality there is no umpire, no arbiter or judge; it is of the essence of morality that we confront each other directly. In the political, public realm, on the other hand, the normal situation is one where official "interpreters" are supplied by the society to tell the individual what the law or Constitution says, whether he has or has not committed grand larceny. But what happens at times of resistance or revolution is precisely that these normal official interpreters are themselves called into question. We are both bound by, and yet sometimes free to challenge or change all our obligations; but political obligation has an additional complexity, in that its *content* seems to be a subordination to the judgment of others.[22]

But if normally law and authority oblige and resistance requires

---

[22] Compare Tussman, *op. cit.*, pp. 86–95. It is tempting to construe the problem in relation to Hannah Arendt's discussion of action: *The Human Condition* (1958), Part V. The human situation is precarious, and human action fallible in unpredictable ways. Both privately as individuals, and collectively as a society, we try to some extent to overcome this uncertainty, this fallibility. We make commitments, tie ourselves down for the future. As individuals, for example, we make promises. As a society, for example, we try to act and plan beyond the lifetimes of individuals, through the education of our children, or through the establishment of laws and institutions. As we reduce the uncertainty of private future action by telling others what we will do so that they can count on it, so we reduce the uncertainty of public future action by telling others and ourselves what we will do and how, so that we all can count on it. Yet in both private and collective action, uncertainty remains and things go wrong. We do not always live up to our commitments, and promised actions do not always accomplish their intended purpose. Institutions do not always function as intended either; they produce quite different goals, pursue other principles than those they were supposed to embody. Thus sometimes we need to review, re-

justification, and if normally judgment is to some extent subordinated
to that of the authorities, and if revolutionary situations are precisely
the ones that are not normal in these respects, then the crucial question seems to be: *who is to say?* [23] Who is to say what times are normal and what times are not, when resistance is justified or even obligatory? If we say "each individual must decide for himself," we seem
to deny the normally binding character of law and authority. If we
say "society" or "the majority" or "the duly constituted authorities decide," then we seem to deny the right to resist, since it may be the
majority or the authorities themselves that need to be challenged. Yet
these seem to be the only two alternatives.

The matter is very difficult, though the question seems so simple.
This essay will only briefly indicate a direction in which a solution
might be sought. What needs to be said seems to be this: the decision
both is and is not up to each individual. Each individual does and
must ultimately decide for himself and is responsible for his decision;
but he may make a wrong decision and thereby fail to perform his
obligations. But then who is to say someone has made a wrong decision? Anyone can say, but not everyone who cares to say will judge
correctly; he may be right or wrong. And who decides that?

Each person decides for himself what to say and do; yet people
sometimes speak and act in ways that are cowardly or cruel, thought-
less or irresponsible. And it is not merely up to the actor to assess his
own action in this respect. Other people who want or need to assess
the action may also do so; each of them will make a decision for
which he bears responsibility, yet none of these decisions is absolutely
definitive. The judge trying a would-be rebel makes a decision; the
foreign onlooker asked to give money for a revolutionary cause makes
a decision; the historian examining the record in a later generation
makes a decision.[24] Each of us who talks or thinks or acts with regard

---

place or reject commitments we have made; sometimes it must be right for us
to do so.

And where do human beings get the standards by which on such occasions
they assess their government and find it wanting? Well, surely from the very society which they criticize with these standards. That this is possible—that we
learn both the existing rules and criteria for assessing rules *together*, and yet can
use the latter on occasion to criticize the former—may well be the most important single fact about social life.

[23] Compare Tussman, *op. cit.*, pp. 44–46.

[24] Thus not only citizens, but also bystanders and commentators may need to decide about a government. Their problems are not the same, to be sure. The citizen must decide whether to obey or resist; the bystander never had an obligation to obey, so he at most must decide whether or whom to assist; the
commentator only makes a judgment. Therefore the evaluation of governments
as to their legitimacy, their entitlement-to-be-obeyed-by-their-subjects, is a
topic that ranges beyond problems of political obligation.

to the situation assesses it, and no theory or God or Party can get us off that hook.

But that does not mean that all judgments are arbitrary or merely a matter of personal preference or whim. Some decisions are made arbitrarily or whimsically or selfishly or foolishly; others are made on principle, rationally, responsibly. These are ways or modes of deciding; none of them characterizes decision as such. And an individual's decision does not become rational, responsible or right merely because he thinks it is, merely because he urgently wants it to be. What is ultimately needed here is a better understanding of the role played in our language and our lives by assessments like "he was right," "he made a bad decision," "he betrayed the cause," and the like.

Who is to say? I want to answer, each person who cares to, will say—not merely the one who acts, not merely his associates, not merely those in authority over him, not merely the detached historian or observer. No one has the last word because there is no last word. But in order to make that clear, one would have to say a great deal more about how language functions, and why we are so persistently inclined to suppose that there must be a last word.

7 / Hobbes

E. F. CARRITT

Medieval and Renaissance writers seem often to have prided themselves upon eclecticism as a mark of learning more than upon consistency. In this tradition Hooker gives so many characteristics which deserve obedience that he seems to hope some of them may possibly be found in actual laws. If laws are derived from the Law of Reason or the law of God, or if they promote happiness or virtue, or if we have given our consent to them, or if they prevent disputes, or are fit or convenient, we ought to obey them.[1] It is the contrast with such vagueness which gives half its im-

SOURCE: *Morals and Politics* (Oxford: the Clarendon Press, 1935), ch. 3, pp. 25–39. Reprinted by permission of the publisher.

[1] *Ecclesiastical Polity*, I. x (1594). Hooker's merit is to hold clearly that natural reason draws certain rules for the conduct of men to men as equals even as they are men, though they should have no settled fellowship or agreement. Desiring fellowship, they draw up other rules whose authority depends upon consent.

pressiveness to Hobbes's unhesitating intransigence; the other half is due to his incomparable philosophical style, to one adroit ambiguity and one grain of truth.

If Plato had been treated in the spirit of Old Testament commentary we should perhaps regard Thrasymachus as the antitype of Hobbes. What in the first book of the *Republic* we see as in a glass darkly we meet in the *Leviathan* face to face. Might is right. The name of justice is given to obeying the commands of any who can enforce them. Those who issue commands issue them in their own interests, and we obey them, however loath, for fear of a worse fate. But Hobbes's picture is darker still; he entangles us more inextricably in our slavish fate. The fear that constrains us is not only our fear of the tyrant, which might be tempered by assassination, but our fear of our fellow slaves. *Homo homini lupus,* and the whips of any despotism are better than the scorpions of that anarchy, to escape which we sold ourselves into bondage. The most important difference is that the timid Hobbes thinks men so equal in intent and capacity to injure that all are gainers by the general loss of liberty.[2] Thrasymachus, with a more childish self-confidence, thinks that the establishment of laws only confirms and strengthens that advantage which the strong and cunning had always held.[3] They therefore gain by the establishment, while the weaker lose; though, once it has been made, the confirmed strength of the stronger makes it still more the interest of the weaker to obey when they cannot escape detection.[4]

'Whatsoever is the object of any man's appetite or desire, that is it which he for his part, calleth *good,* and the object of his hate and aversion *evil. . . . Pleasure* therefore (or *delight*), is the apparance or sense of good.'[5] Here Hobbes unequivocally adopts our second main theory, and from this all the rest follows of course. 'No man obeys whom [*sic*] they think have no power to help or hurt them.' Our motives for obedience are, besides fear, desire of ease and sensual delight, and also of knowledge and the arts of peace.[6] It is absurd to speak of a moral obligation to obey, for 'Where there is no common power (and there is no common power over the sovereign and his subjects), there is no law; where no law, no injustice.'[7]

There is one right of nature:

> the liberty each man hath to use his own power, as he will himself, for the preservation of his own nature; that is to say of his own life. . . . And because the condition of man . . . is a condition of war of every one against every one, . . . every man has a right to everything; even

[2] This is like the position of Glaucon. Plato, *Rep.* ii. 359.   [3] Ibid. i. 340.
[4] Adeimantus emphasizes the point that nobody would be just if he could escape detection. Ibid. ii. 363–367.
[5] *Leviathan* (1651), vi.   [6] Ibid. x, xi.   [7] Ibid. xiii.

to one another's body. And therefore, as long as this natural right of every man to everything endureth, there can be no security to any man, how strong or wise soever he be, of living out the time which nature ordinarily alloweth men to live. And consequently it is a precept, or general rule of reason, *that every man ought to endeavour peace as far as he has hope of obtaining it; and when he cannot obtain it, that he may seek, and use, all help, and advantages of war*. . . . Of the voluntary acts of every man, the object is some *good to himself.*[8]

The obligation of subjects to the sovereign is understood to last as long, and no longer, than the power lasteth by which he is able to protect them. . . . The end of obedience is protection, which, wheresoever a man seeth it, either in his own or in another's sword, nature applieth his obedience to it, and his endeavour to maintain it.[9]

This is all quite clear and quite consistent [10] and, I think, quite wrong. What is called our duty or obligation to obey the laws is the fact, when it is a fact—and Hobbes thinks this very often—that it is to our advantage to do so. It is to our advantage because disobedience will either be punished or issue in rebellion, between whose bloody motion and its event must intervene that State of War in which the best to be said about man's life is that it is short.

Such an account would hardly have commended itself without the ambiguity, which, in speaking of Hobbes, it seems more charitable to call adroit than lucky.[11] He undertakes to tell us, though it does not affect his theory, how this sovereign, which we are so much interested to obey, came to be there.

From man's first miserable state, with its two rights, vainly to seek peace and by all means he can to defend himself, it follows:

that a man be willing, when others are so too, as far-forth, as for peace, and defence of himself he shall think it necessary, to lay down this right to all things; and be contented with so much liberty against other men as he would allow other men against himself. . . . And when a man hath abandoned or granted away his right; then is he said to be *obliged,* or *bound,* not to hinder those, to whom such right is granted or abandoned, from the benefit of it: and that he *ought* and it is his *duty,* not to make void that voluntary act of his own: and that such hindrance is *injustice* and *injury.* . . .[12]

---

[8] Ibid. xiv.   [9] *Leviathan,* xxi.

[10] Once granting the fantastic meanings he has given to the phrases 'right of nature' (=power) and 'rule of reason' (=prudent calculation), and keeping out of mind their usual meanings, which he probably intends still to influence us, and which perhaps still influenced him.

[11] For he means by charity the feeling of power. And it gives a greater sense of power to detect a cunning sophism than a stupid blunder. See below, pp. 33–34.

[12] Ibid. xiv.

> A *commonwealth* is said to be *instituted*, when a *multitude* of men
> do agree, and *covenant, every one, with every one,* that to whatsoever
> *man* or *assembly of men,* shall be given by the major part, the *right* to
> *present* the person of them all, that is to say, to be their *representative;*
> every one, as well he that *voted for it,*[13] as he that *voted against it,*
> shall *authorize* all the actions and judgements of that man, or assembly
> of men, in the same manner as if they were his own. . . . Because the
> right of bearing the person of them all, is given to him they make sov-
> ereign, by covenant only of one to another, and not of him to any of
> them; there can happen no breach of covenant on the part of the sov-
> ereign; . . . whatsoever he doth it can be no injury to any of his
> subjects.[14]

It is a law of Nature 'that men keep their covenants made.' [15] And the
covenant is eternal on both sides.

> There is no perfect form of government where the disposing of the
> succession is not in the present sovereign.[16]
> He that hath the dominion over the child, hath dominion also over
> the children of the child; and over their children's children. For he
> that hath dominion over the person of a man, hath dominion over all
> that is his.[17]

It is easy to see how commentators on Hobbes have often supposed
that he really based the obligation to obey the sovereign upon a contract, and accordingly should come under that heading in our classification of theories rather than among the hedonists. And in truth
Hobbes allows that a man may be in conscience (*in foro interno*)
bound to keep even an unprofitable covenant,[18] for it is commanded
by God, and 'the right of afflicting men at his pleasure belongeth naturally to God Almighty . . . as omnipotent. . . . The right of afflicting
is not always derived from men's sin but from God's power.' [19] Yet
even in this peculiar sense of the word conscience, 'the laws of Nature
oblige *in foro interno;* that is to say, they bind to a desire they should
take place; but in *foro externo;* that is, to the putting them in act, not
always.' [20]

Critics who have taken this view of Hobbes have consequently
often confined themselves to questioning his cynical psychology, to
doubting the fact of such a covenant, or to asking why, if made, it
should not be a covenant on terms, and why it should bind the makers' children. The furthest they have gone is to ask how there could
be any obligation to keep a covenant made among men with no obli-

[13] i.e. for the elected sovereign, not for the original covenant, for which all must
have voted.
[14] Ibid. xviii.   [15] Ibid. xv.   [16] Ibid. xix.   [17] Ibid. xx.   [18] Ibid. xv.
[19] Ibid. xxxi.   [20] Ibid. xv.

gations one to another—*inter homines hominibus lupos.*[21] But all such skirmishing leaves Hobbes's central position unthreatened, for the 'obligation' to keep the covenant is only the 'obligation' of self-interest. 'Covenants, without the sword, are but words, and of no strength to secure a man at all.' [22] 'The opinion that any monarch receiveth his power by covenant, that is to say, on condition, proceedeth from want of understanding this easy truth, that covenants being but words and breath, have no force to *oblige,* contain, or protect any man.' [23] 'Justice therefore, that is to say, keeping of covenant, is a rule of reason, by which we are forbidden to do anything destructive to our life; and *consequently* a law of Nature.' [24] The only reason given why we 'ought' not to disobey where we think we can escape or defy detection is that even 'though the event (i.e. advantage) follows, yet it cannot reasonably be expected.' [25]

How little Hobbes in fact relied upon the covenant is shown in his placing commonwealths by acquisition, that is, where the sovereign power is got by force, on precisely the same footing as a commonwealth by institution. In them either the vanquished has made an unconditional covenant to obey the victor, or a child has expressly or 'by other sufficient arguments' declared its consent.[26]

Finally it is clear that no covenant binds contrary to interest, since for Hobbes it is impossible even to make a contract which it must be contrary to our interest to keep, as for instance, to endanger our lives or to obey one who is not strong enough to protect us in return. 'The end of obedience is protection, which, wheresoever a man seeth, either in his own or in another's sword, nature applieth his obedience to it.' [27] Hobbes even seems to allow that if the sovereign make any distribution of lands in prejudice of peace and security, and consequently contrary to the will of all his subjects that committed their peace and security to him, such distribution may be reputed void.[28] There is then no obligation except self-interest; that is to say, no obligation at all. Hobbes was justly as well as temperamentally frightened at the spread of the revolutionary doctrine that a man should obey no laws not approved by his own conscience, a doctrine which had proved as troublesome to Cromwell as to Charles Stuart,

---

[21] Though the sovereign cannot behave unjustly he can iniquitously, i.e. disobey God (ibid. xviii). Hobbes really admits there is no obligation to keep the first covenant (which precedes the election of the sovereign) until the sovereign is elected to enforce it and does so. But a covenant which, when made, there was no obligation to keep, has a questionable past. He tries to deduce a duty to keep covenants from a duty to obey and vice versa.

[22] Ibid. xvii; cf. xiv.   [23] Ibid. xviii. (*My italics.*)

[24] Ibid. xv. (*My italics.*) Laws of Nature or of Reason, as distinct from the Right of Nature, are reasonable maxims for securing peace, 'hypothetical imperatives.' Cf. xiii, xiv.

[25] Ibid. xv.   [26] Ibid. xx.   [27] Ibid. xiv, xxi.   [28] Ibid. xxiv.

and which must have given to lovers of security the same sense of vertigo which has been produced in our own day by bolshevism. It was too late to appeal to the authority of the church for obedience to God's anointed, or so it seemed to Hobbes, judging other men's scepticism, as he did their timidity, by his own. Moreover, there were now rival churches, and the dangers of ecclesiastical intrigue against secular power were increased. But he thought that in self-interest he had found a motive of obedience that would be a universal substitute for spiritual authority. Unfortunately men's opinions as to where their interest lies are as divergent as their consciences. Hobbes himself had to allow that each must judge when the sovereign's orders endanger his life or property, or when the security offered is even less certain than the hopes of successful rebellion.[29] Moreover, men are apter to take risks than he supposed, and much apter to take them for generous motives.

This cynical psychology is very well refuted by Bishop Butler in the passage [30] where he criticizes Hobbes's [31] identification of charity with love of power:

Is there not often the appearance of men's distinguishing between two or more persons, preferring one before another, to do good to, in cases where love of power cannot in the least account for the distinction and preference? For this principle can no otherwise distinguish between objects, than as it is a greater instance and exertion of power to do good to one rather than to another. Again, suppose good-will in the mind of man to be nothing but delight in the exercise of power: men . . . would have a disposition to, and delight in mischief, as an exercise and proof of power. And this disposition and delight would arise from, or be the same principle in the mind, as a disposition to and delight in charity. Thus cruelty, as distinct from envy and resentment, would be exactly the same in the mind of man as good-will: That one tends to the happiness, the other to the misery of our fellow creatures, is, it seems, merely an accidental circumstance, which the mind has not the least regard to. These are the absurdities which even men of capacity run into, when they have occasion to belie their nature. . . . Could any one be thoroughly satisfied, that what is commonly called benevolence or good-will was really the affection meant, but only by being made to understand that this learned person had a general hypothesis, to which the appearance of good-will could no otherwise be reconciled?

The definition of pity as 'an imagination, or fiction, of future calamity to ourselves, proceeding from the sense of another man's calamity' [32] is similarly criticized.[33]

[29] Ibid. xiv, xxi, xxiv, loc. cit.   [30] Sermon, i, note.   [31] Of Human Nature, § 17.
[32] Hobbes, Of Human Nature, § 10.   [33] Butler, Sermon, v, note.

Hobb's, after having laid down that pity, or compassion, is only fear for ourselves, goes on to explain why we pity our friends in distress more than others. Now, substitute the *definition* for the word *pity* in this place, and the inquiry will be, why we fear our friends. . . . The very joining of the words to *pity our friends* is a direct contradiction to his definition of pity. . . . Had he put the thing plainly, the fact itself would have been doubted that *the sight of our friends* (or the innocent) *in distress raises in us greater fear for ourselves, than the sight of others in distress.* And, in the next place, it would immediately have occurred to every one, that the fact now mentioned, which, at least, is doubtful, whether true or false, was not the same with this fact, which nobody ever doubted, that *the sight of our friends* (or the innocent) *in distress raises in us greater compassion than the sight of others in distress;* every one, I say, would have seen that these are not the *same,* but *two different* inquiries; and, consequently, that fear and compassion are not the same. Suppose a person to be in real danger, and by some means or other to have forgotten it, any trifling accident, any sound might alarm him, recall the danger to his remembrance, and renew his fear: but it is almost too grossly ridiculous to speak of that sound, or accident, as an object of compassion; and yet, according to Mr. Hobbs', our greatest friend in distress is no more to us, no more the object of compassion, or of any affection in our hearts. Neither the one nor the other raises any emotion in our mind, but only the thought of our liableness to calamity, and the fear of it; and both equally do this. It is right such sorts of accounts of human nature should be shown to be what they really are, because there is raised upon them a general scheme, which undermines the whole foundations of common justice and honesty.

It would be hard to find a better instance of the definite refutation of sophistry or of definite philosophical advance. It is disappointing that most subsequent writers on political philosophy have neglected it, and have continued to assume that the only human motive is a desire for personal good.[34]

In endeavouring to bridge the really impassable gulf between his assertion that 'reason directeth man to his own good' (good being 'the object of any man's appetite or desire,' and our strongest desires being for security and power) and his assertion that we are under *obligation*[35] to obey the sovereign, Hobbes insinuated an ingenious way of talking which has had an incalculable influence on the history of our subject. Having supposed that our ancestors, in order to escape dangers, voluntarily contracted either with one another (by institu-

[34] Cf. p. 128, Carritt, *Morals and Politics.*

[35] If Hobbes and his readers could really keep their minds quite clear of the ordinary meaning of this word, and take it simply to mean self-interest, there would be no gulf to bridge. But then, I think, the great *Leviathan* would only be a museum piece.

tion) or with a victor (by acquisition) or with a parent (by generation) to obey the sovereign, he concludes that all the acts of the sovereign are our own. If the sovereign injures me I am injuring myself, and, by the same argument, if I injure him I must be injuring myself, so that there is no difference between the two injuries. The implication really seems to be that all the unforeseen consequences of my contractual act are, in the same sense, my acts.

A person is he, "whose words or actions are considered, either as his own, or as representing the words or actions of another man, or of any other thing, to whom they are attributed, whether truly or by fiction." When they are considered as his own, then is he called a "natural person": and when they are considered as representing the words or actions of another, then is he a "feigned" or "artificial person". . . . A multitude of men are made "one" person, when they are by one man or one person represented, so that it be done with the consent of every one of that multitude in particular. . . . And "unity" cannot otherwise be understood in multitude.[36]

The only way to erect such a power, as may be able to defend them from the invasion of foreigners, and the injuries of one another, . . . is to confer all their power and strength upon one man, or upon one assembly of men, that may reduce all their wills, by plurality of voices, to one will: which is as much as to say, to appoint one man or assembly of men, to bear their person. . . . This is more than consent or concord; it is a real unity of them all in one and the same person. . . . This done, the multitude so united in one person is called a "commonwealth," in Latin *civitas*. This is the generation of that great "Leviathan," or rather, to speak more reverently, of that "mortal god"; [37] . . . and he that carrieth the person is called "sovereign."

If he that attempteth to depose his sovereign, be killed, or punished by him for such attempt, he is author of his own punishment, as being by the institution, author of all his sovereign shall do.[38]

Though he that is subject to no civil law sinneth in all he does against his conscience, because he has no rule to follow but his own reason; yet it is not so with him that lives in a commonwealth; because the law is the public conscience, by which he hath already undertaken to be guided.[39]

---

[36] *Leviathan*, xvi. Cf. Bosanquet, *Philosophical Theory of the State*, p. 59. 'The terms of the paradox of self-government become irreconcilable . . . so long as to every individual, taken as the true self, the restraint enforced by the impact of others is alien.'

[37] Cf. Hegel, *Philosophie des Rechts*, § 258. 'The existence of the state is God's process in the world. The Idea of the state is the true God, but as the most villainous cripple is a man, so with states.'

[38] *Leviathan*, xvii. Though it is impossible to covenant away one's life or liberty (xiv, xxi). Cf. Green, *Political Obligation*, § 186: 'The criminal sees that the punishment is his own act returning on himself.'

[39] *Leviathan*, xxix.

If we consider the motives of that undertaking, they will not seem unworthy of being invoked as a conscience to justify the most infamous obedience.[40]

Such are the consequences of assuming that there are no bonds either of love or duty between persons: the great Leviathan must be one person, but, we may remember, a feigned or artificial person; a fabulous monster. It was left for Rousseau to deny that the 'moral person' or 'common self' which he identifies with the state was a *raison d'être*.[41]

The grain of truth which may be attributed to Hobbes is that a duty to obey, when commanded to do actions which we should not otherwise have thought right, might depend on one of two things, either that we had promised obedience to the commander, or that his authority would be impaired by our disobedience, and is an authority that, upon the whole, secures to our fellow men a justice and a wellbeing which we see no better way of affording them. In the latter case our obligation to the sovereign *is* roughly proportionate to its efficiency.

8 / "The Consent of the Governed" in Two Traditions of Political Thought

Fred H. Willhoite, Jr.

This essay is an attempt to explicate the meaning of "the consent of the governed" in two of the principal traditions of Western political philosophy—classical-Christian rationalism and secular, naturalistic voluntarism. These fundamentally divergent views of man's nature and purposes have co-existed in tension and conflict at least since the time of Socrates' running arguments with Sophists.

[40] '*2nd Murderer:* Come, he dies: I had forgot the reward.
  1st Murderer: Where's thy conscience now?
  2nd Murderer: In the Duke of Gloster's purse.'
                                        Shakespeare, *Rich.* III, I, iv.
[41] *Contrat Social,* I. vii.

SOURCE: *Southwestern Social Science Quarterly* (June 1965), 59–66. Reprinted by permission of the author and the publisher.

In the rationalist tradition—herein represented by Cicero, Aquinas, Calvin, and, equivocally, by Locke—reason is considered to be man's highest and most distinctive faculty. In the Greek and Roman Stoic view it is the characteristic man shares with the gods. The rationalist strain in medieval theology incorporates this idea, virtually identifying man's rational faculty with the *imago dei*. Man is not purely a "thinking creature," but reason is conceived to be the controller of the passions, the proper guide for man's will. Reason is capable of discerning the natural ends of human life, of charting the pathway to the full moral and spiritual development of the person. It is man's duty to conform his acts to this regulative reason in order to live the good life, and in Christian rationalism to prepare for the supernatural end of eternal life.

The foundational assumption of voluntarism—as seen, for example, in the thought of Marsilius of Padua, Hobbes, and Rousseau—is summarized in Hume's declaration that "reason is and ought only to be the slave of the passions and can never pretend to any other office than to serve and obey them." [1] Reason is essentially a highly developed form of animal cunning; it is the tool which enables man to calculate how to get what he wants, but it is incapable of instructing him in what ought to be the goal of his desiring and doing. Reason does not control the passions but is inevitably directed by them; it is the servant of man's will.

THE NATURE OF CONSENT
IN THE TWO TRADITIONS

In a politically significant sense, "consent" appears to have three general meanings, which may be designated continuing consent, formative consent, and consensus. Because of their close interrelationship in the voluntarist tradition, the latter two categories will be considered together.

"Continuing consent" refers to an ongoing process, undergirding the lawmaking and law-enforcing functions of government. That is, the legitimate operations of legislative and executive authority are conceived as based upon the electoral mandate of the governed. This is, of course, the common contemporary meaning of political consent. Political philosophers in the rationalist tradition generally place little emphasis on institutionalized consent; they are concerned more with

[1] David Hume, "Treatise of Human Nature," in *Hume's Moral and Political Philosophy,* edited by Henry D. Aiken (New York: Hafner Publishing Company, 1948), pp. 24–25.

the ends served by human laws and political institutions rather than the means of legislating and governing. The reverse holds true of voluntarist theories.

The concern of rationalists for ends rather than consensual means is apparent above all in their recurrent emphasis upon natural law discovered by right reason. Cicero's eloquent statement of the rationalist faith in a universal teleological order transcending human will and serving as the judgmental standard for human acts is convincing evidence of this point.[2] Aquinas also quite obviously subordinates consent to wisdom in his doctrine of law, declaring that a human enactment is not truly a law, regardless of the process or human authority that produced it, if it contravenes that part of God's eternal law in which rational creatures are able to participate—the natural law.[3] Both Aquinas and Cicero look with favor upon some forms of institutionalized consent—but only as means which prudence may dictate as essential under certain conditions for the attainment of political order, and not as requirements for legitimate political institutions.[4]

A primary concern for the ends served by governmental authority likewise characterizes Calvin's political thought. Every government, whatever its form, has been established by God and commands the willing obedience of its subjects.[5] But Calvin's profound sense of human depravity led him to see the value of consensual institutions as checks upon the exercise of arbitrary power, and he thought preferable a "mixed" regime in which the people, as the earthly depository of God's political authority, elect their own magistrates.[6]

In general principles and apparent intent Locke evidently agrees with the rationalist tradition that positive law is to be evaluated not by the presence or absence of the consent of the governed in making it but by eternal standards of natural justice. However, political order can be established and maintained only by the consent of those to be governed, and some kind of representative process is required to protect the interests of men who have surrendered their natural freedom and equality in return for security for their lives, liberties, and property. In a sense, then, valid law requires a consensual basis, but this requirement is in turn derived from the rational law of nature as Locke conceives of it, namely that no man should harm another's life,

---

[2] *De Republica* iii. 22. See also *De Legibus* i. 6.

[3] *Summa Theologica*, I–II, qu. 90, art. 1, ad 3um; I–II, qu. 95, art. 2, concl.

[4] For Cicero, see *De Republica* i. 45; *De Legibus* iii. 12, 17. For Aquinas, see *Summa Theologica*, I–II, qu. 97, art. 3, ad 3um; also Thomas Gilby, *The Political Thought of Thomas Aquinas* (Chicago: University of Chicago Press, 1968), p. 294.

[5] *Institutes* iv. 20.22.   [6] *Ibid.* iv. 20.8; cf. commentary on Micah 5:5.

liberty, or property.[7] In sum, the just ends of law, rather than consensual means, remain in Locke's thought the principal criterion for the evaluation of positive laws and political institutions.

Theorists more unambiguously voluntarist than Locke tend to make institutionalized consent an essential component of the political order. Marsilius of Padua avers that men live in civil society to preserve themselves against the perils of natural disaster and predatory anarchy. He assumes that the "weightier part" (mainly quantitative, but with some qualitative implications) of the people will always be concerned with maintaining the social fabric and is therefore the best judge of the means to the end of self-preservation. Thus the whole people, organized on the basis of social classes, elects a "secondary legislator" of citizens who have the ability and leisure to draft proposed legislation, but no law can be promulgated until approved by the whole people acting as the "primary legislator." And further, only human positive law enacted through this representative process has juridical or normative status.[8] Marsilius stresses the sole legitimacy of a form of political organization which makes the consent of the people the measure both of necessity and of justice.

It is even more obvious in Rousseau's thought, despite the ambiguity of his concept of the general will, that particular institutional means and procedures embodying the active, on-going consent of the governed are the hallmark of political legitimacy. Man's basic guiding passion for the freedom to preserve himself and advance his own interests [9] requires the institutionalization of consent to be accomplished in the most literal and thoroughgoing manner imaginable. Though the assembled people may sometimes err in attempting to discern the general will, it cannot be discovered at all aside from the decisions of the entire citizen-body gathered as the sole legislative authority. The means of governance is of crucial importance for Rousseau. True political legitimacy cannot be attained by large states, monarchies, or aristocracies; they cannot give institutional expression to the participant will of each individual. Nothing but actual popular sovereignty can gratify man's essential passion for freedom.[10] Rousseau calls the only fully legitimate form of government "elective aris-

---

[7] *Second Treatise of Civil Government*, secs. 124, 135, 173. See also John W. Gough, *John Locke's Political Philosophy* (Oxford: Oxford University Press, 1950), p. 113.

[8] *Defensor pacis* i. 10.4; i. 12.3; i. 5.1, i. 12.3, i. 12.5, i. 13.8, i. 15. 1–2.

[9] "A Discourse on the Origins of Inequality," in *The Social Contract and Discourses*, translated and edited by G. D. H. Cole (New York: E. P. Dutton, 1950), p. 208; *Social Contract*, i. 2.

[10] *Social Contract*, ii. 6.

tocracy," but this means simply that a few executive officials should be elected by the assembled people to carry out the laws decreed by the whole body.[11] Standards of rational justice are no substitute for the legitimate means of government, the active sovereignty of the whole people.

Although his voluntarist perspective is akin to Marsilius's and Rousseau's, Hobbes does not equate the passion for self-preservation with the competence to evaluate alternative means of gratifying this basic human desire. Men are so much the slaves of their impulses, appetites, and fears that the dependence of governmental institutions and processes upon continuing consent would be hazardous to the maintenance of social order itself. Therefore the sovereign is appointed to be the permanent "representative" of all the people; in agreeing to establish the sovereign power the people consent once and for all to be guided by the commands of the authority that possesses supreme coercive power in the community. Hobbes in effect denies the existence of any transcendent moral law by wholly replacing the content of traditional natural law with "theorems" of reasonable action derived from the desire for self-preservation.[12] If all men were lucidly rational at any one time they would then willingly consent, as the only hope for social peace, to the establishment of unrestrained authority to hold in check their destructive impulses by the use or threat of overwhelming coercive force. Hobbes thus joins other voluntarists in insisting that the means of government—institutionalized consent—overrides in significance the political end of transcendent justice which is the primary concern of classical-Christian rationalism.

The remaining two meanings of "the consent of the governed"—formative consent and consensus—may be fruitfully considered in tandem. Formative consent designates the kind of agreement voluntarists consider essential to the creation and maintenance of social and political life, the necessary and sole legitimate instrument for welding individuals into ordered and authoritatively structured society. Seen with particular clarity in the teachings of Hobbes and Rousseau, this view denies the existence of any natural right of rulership, whether based on wisdom or on any other intrinsic criterion. By nature individuals are free and independent, and in some sense they must consent to the very existence of authority if it is to be considered legitimately established.

In Hobbes's version, men are moved by their fear of violent death at one another's hands to consent to the creation of a supreme author-

[11] Ibid., iii. 5.
[12] De Cive, ii. 1; Elements of Law, i. 15.1; Leviathan, edited by Michael Oakeshott (Oxford: Basil Blackwell, 1947), p. 84.

ity possessing a virtual monopoly of coercive force.[13] Hobbes's "formative consent" is actually hypothetical; he assumes that men would give it to unlimited governmental authority in their most rational moments. Society sprang in fact from conquest and is maintained by the use or threat of supreme force against potential rebels.

Rousseau asserts that men were originally independent and asocial and that the founding of political society brought great misfortune to the human race. Man's *summum bonum* is freedom—total liberty to do as one sees fit to preserve his life and fulfill his desires. This fundamental passion for freedom, given the impossibility of returning to the state of nature or of primitive society, motivates a quest for a kind of civil society in which men may enjoy the advantages of communal life without becoming subservient to any of their fellows. Only a free society, of which the unalterable social contract serves as the ontological basis, can be considered legitimate; it is established and maintained solely by the voluntary consent of its members.

Consensus designates that which a people fundamentally agree upon, perhaps implicitly, as the essential framework of principles and practices that bind together their political life.[14] For voluntarists, the passions which move individuals to "give" their "formative consent" to civil society constitute also the focal point for political consensus. In Hobbes's view, the desire for self-preservation, which impels men to flee from the "war of every man against every man," likewise results in reliable, continuous agreement to obey governmental authority—the alternative is to expose oneself to the terrible punitive force exercised by Leviathan. In Rousseau's doctrine, the passion for self-determination leads men to submit themselves to the rule of the "general will" (in one sense at least the "real will" of each citizen); as in the case of Hobbes, the essential content of political consensus is the basic human passion which makes possible and necessary the formation of civil society.

Theorists in the classical-Christian rationalist tradition do not conceive of any common passion as the focus of political consensus, for they reject the notion of formative consent. Because men require each other's company for the mutual fulfillment of material and psychological needs, and because they are distinctively rational creatures, structures of ordered authority are essential to communal existence. Cicero, for example, declares that nothing else so completely accords

---

[13] *Elements of Law*, i. 14.6–7; *De Cive*, i. 2, v. 8; *Leviathan*, p. 109. Cf. Leo Strauss, *The Political Philosophy of Hobbes* (Oxford: Oxford University Press, 1936), pp. 17–18.

[14] For an analysis of the meanings of consensus, see Fred H. Willhoite, Jr., "Political Order and Consensus: A Continuing Problem," *The Western Political Quarterly*, XVI (June, 1963), 294–304.

with the demands of human nature as does government, which is necessary to the functioning of every human group from the household to the nation.[15] Aquinas and Calvin likewise maintain that civil society is the product of man's nature and not of his willful consent.[16]

Consensus is certainly as important to rationalists as to voluntarist thinkers, but its content consists not of the motivations for the establishment of the political order but of the transcendent ends that order is to fulfill. In Cicero's version, a "common agreement about law and rights" undergirds civil society.[17] The people expect that the government will seek to realize the rule of rational justice in practical affairs. Political discussion and disagreement are focused on differing ideas about the means for realizing justice and about the meaning of justice in particular contexts. Citizens assume that government has a moral purpose set for it by the transcendent natural law.

Locke's straddling of the philosophic fence between rationalism and voluntarism is especially noticeable on the issues of formative consent and consensus. Man is indeed by nature a creature of society; he is under strong impulsions of necessity, convenience, and inclination to live in community with his fellows.[18] But structures of governmental authority are not so simply a concomitant of human nature; they cannot be legitimately grounded in differences of virtue and wisdom. For by nature men, though inclined to live in society, are free and equal.[19] Locke's individualism causes him to subscribe to the necessity of consent for the creation of legitimate governmental authority.

In a somewhat misleading quantitative form Locke also emphasizes the necessity of consensus for political order. This seems to be a legitimate interpretation of his defense of the right of the majority to establish the institutional form of civil society.[20] Most members of society agree on their particular form of government because and so

---

[15] *De Legibus* iii. 1.

[16] Aquinas's acceptance of the Aristotelian view of man as a political animal is well known. But less generally recognized is the essential rationalism of Calvin's political perspective, manifested in his view that God has created man a naturally sociable creature capable of living in earthly fellowship with other men and of ordering mundane affairs in a generally tolerable fashion despite the debilitating effects on his will and reason of original sin. (*Institutes* ii. 2.13; iv. 20.16.)

[17] *De Republica* i. 25.

[18] *Second Treatise of Civil Government,* sec. 77; *Essays on the Law of Nature,* edited by W. von Leyden (Oxford: Oxford University Press, 1954), pp. 157–159.

[19] *First Treatise of Civil Government,* sec. 67; *Second Treatise of Civil Government,* secs. 4, 54.

[20] *Second Treatise of Civil Government,* secs. 96, 98.

long as it seems to them best suited to fulfill the essential purposes of public authority—the preservation of life, liberty, and property. This consensus oriented by the law of nature will break down, resulting in justifiable revolution, should the government alienate a majority of the people by consistent deviation from the standards of transcendent morality.[21]

CONCLUSION

Clearly there is a direct relationship between voluntarism and the central importance of political consent in general, and an inverse relationship between this conception and rationalism. But more particularly these relationships hold for formative and continuing consent.

Rejecting the rationalist view of man as a social and political creature naturally suited to ordered structures of authority, voluntarists find no other basis for the "original" establishment of civil society (its ontological structure) than the consents of naturally discrete individuals. Political order is a contrivance of human will and the instrumental reason motivated by will and passion. Where, as in Locke's thought, rationalist and voluntarist motifs uneasily coexist, the logical outcome is a view of man as naturally sociable but made political only through consent.

Active institutionalized consent clearly accords with a view of man as essentially volitional, and voluntarist thinkers do in fact tend to emphasize continuing consent as the ethical criterion for political institutions and law. But although there is no direct relationship between rationalism and continuing consent, neither is there any necessary inverse relation. Certainly rationalists emphasize the transcendent natural law discovered through right reason, and not consent, as the ultimate criterion of governmental acts. However, rationalists also recognize the necessity of reconciling wisdom, or the discernment of justice, with the social requirement of consent.[22] It is perfectly legitimate to give the whole people some kind of representative voice in government, but this is not, as it is for voluntarists such as Marsilius and Rousseau, a *sine qua non* of political legitimacy.

There is no significant rationalist-voluntarist divergence on the importance of consensus. In fact this is the most significant meaning of consent for thinkers in the classical-Christian rationalist tradition. Political order is undergirded and wholly interpenetrated by agreement

[21] *Ibid.*, secs. 199, 202, 209, 211, 212–223, 228–229.
[22] For a clear statement of the rationalist view of this fundamental political problem, see Leo Strauss, *Natural Right and History* (Chicago: University of Chicago Press, 1953), pp. 140–143.

to rule and be ruled by standards of natural justice inherent in the cosmic scheme of things. While rejecting the content of rationalist consensus in favor of a common focal passion-derived motivation, voluntarists agree on the necessity of some fundamental accord to unify the diverse human elements of civil society. This shared characteristic of two of the most important streams of Western political thought may well point to a genuine need that a people hold something in common for community itself to exist and endure.

It should now be apparent that the meaning and implications of "the consent of the governed" are not univocal and self-evident, as is so generally assumed in contemporary thought. Nor is a concern for the role of political consent peculiar to democratic theorists. The nature and functions of consent have presented fundamental problems to all thinkers who have genuinely endeavored to understand the foundations of political order and prescribe therapy for man's social and political disorders.

Furthermore, the differences among the ideas of major theorists who have dealt most significantly with political consent may be traced to basic divergences between the anthropological and ethical perspectives of classical-Christian rationalism and of naturalistic voluntarism. From the profoundest thinkers in both traditions we must learn that before we can adequately consider the significance of "the consent of the governed" in the political life of our times, we must grapple with more fundamental issues—the perennial questions of man's nature, purposes, and destiny.

ORGANICISM

Whoever refuses to obey the general will shall be
constrained to do so by the whole body.

—JEAN JACQUES ROUSSEAU, *Social Contract*

G. W. F. Hegel has been de-
scribed as the preeminent theoretician of the organic state. In his
analysis of Hegel, E. F. Carritt describes the Hegelian justification for
individual subordination to the rational "higher-self" as it is embodied in the State. For Hegel even imperfect "phenomenal" states possess the pure or essential characteristics of the State-in-itself—pure
rationality, objective justice, and the moral guidance of a divinity—
and thus must be obeyed if man is to achieve "true freedom." Needless to say, this kind of conceptualization reduces such checks on unbridled state action as the need for popular consent or the utilitarian
norm of general happiness to mere subjective obstacles to the state in
the performance of its "historical mission."

By sacrificing individual preferences and individual moral standards to the so-called objective rationality of the state, Hegelian organicism reduces human fulfillment to loyal citizenship. It leaves no
room for resistance to perceived evil. Moreover, the fact that Hegel's
thought is supported by a historicist dialectical metaethical theory
has allowed some self-styled "disciples" to apply aspects of his
thought to justify cruel and barbarous political acts on the ground
that they are merely one dimension of a historical conflict that inevitably will lead to a higher synthesis or fulfilled "world mission."

Perhaps the Organicist who has had the greatest impact on American political thought is T. H. Green. Unlike Hegel, who assigned primarily negative functions like the police powers to the state, Green is
regarded as the precursor of the modern social welfare state. He has
had a profound influence in changing the nineteenth-century liberal
concept of freedom from the negative "freedom from" to the positive
"freedom to"—i.e., from the desirability of the absence of restraint to
the need for social welfare and individual development. In the selected excerpts from his book *The Politics of Conscience: T. H. Green
and His Age*, Melvin Richter comprehensively analyzes Green's
theory of political obligation. Green invested citizenship with a moral
sanction. Although he felt the state could never make men good directly, since good acts must be *voluntary*, he argued that it most cer-

115

tainly could do so indirectly by removing impediments to free choice. Freedom in the positive sense, for Green, is liberation of the powers of all men equally for their contributions to a common good. Accordingly, no person or group should be free—i.e., unrestrained—to do anything that contravenes the common good or public interest. Individual and group actions should be subject to regulation if they militate against the social body. The state becomes the harmonizer of conflicting interests, and thus its laws and regulations ought to be obeyed. Metaethically, Green believed that men would tend to obey the state because they possess a common rational will to act together for common ends.

The philosopher par excellence of Italian Fascism, Giovanni Gentile, has carried political organicism to its ultimate extreme in his famous article "The Philosophic Basis of Fascism." Here the state becomes all-embracing, outside which no human or spiritual values can have worth or even exist. For Gentile, the State is a living organism, a synthesis of all human values that defines, interprets, and develops the whole life of a people. In this extreme form of organicism, the State is not satisfied with establishing certain limits to individual activity. It exists to permeate the will no less than the intellect of the whole man, shaping his entire personality. The individual is fully submerged.

9 / Hegel

E. F. CARRITT

Hegel says that the historical origin of the state is irrelevant [1] but that Rousseau had the merit of proposing the rational will as the essential principle of political allegiance. Rousseau's mistake was to think of the will as an individual will, and of the general will as merely the common element emerging from conscious particular wills, instead of as the fully realized rational element in will.[2] Consequently he made the union of individuals in a state a contract, based on voluntary choice and consent, thus

SOURCE: *Morals and Politics* (Oxford: the Clarendon Press, 1935), ch. 9, pp. 105–122. Reprinted by permission of the publisher.

[1] Werke, viii (Berlin), *Philosophie des Rechts* (1821, trans. Dyde), § 258. As we shall see, he thinks the philosophy of the history of states relevant.
[2] 'Das an und für sich Vernünftige.'

compromising the state's essential divinity and absolute authority and majesty. The result of such abstraction was the scheme, for the first time in history, to found a constitution *de novo* on pure theory, with all the horrors incident to such an attempt. If the state were to be identified with the bourgeois society whose only aim is the protection of property and individual liberty, then the well-being of individuals could be the one purpose of this union,[3] and membership of a state would be optional. But in fact it is the highest duty of an individual to be a member of his state; only thereby has he any reality, truth, or goodness.[4] That is his true end, and the condition of any other activity or satisfaction. Against the view that particular wills are real and responsible for the state, it must be maintained that the universal or objective will is implicitly rational, whether it be recognized and assented to by individuals or not. The state is the moral world; it is the actualization of freedom. For in freedom we must not start from individual self-consciousness but from the essence [5] of self-consciousness, which, whether men recognize it or not, realizes itself as sovereign might, in which individuals are only moments. In the existence of the state we see God walking upon earth; [6] its foundation is the might of reason actualizing itself as will. In conceiving of the state we must not look at particular states or constitutions, but rather consider the ideal, the actual God, by itself.[7] Every state, however bad it may be from some particular point of view, whatever its faults, if it is a developed contemporary state, has the essential characteristics of a state.[8] It is easy to criticize, but even the most loathsome human being, diseased, crippled, criminal, is a man; and so it is with states.[9]

In this passage we find clearly exhibited the influence of Rousseau, modified by Kant in two ways: first by the distinction between phenomenal wills and the will-in-itself, and secondly by the conception of a divinity that shapes our ends, rough-hew them how we will.

In the same vein we find the state identified with the ethical world [10] and also with reason, and its commands with objective justice.[11] The complaint is made that, though justice thus realized in the state is as much an objective fact as the physical world is, subjective

[3] This is what Kant denied; he thought the purpose should be justice.
[4] 'Objektivität, Wahrheit, Sittlichkeit.'   [5] 'Das Wesen.'
[6] 'Es ist der Gang Gottes in der Welt, dass der Staat ist.'
[7] 'Die Idee, diesen wirklichen Gott, für sich betrachten.'
[8] 'Die wesentliche Momente seiner Existenz in sich.' Yet in the *Philosophie der Geschichte*, Werke, ix, we are told that England has practically no freedom. The translation by Sibree is from the 2nd edition (K. Hegel, 1840) which differs considerably from the 1837 text of Gans.
[9] *P. d. R.*   [10] 'Die sittliche Welt.'
[11] 'Das substantielle Recht,' *Philosophie des Rechts*, Vorrede, pp. 7–8, cf. § 140, note.

conscience ventures to criticize it, and philosophy, whose proper exercise is in the service of the state,[12] has lent its aid. But the unperverted mind is said intuitively to recognize the compulsion of social institutions as fundamentally its own.[13] In ethical society man's only duties are the well-known duties socially prescribed him by his station.[14] In civil society law expresses what is intrinsically right.[15] This being the nature of the state, it has no need to found its claim to obedience on any kind of contract or popular assent.[16] It does not even seem necessary that the state should consult the well-being or happiness of its subjects if that conflicts with its own greatness.[17] Indeed war is justified on the grounds that by it domestic discontent and hankerings after liberty are quelled, and the inconsiderable nature of individual life and happiness demonstrated by 'hussars with shining sabres'.[18]

Yet Hegel held that in implicit obedience to such absolute authority man finds his true freedom, since he is obeying the state, which is objectified reason. The ideas that freedom consists in doing what one likes [19] and that morality consists in doing what one believes right [20] are said to belong to the crudest level of thought; but it is not explained how we escape this 'subjective caprice' if we decide that the state knows better than we do. It is admitted to be an advantage if the state can conciliate the convictions of its subjects, but that is not essential.[21] This conception of freedom clearly depends on an identification of my real will with that of the state, and that, no doubt, depends ultimately upon Hegel's doctrine of the concrete universal, so that we can hardly expect to understand or accept the former without the latter. We may say here that either that doctrine does not really involve the consequences for political theory which Hegel and his followers often draw, or, if it does, we have very good ground for rejecting it.

The same doctrine is set out in the earlier *Phenomenology of Spirit* [22] in a more modest form. In national life self-consciousness is realized, for there men have the sense of complete unity with one another in independence, and each becomes conscious of self by sacri-

[12] Loc. cit. p. 13.   [13] *P. d. R.* § 147.   [14] *P. d. R.* § 150.
[15] 'Das Gesetz ist das Recht, als das gesetzt, was es an sich war,' *P. d. R.* § 217.
[16] *P. d. R.* §§ 75, 100 (note), 258, 281.
[17] *P. d. R.* § 100. Cf. the odd remarks on marriage in *P. d. R.* § 162 where it seems to be stated that what is 'of infinite importance' to the individuals concerned is of none 'in itself'. For a more moderate statement, cf. §§ 261, 270.
[18] *P. d. R.* § 324.   [19] *P. d. R.* § 15 note.   [20] *P. d. R.* § 140e.
[21] *P. d. R.* § 206. Quite inconsistently Hegel praises freedom, in the ordinary sense of immunity from state interference, in the *Kritik der Verfassung Deutschlands,* p. 20.
[22] *Phänomenologie des Geistes* (1809, vol. ii, trans. Baillie C(AA)B.

ficing it to the universal self, which is the nation, and which maintains the welfare of all. So in the free states of Greece it was held wisdom and virtue to live by the customary law of the city. This naïve sense of union has indeed to be outgrown, as we pass from an instinctive good-citizenship[23] to conscious morality,[24] but that is only a stage, marked by loss as well as gain, in the progress to conscious good-citizenship,[25] to perfect identification of the self with a state in whose actual institutions we can recognize the realization of our own moral ideals.[26] In this progress the individual consciousness first comes to contrast itself with an outer world, hostile, but to be moulded to its desire. In seeking to satisfy itself in this world it discovers that it cannot do so as an isolated individual, but only as united or identified with others, and indeed as being more than an individual, and as having the necessity or law of union in itself. In carrying out this law it learns that to save its life it must lose it, and so it passes into virtue.[27] But virtue finds that its ideal is no far off event, but is realized in its own activity; well-doing is well-being.[28]

This is a Hegel, a still quasi-Kantian Hegel, to whom, whether we agree with him or not, we might appeal from some of his later utterances, like that already quoted. But it leads us to the crucial distinction between conscientiousness (*Moralität*) and an alleged higher stage of good-citizenship (*Sittlichkeit*), which is further developed later in the same work.[29] I understand Hegel to be criticizing the Kantian view of our obligations to other men as a law or laws, recognized by our individual reasons, a law which demands both the sacrifice of our desires and happiness and also sometimes a revolt against the laws and conventions of a society that has grown up partly out of accident and partly out of the selfish interests of men. He grants that this view, puritanical and pessimistic as he thinks it, is in some respects an advance upon the life of mere instinct and custom, but he holds that it must give way to a recognition that both our own desires and sympathies, and also the laws and institutions of society, were

---

[23] 'Die an sich unmittelbare Sittlichkeit.'   [24] 'Moralität.'

[25] 'Die Sittlichkeit für sich.'

[26] Cf. *P. d. R.*§ 260. Possibly Hegel would have thought his three stages (which apply to individuals as well as societies) exemplified in Wordsworth's patriotic boyhood, revolutionary youth, and elderly idealization of the British constitution and established Church.

[27] *Tugend*. (I do not distinguish this from *Moralität*.) In pre-Hegelian language, I suppose, following out the law of nature or reason, men sacrifice all their natural rights or powers and make them over to the general will.

[28] 'Das Thun selbst das Gute ist.' In Kantian language, I suppose the good will is the only unconditionally good thing. The service of the general will is perfect freedom. Cf. C(AA)B, c.

[29] C(AA)B, c.

only other manifestations of the same universal reason which manifests itself in our conscience. In other words he turns Kant's philosophy of history against Kant's moral philosophy; tells us that the very
greed and cruelty, on which states are founded and which our conscience revolts against, all work together for good and are therefore
manifestations, perhaps better manifestations, of the same rational
will which appears in us; and draws the conclusion that to be a loyal
citizen and to fulfil one's station is wisdom, freedom, goodness, and
happiness.[30]

We have already come across a certain ambiguity in Hegel's protests, that when he speaks of the state he means the ideal state and
that, at the same time, his remarks apply to all states.[31] And according as we emphasize one or the other of these statements, the doctrine just expounded might be taken to mean either that a perfectly
good man would conscientiously obey a perfectly good state, or that
he would blindly obey any state. We must try to discover which is
Hegel's predominant meaning. The first meaning might seem indicated by his criticism of religious formalism, of slavery, and of Plato's
ideal Republic as lacking in subjective liberty; [32] and also by his concession that the piety and morality of a peasant have infinite worth
untroubled by the drums and tramplings of world history in its necessary progress,[33] which seems inconsistent with the argument that the
rise of a state to power confers on it a monopoly of worth and reality
and thereby a claim to unquestioning obedience. But evidence on the
other side is strong.

A noble or governing class, we are told, represents the absolute
universal spirit of the others; it is the manifestation of God. That it
should be elected by the people or have the supreme authority conferred upon it would rather diminish than increase its sanctity.[34]
States are not historically founded on contract but by force, not the
physical strength of the tyrant, but his ability to impose his will on
that of individuals. This is 'sheer frightful tyranny', but it is necessary
and therefore *justified*,[35] since it is the foundation of the state. This

[30] Cf. Bradley, *Ethical Studies, My Station and its Duties.*
[31] It might be argued from the statement in *P. d. R.* § 274, 'Every nation has the
constitution which is best suited to it', that all states are ideal states.
[32] *Philosophie des Geistes*, 503: 'Moral and religious principles must not only lay
claim on the individual as external laws, but must find assent and justification in
his heart and conscience.' Cf. 552: 'From externality in religion arises a laity receiving its knowledge of divine truth, as well as the direction of its will and
conscience from another order. It generally leads to contentment with outward
conformity. The spirit is radically perverted; law and justice, conscience and responsibility are corrupted at the root.' The same story can be told of states.
[33] *Phil. der Geschichte*, Einleitung.
[34] *System der Sittlichkeit*, ed. G. Mollat, 1893, iii, iii.   [35] 'Gerecht' (*my italics*).

state is the simple absolute spirit, confident in itself, against which
nothing finite has standing, no ascription of good and evil, of infamous villainy or of cunning treachery. It is superior to all these, for in
it evil is reconciled with itself. It was in this lofty strain that Machiavelli wrote his *Prince*. . . . Men pretend to kill tyrants for their cruelty, but in fact only because their work is done; they are divine,
though only with the divinity of beasts, a blind necessity as terrible
as evil itself.[36]

It can, of course, be urged that in all this Hegel is so far from describing the ideal state that he is only tracing the unhappy course of
its development in the past. Yet if his words mean anything, he *justifies* any crime by its fortunate results and belittles or blames the conscientious scruples of those who resist it. Whether he would justify
the crimes of a would-be dynast who failed through no fault of his
own, or would blame those who successfully foiled him, is hard to
say. For as Kant's use of the philosophy of history was to give us
hope that the future will be better than the present, however little we
deserve it, Hegel uses the other end of the same stick to prove that
the power which brought us out of the horrible pit and ordered our
goings must have all that it imposed upon us on the way, or is still
imposing, wickedness as well as suffering, counted to it for righteousness. Indeed the section III, iii, c of the *Philosophie des Rechts*, entitled *Die Weltgeschichte*, by adopting as its motto Schiller's famous
epigram 'Die Weltgeschichte ist das Weltgericht', frankly identifies
might with right and claims an undialectical finality, as if ours were
the Judgement Day. Since spirit or reason rules the world, all that
succeeds must be good, and the more *de facto* power anything has,
the more right. And the state has great power. This position is explicitly defended in the introduction to the *Philosophy of History*.[37]

What the absolute [38] aim of Spirit requires and accomplishes, we
there read, what Providence does, transcends the obligations and responsibilities of persons, to whom good or bad moral motives can be
imputed. Those who, on moral grounds and from noble motives, have
resisted what the progress of the Idea of Spirit necessitates, are, no
doubt, *morally* superior to those whose crimes have been employed
by a higher dispensation to effect its purposes; but in such struggles
both parties, *generally speaking*, stand on the same level of imperfec-
tion. Consequently it is merely formal justice, abandoned by the

---

[36] *System der Sittlichkeit*, Anhang.
[37] Gans, vol. ix, p. 67; Eng. Trans., p. 70. Cf. *P. d. R.*, Vorrede, p. 18. What is, is
   not only intelligible (?*vernünftig*) but is reason (*Vernunft*) and what *is*, is no *ideal*
   state. Cf. *Phil. d. Geschichte*, 'The world is as it ought to be.' E. T., p. 38.
[38] 'An und für sich seyende.'

Spirit and by God,[39] that these self-righteous apologists defend. The deeds of great men, therefore, of the individualities of world-history, might be justified not only by their unconscious inner significance but even from a human point of view. Yet the deeds of supermen [40] are really exempt from the claims of morality. Against them we must not raise the litany of private virtues, of decency, modesty, humanity, and charity.[41] World-history is justified in rising superior to the sphere of morality with its hackneyed distinction between morals and politics,[42] not only because it does not judge—though its principles, and the necessary relation of actions to them, are judgement enough—but also because individuals fall outside the sphere of its notice. Its judgements are passed upon the deeds of the Spirit of Peoples. A nation is moral, virtuous, vigorous (and, I suppose, approaches the ideal State) so long as it is realizing its grand object, for example to possess the world's commerce, the wealth of the Indies, parliaments, juries.[43] Caesar, acting for his own interest, was a blind but inspired instrument for fulfilling the mission of Rome. A superman may treat great, even sacred, interests inconsiderately—conduct which is indeed obnoxious to moral reprehension; for so mighty a force must trample down many an innocent flower.[44]

What such a theory of justification by success fails to explain is the presence in the world's course of unsuccessful or disastrous episodes, vain crimes and useless martyrdoms, great civilizations whose memorial has perished, and happy island races which are as though they had never been. Is it best called laziness or snobbery to dismiss all these, as well as all individuals, as 'unhistorical' [45]—beneath the notice of philosophy? Providence seems to be pictured in the philosopher's own image, as the manager of a business so large that some of its details escape his attention; those subordinates who are too honest

[39] *My italics.* 'Generally speaking' has dropped out. Cf. *Victrix causa deis placuit, sed victa Catoni* and 'What God abandoned these defended', A. E. Housman, *Last Poems,* xxxvii. Cf. also Marx, *La Misère de la philosophie,* Pref. to German Trans.: 'Morality only condemns what has already been condemned by history.' Cf. *P. d. R.,* § 345.

[40] 'Welthistorische.'

[41] Nearly Plato's political virtues of αἰδὼς καὶ δίκη. *Prot.* 322 more exactly Nietzsche's 'slave virtues.'

[42] Contrast Kant, *Perpetual Peace,* App. I. 'On the Discrepancy between Morals and Politics.' 'The guardian divinity of right need not bow to the Jupiter of might, who also awaits the ultimate decree of fate', i.e. 'das Weltgericht'.

[43] E.T., p. 77, not in Gans text. Cf. *P. d. R.,* §§ 342–6. 'World-history is realized reason. Its plan is knowable. It entrusts to particular nations missions which transcend justice and morality' (summarized).

[44] E.T., p. 34, not in Gans text.

[45] *P. d. R.,* § 347, *Phil. der Geschichte,* Einleitung. And even history is only appearance. *P. d. R.,* § 258.

to carry out his schemes he dismisses, with a character. And no doubt, if we exclude from world-history all the exceptions, world-history will prove our rule. 'The real is rational', but then the actual, so far as we cannot 'rationalize' it, is not real.

Fortunately our purpose can be attained without discussing the whole foundation of Hegel's philosophy. It is enough if we have convinced ourselves that his account of allegiance is monstrously incredible unless applied to an ideal State, and that, for all his protests, he in fact applies it to very ordinary states. If any further witness is needed on the last point, we may consider briefly his account of the international relations of the State—the same state 'against whose substantial goodness subjective morality must not raise its puling litanies'.

International relations, Hegel asserts, are not merely moral like those of private persons who live under a tribunal which can enforce what is in theory [46] just. Consequently in international relations justice must remain in the realm of theory.[47] States are superior to their pledges. In this world right must have might. A people as state is Spirit in realized rationality and actuality: it is the absolute might on earth.[48] States are independent wills, and the will of the whole is for its own well-being. That, then, is their highest law [49] in their mutual relations, for in a state the distinction between the formal rightness of the will and its actual object is transcended. The object of a state in all international relations, and the justifying principle for all wars and treaties, is its own actual private welfare, no universal philanthropy. Since the state is itself morality actualized, its very being, which is the same thing as its right, is a concrete reality, no abstraction like the so-called principles of morality; and this is the principle of its conduct. To accuse statecraft of injustice is a mark of shallowness.[50] When a people has a world-mission to fulfil, no other has any right against it; those whose mission is fulfilled count no more in world-history.[51] The might of a state is its right because there is no general will actualized in a coercive power above it. Its only superior is the World-spirit which judges by success.[52]

On the balance, then, of irreconcilable contradictions, Hegel's most consistent views emerge, I think, as closely resembling those of Hobbes and Spinoza.[53] The state has just so much right, both against

[46] 'An sich.'   [47] 'Beim Sollen bleiben.'

[48] *P. d. R.*, §§ 330, 331, 333, and cf. § 337, a passage presumably directed against Kant's contention that politics should conform to morality, which is described as a shallow view. Cf. Kant, *Perpetual Peace* and *Theory and Practice*.

[49] *P. d. R.*, § 336.   [50] *P. d. R.*, §§ 336–7.   [51] Ibid., § 347.

[52] Ibid., §§ 333, 340.

[53] Cf. Wallace, *Hegel's Philosophy of Mind*, p. clxxxii, a good statement of the whole theory.

its subjects and against other states, as it has power. The 'superman', like Caesar, 'has a right to oppose its will, because he is able to impose his will on it; and all this is as it should be.

Nor is it surprising that the conclusions should be similar since the premises were not unlike. On Hegel's view all moral principles and claims, including, I think, obligations, are merely abstract and 'ideal'; however 'true', they are not yet actualized; the only thing that can actualize them is the will, that is to say, the needs, desires, impulses, and affections of man; if I am to bring anything about I must find my satisfaction in the achievement. 'The absolute right of personality is to satisfy itself.' Its interest may be 'unselfish', but nothing is done except by persons seeking their own satisfaction, nothing is done without passion.[54] Obligation is 'moralisch, ein blosses Sollen'. The context will not allow us to include in these admitted interests Kant's 'intellectual interest' or 'reverence for the moral law'.

But it would be a mark of impatience to relegate Hegel summarily to the same class of moral philosophers as Hume, with those who describe obligation as an interest (one among others) which we take in the welfare of all men and in the execution of justice and the maintenance of a civil state, as a means thereto. He had before him, what Hume had not, the directly contrary view of Kant; and he cannot be accused of failing to consider it.[55] He regards it as unsatisfactory and as definitely superseded. Whether he means that it is a false account of the moral experience, though an account which in a certain stage of philosophical insight men necessarily gave; or whether he means that it is a true account of an experience which every man in the course of his development necessarily goes through, or of one which was the highest attainable by men before his own day, I am not sure. His main criticisms of it, so far as I understand them, seem to be that, for several reasons, it makes morality self-contradictory or absurd:

1. That there would be no guarantee that the moral man would succeed in effecting the changes he tried to bring about, and certainly not in perfecting the world.
2. That if *per impossible* he did so succeed he would thereby destroy the possibility of further morality; there would be no more changes which he ought to effect.

---

[54] *Phil. der Geschichte*, Einleitung. For modern versions of the Hegelian political philosophy, see Treitschke, *Politik;* Ritchie, *The Rationality of History (Essays in Philosophical Criticism);* Marx, *Critique of Political Economy;* Engels, *Socialism, Utopian and Scientific.* Cf. *P. d. R.*, § 261.

[55] In *Encyklopädie*, 95, 503–16, *Phänomenologie des Geistes*, C(BB) and many other places. I am not always sure whether Hegel has before his mind in these criticisms mainly Kant's moral doctrine or the metaphysic of Fichte, e.g. *Vom Ich als Prinzip der Philosophie.* Anyhow he seems to mean that if I think I ought to try (or to refrain from trying) to affect the course of events, I am mistaken.

3. That still less can he hope to become perfectly moral, to resist all desires contrary to duty, and certainly not to eradicate his desires.
4. That if *per impossible* he did so succeed he would again destroy the possibility of morality, which consists in the struggle to resist desires.
5. That consequently the moral condition is one of necessary self-frustration and unhappiness.
6. That there are conflicting obligations which cannot all be fulfilled.[56]
7. That the moral man aims at doing right, but can at best only do what he thinks right; he therefore claims that the good will is all that matters, and yet that the good will is the will to bring about good.[57]

The first five of these objections, in any sense in which they are true, seem to involve no self-contradiction or absurdity. There is no absurdity involved in saying that the ideal of the coercive State is to make itself unnecessary and that we ought to try to bring this about whether we can completely succeed or not; [58] nor yet in saying that we ought to try to cure our bad habits so long as we have any. What *is* involved is the conclusion that we find ourselves in a world which is not quite what we should, perhaps unwisely, wish, nor what we ought to try to make it. The last two (6 and 7) objections raise difficulties which seem to depend, as I have indicated, on misdescriptions of morality. If they were real difficulties I should not be inclined to try to remove them at the cost of failing to distinguish obligation from self-interest.

I am, then, reduced in the end to the conclusion that, if Hegel is right in holding Kant's distinction between desire and duty to be a crude abstraction, then it is a world of crude abstraction with which political philosophy has to deal. But, on the contrary, I think that the

[56] The fact which is troubling Hegel has been described by saying that in a given situation we may have several *prima facie* duties of which, on reflection, we shall see one to be our actual duty. (Ross, *The Right and the Good*, pp. 18–36, &c.) It might be better to say that there are several claims upon us, to each of which corresponds a responsibility, the strongest of which (or that which we believe to be strongest) it is our duty to fulfil.

[57] As Hume showed it does not seem true that our only obligation is to produce good. I may have an obligation *to do what seems to me most likely* (i.e. to try) to bring about a state of affairs (e.g. the receipt of money by my creditor) which nobody else would have any obligation to try to bring about. Kant was, no doubt, wrong if he contended that we always know we ought not to break a promise. But so was Hegel, if he contended that we always know we ought to obey the state. 'Ethical goodness' only seems to escape the 'subjectivity' objected to 'morality' so long as it is instinctive; and then it may be ethical badness.

[58] Kant was perhaps following the same train of thought as Hegel in arguing (if that is what he really meant) that there is a self-contradiction in doing anything (e.g. making a fraudulent promise), even when some other people do not, if it would be impossible or futile to do it, when everybody else did it, or tried to do it.

chief cause of the staggering paradoxes in Hegel's political philosophy, and of their shameless practical application by some alleged disciples, is his failure to recognize this distinction.

10 / T. H. Green: The Principles of Political Obligation

MELVIN RICHTER

It is not easy to arrive at a just ap-
preciation of Green as a political philosopher. His style verges on the
impenetrable, and some of his problems were not political at all, but
metaphysical and theological. Even when he made his meaning relatively clear, his form of statement created logical and linguistic difficulties. Yet in his political philosophy, the whole is somehow superior
to the sum of its parts; the conclusions are still alive in a way that
their metaphysical and ethical 'foundations' are not. Green was stating his vision of what a free and just society ought to be, and this has
not dated as much as the philosophical form in which it was put. And
he was against ideas which needed to be criticised, although not always for the reasons he stated. Thus he directed his polemic against
social Darwinism, which had all the glamour and danger of pseudo-
science; against chauvinism and imperialism; against the dogmatic individualism and insensitivity to human suffering of a Herbert Spencer; against Utilitarianism, which he put on another plane as a
doctrine which had once performed commendable services, but could
now no longer be seriously maintained. Another source of strength in
Green's writing about politics was the strong sense of personal responsibility which led him to relate his technical work to concrete
problems and the intellectual puzzles which grew out of the attempt
to apply political theory to their resolution. His faith in citizenship
had led him to participate in actual politics, although never at the exalted level more usually associated with the Balliol of his period.
From these activities he acquired practical judgment and a not in-

SOURCE: *The Politics of Conscience: T. H. Green and His Age* (Cambridge, Mass.:
Harvard University Press, 1964), ch. 8, pp. 222–223, 230–248, 252–253,
262–265. Copyright © 1964 by the President and Fellows of Harvard College.
Reprinted by permission of the publishers and Melvin Richter, Professor of Political Science, City University of New York Graduate Center and Hunter College.

considerable knowledge of how politics appeared to the ordinary citizen. These qualities tempered the doctrinaire and abstract aspects of Idealism, which became in his hands the nearest equivalent to an empirical study of politics then available. Aware of the socially shared values that underlie law and political machinery, Green thought it important to understand how the individual is affected by membership in groups, a relationship which ought to be, but seldom is, considered by theorists of rights and duties. Thus the problems he posed were significant, as were the answers he suggested. These still merit serious consideration, when translated out of the technical terms of his system. . . .

Green centred his discussion on the problem of 'political obligation.' This term stood for a cluster of issues, which although not new to the subject, had not previously been put in this central position. Indeed so learned a historian of ideas as Professor d'Entrèves, has attributed to Green the first use of this phrase. This occurred when Green began his lectures by asking the question, 'Why ought I to obey the law?' This arises in terms of the obligation to obey or disobey on the part of a subject towards his sovereign; on the part of the citizen towards the state; and the obligation of individuals to each other as enforced by a political superior. The sort of answer Green was bound to give had been indicated by his decision in his ethics to adopt a teleological theory in which such terms as 'obligation' are always referred to man's purpose, present in his consciousness as the form of his ideal self. This subordination of obligation to purpose is inherent in teleological, as it is not in deontological, theories, which makes duty rather than purpose into the fundamental question of ethics. To later deontological theorists such as Prichard, it appeared that Green was saying that duty or obligation needs some other ground or foundation; no act is worth doing for its own sake.

The *Lectures on the Principles of Political Obligation* are divided into three parts: a definition of law and its essential function; a criticism of the principal alternative theories of political obligation then current in Europe; and a consideration of the chief rights and obligations actually enforced by law in civilised states and the grounds for justifying obedience to such law. Green thus assumed that European society was equitable, and from its practice he could be guided to the proper ground of obedience to law. This in any case, he would go on to argue, would coincide with the general principles of morality. By this contention that the duties of the good citizen and the good man coincide, that, properly understood, there is no conflict between what is demanded by the state and the individual's conscience, Green once again underlined his notion that there exists a spiritual principle which acts upon both. The *telos* or goal is the development of a good character in individuals (good having been defined in Green's lectures on ethics). By this criterion laws and institutions are to be judged. Their value is to be estimated by the extent to which they give reality to the capacities of will and reason by giving men scope for their exercise.

Although Green was moving in the direction of a theory of community, a strong residual individualism derived both from his theology and his liberalism led him to deny that morality can be attributed to anything other than the character of individual men. This denial straightaway creates a presumption against action by law. Law can force men to perform certain actions. But these actions are external. No law can make men moral, for morality depends upon a freely-willed motive, upon performing an act for the right reasons. Hence there is a presumption against the use of law when voluntary action is possible. The business of law is to maintain the conditions under which will and reason may be exercised. Those acts only should be enjoined by law that are 'so necessary to the existence of a society in which the moral end stated can be realised that it is better for them to be done or omitted from that unworthy motive which consists in fear or hope of legal consequences than not to be done at all'. Obviously, the fewer such laws, the better for moral development.

Yet Green's attitude towards the proper function of law and institutions was not the pure negativism of the Spencerian individualist. Rather he felt with Arnold Toynbee that, 'to a reluctant admission of the necessity for State action, we join a burning belief in duty and a deep spiritual ideal.' In short, this entailed the reconciliation of individuality with community. The older individualism had based its theory of political obligation on natural rights. It was supposed that political society had been established to secure these rights. Thus was determined the standard for defining the proper relation among men as well as the conditions under which individuals ought to submit to the state. Of this style of thought Green said with evident distaste:

> The popular effect of the notion that the individual brings with him into society certain rights which he does not derive from society . . . is seen in the inveterate irreverence of the individual towards the state, in the assumption that he has rights against society irrespectively of his fulfilment of any duties to society, that all 'powers that be' are restraints upon his natural freedom which he may rightly defy as far as he safely can.

Such a theory provides 'a reason for resisting all positive reforms, all reforms which involve an action of the state in the way of promoting conditions favourable to moral life'.

Thus Green had to erect a theory which did not base law upon natural rights, in the older sense. What, then, is the proper ground of law and obedience to it? Why should the subject obey his sovereign and the citizen his state? What should be the obligations of individuals to each other as enforced by law? These are the essential questions that must be decided by a theory of political obligation. To them the natural rights theorists had answered in terms of rights secured by a covenant antecedent to society. The Utilitarians had answered that men should have their civil rights respected and they should respect the law because 'more pleasure is attained or pain avoided by the general respect for them; the ground of our consciousness that we ought to respect them, in other words their ultimate sanction, is the fear of what the consequences would be if we did not'.

Both these theories of political obligation Green declared inadequate and returned to his ethics to find the proper principle. Society is based, not on contract or utility, but upon the spontaneous recognition by persons of other persons as ends in themselves and the further recognition that the interests of those others is involved with their own interest. Such recognition of a common good is the essence both of morality and political obligation.

Power cannot create right. Therefore any normative theory must be able to distinguish what is from what ought to be. The great defect of natural rights and Utilitarian theories of political obligation is that they cannot account for such a distinction. Their error, as Green diagnosed it in the *Prolegomena,* is their belief in the possibility of a natural science of ethics. But such theories cannot account for the use of 'ought' in cases where a moral obligation exists to resist the powers that be, or to take an action that leads to unpleasant consequences. Here again, Green is criticising the older theories of reform for two reasons: their failure as ethical principles and their obstructive effect upon the moral initiative of reformers under the conditions of his day.

His own theory began with a subject who has a conception of himself as in an ideal unattained condition. This he seeks to realise in moral action. His power to do so is recognised by other conscious moral agents who regard such powers as a means to that ideal good of themselves which they also conceive. 'No one therefore can have a right except as a member (1) of a society and (2) of a society in which some common good is recognised by the members of the society as their own ideal good.' Some form of community founded on such unity of self-consciousness, on such capacity for a common duty or common good must be presupposed in any grouping of men from which the society we know could have developed. The idea or the common good underlies the conception both of moral duty and legal right. Both imply the twofold conception (a) 'I *must* though I do not like', (b) 'I must *because* it is for the common good'.

What, then, is the proper rationale for law? It is the moral function of law that alone can justify obedience to it. Function, not origin, is the criterion. 'A law is not good because it enforces "natural rights" but because it contributes to the realisation of a certain end.' Here Green re-introduced his teleological definition of goodness as the proper ground for political obligation:

> The claim or right of the individual to have certain powers secured to him by society, and the counter-claim of society to exercise certain powers over the individual, alike rest on the fact that these powers are necessary to the fulfilment of man's vocation as a moral being, to an effectual self-devotion to the work of developing the perfect character in himself and others.

And Green calls such powers, when recognised by society, 'natural rights' on the ground that they are essential to the realisation of man's true nature. This is a translation which utterly transforms. Green's appropriation of this term with its numerous and conflicting associations has caused many a reader to wonder what this Idealist version of 'natural right' can possibly mean. Green first suggested it as an equivalent for *jus* or *Recht*, 'a system of correlative rights or obligations actually enforced, or that should be enforced by law'. But this formulation is ambiguous, for it leaves unanswered two questions: Are there rights and obligations which ought to be enforced, although not recognised by law? If so, what can be the standard by which such powers are to be considered as legitimate in the absence of such recognition? To the first query Green answered that no actual system of rights and obligations is all that it should be. The statute book may not incorporate all the claims acknowledged as legitimate by the society. To the second query Green answered, changing his ground, that there is a meaningful sense in which it may be said that rights and obligations ought to be maintained by law, although they are not. And that sense is teleological: such rights and obligations are 'natural' because necessary to the end which it is the vocation of human society to realise.

At this point Green creates the impression that the most important aspect of any power conceded to be a right is its relation to the 'moral end, as serving which alone law and the obligations imposed by law have their value'. A law is good not because it enforces natural right but because it contributes to the realisation of a certain end. We only discover what rights are natural by considering what powers must be secured to a man in order to attain this end. Green thought that any objection to calling such rights 'natural' would be removed if he avoided two errors made by earlier theorists: he would admit that rights are not the arbitrary creations of law or custom; and, on the other hand, deny that there are rights antecedent to society, rights which men brought with them into a society formed deliberately by contract among themselves. Thus rights are natural 'in the same sense in which according to Aristotle the state is natural; not in the sense that they actually exist when a man is born and that they have actually existed as long as the human race, but that they arise out of, and are necessary for the fulfilment of, a moral capacity without which a man would not be a man'. Innate rights exist in the same sense as innate duties: both are equally necessary to the realisation of moral capacity.

Nothing could appear less equivocal than this teleological statement of rights. Unfortunately, later in his exposition Green changed his formulation of this concept when he gave the following definition: 'A right is a power of which the exercise by the individual or by some body of men is recognised by a society, either as itself directly essential to a common good, or as conferred by an authority of which the maintenance is recognised as so essential.' Here the criterion was expanded to include three further considerations: whether a claimed right is or is not essential to a common good; whether it is conferred by a power, the maintenance of which is considered essential; and, finally, whether in both of the foregoing cases, the society has registered its recognition. Of course, it may be that Green meant to identify the 'common good' with 'the fulfilment of a moral capacity without which a man would not be a man'. But if this was the case, then he could not have meant what is ordinarily conveyed by the phrase 'common good': something benefiting the members, or most of them, of a given political community. Rather 'common good' must mean 'the realisation of a given type of character'. What 'recognition' may mean is at this point not yet clear. At first Green seems to have been saying that a claim to rights must be acknowledged by whatever procedure is used for making law in a society; but then he asserted that the existing social relations of a society may be said to embody moral principles not yet registered in its laws.

In his introductory remarks, he touched upon rights only so that he could clarify the proper rationale for law and this, in his view, was moral and teleological. Thus he had set out at the beginning both the ground for obedience to law and the appropriate field for state action. At this point, he was not so much developing new arguments as illustrating the political application of the principal conceptions of his metaphysics and ethics. This was meant to demonstrate to his audience the wholeness of his view of life. On essential points his statement maintained a continuity with the individualist tradition of Liberalism; yet it provided a new emphasis when it acknowledged that the state must maintain conditions favourable to moral life and even actively promote the development of character by removing all possible hindrances. This is a negative standard justifying 'positive reform'. Does it really provide an unambiguous standard? Surely contradictory inferences are easily drawn from it. A person, applying this criterion to a proposed enactment, might not know whether to emphasise its negative or its positive aspects: whether to be on his guard lest he impair self-reliance and voluntary action; or whether to consider the added contribution to the common good by state action. If compulsory education is to be justified, should this not be done on the positive ground of contributing to the common good rather than the negative one of removing hindrances? Green was seeking a balanced position intermediate between two views of state action which he regarded as equally extreme and one-sided. But, in these lectures, his own views were more evident in his rejections and qualifications than in any positive alternative to competitive theories. Just as he had denounced the theory of natural rights because it stimulated individuals to make claims upon the state without assuming any corresponding duties, so he denounced paternalism because it lessened the scope for self-imposed duties:

> It is one thing to say that the state in promoting these conditions [favourable to moral life] must take care not to defeat its true end by narrowing the region within which the spontaneity and disinterestedness of true morality can have play; another thing to say that it has no moral end to serve at all, and that it goes beyond its province when it seeks to do more than secure the individual from violent interference by other individuals. The true ground of objection to 'paternal government' is not that it violates the 'laissez faire' principle and conceives that its office is to make people good, to promote morality, but that it rests on a misconception of morality. The real function of government being to maintain conditions of life in which morality shall be possible, and morality consisting in the disinterested performance of self-imposed duties, 'paternal government' does its best to make it impossible by narrowing the room for the self-imposition of duties and, for the play of disinterested motives. . . .

Having applied his ethical theory to the function of law, Green moved on to examine the chief doctrines of political obligation then current in Europe. Such polemics played an important part in the exposition of his own views, for in this way he could achieve three objectives at once: he could develop the substance of his own teaching, demonstrate his philosophical method in action, and discredit other political philosophers in the field. His analysis was never a point-by-point examination of the author within his original framework of assumptions. Rather Green took up the unresolved dilemmas of earlier thinkers or the basic assumptions which he thought had led them astray. Spinoza, Hobbes and Locke he represented as fully involved in a social contract theory. In Rousseau the concept of social contract was at war with another and more rewarding concept, that of the general will. Austin's theory of sovereignty was not wrong but incomplete, a defect which has provoked mischievous inferences.

The major criticism Green made of social contract and natural rights theories was that they assumed rights said to be inherent in the individual quite apart from his performance of any duties. On the basis of his own ethics, Green argued that political obligation cannot be validly derived from contract. Just as any contract presupposes the recognition by its parties of a good common to them both, so all other obligations involve a similar acknowledgment. Only the teleological view of man and society can provide an adequate theory of rights. It was because Plato and Aristotle conceived the *polis* as the *telos* of the individual that any true theory of rights must build on the foundation of their root concepts.

Green attacked Hobbes because he wished to derive from a contract of all with all the sovereign's right to power over his subjects. This argument will not do. For, in its notion of a contract, it presupposes just that state of affairs it claims to account for—a régime of recognised and enforced obligations. Locke's treatment of social contract had the same defect. And this consisted in its presuppositions, not in its truth or falsity as an account of a historical event. The concept of a 'state of nature' cannot validly be distinguished from that of a political society. It is inconceivable that men should suddenly contract themselves out of one into another unless the state of nature were virtually identical with a political society.

Only when men are conscious of the law of nature are they bound by it. But then it ceases to be a law of nature. 'It is not a law according to which the agents subject to it act necessarily but without consciousness of the law. It is a law of which the agent subject to it has a consciousness, but one according to which he may or may not act; i.e., one according to which he *ought* to act.' From this law all those theorists derive the obligation to submit to civil government.

At this point, Green springs his trap. If it is acknowledged that the law of nature is an ethical law based on consciousness, then two questions must be asked: How can the consciousness of obligation arise without recognition by the individual of claims on the part of others? Secondly, given such a society of man capable of the consciousness of obligation, how does it differ from a political society? The first question, aimed at Hobbes, involves Green's recognition theory of rights; the second, aimed at Locke and Rousseau, raises the issue contained in Green's theory that every society, however primitive, already presupposes the idea of a common good. Thus the social contract theory 'must needs be false to itself in one of two ways'.

To account for the possibility of a social contract based upon the compact of all with all, its theorists must assume a society subject to a law of nature, prescribing the freedom and equality of all. But such a society governed by such a law would have no reason to establish civil government. Hobbes attempted to supply a motive for change when he represented the state of nature as a state of war in which no reciprocal claims are recognised. When Hobbes denied that recognition of claims exists in the state of nature, he thereby destroyed the only basis for the obligation to honour the social contract. The absence of recognition means the absence of obligation.

On the other hand, if, as in Locke, it is denied that the state of nature is a state of war, then it becomes possible to have a theory of obligation. But in that case there is no motive to establish civil government. If in the state of nature men were free and equal and governed by a law of nature, from this 'political society would have been a decline, one in which there could have been no motive to the establishment of civil government'. Thus Green claims to have destroyed the theory of social contract. However his argument is based upon his own definitions of terms rather than upon those of the authors he criticises. For someone who accepted Green's position, its plausibility was increased by this sort of exercise. But it is of dubious value to someone who does not accept Green's philosophical method. Apparently Green was willing to concede the difficulties which remained unresolved in his own translation of the issue, for he added a startling remark, a paradox which involved him in a position even more unusual than before:

> Whether or no any particular government has on this ground lost its claim and may be rightly resisted, is a question, no doubt, difficult for the individual to answer with certainty. In the long run, however, it seems generally, if not always, to answer itself. A government no longer serving the function described . . . brings forces into play which are fatal to it.

Suddenly Green introduced the notion of a self-regulating mechanism at work in history, in this case operating to remove any government no longer serving its true function. This was the theodicy of his political faith. It had previously made its appearance when he discussed the reasons for the decline of the Greek *polis:*

> There is no clearer ordinance of that supreme reason, often dark to us, which governs the course of man's affairs, than that no body of men should in the long run be able to strengthen itself at the cost of others'

weakness. The civilisation and freedom of the ancient world were shortlived because they were partial and exceptional.

Except for this remark, Green's consideration of earlier political philosophers had been destructive. But when he came to Rousseau, his method and tone altered. For in the conception of the general will, Green had long ago found the clue to the problem of political obligation. All that remained was to bring out the essential truth by extricating it from the formula of the social contract. Or so he said. What he really did was to rephrase Rousseau so as to make him appear as a predecessor of Idealism in the form Green gave it.

It was Rousseau's merit to have seen what other members of the social contract school had missed. They had all approached the problem of political obligation in the same way. Their substantive errors followed from this defective method. They never paid sufficient attention to society and its effect upon the development, moral and political of its members. In short, all they saw was a number of individuals regulated by a supreme coercive power. They never apprehended what a true political community is, and thus failed to see how men are made moral by it: the process by which men have been clothed with rights and duties and have come to be conscious of their obligations. Consequently philosophers had defined the issue as though their problem was to reconcile the claims of formed, self-sufficient individuals with those of the political sovereign. When so put, this problem can be dealt with only by representing the individuals governed as consenting to the exercise of government over them. This consent no doubt exists so long as there is no conflict between the individual and government. But the principle of obligation must explain how an individual can feel compelled by his own principles to obey even in the event that his inclination or interest runs counter to that of the government. Such a case cannot be covered by the theories of political obligation just surveyed. So long as government is conducted according to the wishes of its subjects, they consent to it. But this is only to discuss those occasions when there is no interference by the government with the 'natural liberty' of its subjects to do as they like. The test of the theory comes when this liberty is interfered with.

When such conflict occurs, the political philosopher must square the sovereign's right with the natural right of the individual. It is just then that it becomes clear how inadequate is the theory that the right of the sovereign is founded on consent. For it cannot handle issues of conflict. The theory of consent is a fiction which is created to compensate for the original error in the framing of the issue: 'the power which regulates our conduct in political society is conceived in too abstract a way, on the one side, and on the other are set over against it, as the subjects which it controls, individuals invested with all the moral attributes and rights of humanity'. Here Green is repeating the *a priori* argument of the *Prolegomena* and these lectures. Only as members of a society, as recognising common interests and objects, do individuals come to have these moral attributes and rights of humanity. The power, which in a political society they have to obey, is derived from the development and systematisation of those institutions for the regulation of a common life without which they would have no rights at all. This, Green reminds us, is involved by the balance he had argued at such length: without society, no individuals; without individuals, no society. . . .

It was in terms of Rousseau and Austin that Green set out his own theory of sovereignty. Rousseau had provided a theory which could do justice to the experience of the citizen: the state is founded on a general will, which is not to be confused with the mere majority, or the will of all. For the general will is always rational and always for the good, however imperfectly actual government may express it. From this will, both outside the individual and within him, he derives his capacity for right, freedom and duty. And Green declared, with his usual kind of preemptive claim, the general will provides the only principle by which we can make any sense of the relation between man's self-consciousness and social relations. When rephrased into Idealist concepts and purged of the elements Rousseau had retained from earlier discussions of right, his theory would serve as the cornerstone of Green's own statement of what he understood by sovereignty.

Locke had conceived of the sovereignty of the people as held in reserve after its first exercise in constituting a government. Sovereignty was to be exercised again only if the legislature were false to its trust. Rousseau, in contrast, supposed the sovereignty of the people to be constantly exercised. By its act of organisation the society becomes a sovereign and continues to be so. Rousseau put a new content into the theory of sovereignty. He was not aware that he had done so. He still confused it with the older notion of it as the supreme coercive authority with power to compel obedience. To this legal conception of sovereignty, Rousseau adds the notion of a common will that wills nothing but what is for the common good. But those readers of Rousseau who know only this legal theory will come away with the notion that the essential attribute of sovereignty is the supreme coercive power. And thus they will ignore that attribute of pure disinterestedness which, according to Rousseau, must characterise every act that can be attributed to the sovereign.

Thus Rousseau creates the impression of treating sovereignty in the sense of some power of which it could be reasonably asked how it was established in the part of government where it resides, when and by whom and in what way it is exercised. Yet Rousseau had in mind something essentially different. His idea was what Plato and Aristotle would have said 'is the source of the laws and discipline of the ideal policy, and what a follower of Kant might say of the "pure practical reason", which renders the individual obedient to a law of which he regards himself, in virtue of his reason, as the author, and causes him to treat humanity equally in the person of others and in his own always as an end, never merely as a means'. Yet Rousseau himself thought that he was treating the sovereign just as had other philosophers of the social contract; he did not perceive how incompatible this treatment was with his real innovation—the notion of a supreme and disinterested reason. What he should have done was to have based his case on the conception of the sovereign as entitled to obedience because it represents the general will of the society.

At first glance, there seems to be a considerable gap between Rousseau's and Austin's theories of sovereignty. For Rousseau the essence of sovereignty is the general will; for Austin, the power of a determinate person or persons to put compulsion without limit on its subjects, to make them do exactly what it likes. But the general will cannot be identified with the will of any determinate person or persons. According to Rousseau, it can be expressed only by a vote of the whole body of subject citizens. And even when they have been assembled there is no certainty that their vote does express the general will. Nor does their vote necessarily command any power.

Although these two views seem mutually exclusive, Green treated them as complementary. His own theory of sovereignty rested neither upon consent alone nor upon coercion. The sovereign is habitually obeyed by its subjects because of their feeling that by doing so they secure certain ends. Austin was right both in pointing out the importance of habitual obedience and in asserting that a fully developed state implies a determinate supreme source of law. But the error of Austin was his subsequent assertion, that the essence of sovereignty lies in its power to compel obedience. For if by 'sovereign power' is meant the influences which really make the members of a state obey, then this power must be sought in the general will. The essence of sovereignty is, will not force'. . . .

. . . Green argued that the cause of men's obedience is their free recognition that custom, law and institutions embody, however roughly, a notion of right which they share. The legal sovereign does not exercise an unlimited power of compulsion. It is effective only to the extent that it is supported by the subjects' conviction that the government is contributing to the common good. . . .

Green's purpose in this discussion can be understood as disposing of two alternative answers to the question of why men obey: one answer, identified with Austin, is that men obey because of their fear of a supreme power. This is met by Green's assertion that the aggregate influences which make men obey are moral. Another answer is that men obey because they in some sense have consented to laws. This Green denied by pointing out that such a theory cannot explain an obligation to act against personal inclination or interest. Yet this is what we mean when we talk of being obliged to do something.

Green, having eliminated, to his own satisfaction, all alternative explanations, is left with his own. He was sufficiently self-critical to acknowledge that it was not without difficulties, particularly on the question of when, if ever, the individual is justified in resisting his sovereign. This was for him a thorny issue because it raised the problem of how to reconcile what was worth preserving in the individualist tradition of Liberalism and Protestantism with his Idealist emphasis upon the common good and social recognition of rights. Two questions confronted him: Must not the individual judge for himself whether a law is in the common good? And if he decides that it is not, does he then have the right to resist it? The first issue is the right of private judgment on the part of the citizen, always assuming that he exercises this right on the proper basis (in Green's terms, by judging the law in terms of its effect upon the common good). The answer comes back that certainly every citizen should decide for himself whether a given enactment meets that test. Otherwise he would not be an intelligent and committed citizen obeying laws because they embody rights acknowledged by himself as just.

Suppose that after such an exercise of individual judgment and conscience, the citizen decides that the law violates the common good. He has then to decide how to register his protest. Green thought that in a country such as England, with a popular government and settled methods of enacting and repealing laws, the answer of common sense is quite good enough. The citizen, by legal methods, should do all he can to have the law repealed, but he should not violate it. For the common good would suffer more from resistance to the legal authority than from the individual's conformity to a bad law.

This is, however, not a hard case. Genuine difficulties arise in other circumstances, among which Green discriminates four types: when a law is issued by a sovereign whose legal authority is questionable; when the government is of such a kind that no means short of resistance can be found for obtaining the repeal of the law; when the whole system of law and government is so dominated by private interests hostile to the public that there no longer is any common interest in maintaining it; and when the authority issuing the law is so easily separable from the forces which really maintain public order and rights that this authority may be resisted without danger to order and rights. This fourth instance raises no real issue and may be dismissed without further consideration. In discussing the remaining contingencies, Green, although doing so in an abstract fashion, clearly had in mind American examples dating from the conflict about slavery and the outbreak of the Civil War. If a man belonged to a seceding state, did he not have as much a right to fight for his state as for the Union? This illustrates the difficulty of deciding rights in cases where it is not easy to determine the legitimate sovereign. For all modern states have experienced similar occasions when men have deemed themselves entitled to resist an authority which on its side claimed the right to enforce obedience and turned out actually to be able to do so. Which side was, then, in the right? Somewhat surprisingly, Green decides that in such instances there was nothing amounting to a right on either side. There being no recognition sufficiently general to confer the right of compulsion or resistance, right was in suspense on the point at issue. But then, returning to the case of the citizen of a seceding state in the American Civil War, he makes the remark that although there may not be a right on either side, this does not mean that there is not a better and worse choice on the basis of the probable effects upon the common good. Since the seceding states had a special interest in maintaining slavery, the side of the Union was the one which ought to have been taken.

This lame conclusion derived from the fact that Green's definition of rights was based upon a combination of two criteria and that he has been honest enough to choose an embarrassing instance where only one condition could be met. A right is a power which will, if granted, contribute to the common good, and which is so recognised by the society. Since recognition was here lacking, there was no right, although there was a good and an evil choice. The reader does not know whether to applaud Green's candour in admitting difficulties or to wonder why he thought that he had so improved upon the older natural right philosophers. Probably no political philosophy can deal adequately with exceptional cases by the principles it applies to ordinary ones. But Green thought that he could, on the basis of his argument, make resistance into a right. Thus he actually raised the standard for such a theory and claims that it should provide, not only for a right to resist, but for the duty to do so. Despite the troubles he has himself encountered thus far in the exposition of his doctrine, he once more attacked the writings of the seventeenth and eighteenth centuries. There the question was never put on the right basis. It was not asked when, for the sake of the common good, the citizen ought to resist the sovereign, but what sort of injury to person or property gave him a natural right to resist. But on the ground Green now provided there can be no right to do anything unless it is for the common good, and in such a case there is a duty.

This seems to offer hope for new light on the case of resistance to a despotic government when no law, written or customary, can be appealed to against a command contrary to the public good, when no rival agent of sovereignty exists, and when in the absence of any participation by the people, there is no means of repealing the law by legal means. The duty of resistance, Green tells us, is equally possible for a majority or minority. To oppose a law may be a duty before a majority of citizens so conceives of it; and the fact that a majority does conceive of opposition as a duty does not necessarily make it such. That is, in the first instance there might be a law contrary to the common good; and in the second, there might not. But what of recognition, the other criterion? When this is taken into account, we are told, a presumption is created that 'resistance to a government is not for the public good when made on grounds which the mass of the people cannot appreciate; and it must be on the presence of a strong and intelligent popular sentiment in favour of resistance that the chance of avoiding anarchy . . . must chiefly depend'. Once again the two criteria may produce conflicting judgments. And the possibility of this is increased by still another admission by this author who here appears almost morbidly anxious to produce points damaging to his theory. For 'it is under the worst governments that the public spirit is most crushed; and thus in extreme cases there may be a duty of resistance in the public interest, though there is no hope of the resistance finding efficient public support. (An instance is the Mazzinian outbreaks in Italy.)'

On his own showing, Green concludes that no precise rule can be laid down on just what conditions create the duty to resist a despotic government. He does offer some prudential guides but concedes that they are not likely to be considered in times when revolution is being considered. Indeed the effort to use such yardsticks, he admits, would paralyse the revolutionary's power of action. No critic could make out a better case against using Green's double criterion. Throughout he has been sober and realistic. But he did not demonstrate the superiority of his own principles. Perhaps he should have taken the line that a theory of obligation applicable to the ordinary situations which arise in a constitutional democracy cannot offer guidance in extreme instances. His theory of progress, here, as elsewhere, a barrier to realism, led him to believe that revolutionary situations were not likely to arise again.

. . . Green's philosophy of history is worth consideration at this point because he himself attempts to save his theory of rights and obligation by resorting to his theodicy: the assertion that in proportion to the amount of good citizenship in any political movement, whether in rebellion or in more peaceful times, there will be a good result of that movement. One way of putting the point is that there is no better way of proceeding in politics than by consulting the criterion of the common good; another, and the author's language indicates its theological quality, is the following: '. . . we can only fall back on the generalisation that the best man—the man most disinterestedly devoted to the perfecting of humanity . . . —is more likely to act in a way that is good as measured by its results, those results again being estimated with reference to an ideal of character. . . .'

This argument occurs at the end of the chapter called 'Sovereignty and the General will'. It is a vindication of good citizenship defined in terms of devotion to the common good and represents a reassertion at this critical place of the philosophy of history found in his theology and ethics. In the next chapter, perhaps the best known in his lectures, Green is arguing not only that 'Will, not Force, is the Basis of the State', but also that devotion to the common good, produces beneficient political results, while devotion to selfish interest can, despite appearances, produce only the contrary result. . . . What is involved in claiming that will is the basis of the state is Green's secular religion of citizenship, with its teaching of altruism and its prescription of self-sacrifice to duty. His view of the world depends on the idea of God, as a spiritual principle, realising himself in the establishment of obligations by law and authoritative custom and the gradual recognition of moral duties by individuals. In this scheme the idea of the common good plays a crucial rôle. Green makes it into the criterion of political obligation. He contends that this idea progressively realises itself in history. Hence he is committed to a theodicy indicating the general implications of his conception of the common good. How all these notions are related to political obligation, as Green defined it, may be seen from the passage with which he closed his lectures on that subject:

I am properly *obliged* to those actions and forbearances which are necessary to the general freedom, necessary if each is not to interfere with the realisation of another's will. My *duty* is to be interested positively in my neighbour's well-being. And it is important to understand that, while the enforcement of obligations is possible, that of moral duties is impossible. But the establishment of obligation by law or authoritative custom, and the gradual recognition of moral duties have not been separate processes. They have gone on together in the history of man. The growth of the institutions by which more complete equality of rights is gradually secured to a wider range of persons, and of those interests in

various forms of social well-being by which the will is moralised, have
been related to each other as the outer and inner side of the same
spiritual development. . . . The result of the twofold process has been
the creation of the actual content of morality.

Thus Green argues that to promote the common good is the essential characteristic of a state. He asserts further that such an idea has
been a determining element in the consciousness of even the most
selfish men who have been instrumental in the formation or maintenance of states. Napoleon did good to the extent that in seeking his
own ends he had to further those of the French Revolution. 'His selfishness gave a particular character to his pursuit of these ends, and
(so far as it did so) did so for evil.' 'Caesar again we have learnt to
regard as a benefactor of mankind, but it was not Caesar that made
the Roman law, through which chiefly or solely the Roman Empire
became a blessing.' The assertion, then, that an idea of social good is
realised in the formation of states is not to be met by the selfishness
and bad passions of men who have been instrumental in forming
them.

In this way, Green established to his own satisfaction that the idea
of the common good provides the basis of the state. The fact that the
state implies a supreme coercive power has produced the erroneous
view that coercion is its essence. Actually just the reverse is true.
There can be a supreme coercive power only because it is recognised
by citizens as serving a proper function. A state is not to be defined
as an aggregate of individuals under a sovereign but as a society in
which the rights of man are defined and harmonised. Thus the state
does not create rights but gives fuller reality to rights already existing. A state presupposes other forms of community with the rights
that arise out of them, and exists only in sustaining, securing and
completing them. Once the state has come into existence, new rights
arise in it. It leads to a further moral development of man. The citizen can claim rights but only those which are contributory to some
social good which the public conscience is capable of appreciat-
ing. . . .

. . . The state regulates and harmonises rights. The other forms of
community which precede the state neither continue to exist outside
it, nor are they superseded by it. They continue within it, but attain a
new fullness as they come into the harmony produced by its action.
Thus the citizen cannot properly claim a right against the state as
natural rights theorists would do. No one can make such a claim except as a member of a society, and the state is for its members 'the society of societies, the society in which all their claims upon each
other are mutually adjusted'.

Where does this leave the citizen who regards the laws of his state as unjust because violating the rights of some who live within it? Does this mean that he, under no conditions, has the right to disobey? To these questions Green replies as he had earlier in considering the justifiability of resistance to an ostensible sovereign. Again there is no clear-cut answer. The state may be disobeyed only for the purpose of making its actual laws correspond more closely with its inherent tendency and idea—the reconciler and sustainer of the rights arising out of men's social relations. Green is in the curious position of defining the state in terms of its idea, while admitting that this idea is never in fact completely realised. Thus he explicitly denies the Hegelian version of the Idealist theory. If the state fulfils its ideal function, the individual would be obliged to regard its laws as having absolute authority. But since this is never the case, the unconditional obedience to the state demanded by Hegel is inappropriate. The principle that a citizen should never act otherwise than as a citizen does not carry with it the obligation to obey the law of his state in any and all conditions. Disobedience must be based on an acknowledged social good. Whether a citizen chooses to claim a right by obeying or disobeying the law is a matter of circumstances. A citizen may properly attempt to repeal laws which prohibit the instruction of slaves or assisting runaways; but although there is always a presumption in favour of obedience even to bad laws, the public interest may be best served by violating an existent law. Such was the case when the public conscience recognised that slaves had a capacity for right which was being denied them because a powerful class in its own interest resisted any alteration of the law. And because of such recognition, there was no danger that disobedience will create a breach in popular obedience to law.

But what if no recognition of the implicit rights of the slave can be elicited from the public conscience? Has the citizen still a right to disregard these legal prohibitions? Green, who has been wavering throughout this discussion, once again takes an unexpected position. In the absence of recognition, the right of helping the slave may be cancelled by the duty of obeying the prohibitory law. This, he is prepared to say, would be the case if the violation of the law in the interest of the slave were liable to produce general anarchy. 'Such a destruction of the state would mean a general loss of freedom, a general substitution of force for mutual good-will in men's dealings with each other, that would outweigh the evil of any slavery under such limitations and regulations as an organised state imposes on it.' . . .

How adequate was the theory of rights presented in his work? It is not unfair to say that all the unresolved difficulties in Green's theory of the common good recur in his treatment of rights. For he attempted to shift the basis for rights from the theory of consent used by natural rights theorists to his own version of the common good. And he introduced the Idealist notion of social and conscious recognition as an essential ingredient of rights. A right is a claimed power which should be granted if it promotes a good common to all those within a given political society. More: this power must be perceived as so doing by the members of the society, or be implied by existing practices and relationships themselves recognised as legitimate. Professor Sabine has rephrased this point in its most plausible form: 'A moral community . . . is one in which the individual responsibly limits his claims to freedom in the light of general social interests and in which the community itself supports its claims because the general well-being can be realised only through his initiative and freedom.' Green neither wished to gain recognition for new rights, nor to discard those already in force, but rather to provide a more adequate account of the process actually operative in communities such as his own, and in citizens such as himself. It may be doubted whether, for all his criticism of J. S. Mill's work, a list of substantive rights Green himself believed in would have differed much from a similar one drawn up by Mill. But Green thought that his own system could provide a rationale of these rights which was consistent with itself in a way not open to Mill. Was this in fact the case?

When Green's own analysis of particular cases was examined earlier, it turned out that the two criteria he prescribed did not always yield the same result. A claimed power may in fact contribute to some good common to all the members of a society, but not be acknowledged; again, such a power may be implied by existing social relationships, but to resist existing laws which deny the claim, may demonstrably produce results inimical to the good of the society as a whole. Nor is Green's account of 'recognition' sufficiently clear. In ordinary instances, he tells us, regular legislative practice in a constitutional state is quite good enough as an indication of what is recognised. But, as we know, it is not an ordinary instance that provokes genuine bewilderment or conflict about the status of a right. Neither majority nor minority views are necessarily decisive in such a case, and so we must look at existing social relationships. Here Green's account of a slave in a society which otherwise grants full rights to all its members again seems unrevealing. The slave, by having a full, human relation to some persons such as his family, is said to have demonstrated his right to be a member of the larger community, which is thus obliged to recognise his claim. But has not 'recognition' been transformed here from the criterion of right into a process itself considered to be subject to a higher standard? This is to assert that some rights are tacitly, but not legally, recognised. And what constitutes tacit social recognition? The existence, we are told, among men of relationships which imply certain rights. Those individuals who do in fact enjoy them may not deny them to others without denying the basis of their own claim. But surely this is to introduce a question of logic into what previously has been defined as a matter of fact. What if slave-owners fail to recognise their slaves' claim to rights? In the presence of conflicting views about which rights ought to be recognised, who will decide what are the rights immanent in the existing social system?

. . . Strictly speaking, a theory of rights, defined purely as socially acknowledged claims, says nothing about their content. If the members of a society recognised cannibalism as a practice, not only justified but mandatory in certain circumstances, no one using Green's criterion would have a right to object to being eaten under such specified conditions. Indeed, as in Hegel's illustration of his own theory of punishment, a person who was treated otherwise than by the recognised usage of the society might properly complain that he was being treated as something less than a full member of it.

Nothing could be more certain than that Green would have repudiated any practices substantially at variance with the values of his own society. Yet on the basis of recognition alone, he could not have excluded what he manifestly would have wished to exclude. Nor is this the worst which can be said about Green's theory. For it is simply inconsistent with itself. It is impossible to reconcile the assertion that rights are such only when socially recognised, with the contrary view that there exist rights which ought to be granted, whether or not they are in fact recognised. . . .

Everything which has already been said about his theory of rights applies equally well to that of obligation. When ought a subject to obey his sovereign? When ought he to resist commands and on what basis? Here again Green's proposals for the sort of dialogue which a conscientious citizen might carry out with himself or others is excellent as a list of difficulties to be explored, but remains inconclusive as answers to them. He himself admits that his theory *qua* theory does not resolve the contradictions or remove the doubts confronting the actor in an extreme situation. Indeed, at one place, Green concedes that the very effort to perform the sort of analysis he recommended would probably paralyse the actor in his effort to reach a decision. Again, the reader may conclude that possibly there is no help which the philosopher can render beyond analysing the alternatives and assessing their likely consequences in relation to the actor's goals. To clarify possible courses of action, to discredit loose thinking and dubious argument—these are not small services in such situations. But it is no good pretending that any philosophical reasoning can eliminate the pull of conflicting loyalties, which characterise those occasions when men must choose between an established government and its revolutionary rival. Some modern 'crisis philosophers' have attempted to construct theories resting upon the assumption that extreme situations are the paradigm of human experience; Green's thought is predicated on the opposite view, which denies the significance of such situations. Surely this attitude stemmed from a religious need. For, in one part of his mind, he knew well enough that political life abounds in conflict of duties and in situations where neither right nor advantage to the common good are easily decided. From his own civic experience he was acquainted with the fact that decisions must often be made, not on the basis of some substantial and indubitable good, but rather as the result of calculating a merely marginal advantage, which is the best which can be made out of things as they are. But he had invested citizenship with a moral sanction and an urgency which brooked no qualification. In fact his political philosophy was less an analysis of English political life than a vision of what it might be. . . .

11 / The Philosophic Basis of Fascism

GIOVANNI GENTILE

The politic of Fascism revolves wholly about the concept of the national State; and accordingly it has points of contact with nationalist doctrines, along with distinctions from the latter which it is important to bear in mind.

Both Fascism and nationalism regard the State as the foundation of all rights and the source of all values in the individuals composing it. For the one as for the other the State is not a consequence—it is a principle. But in the case of nationalism, the relation which individualistic liberalism, and for that matter socialism also, assumed between individual and State is inverted. Since the State is a principle, the individual becomes a consequence—he is something which finds an antecedent in the State: the State limits him and determines his

SOURCE: *Foreign Affairs*, VI (January 1928), 301–304. Copyright by the Council on Foreign Relations, Inc., New York. Reprinted by permission of the publisher.

manner of existence, restricting his freedom, binding him to a piece of ground whereon he was born, whereon he must live and will die. In the case of Fascism, State and individual are one and the same things, or rather, they are inseparable terms of a necessary synthesis.

Nationalism, in fact, founds the State on the concept of nation, the nation being an entity which transcends the will and the life of the individual because it is conceived as objectively existing apart from the consciousness of individuals, existing even if the individual does nothing to bring it into being. For the nationalist, the nation exists not by virtue of the citizen's will, but as datum, a fact, of nature.

For Fascism, on the contrary, the State is a wholly spiritual creation. It is a national State, because, from the Fascist point of view, the nation itself is a creation of the mind and is not a material presupposition, is not a datum of nature. The nation, says the Fascist, is never really made; neither, therefore, can the State attain an absolute form, since it is merely the nation in the latter's concrete, political manifestation. For the Fascist, the State is always *in fieri*. It is in our hands, wholly; whence our very serious responsibility towards it.

But this State of the Fascists which is created by the consciousness and the will of the citizen, and is not a force descending on the citizen from above or from without, cannot have toward the mass of the population the relationship which was presumed by nationalism.

Nationalism identified State with Nation, and made of the nation an entity preëxisting, which needed not to be created but merely to be recognized or known. The nationalists, therefore, required a ruling class of an intellectual character, which was conscious of the nation and could understand, appreciate and exalt it. The authority of the State, furthermore, was not a product but a presupposition. It could not depend on the people—rather the people depended on the State and on the State's authority as the source of the life which they lived and apart from which they could not live. The nationalistic State was, therefore, an aristocratic State, enforcing itself upon the masses through the power conferred upon it by its origins.

The Fascist State, on the contrary, is a people's state, and, as such, the democratic State *par excellence*. The relationship between State and citizen (not this or that citizen, but all citizens) is accordingly so intimate that the State exists only as, and in so far as, the citizen causes it to exist. Its formation therefore is the formation of a consciousness of it in individuals, in the masses. Hence the need of the Party, and of all the instruments of propaganda and education which Fascism uses to make the thought and will of the *Duce* the thought and will of the masses. Hence the enormous task which Fascism sets itself in trying to bring the whole mass of the people, beginning with the little children, inside the fold of the Party.

On the popular character of the Fascist State likewise depends its greatest social and constitutional reform—the foundation of the Corporations of Syndicates. In this reform Fascism took over from syndicalism the notion of the moral and educational function of the syndicate. But the Corporations of Syndicates were necessary in order to reduce the syndicates to State discipline and make them an expression of the State's organism from within. The Corporations of Syndicates are a device through which the Fascist State goes looking for the individual in order to create itself through the individual's will. But the individual it seeks is not the abstract political individual whom the old liberalism took for granted. He is the only individual who can ever be found, the individual who exists as a specialized productive force, and who, by the fact of his specialization, is brought to unite with other individuals of his same category and comes to belong with them to the one great economic unit which is none other than the nation.

This great reform is already well under way. Toward it nationalism, syndicalism, and even liberalism itself, were already tending in the past. For even liberalism was beginning to criticize the older forms of political representation, seeking some system of organic representation which would correspond to the structural reality of the State.

The Fascist conception of liberty merits passing notice. The *Duce* of Fascism once chose to discuss the theme of "Force or Consent?"; and he concluded that the two terms are inseparable, that the one implies the other and cannot exist apart from the other; that, in other words, the authority of the State and the freedom of the citizen constitute a continuous circle wherein authority presupposes liberty and liberty authority. For freedom can exist only within the State, and the State means authority. But the State is not an entity hovering in the air over the heads of its citizens. It is one with the personality of the citizen. Fascism, indeed, envisages the contrast not as between liberty and authority, but as between a true, concrete liberty which exists, and an abstract, illusory liberty which cannot exist.

Liberalism broke the circle above referred to, setting the individual against the State and liberty against authority. What the liberal desired was liberty as against the State, a liberty which was a limitation of the State; though the liberal had to resign himself, as the lesser of the evils, to a State which was a limitation on liberty. The absurdities inherent in the liberal concept of freedom were apparent to liberals themselves early in the Nineteenth Century. It is no merit of Fascism to have again indicated them. Fascism has its own solution of the paradox of liberty and authority. The authority of the State is absolute. It does not compromise, it does not bargain, it does not surrender any portion of its field to other moral or religious principles which may interfere with the individual conscience. But on the other hand, the State becomes a reality only in the consciousness of its individuals. And the Fascist corporative State supplies a representative system more sincere and more in touch with realities than any other previously devised and is therefore freer than the old liberal State.

UTILITARIANISM

. . . obey . . . so long as the probable mischiefs of obedience are less than the probable
mischiefs of resistance.

—JEREMY BENTHAM, A *Fragment*
on Government

Jeremy Bentham is considered one
of Western philosophy's most influential empiricists. In "Behavioural
Factors in Bentham's Conception of Political Change," Warren Roberts, Jr., discusses Bentham's search for the empirical "means, techniques or tactics"—the positive and negative *sanctions*—appropriate
to induce desired political change. Bentham seeks to elaborate incentives that may encourage the "ruling few," who control most power
resources in the society, to institute policies beneficial to the "subject
many." Among the political tactics mentioned by Bentham are included political education, propaganda, and pressure-group activities
by informed elites to counteract governmental influence over the
communications media, passive resistance tactics such as a general refusal to pay taxes, and the threat or resort to revolutionary violence
by a majority.

Bentham's entire analysis rests on the utilitarian assumption that
man's dual master is pleasure and pain, and accordingly, that
"sanctions"—i.e., threats of pain or promises of pleasure—will be sufficient incentives to motivate both the many and the few. Although
Bentham's "rational self-interest" theory of motivation has been criticized as insufficiently inclusive of the range of human sentiments, his
empiricist approach combined with his "general happiness" standard,
at very least, forces the close student of political obligation to trace
out thoroughly and accurately the probable consequences of obedience or resistance, using observable indicators whenever possible.

John B. Stewart's book *The Moral and Political Philosophy of
David Hume,* from which the article that appears here is taken, offers
an incisive discussion of Hume's analysis of civil reform. For Hume,
the social contract theory of the origin and development of civil society is a mere myth. Habit, trial and error, and practical results
comprise the long process by which men work out viable sociopoliti-
cal relationships. Therefore, Hume cautions circumspection in at-

tempts to alter those arrangements. Hume's evolutionary common-sense utilitarianism leads to basically conservative conclusions—for if, on balance, what survives is functional and if utility is the standard of goodness, then it is difficult to avoid the conclusion "That which is, is good."

12 / Behavioural Factors in Bentham's Conception of Political Change

WARREN ROBERTS, JR.

The purpose of this paper is to analyse in systematic fashion Jeremy Bentham's conception of the factors involved in the process of bringing about political change, and in so doing to emphasize the political and behavioural side of his thought. Bentham himself does not treat the subject of political change systematically, but he does give us a clue as to how he might have done so if he had so chosen. For he indicates as early as *The Theory of Legislation* that he considers the three fundamental factors or elements—will, knowledge, and power—to be involved in human action of any sort; and clearly this concept is broad enough to include actions designed to bring about change. Moreover, as late as his *Logical Arrangements* he includes the theory that human action is based on these factors as one of his fifteen basic ideas or 'instruments of invention and discovery'. In terms of these three factors, then, a model for political change will be built and Bentham's conception of the means, techniques, or tactics used in bringing about change indicated. The relative significance of each of the three factors varies, however. As time passes he places more and more emphasis upon the power factor and consequently upon what today might be called political behaviour. How and why this change takes place will be indicated in the first section of this paper. For the moment it should be pointed out that his contributions to the study of political behaviour are much greater than have hitherto been realized. These contributions are to be found in both published and unpublished works, espe-

SOURCE: *Political Studies*, X (June 1962) 163–179. Reprinted by permission of the Clarendon Press, Oxford.

cially in the latter.[1] No doubt the fact that so much of this material is unpublished helps to explain why his contributions here have not been appreciated as much as they should have been. But this is not the only reason, since much of what Bentham has to say has been published. The writer would argue that the tradition of regarding Bentham in legal and institutional terms has hampered the development of an adequate appreciation of the political and behavioural side of his thought. To readjust the balance, then, is one of the primary purposes of this paper.

I

Although Bentham's conception of political change is always conceived in terms of the three basic elements in human action (will, knowledge, and power), his attitude towards the significance of each varies. In his earlier period, his emphasis is upon the first two factors, although the third is by no means ignored. On one level, he seems to believe that knowledge of the goals is the most important single factor—hence his emphasis upon his codes. If he can just persuade the sovereign to adopt his codes, that is, if the sovereign wills to do so because of some reward he will receive (say, the gratitude of his subjects or the verdict of history that he was enlightened and benevolent) then all will be well, since obviously the sovereign has the power to act. In this approach the emphasis is upon initiating change: clearly this is done by the legislator (or sovereign) through laws which change institutions which in turn will change behaviour,

---

[1] Considered in terms of their contributions to political science, and especially to theories of political behaviour as it relates to the change process, his most important published works are his *Constitutional Code, Plan of Parliamentary Reform, Securities Against Misrule, Codification Proposal Addressed to all Nations Professing Liberal Opinions, Justice and Codification Petitions, A Table of the Springs of Action, The Book of Fallacies, Pannomial Fragments, Logical Arrangements,* and *Official Aptitude Maximized; Expense Minimized.* There are at least a score of additional works with varying degrees of significance. For each of these works there are many pages of unused manuscript material, sometimes as much as in the published version, or even more in at least one case. In addition there are the following related unpublished works, all of which are important for the purposes of this paper (composition dates are indicated in parentheses): *Thoughts on Sinecures* (1810), *Influence* (1809–14 largely), *Government as Viewed at 27 and at 70* (1817–18), *Picture of Misrule* (1818), *Defence of the People Against Lord Erskine* (1819), *Law Amendment* (1827–28). There are numerous works of lesser importance, including various letters to editors and other open letters, as well as correspondence with public officials and others.

thus creating improvement all along the line. Conceived in terms of
the will, the purpose of these institutional changes is to create a situation in which men will be more apt to will to do what they ought to
do. On this level, that of continuing the process of change once it is
initiated, it seems that the will is the most important factor, since it is
the will to act more ethically that is of such primary concern. But obviously one can only do this if one has the knowledge and the power
to do so. In sum, in his earlier period his emphasis is upon knowledge
and will, or, in other words, upon the development of the science of
jurisprudence and the establishment of the proper institutions to influence the will. So far as power is concerned, change is to come from
the top, or from the power holders; and since change benefits the people, obviously they will acquiesce or at least not resist.[2] This entire
approach presupposes that in spite of the prejudices and conflicting
interests of power holders, somehow it will be possible to appeal to
their 'better selves' and get the reforms essential to the furtherance of
the principle of utility.

Once Bentham discovers that this presupposition is too optimistic,
then quite clearly he has to change his emphasis. The problem becomes one of creating the power to make the changes; hence his emphasis in his later period is upon power. Knowledge and will are still
important, but here again there is a difference. For the knowledge
that most concerns him is not the science of jurisprudence; rather it is
the science of politics and in particular of political behaviour. This is
what must be known in order to get power to make changes. So far as
the will is concerned, rather than thinking primarily in terms of creating institutions to change the will, he is more concerned with the
problem of creating the will to change institutions. In other words,
there is a shift in emphasis from the legal and institutional to the political and behavioural. This is not to say that the political and behavioural are ignored in his early period; on the contrary, he has a
great deal to say about power even then, and the institutional
changes which he advocates are designed to influence the will to act
—that is, to influence behaviour. Nor is it to say that legal and institutional factors are ignored in the later period; actually they are not,
as will become apparent. Rather it is simply to say that there is a
shift in emphasis in his approach. Just how this is worked out will be

---

[2] It would be a mistake, however, to say that he ignores the problem of public
support. At times he specifically refers to the need for an informed public opinion (U.C. MSS, box 154a, pp. 36–47). Indeed on one occasion he says: 'It is
for the people to arise and cast out these seeds of corruption' (ibid., box 5, p.
31). This is atypical, however, since his usual emphasis in this period is upon
change from above rather than from below.

seen in the ensuing sections in which each of Bentham's three factors involved in change will be considered separately and his specific proposals indicated in each case.

II

The first basic factor in the change process is the will to bring about change. In Bentham's opinion, the will to act is ultimately the result of the operation of one of the sanctions.[3] A sanction is an 'efficient cause' of action which in the last analysis is backed up by the 'final cause' of all actions—i.e. pleasure or avoidance of pain. In other words, if we will to do whatever is required by the sanction, pleasure will be the result; if not, pain will result. The ultimate sanction is the physical, which arises from the nature of man and includes both physical and psychical factors. There are in addition three other sanctions: the political, which emanates from government; the moral, which comes from public opinion; and the religious, which comes from 'a superior invisible being'. In his early period Bentham's emphasis is upon the political sanction as the source of change. Through legislation institutions will be changed and as a consequence men will be more apt to will to do what they ought to do. When he discovers that the change is not forthcoming, he shifts his emphasis to the moral sanction as the chief instigating factor in bringing about change. Through an aroused public opinion those in power will be persuaded to change. In the last analysis the moral sanction depends on the physical sanction, but as a result of the misuse of the political sanction there is much suffering and the physical sanction is thus playing its role as the ultimate efficient cause of change. In a sense this suffering, then, is the basic factor in creating the will to change.

On a less ultimate level, the will to action is the result of motives which influence the will and serve as a means of determining the action taken on any given occasion. The catalogue of motives corresponds to that of pleasures and pains—in other words, for each pleasure or pain there is a corresponding motive inciting man to action. For example, for the pleasure of eating there is the desire or motive of hunger; for the pleasure of sympathy, there is the motive of good will; for the pleasure of power, there is the motive of love of power. Quite clearly Bentham is here concerned with motivational or psy-

[3] The ensuing is adapted from the analyses of sanctions in the following works: *An Introduction to the Principles of Morals and Legislation*, ch. 3; *The Theory of Legislation*, pp. 27–30; *Logical Arrangements, Works*, vol. iii, pp. 290–3; *Deontology* (2 vols.; Edinburgh, William Tait, 1934), vol. ii, pp. 2–4; as well as from miscellaneous manuscript material.

chological factors in political behaviour. He has much to say on the relation between motives and other factors, such as intentions, consciousness, disposition, habits, desires, aversions, hopes, fears, wants, needs, and interests; but limitations of space prevent a consideration of this. From the point of view of this paper, what is important is the use to which motives may be put in bringing about change. In general Bentham emphasizes appeals to motives which result in rewards, especially political rewards. The desire for, or love of, liberty, security, country, power, reputation, good will, amity, ease, peace, and many related pleasures is clearly more important to him than the desire for or love of wealth. This is not to say that economic motives are not important or that the economic factor is not emphasized. Indeed, wealth is closely related to power and in one sense may be considered one of the elements of power. Moreover, he makes quite a point of the inviolability of the property of the present power holders, and assures them that they have nothing to fear from reform on this score, that they will continue to receive these rewards. But his more positive appeals are conceived in terms of the development of greater sympathy for one's fellow man—of 'other-regarding' motives, in other words. These would not only give power holders a sense of moral well-being, but would also earn them the respect of the community and such rewards as honour, dignity, reputation, and good will. He also appeals to them in terms of love of knowledge, talent, and similar power-related motives. Appeals to the 'subject many' are similar to those to the 'ruling few' except for necessary modifications because of their different statuses. Although the emphasis is upon motives which bring rewards both to the power holders and to the people generally, there are also threats of punishment, especially to the more 'wicked' of the present ruling few. If they continue in their present course, they may lose everything: power and all that goes with it, including rank, wealth, reputation, dignity, ease, and possibly even their lives, in the event of a violent revolution. Appeals based on fear, intimidation, vengeance, or punishment are thus not to be ignored, even though they are less emphasized than those based on reward.

The entire problem of creating the will to change may be conceived in terms of interest. In this case the problem is primarily one of creating a situation in which it is in the interest of the power holders to change. As time passes, Bentham becomes more and more convinced that given the irresponsibility of the present power holders this can only be done by bringing about a change in power relations: only if a new power balance is created will the present power holders see that it is in their interest to change, or at least not to prevent change by force. Once this is done and changes are agreed upon that make the governors responsible to the governed, then in the future the will to change will in effect be built into the political system. This will result from the fact that it will be in the interest of the governors to will to do whatever is conceived to be in the general interest, and since we live in a dynamic society, quite clearly change will be in the general interest. Expressed in different terms, the will to make changes in the common interest will be in the self interest of the power holders if they are to stay in power. In a sense, then, by making them responsible Bentham is also making them conceive their self-interest in more enlightened, long run, other-regarding terms rather than in narrow, short run, self-regarding terms.

III

The second basic factor in the change process is knowledge. Through the development of science we will have knowledge both of the ends to be sought in bringing about change and of the means to be used in achieving these ends. Among other things the development of science means getting the facts, and Bentham concentrates upon ways and means of doing this. Although an avaricious student and collector of the existing literature, whether in the form of histories, biographies, newspapers, journals, law books, parliamentary reports, committee reports, political works (especially on constitutional questions), or from some other source, he finds that these are not adequate for his purposes. In particular there is not enough specific data, especially quantified data. To remedy this he himself sends out questionnaires on various subjects and suggests that others, both individuals and groups, do the same. He is particularly impressed by the 'newly cultivated' science of statistics and makes many suggestions for governments to follow in the collection of statistics.

His emphasis upon knowledge is not limited to the development of science, however: equally important is the diffusion of this knowledge through education. He is particularly interested in the teaching of useful subjects in the schools, both public and private, and at all levels, even including the college level. This would mean a greater emphasis upon the natural and social sciences, especially upon political science. With such education, the chances of getting the changes which he considers necessary are much improved, since there is a very close relation between the understanding and the will. Given a greater understanding of their 'true' interest, people are more apt to will to do whatever is needed in this interest. Indeed, perhaps the main reason for the masses' apathy towards change may be found in their ignorance of their real interest and what they can do to further it. This is traceable not only to lack of education but also to the spread of false ideas by those in power. The opinions of the average person on public matters are determined to a large extent by the ruling few who control so much in the society, in particular, the media of communications, the instruments of government, the standards of taste, and to some extent the means of livelihood. Moreover, in an irresponsible government the ruling few develop 'sinister interests' and 'interest-begotten prejudices' to 'justify' these sinister interests. Such 'fallacies' must be exposed by those in favour of change if the 'delusions' of the public are to be dispelled. To do so will require the establishment of their own newspapers, magazines, publishing houses, and other communication facilities. In other words—in present-day terms—propaganda will have to be combated with propaganda in order to get an informed public opinion. Moreover, this is essential if the moral sanction is to play its role in bringing about change. Actually, this kind of education is not limited to the general public. Appeals are also made to the ruling few to develop a more enlightened view of their interest. Such appeals are addressed in particular to the more independent, the less active, the more moral, and the more intelligent, among the power holders. In his terms, 'intellectual aptitude' is essential to good government; consequently it is important that it be developed as much as possible even in a 'bad' government. For if it is, the probabilities of peaceful, non-violent change are considerably enhanced.

IV

The third factor in the change process is power, a subject which, as has been indicated, becomes increasingly important for Bentham. He defines power as 'the faculty of giving determination either to the state of the passive faculties, or to that of the active faculties, of the subject in relation to and over which it is exercised'. The passive faculties are the physical characteristics of a person or a thing; the active are the psychical, motivational, or volitional characteristics of men. In government 'determination' is usually given by means of a command which is enforced by a sanction. The person giving the determination is the 'power holder' or 'director'; the person to whom it is given is the 'correlative subject' or 'directee'. Under all forms of government, even including democracy, there have always been, and probably always will be, only a few power holders: in a sense this is in the nature of power, since if everyone issued commands there would be anarchy. Granted that there will always be the few and the many, the leaders and the led, then clearly, if there is to be change, leaders must be won over: leadership is essential in any effective attack upon the *status quo*. Some leaders may come from the existing power holders, if they can be won over through appeals to motives or interests which they have or might have, that would be favourable to change, through education and propaganda, and through various political activities to be indicated subsequently. If, however, an insufficient number are won over through these devices, then emphasis would have to be placed on enlarging the number of the ruling few by adding to the existing members new members in favour of change. In this way a new balance of power would be created with the backing of the people and the probabilities of change would therefore be increased.

One method of determining who might be included in the new group, as well as which ones of the old might be won over, is that of ascertaining the criteria for membership in the ruling few, and then finding which of these criteria would be most apt to characterize a person in favour of change. Bentham finds that in varying degrees wealth, rank, reputation, knowledge, talent, and moral worth seem to be the characteristic endowments of power holders. Among the existing power holders the first three characteristics are the most significant, reputation being based on wealth or rank, especially titles of nobility, rather than upon one of the last three criteria. Clearly these people do not have an interest in change—that is, unless they are morally superior, and think in enlightened terms, and are leaders of ability. Moral worth, knowledge, and active talent, then, are the three criteria which leaders in favour of change would and should have; therefore these must be found or created if change is to be promoted. There is a good chance of doing so by 'awakening the potentially independent few'. Newspaper editors, writers, scientists and other intellectuals already are enlisting in the cause; still others could and should be found. Nor should men of great national prestige be overlooked. It is possible to win over such outstanding leaders especially if they can be persuaded that parliamentary reform is inevitable, or, if they are in Parliament and lose influence there, that they will have greater influence outside Parliament as a result of changing their position. If the class origin of the leaders is considered, then Bentham seems to believe that a few would come from the upper class, the majority from the middle class, and a few from the potentially more 'active' among the lower class. By appealing to these people, then, the chances are that leaders can be found.

Ultimately, in order to get a change in the power balance, it is necessary to have a change not only among the leaders but also among the led. Unless there are 'correlative subjects' over whom power is exercised, the 'power holders' will cease to have power. As Bentham puts it, 'Power on the one part is constituted by and is in greater or less proportion to obedience on the other. It is in direct ratio of the obedience and in the inverse ratio of resistance.' [4] The classes from which this resistance is to come are really the same as those from which the leaders are to come—that is, the middle class and a few from the upper and lower classes. That this is his position may be seen from his suggestions with regard to negative disobedience or passive resistance. If the situation gets bad enough to warrant it, then he suggests that as a first step in resistance there might be a general refusal to pay taxes.[5] On another occasion he adds that rather than undergo the terrors of such popular actions as breaking the bank, not paying taxes, and the consequent loss of public credit, etc., the ruling few might give in.[6] Quite clearly such actions would have been primarily middle-class actions since the lower classes did not pay taxes, and were in no position to break the bank. But this should not be construed to mean that Bentham is a middle-class reformer uninterested in the working or lower classes. He is interested in the happiness of all people, especially that of the subject many whether of the middle or lower class. Nor should it be construed to mean that he would advocate resistance if only a minority wanted it. It is true that each person must make his own decision about the 'relative mischiefs of disobedience' but Bentham specifically says that only if the majority agree should there be disobedience or revolution.[7] Not only would the middle classes be the backbone of the resistance to abuses of authority, they would also be the chief supporters of the reform leaders on a less extreme basis—e.g. they would form the numerical base for the operations of the moral sanction or for the demands of public opinion. Thus the leaders would have the followers needed to support the new power balance.

Power is not simply a question of 'who'; it is also a question of 'how'. On this question Bentham is especially concerned with the tac-

[4] *Securities Against Misrule, Works*, vol. viii, p. 572. See also U.C. MSS, box 167, p. 4.

[5] Ibid., box 232, p. 159. To be exact, this action is to be taken only after a petition to Parliament in which it is indicated that the action will be taken if Parliament does not act favourably upon the petition.

[6] U.C. MSS, box 232, p. 442.

[7] See, for example, ibid., box 132, p. 453; *Deontology*, vol. ii, pp. 288–90. This latter reference would exclude a Marxist-type revolution led by an elite without the expressed consent of the majority. He has little to say about positive disobedience or active resistance involving the use of external physical force, largely because he does not believe that this will be necessary; or at least such is my interpretation. On one occasion he says that if violence does become necessary the people should be discriminating, not burn houses and property as in backward countries, nor harm the persons of the ruling few, since mischief to person is worse than that to property—perhaps threats to milord's art would be effective! See U.C. MSS, box 132, pp. 467–70.

tics or techniques used by power holders to maintain themselves in power, and how these may be countered if change is brought about. Corruption is one of these and although there will always be some corruption, at least the amount would be reduced if the 'matter of corruption' in the hands of the corruptionists were decreased. Changes in election laws would also help to decrease corruption, as would changes in the structure of government that would make for responsibility. Delusion is another technique used, and this may be countered by education and propaganda, as was indicated in the preceding section. Intimidation is a third tactic, which in the last analysis is based upon force and may be conceived as force applied to the mind. Clearly if intimidation is to be lessened there must be a change in the force at the command of the government. Undoubtedly force is needed for defence, but defensive forces should be changed in make-up so that there would be only a small number of professional military forces or 'stipendiaries', and a large number of other forces or 'radicals'. The radicals would consist of every one who could bear arms, and these would be provided them. Their primary purpose would be defence, but they would also aid in maintaining order internally. In terms of a change in power relations, Bentham obviously thinks of these forces as a counter force against the force at the command of the present power holders. Ultimately power depends on force and if control over force can be changed either in this way or in some other, then chances of peaceful change will be improved. A fourth tactic is depredation, which is not defined precisely, but which seems to mean not only despoiling or making inroads into property but also preying upon the subject many in any fashion. Of primary importance here is the state of the law and the role of lawyers. Bentham's proposals for remedies in each case are well known. They include such things as the codification of law and changes in judicial organization and procedures which would alter considerably the role of lawyers and hence make depredation more difficult. A fifth tactic is oppression, and in Bentham's view this is closely related to depredation, the chief difference being that oppression arises only when those suffering from depredation are forbidden to communicate concerning their suffering. In order to fight oppression, then, freedom of speech, press, and assembly are essential. Among other things, this means that libel laws must be changed; otherwise those in favour of change will be imprisoned or fined as libellers of the power holders.

These freedoms are also essential in combating another kind of technique of the power holders—their ability to act in concert. Clearly there is an alliance between 'the throne, the altar, and the bench', or between 'the soldier, the lawyer, and the priest', and this is an underlying cause of the success of the power holders in employing corruption, delusion, and intimidation. This may be combated by trying to make cracks in this 'unholy' alliance (e.g. by appealing to one against another) and in general attempting to decrease their power, or by trying to increase the power of those in favour of change. To accomplish such objectives it is necessary for those in favour of change to organize what would now be called pressure groups and through their 'combined public exertions' change the power balance. Among other things they would concentrate on pressing government—through the use of petitions, for example—and influencing public opinion.[8] Not only is it necessary to have pressure groups but, given the situation with regard to the Whigs and the slim chance of winning over the party as a whole, it is also necessary to organize a third party dedicated to bringing about changes in the people's interest. Even though its candidates may not be winners, at least at the beginning, it is important that it be supported by those who favour change. These, then, are the things that must be done if there is to be a change in power relations in favour of reform. And clearly a change in power relations is essential, in his view, if there is to be reform.

V

From what has been said, it should be apparent that Bentham's theory of change, especially in his later period, is conceived primarily in political and behavioural terms. Power is of the essence of his approach, but will and knowledge are also included since each is essential to change and especially to a change in power relations. Moreover, all three are conceived primarily, but not exclusively, in psychological or behavioural terms. It is submitted that in Bentham's theory we find an early example of the behavioural approach so much in vogue today, especially in the United States. It is an example which focuses upon power rather than group, decision-making, political participation, or some other concept. On this score he finds himself in company with many contemporary political scientists, both behaviouralists and non-behaviouralists.

His approach, however, may be considered rather crude in comparison with that of the typical modern behaviouralist in that he fails to state his assumptions as clearly as they would demand, he

[8] He proposes petitions on any number of occasions, even publishes a polemic entitled *Justice and Codification Petitions, Works,* vol. v, pp. 437–548. In an analysis of the value of petitioning, he observes that it not only makes the petitioners' desires known, but also acts as a means of bringing the petitioners together and cementing their relationships. See U.C. MSS, box 125, p. 176.

fails to use rigorous methods of data collecting, and he is not as precise and cautious in his conclusions as they would require. For example, his study of the party situation in his unpublished *Defence of the People Against Lord Erskine* is anything but what most modern behaviouralists would demand: assumptions and hypotheses are not clearly stated, terms are not operationally defined, no questionnaires are sent out on the basis of which quantitative data could be assembled, analysed, and cautiously interpreted. Instead, his generalizations are in rather sweeping terms, based largely on his general knowledge of past behaviour, and include a large intuitive element. His treatment of pressure groups is similar and probably helps to explain his unduly sanguine views concerning the effectiveness of the Parliamentary Candidate Society and Law Reform Association. This is not to say that the contemporary behaviouralists are right in their insistence upon such precision, rigour, and caution. It may well be that their critics are right in denying that politics can be studied effectively in this manner. But insofar as Bentham agrees with the contemporary behaviouralist on method, we can say that his treatment of parties and pressure groups, for example, falls considerably short of his own ideal, to say nothing of being rather unsophisticated from the contemporary point of view.

On the other hand, Bentham's theory has the advantage of being part of a general theory of man and society which is conceived in terms of both the is and the ought, and includes not just politics and behaviour, but also law and institutions, and much of the other material which goes to make up the total complex with which we are concerned in political science. It thus avoids the narrowness both in scope and method which seems characteristic of some contemporary behavioural theories. This narrowness in scope is often found nowadays in a refusal to consider ethical questions at all or at best in a consideration of such questions only on the level of is, not on the level of ought. It also manifests itself in an adequate emphasis upon institutions, especially upon legal institutions, an inadequate emphasis upon history, and an inadequate emphasis upon philosophy, especially upon metaphysics or upon 'first principles' of any sort. As for method, all too often its method is that of the natural scientist, and with such techniques it is difficult if not impossible to consider adequately many political phenomena, since only certain aspects of man's political relations with his fellow man in society can be considered in this manner. Insofar as Bentham is not guilty of such narrowness, either in scope or in method, he may be cited as an example of a broader approach worthy of consideration, if not emulation by certain contemporary behaviouralists.

13 / David Hume: Civil Reform

JOHN B. STEWART

Le mieux est l'ennemi du bien.

—VOLTAIRE, *Dictionnaire philosophique*

It is from habit, and only from habit, that law
derives the validity which secures obedience.
But habit can be created only by the passage
of time.

—ARISTOTLE, *Politics* 1269a

The scope and profundity of
Hume's thought are exceptional; yet when we try to define his position in the history of modern political philosophy, it seems fair—as
fair as such generalizations ever are—to say that he was a typical
eighteenth-century liberal.

He distinguishes, as we have seen, between family, friendship, and
humanity, on the one hand, and the civil relationships, society and
state, on the other. The former are the direct results of the feelings
men have for others, and therefore they can be called "natural." The
latter are artificial: when men are seeking scarce economic goods the
natural relation among them is competition, and society and state are
the framework within which this competition can go on with results
most satisfactory for all. In this chapter, in which we are dealing with
Hume as a reformer, our attention will be concentrated on the civil
relationships. Since human nature, which is expressed directly in the
family, friendship, and in acts of humanity, remains quite constant,
the noncivil relationships are not susceptible to much alteration.

From the time of the Sophists the proper civil relationships among
men have been discussed again and again by political philosophers in
terms of artifice and nature, and although these terms have been
given a multitude of different meanings—witness Hume's own distinction just referred to—the contrast is useful still. There are, we
may say, two basic (and extreme) ways of viewing these relation-

SOURCE: *The Moral and Political Philosophy of David Hume* (New York: Columbia University Press, 1963), ch. 13, pp. 302–303, 305–309, 311–320, 323–324.
Reprinted by permission of the publisher.

ships; first, as properly an artificial order, and, second, as properly a natural order. (Few, if any, of the theorists who make this distinction go to either extreme.) The former view—emphasizing artifice— presents the relationships as maintained immediately by men, that is, either, first, by one man (or a group of men) deliberately or, second, by the many acting under the influence of accumulated customs and prejudices. It emphasizes, not spontaneous individual conduct, but the limits that must be placed on such conduct if a war of all against all is not to erupt. In contrast, in the latter view—emphasizing nature —the focus is on the efforts of individuals to obtain whatever each deems good; the consequent competition among individuals is ex- tolled; and the emergence without the aid of human laws of a gener- ally good result from this selfish competition is asserted.

The difference between the two kinds of artificial regulation is im- portant. One insists on the need for laws made by a human ruler, i.e., written laws, but does not necessarily prescribe the specific content of those laws. It does not necessarily say what relationships among men —what order of public life—are to be commanded and enforced by the government. But the second theory of artifice, that of "unwritten law," does prescribe the proper relationships for any time, to a great extent. Its basic maxim is that men are to acquire their different places (and rights and duties), not by competition, but by customary rules of inheritance; consequently, the good social and political order is the one received from the past. . . .

When we think of the debate during the eighteenth century be- tween the proponents of competition and the proponents of custom (those who would have public policy incline to one instead of the other), we often use the terms "Liberals" and "Conservatives." These terms seem as useful as any, despite obvious disadvantages: few men of that century would have known our meanings of the terms, and we ourselves, now that we have undergone various new liberalisms and various new conservativisms, and have endured the tussles of political parties that call themselves, not necessarily accurately, liberal and conservative (or in some countries, Liberal and Conservative), proba- bly find that they do not mean exactly the same for each of us.

Edmund Burke is perhaps the most outspoken exponent of conser- vative thought in eighteenth-century Britain. When he looks at the social and political order in Britain or in France, he sees first, not the individual, but a whole "People." For him, this relationship, that by which men are related as a "People," is the cardinal one; and for him, this relationship is a complicated hierarchy of unequal players, at any moment the end product of inheritance. To the maintenance of this great historic relationship, the People, all public policy, both eco- nomic and political, should be directed.

In contrast, Hume in his analysis of the structure of the social and political order is antihistorical. Concerned as he is to advance the study of moral subjects by examining human nature, he looks at the whole human scene from the other side: he sees the individual first. Accordingly, it is not surprising that he distinguishes between those relationships that individuals enter because of their inherent value and the civil relationships, society and state, which are merely useful. Moreover, since for Hume, unlike Thomas Hobbes, the usefulness of society and state is chiefly economic, the process and institutions of the former are primary. The first rule of public life is that society (the economy) ought to be allowed to function as fully and as efficiently as possible; it follows, therefore, that no government that either fails to promote the economic process or interferes with the proper activities of the individual can be called a genuine government. When we examine Hume's view of the civil sphere, it becomes clear that he presupposed that competition is the basic process of this sphere. Because he finds that uncontrolled competition frustrates itself, he sets forth the principles of justice, principles entailing three institutions, property, trade, and contract, by which competition can be rendered orderly. And since these institutions probably will not be respected when competition becomes keen, governments are necessary to buttress artifice (justice) with further artifice (human laws). The principles of justice and governance constitute the legal framework within which he would allow competition to fructify. He believed that competition ought not to be left uncontrolled, but at the same time he would have it regulated only in ways, and to the extent, that would permit it to be most fruitful. His theory combines nature (competition) and artifice, but because artifice is to supplement nature, the proper content of the human laws is fixed neither by custom nor by the whim of the government; rather, the content is implied by the natural process which those laws are to supplement.

It might be assumed that, given this beginning, Hume would have proposed a thorough reformation of the existing society and state. It even might be thought that he would have urged the creation of a single system of free, world-wide commerce, based on a world-wide division of labour; second, that he would have advocated the replacement of the old governments by a single world government, or, if one government would have been overworked, by a system of regional governments, each with a jurisdiction scientifically designed, each located conveniently, like a chain of highway service stations; and third, that he would have insisted that this government (or each of these governments) should have the ideally best form of constitution. Such proposals would have been consistent with his analysis of society as a system of relations among owners, traders, and contractors, a system in which the greatest supply of goods would be produced by the natural (world-wide) division of labour and the natural (world-wide) flow of commerce, and it would have been consistent with his analysis of the essential work of government as the enforcement of the rights necessary for fruitful competition. But. although Hume does recommend some very important reforms, he stops far short of anything so unhistorical and rationalistic.

If the principles of justice and governance, which remain the same always, are to be followed, their validity must first become known generally. They can be known in two ways. First, the causal connection between acts of justice and governance and their good results can be traced, so that acts of justice and governance, which otherwise might seem a bother, or even bad, seem good. They are found good because it is believed that they will lead to certain good results. In short, they are found good because of their usefulness. In this case, the obligation to observe the principles is simply "rational." Second, through the mechanism of sympathy men feel the pleasure others feel, and the pain they feel, when their expectations are fulfilled or disappointed, so that without relying on their direct experience, and without tracing the connection between acts and their effects, they come to know, regardless of their private interests, that some acts are morally good, and that others are morally bad. The former they feel obliged to do; the latter they feel obliged to avoid. This obligation is "moral."

It follows from Hume's theory that men may be drawn to somewhat divergent courses of conduct by these two different kinds of obligation. The relation between rational obligation and moral obligation in the civil sphere can be summed up by three points. First, in this area moral duties which are not also generally useful to some degree are impossible, for it is the usefulness of justice and governance that gives rise to the moral virtues of the just man and of the good ruler and subject. Second, conformity to the economic and political standards of a civil society in which the principles of justice and governance are not realized perfectly can be morally obligatory; indeed, since no perfect society or state exists, all moral civil obligations known to us are of this kind. The more civilized men become, the more their economic and political systems will conform to the principles of civility, but at every phase in the process of civilization, even at the earliest, when justice is observed only slightly, and even less attention is given to good governance, men will feel some moral obligation, and so have moral duties. Third, there is an obligation to realize the principles of civility to higher and higher degrees, but this is a rational obligation, not a moral obligation. Moral obligation comes into existence only as a result of expectation, and this, in turn, is an effect of the past. The

sense of moral obligation is a cause of many specific (future) acts, but
the feeling of moral obligation and the content of moral duty are
products of experience. The sense of moral obligation cannot introduce new and higher moral standards.

When we turn to the question of civil reformation, this difference
between the two ways of knowing the principles of civility takes on
vast importance. For Hume, a proposal that an ideal civil society be
established would have to be accompanied by a demonstration that
all the participants therein would be self-conscious individuals, that
is, men who understand the nature of beliefs and who, consequently,
refuse to act on the basis of any belief falling short of proof or high
probability. At this point, the difference Hume mentions between
"men capable of true principles" and "the vulgar" becomes relevant.

He finds, we have seen, that men fall into various kinds of groups:
the nobles and the people, soldiers and civilians, priests and laity,
traders and the landed, and so forth. But most important for him, perhaps because he is a philosopher, is the difference between men capable of true principles and the vulgar. The former can distinguish between the several kinds of knowing. They comprehend what belief is,
and can employ the rules by which legitimate beliefs are distinguishable from fancies. They can trace the causal connection between justice and governance, on the one hand, and peace and prosperity, on
the other, and therefore can know that justice and governance are
usefully good. Quite apart from moral obligation, they feel obliged to
support civility. The vulgar, in contrast, although they know in the
several ways, are incapable of being scrupulous in distinguishing
among those ways. They do not test their beliefs against rules based
on the nature of belief, so that although many of their beliefs are
valid, many are not, or are only partly so. They have undergone civilization, and have learned to live by the principles of civility to some
extent; yet they cannot state those principles or explain their basis.
They know the principles only in terms of morality. They, in short,
are not conscious of the nature of knowing; nor are they self-conscious.

We have seen that it is because he thinks that the vulgar cannot
distinguish between true and false beliefs that Hume finds that they
tend to run either to superstition or to enthusiasm in their religion.
Wise governors, we have been told, will establish procedures by
which those religious passions that are dangerous to the civil order
can be grounded and dissipated.

The vulgar, or more exactly, those just above the very lowest rank
of men, who do little or no thinking whatsoever, because they cannot
distinguish between true and false belief are liable to think in terms
of ideologies. The attainment of true principles is beyond them;

therefore, they fly to simple, impractical theories such as divine right or popular sovereignty.

The vulgar often act on prejudices. No man brought up in a cold climate, however unobservant, would ever expect to be warmed by ice. Nevertheless, that same man, after talking with two lugubrious men from Dublin, may jump to the conclusion that all Irishmen are lugubrious. He forms his judgment of Irishmen before he has had experience with an adequate sample. Cautious, careful men, men of moderate scepticism, consciously make an effort to reserve judgment until they know well what they are talking about.

It may be desirable at this point to observe that although Hume never tries to put down a concise definition of "the vulgar," and, indeed, assumes that his readers need no extensive description, it is obvious that this rank is not very exclusive. . . .

The civilization of men is the process by which they have acquired beliefs about what economic and political conduct is good and bad. Civilization is not something that men have done to themselves; rather, they became civilized by becoming experienced. It is through experience, mainly, bitter experience, that they have acquired their moral beliefs. They were backed into civility. Now, although some men think through the principles of civility, just as some think through the principles of physical nature, it is through the moral sense that most men find justice and governance good. They simply accept their moral judgments, and act according to them. They act in their economic and political affairs very much as they behave in the physical universe. The experienced man, even though he is not a physical philosopher, normally avoids colliding with stoves, stepping into large, dark puddles, and standing near precipices. He has learned what to do and what not to do. Similarly, the highly experienced man normally condemns injustice and misgovernance without the benefit of dissertations from the pens of moral philosophers. In each case, experience has established strong, valid beliefs, and it may be quite as difficult for an ordinary civilized man to bring himself to steal or to revolt as to comport himself without trepidation on a towering height.

But there is an important difference between beliefs about correct behaviour in relation to the physical universe and beliefs about correct conduct in economic and political affairs. Whereas the physical universe does not depend on the opinions of men for its existence, every society and every state does. The principles of justice and governance, insofar as they are embodied in any existing political order, will work, no matter who plays each of the several roles; therefore, in terms of the order, men can be referred to as "individuals." But the men who exist are never mere individuals; rather, they are particular men. If there is to be a working economic and political system, the several roles have to be filled by those particular men; and assuming that all perform reasonably well, although who plays what role makes no appreciable difference in the successful operation of the system, his role—whether as a king, a subject, the owner of this large, fertile field, the owner of that large, stony hill—does makes a difference to each man involved. The principles are the rules of the game. They state the rights of those who play in each different position. But the beginning and the continuation of the game require presupposition or opinion: let Andrew, Robert, and Duncan be the players in each of the positions, and let each have the rights appropriate to his position. Unless this basic, casting presupposition is made there will be rules for a game, but there will be no players, no rights, and, therefore, no game. An economic and political system is founded on presupposition, not on prior right. This does not mean that an economic and political system based on the principles of civility is arbitrary in its form and processes. The principles always are the same, for the way of the greatest utility always is the same, but who will play the particular, different roles is a question not answerable by logic.

Those who know full well that the economic and political orders are good because useful—if indeed there are such men—would be willing to recast the game if the present one were to stop. They would see the need to assign rights and to begin again. In contrast, those who know the principles of civility only as moral beliefs could not possibly begin again deliberately. They might continue to believe that the rights of owners and the rights of rulers ought to be respected, but would find nobody with such rights. Since they would not know the (useful) good of rights, they would not be able to start civil society again by a deliberate act of presupposition. That the vulgar should be helpless if divorced from the present arrangement of possessions and power is inevitable, and it poses a danger to which all reformers should be closely attentive.

It is no accident that in selecting the factual conditions which should be considered when rights to things are to be assigned, the goal Hume set for himself was to discover the assignment that would be least likely to cause protest and objection. The more perfectly the legal relations between men and goods follow the natural association tendencies of the human mind, the better is the distribution of goods. Any gap between these two serves only to reveal the truth that all rights to goods have their origin in opinion. Similarly, it is no accident that in selecting the considerations to be examined when rights to govern are to be assigned, Hume tried to find the most acceptable governor(s). Again and again he reiterates that authority rests finally on opinion.

We may say that as a scientist, Hume feels obliged to promote the full realization of the ideal civil society. How is this obligation to reform both society and state modified by his view that most men are not scientists? . . .

. . . The essential task of governments is to enforce justice. The state is inferior to the economic order: justice is good because it is the means by which competition is made fruitful, but the state, in turn, is a means to justice. Accordingly, any government which cannot or does not do its work, we might think, is liable to be discharged and replaced. But we must not move too fast.

First, are not some governments disqualified by their forms? It is Hume's view that in modern times, when civilized standards prevail, a government of any form can govern well, but that absolute monarchies and mixed governments still have disadvantages, and, consequently, are less likely to govern well over a long period than are well-contrived commonwealths. Yet it is the present government, whatever its form, that has the right to govern, in the opinion of the vulgar. Ordinarily they believe, fortunately, that it would be morally wrong to overthrow that government. Consequently, there always is a *prima facie* rational argument in favour of that ruler or set of rulers who access to office is most expected. Constitutional changes can be made, often should be made, but such changes should be brought about by such gentle, imperceptible alterations and innovations as will not show that the constitution ultimately is a matter, not of right, but of opinion.

Second, should *national* or *dynastic* governments imposed on the present by the past, governments whose jurisdictions may have no direct relevance to the task of enforcing justice in a world-wide market, be retained? This is a question that Hume himself does not treat, although it is one that rises directly from his analysis of civil society. His answer, clearly, would have been that while some adjustments, such as the union of England and Scotland, are feasible, the obedience of most people is primarily a matter of moral obligation, and that it is their old, familiar rulers whom they feel have a right to be obeyed. A more rational, but novel, scheme probably would become established only after the strenuous exertion of force over a period of three or four generations.

And third, should efforts be made to overthrow bad governments? No constitution, however ingeniously contrived, can be an adequate cause for believing that those in authority under it will always act properly. This is true even in an ideal commonwealth, wherein the due processes of governing have been devised with consummate care to keep rulers from acting to promote either partial or eccentric interests. Obviously, in an absolute monarchy or a mixed government the acumen and industry of the ruler(s), at any time, are extremely important. Rulers are only normal men. Virtue and vice vary as greatly among them as among ordinary men. No dynasty can be relied on to produce a succession of wise and competent governors. Moreover, a man, upon assuming a political office, receives no special access of wisdom and knowledge. The main factor making for good governance is not that rulers, whether they come to office by birth or by election, can be expected to have extraordinary personal virtue, but that they have a neutral, disinterested stand. They are free from many—the more, the better the constitution—of the needs and aspirations that tempt their subjects. They are so placed—unless the constitution is extremely bad—that they are apart from their subjects, and have a more immediate interest in the enforcement of the principles of civility. But rulers do not always adopt the view suitable to their position. The neutral place of the ruler(s) will tend to make him favour justice and the peace, but not invincibly. The character of the ruler(s) may overpower his place: a ruler may be so fully possessed by interested favourites or by ulterior ambitions, or else be so indolent, that he will ignore what lies plain before him, and thus embark upon programs of domestic intervention, either economic or religious, or on military adventures, or waste his time in hunting, carousing, and similar vain pleasures. In short, although rulers in general may be expected to have a greater concern for justice and the peace than ordinary men, the quality of rulers will vary from one to another; and some may be swept by violent passions to such outrages of cruelty and ambition that they, in truth, will cease to perform the office of rulers.

We have seen that in the case of rights to goods, too, we cannot be sure that the general rules will provide the most virtuous men with the greatest, or even with adequate, possessions, but also that it would be wrong to tamper with the assignment of goods produced by those general rules. But here, where we are concerned with the right to govern, Hume lays down no such flat prohibition. These two kinds of rights differ in three ways. First, rights to goods are private and numerous, while rights to govern are public and are limited to a few men, at the most. Second, while in the economic order the character of one man or a few can have only small consequences, in the political order the character of the ruler or rulers may be of the greatest importance. The third difference, the basic one, is that, as we have noticed again and again, the enforcement of justice is the reason for governance. Accordingly, what is not true in the case of economic goods is true in the case of power: from time to time it may be desirable to consider disobedience and rebellion against a king (or a government), and even the overthrow of the constitution, despite his (or their) formal right to rule.

The desirability of rebellion is difficult enough to weigh in an absolute monarchy, but it is even harder, Hume finds, in a constitutional government. An absolute monarch has a complete right to govern, and there never can be a claim that any of his acts is unconstitutional. That his acts are pernicious may be adequate ground for rebellion, but that his acts are *ultra vires,* never. In a constitutional government, in contrast, the right to govern is divided, and occasionally it may be necessary to consider a resort to force to deter one part of the government from altering the constitution by exalting itself permanently. But to ascertain that the acts of any part are *ultra vires* that part, is not easy. First, the right to govern can be allocated to the several parts only in very general language. There are sure to be areas of vagueness and uncertainty, so that different constitutional interpretations are almost inevitable. Second, even if a definite division of powers were possible, insistence on the scrupulous observation of that division at all times, might prove harmful, even disastrous, for the state. It is certain that there will be emergencies, unforeseen events, which can be met expeditiously only if the king and his ministers resort to extraordinary, emergency action, action which may not be provided for in the statutes, or which may even be against the statutes. Now, Hume holds, the emergency power of the day-to-day government should not be defined, for the measures which at one time would be proper and necessary, at another time would be despotic. Any definition of emergency power, therefore, will either make desirable measures illegal or bestow legality on despotism. Emergency power is best left vague. This means that men must use their discretion, and cannot rely on the words of the constitution to discover whether or not the constitution is endangered.

Since no government, whatever its form, always will be perfectly virtuous, and none almost certainly will be entirely vicious, no set of easy tests can be established by which to decide whether or not governors have become "tyrants and public enemies." Many diverse factors should be taken into account by a man as he tries to answer that question. How likely is it that the revolt will succeed? Is it likely that it will issue in a prolonged, bloody civil war? If it is successful, will the new government prove no better, perhaps worse, than the old one? These are questions which should be answered. And malcontents should take up a deeper question, How great will be the corrosive effect of the revolt on the morality of the populace? The vulgar, we know, obey a government chiefly because they think of the established government as having a moral right to be obeyed. A revolt against the established government threatens not only that particular government, but the state, and thus the economic order. Once "the sacred boundaries of the laws" have been violated, nothing remains "to confine the wild projects of zeal and ambition." If the corrosion is extensive, the reestablishment of civility will come to depend largely on the enlightenment of those who, in the event, come to possess coercive power. Besides, not only do rebellions threaten the domestic civil order from top to bottom, but they tend to spread abroad into neighbouring countries, and thus to threaten "universal anarchy and confusion among mankind." There are times when disobedience and even rebellion are proper; obviously, however, one should think seriously of such perilous measures only when tyranny is enormously flagrant and oppressive.

The Tory theory of the divine right of kings is based on a false notion of the nature of constitutions, and the doctrine of passive obedience, the corollary of that theory, is equally false. The Whig theory of original contract also is based on a false notion of the nature of constitutions, and the doctrine of a right of revolution, likewise, is invalid. The right to govern is not a right delegated to the government by a higher legal body, either God or the people; rather, the right to govern is based on opinion. Revolt is permissible, and sometimes desirable, despite what the Tories say. But whether or not there should be a revolt at any specific juncture is not a question that can be answered by inspecting a list of conditions supposedly laid down by the people in an original contract.

Both parties are wrong in their teachings, but, argues Hume, the error of the Whigs is far more dangerous than that of the Tories. The former, by their theory of popular sovereignty and precarious delegation, tend to destroy the popular belief in the right of the government, and thus they promote a situation in which the only way in which the peace can be maintained is by the constant and fierce exertion of force. If the vulgar were not told constantly that they are the source of all rights, they would not lapse into servile dependence. They are prone enough to disobedience without being told incessantly that the government is only their agent.

This argument is repeated by Hume again and again. Perhaps the most felicitous enunciation of it appears in the *History of England*, at the point where he is reporting on opinions subsequent to the trial and execution of Charles I. He writes as follows:

The tragical death of Charles begat a question, whether the people, in any case, were intitled to judge and to punish their sovereign; and most men, regarding chiefly the atrocious usurpation of the pretended judges, and the merit of the virtuous prince who suffered, were inclined to condemn the republican principle, as highly seditious and extravagant: But there still were a few, who, abstracting from the particular circumstances of this case, were able to consider the question in general, and were inclined to moderate, not contradict, the prevailing sentiment. Such might have been their reasoning. If ever, on any occasion, it were laudable to conceal truth from the populace; it must be confessed, that the doctrine of resistance affords such an example; and that all speculative reasoners ought to observe, with regard to this principle, the same cautious silence, which the laws, in every species of government, have ever prescribed to themselves. Government is instituted, in order to restrain the fury and injustice of the people; and being always founded on opinion, not on force, it is dangerous to weaken, by these speculations, the reverence, which the multitude owe to authority, and to instruct them beforehand, that the case can ever happen, when they may be freed from their duty of allegiance. Or should it be found impossible to restrain the licence of human disquisitions, it must be acknowledged, that the doctrine of obedience ought alone to be *inculcated,* and that the exceptions, which are rare, ought seldom or never to be mentioned in popular reasonings and discourses. Nor is there any danger, that mankind, by this prudent reserve, should universally degenerate into a state of abject servitude. When the exception really occurs, even though it be not previously expected and descanted on, it must, from its very nature, be so obvious and undisputed, as to remove all doubt, and overpower the restraint, however great, imposed by teaching the general doctrine of obedience.

It may be that the young Hume hoped to assist in the general enlightenment of the populace, and thus to speed up the process of civilization. His comments on education as a source of false beliefs and his rules for the testing of beliefs, both in the first book of the *Treatise,* have practical implications. His original comment on the edifying influence of the press on "the people" in "Of the Liberty of the Press" seems hopeful. But not the slightest sign of such thinking is to be found in his later writings; indeed, their general tendency is strongly in the opposite direction. He has no notion that the men of true principles will act as a vanguard leading the vulgar to a new order in which all will be cautious and suitably sceptical, and will understand the principles of civility. These men will try to make some changes, such as the abolition of mercantile laws, the destruction of prejudices against the French, the breaking of the English habit of flying into outrageous wars in the name of the balance of power, and the stopping of the feckless accumulation of a great national debt. They will even try to improve the constitution somewhat, in the light of the idea of a perfect commonwealth. But notions of a vast general enlightenment, such as would emancipate men from dependence on custom and prejudice, are vain and silly. . . .

For Hume, customary law, born of accumulating experience, has been man's guide to civility throughout the past. Now, however, the night of subconscious development is at an end. Men of true principles know that civil society is ordered best by competition, and that since total competition is destructive, the proper framework for competition should be established by deliberate artifice. Because the civility of the vulgar remains mainly a matter of custom, the rules of customary law, especially concerning property and the constitution, are not to be jettisoned, but are to be adopted deliberately; that is, customary artifice is to be swallowed up by deliberate artifice. This concession men of true principle will be ready to make in the interests of stability.

The priority Hume gives to the individual, the preeminence and consequent independence he gives to the economy, his faith in the natural harmony of society, his disinterest in folkish emotions, and his readiness to make performance the test both of forms of government and of particular governments are all notable marks of liberalism. Likewise, the strong emphasis on institutions, sometimes called "constitutionalism," as a means of restraining partial interests and of preventing the vulgar from acquiring a dangerous measure of political power, is an eighteenth-century liberal trait. Hume, of course, save on economic matters, is far from being an ardent reformer; the hold of the vulgar on civility is too precarious to permit quick improvements. But even when he sounds least like a reformer, as when he writes about "the sacred boundaries of the laws," Hume is not a conservative, at least not the same kind of conservative as is Burke. For Burke to talk of rapid change is folly because for him, as for the common lawyers, there is no ideal to pose over against the present. By a slow process of trial, error, and success men work out the best arrangements. For Hume, on the other hand, the present, when it falls short of the ideal, is worthy of no great adulation. When improvement is not to be undertaken, it is not because nothing better is presently conceivable, but because the vulgar, given the nature of their civility, cannot be expected to endure overt reformations.

Hume has transcended conservativism: he had come to know competition framed by artifice as the correct process for ordering civil relations among men. At the same time, he, like many other men of the Enlightenment, was apprehensive of the multitude.

PHILOSOPHICAL
ANARCHISM

> I think that the efforts of those who wish to
> improve our social life should be directed to-
> ward the liberation of themselves.
>
> —LEO TOLSTOY

Henry David Thoreau's essay
"Civil Disobedience" must be considered American political thought's
foremost contribution to the corpus of anarchist literature. His doctrine of *individual nullification* holds that individual conscience takes
precedence over all positive laws and governmental actions and that
the central political obligation is the individual's obligation to resist
any governmental law or policy—e.g., the Mexican War and the
taxes required to support the war—that his conscience cannot support. On the ethical level, Thoreau's words affirm the value of individual autonomy in an increasingly interdependent environment. Yet
on the metaethical level, they say little about the subtle psychological
processes by which a man's conscience functions to guide him in
making moral choices. Nor does Thoreau adequately come to grips
with the probable social consequences of universalizing the maxim
"Let your conscience be your guide." Nonetheless, his writings do
seem to have a kind of universal appeal. They espouse the values of
courage and personal integrity in the face of social conformity and
habitual political obedience.

In his letter "Relation to the Government and the Existing Order,"
Count Leo Tolstoy offers a dimension of Anarchist thought quite different from Thoreau's. Whereas Thoreau's arguments may be used in
support of individual acts of nonviolent or even violent political resistance, Tolstoy is an exponent of the theory of *nonresistance* to evil.
He counsels love, contemplation, and *withdrawal* from the sources of
evil. He fears that the individual may *become* the moral equivalent of
what he opposes if he employs force and violence to resist unjust governmental power. In the selection appearing in this volume, he argues
that individuals should not participate in organizations employing
force and violence, which are frequently instruments of the political
regime. Instead, he asks the individual to learn to harmonize his life

with the demands of his consciousness, which is true enlightenment in brotherly love.

"Toward a New Understanding of Anarchism," by William O. Reichert, presents a new perspective on the history of and the reaction to Anarchist thought in America. His discussion of the invalidity of the presumed dichotomy between philosophical (individual) and revolutionary (collectivist) anarchism is particularly perceptive. Emphasizing their shared belief in *social* rather than political revolution, Reichert concludes that both the individualist and the collectivist traditions may be termed "philosophical" in the sense that they both reject force and violence as revolutionary methods.

14 / Civil Disobedience

HENRY D. THOREAU

I heartily accept the motto—"That government is best which governs least"; and I should like to see it acted up to more rapidly and systematically. Carried out, it finally amounts to this, which also I believe—"That government is best which governs not at all"; and when men are prepared for it, that will be the kind of government which they will have. Government is at best but an expedient; but most governments are usually, and all governments are sometimes, inexpedient. The objections which have been brought against a standing army, and they are many and weighty, and deserve to prevail, may also at last be brought against a standing government. The standing army is only an arm of the standing government. The government itself, which is only the mode which the people have chosen to execute their will, is equally liable to be abused and perverted before the people can act through it. Witness the present Mexican war, the work of comparatively a few individuals using the standing government as their tool; for, in the outset, the people would not have consented to this measure.

This American government—what is it but a tradition, though a recent one, endeavoring to transmit itself unimpaired to posterity, but each instant losing some of its integrity? It has not the vitality and force of a single living man; for a single man can bend it to his will. It is a sort of wooden gun to the people themselves. But it is not the less necessary for this; for the people must have some complicated

SOURCE: Hugo Bedau, ed., *Civil Disobedience: Theory and Practice* (New York: Pegasus, 1969), pp. 27–48.

machinery or other, and hear its din, to satisfy that idea of government which they have. Governments show thus how successfully men can be imposed on, even impose on themselves, for their own advantage. It is excellent, we must all allow. Yet this government never of itself furthered any enterprise, but by the alacrity with which it got out of its way. *It* does not keep the country free. *It* does not settle the West. *It* does not educate. The character inherent in the American people has done all that has been accomplished; and it would have done somewhat more, if the government had not sometimes got in its way. For government is an expedient by which men would fain succeed in letting one another alone; and, as has been said, when it is most expedient, the governed are most let alone by it. . . .

But, to speak practically and as a citizen, unlike those who call themselves no-government men, I ask for, not at once no government, but *at once* a better government. Let every man make known what kind of government would command his respect, and that will be one step toward obtaining it.

After all, the practical reason why, when the power is once in the hands of the people, a majority are permitted, and for a long period continue, to rule, is not because they are most likely to be in the right, nor because this seems fairest to the minority, but because they are physically the strongest. But a government in which the majority rule in all cases cannot be based on justice, even as far as men understand it. Can there not be a government in which majorities do not virtually decide right and wrong, but conscience?—in which majorities decide only those questions to which the rule of expediency is applicable? Must the citizen ever for a moment, or in the least degree, resign his conscience to the legislator? Why has every man a conscience, then? I think that we should be men first, and subjects afterward. It is not desirable to cultivate a respect for the law, so much as for the right. The only obligation which I have a right to assume, is to do at any time what I think right. It is truly enough said, that a corporation has no conscience; but a corporation of conscientious men is a corporation *with* a conscience. Law never made men a whit more just; and, by means of their respect for it, even the well-disposed are daily made the agents of injustice. A common and natural result of an undue respect for law is, that you may see a file of soldiers, colonel, captain, corporal, privates, powder-monkeys, and all, marching in admirable order over hill and dale to the wars, against their wills, ay, against their common sense and consciences, which makes it very steep marching indeed, and produces a palpitation of the heart. They have no doubt that it is a damnable business in which they are concerned; they are all peaceably inclined. Now, what are they? Men at all? or small movable forts and magazines, at the service of some unscrupulous man in power? . . .

The mass of men serve the state thus, not as men mainly, but as machines, with their bodies. They are the standing army, and the militia, jailers, constables, posse comitatus, &c. In most cases there is no free exercise whatever of the judgment or of the moral sense; but they put themselves on a level with wood and earth and stones; and wooden men can perhaps be manufactured that will serve the purpose as well. Such command no more respect than men of straw or a lump of dirt. They have the same sort of worth only as horses and dogs. Yet such as these even are commonly esteemed good citizens. Others—as most legislators, politicians, lawyers, ministers, and officeholders—serve the state chiefly with their heads; and, as they rarely make any moral distinctions, they are as likely to serve the Devil, without *intending* it, as God. A very few, as heroes, patriots, martyrs, reformers in the great sense, and *men*, serve the state with the consciences also, and so necessarily resist it for the most part; and they are commonly treated as enemies by it. A wise man will only be useful as a man, and will not submit to be "clay," and "stop a hole to keep the wind away," but leave that office to his dust at least:

> "I am too high-born to be propertied,
> To be a secondary at control,
> Or useful serving-man and instrument
> To any sovereign state throughout the world."

How does it become a man to behave toward this American government to-day? I answer, that he cannot without disgrace be associated with it. I cannot for an instant recognize the political organization as *my* government which is the *slave's* government also.

All men recognize the right of revolution; that is, the right to refuse allegiance to, and to resist, the government, when its tyranny or its inefficiency are great and unendurable. But almost all say that such is not the case now. But such was the case, they think, in the Revolution of '75. If one were to tell me that this was a bad government because it taxed certain foreign commodities brought to its ports, it is most probable that I should not make an ado about it, for I can do without them. All machines have their friction; and possibly this does enough good to counterbalance the evil. At any rate, it is a great evil to make a stir about it. But when the friction comes to have its machine, and oppression and robbery are organized, I say, let us not have such a machine any longer. In other words, when a sixth of the population of a nation which has undertaken to be the refuge of liberty are slaves, and a whole country is unjustly overrun and conquered by a foreign army, and subjected to military law, I think that it is not too soon for honest men to rebel and revolutionize. What makes this duty the more urgent is the fact, that the country so overrun is not our own, but ours is the invading army.

Paley, a common authority with many on moral questions, in his chapter on the "Duty of Submission to Civil Government," resolves all civil obligation into expediency; and he proceeds to say, "that so long as the interest of the whole society requires it, that is, so long as the established government cannot be resisted or changed without public inconveniency, it is the will of God that the established government be obeyed, and no longer. . . . This principle being admitted, the justice of every particular case of resistance is reduced to a computation of the quantity of the danger and grievance on the one side, and of the probability and expense of redressing it on the other." Of this, he says, every man shall judge for himself. But Paley appears never to have contemplated those cases to which the rule of expediency does not apply, in which a people, as well as an individual, must do justice, cost what it may. If I have unjustly wrested a plank from a drowning man, I must restore it to him though I drown myself. This, according to Paley, would be inconvenient. But he that would save his life, in such a case, shall lose it. This people must cease to hold slaves, and to make war on Mexico, though it cost them their existence as a people. . . .

⌐ . . . There are thousands who are *in opinion* opposed to slavery and to the war, who yet in effect do nothing to put an end to them; who, esteeming themselves children of Washington and Franklin, sit down with their hands in their pockets, and say that they know not what to do, and do nothing; who even postpone the question of freedom to the question of free-trade, and quietly read the prices-current along with the latest advices from Mexico, after dinner, and, it may be, fall asleep over them both. What is the price-current of an honest man and patriot to-day? They hesitate, and they regret, and sometimes they petition; but they do nothing in earnest and with effect. They will wait, well disposed, for others to remedy the evil, that they may no longer have it to regret. At most, they give only a cheap vote, and a feeble countenance and God-speed, to the right, as it goes by them. There are nine hundred and ninety-nine patrons of virtue to one virtuous man. But it is easier to deal with the real possessor of a thing than with the temporary guardian of it.

All voting is a sort of gaming, like checkers or backgammon, with a slight moral tinge to it, a playing with right and wrong, with moral questions; and betting naturally accompanies it. The character of the voters is not staked. I cast my vote, perchance, as I think right; but I am not vitally concerned that that right should prevail. I am willing to leave it to the majority. Its obligation, therefore, never exceeds that of expediency. Even voting *for the right* is *doing* nothing for it. It is only expressing to men feebly your desire that it should prevail. A wise man will not leave the right to the mercy of chance, nor wish it to prevail through the power of the majority. There is but little virtue in the action of masses of men. When the majority shall at length vote for the abolition of slavery, it will be because they are indifferent to slavery, or because there is but little slavery left to be abolished by their vote. *They* will then be the only slaves. Only *his* vote can hasten the abolition of slavery who asserts his own freedom by his vote.

 I hear of a convention to be held at Baltimore, or elsewhere, for the selection of a candidate for the Presidency, made up chiefly of editors, and men who are politicians by profession; but I think, what is it to any independent, intelligent, and respectable man what decision they may come to? Shall we not have the advantage of his wisdom and honesty, nevertheless? Can we not count upon some independent votes? Are there not many individuals in the country who do not attend conventions? But no: I find that the respectable man, so called, has immediately drifted from his position, and despairs of his country, when his country has more reason to despair of him. He forthwith adopts one of the candidates thus selected as the only *available* one, thus proving that he is himself *available* for any purposes of the demagogue. His vote is of no more worth than that of any unprincipled foreigner or hireling native, who may have been bought. . . . The American has dwindled into an Odd Fellow—one who may be known by the development of his organ of gregariousness, and a manifest lack of intellect and cheerful self-reliance; whose first and chief concern, on coming into the world, is to see that the Almshouses are in good repair; and, before yet he has lawfully donned the virile garb, to collect a fund for the support of the widows and orphans that may be; who, in short, ventures to live only by the aid of the Mutual Insurance Company, which has promised to bury him decently.

It is not a man's duty, as a matter of course, to devote himself to the eradication of any, even the most enormous wrong; he may still properly have other concerns to engage him; but it is his duty, at least, to wash his hands of it, and, if he gives it no thought longer, not to give it practically his support. If I devote myself to other pursuits and contemplations, I must first see, at least, that I do not pursue them sitting upon another man's shoulders. I must get off him first, that he may pursue his contemplations too. See what gross inconsistency is tolerated. I have heard some of my townsmen say, "I should like to have them order me out to help put down an insurrection of the slaves, or to march to Mexico—see if I would go"; and yet these very men have each, directly by their allegiance, and so indirectly, at least, by their money, furnished a substitute. The soldier is applauded who refuses to serve in an unjust war by those who do not refuse to sustain the unjust government which makes the war; is applauded by those whose own act and authority he disregards and sets at naught;

as if the State were penitent to that degree that it hired one to scourge it while it sinned, but not to that degree that it left off sinning for a moment. Thus, under the name of Order and Civil Government, we are all made at last to pay homage to and support our own meanness. After the first blush of sin comes its indifference; and from immoral it becomes, as it were, *un*moral, and not quite unnecessary to that life which we have made.

The broadest and most prevalent error requires the most disinterested virtue to sustain it. The slight reproach to which the virtue of patriotism is commonly liable, the noble are most likely to incur. Those who, while they disapprove of the character and measures of a government, yield to it their allegiance and support, are undoubtedly its most conscientious supporters, and so frequently the most serious obstacles to reform. Some are petitioning the State to dissolve the Union, to disregard the requisitions of the President. Why do they not dissolve it themselves—the union between themselves and the State—and refuse to pay their quota into its treasury? Do not they stand in the same relation to the State, that the State does to the Union? And have not the same reasons prevented the State from resisting the Union, which have prevented them from resisting the State?

How can a man be satisfied to entertain an opinion merely, and enjoy *it*? Is there any enjoyment in it, if his opinion is that he is aggrieved? If you are cheated out of a single dollar by your neighbor, you do not rest satisfied with knowing that you are cheated, or with saying that you are cheated, or even with petitioning him to pay you your due; but you take effectual steps at once to obtain the full amount, and see that you are never cheated again. Action from principle, the perception and the performance of right, changes things and relations; it is essentially revolutionary, and does not consist wholly with anything which was. It not only divides states and churches, it divides families; ay, it divides the *individual*, separating the diabolical in him from the divine.

Unjust laws exist: shall we be content to obey them, or shall we endeavor to amend them, and obey them until we have succeeded, or shall we transgress them at once? Men generally, under such a government as this, think that they ought to wait until they have persuaded the majority to alter them. They think that, if they should resist, the remedy would be worse than the evil. But it is the fault of the government itself that the remedy *is* worse than the evil. *It* makes it worse. Why is it not more apt to anticipate and provide for reform? Why does it not cherish its wise minority? Why does it cry and resist before it is hurt? Why does it not encourage its citizens to be on the alert to point out its faults, and *do* better than it would have them?

Why does it always crucify Christ, and excommunicate Copernicus and Luther, and pronounce Washington and Franklin rebels? . . .

If the injustice is part of the necessary friction of the machine of government, let it go, let it go: perchance it will wear smooth—certainly the machine will wear out. If the injustice has a spring, or a pulley, or a rope, or a crank, exclusively for itself, then perhaps you may consider whether the remedy will not be worse than the evil; but if it is of such a nature that it requires you to be the agent of injustice to another, then, I say, break the law. Let your life be a counter friction to stop the machine. What I have to do is to see, at any rate, that I do not lend myself to the wrong which I condemn.

As for adopting the ways which the State has provided for remedying the evil, I know not of such ways. They take too much time, and a man's life will be gone. I have other affairs to attend to. I came into this world, not chiefly to make this a good place to live in, but to live in it, be it good or bad. A man has not everything to do, but something; and because he cannot do *everything*, it is not necessary that he should do *something* wrong. It is not my business to be petitioning the Governor or the Legislature any more than it is theirs to petition me; and, if they should not hear my petition, what should I do then? But in this case the state has provided no way: its very Constitution is the evil. This may seem to be harsh and stubborn and unconciliatory; but it is to treat with the utmost kindness and consideration the only spirit that can appreciate or deserves it. So is all change for the better, like birth and death, which convulse the body. . . .

I meet this American government, or its representative, the State government, directly, and face to face, once a year—no more—in the person of its tax-gatherer; this is the only mode in which a man situated as I am necessarily meets it; and it then says distinctly, Recognize me; and the simplest, the most effectual, and, in the present posture of affairs, the indispensablest mode of treating with it on this head, of expressing your little satisfaction with and love for it, is to deny it then. My civil neighbor, the tax-gatherer, is the very man I have to deal with—for it is, after all, with men and not with parchment that I quarrel—and he has voluntarily chosen to be an agent of the government. How shall he ever know well what he is and does as an officer of the government, or as a man, until he is obliged to consider whether he shall treat me, his neighbor, for whom he has respect, as a neighbor and well-disposed man, or as a maniac and disturber of the peace, and see if he can get over this obstruction to his neighborliness without a ruder and more impetuous thought or speech corresponding with his action. I know this well, that if one thousand, if one hundred, if ten men whom I could name—if ten honest men only—ay, if *one* HONEST man, in this State of Massachusetts, *ceasing to hold slaves,* were actually to withdraw from this copartnership, and be locked up in the county jail therefor, it would be the abolition of slavery in America. For it matters not how small the beginning may seem to be: what is once well done is done forever. But we love better to talk about it: that we say is our mission. Reform keeps many scores of newspapers in its service, but not one man. If my esteemed neighbor, the State's ambassador, who will devote his days to the settlement of the question of human rights in the Council Chamber, instead of being threatened with the prisons of Carolina, were to sit down the prisoner of Massachusetts, that State which is so anxious to foist the sin of slavery upon her sister—though at present she can discover only an act of inhospitality to be the ground of a quarrel with her—the Legislature would not wholly waive the subject the following winter.

Under a government which imprisons any unjustly, the true place for a just man is also a prison. The proper place to-day, the only place which Massachusetts has provided for her freer and less desponding spirits, is in her prisons, to be put out and locked out of the State by her own act, as they have already put themselves out by their principles. It is there that the fugitive slave, and the Mexican prisoner on parole, and the Indian come to plead the wrongs of his race, should find them; on that separate, but more free and honorable ground, where the State places those who are not *with* her, but *against* her—the only house in a slave State in which a free man can abide with honor. If any think that their influence would be lost there, and their voices no longer afflict the ear of the State, that they would not be as an enemy within its walls, they do not know by how much truth is stronger than error, nor how much more eloquently and effectively he can combat injustice who has experienced a little in his own person. Cast your whole vote, not a strip of paper merely, but your whole influence. A minority is powerless while it conforms to the majority; it is not even a minority then; but it is irresistible when it clogs by its whole weight. If the alternative is to keep all just men in prison, or give up war and slavery, the State will not hesitate which to choose. If a thousand men were not to pay their tax-bills this year, that would not be a violent and bloody measure, as it would be to pay them, and enable the State to commit violence and shed innocent blood. This is, in fact, the definition of a peaceable revolution, if any such is possible. If the tax-gatherer, or any other public officer, asks me, as one has done, "But what shall I do?" my answer is, "If you really wish to do anything, resign your office." When the subject has refused allegiance, and the officer has resigned his office, then the revolution is accomplished. But even suppose blood should flow. Is there not a sort of blood shed when the conscience is wounded?

Through this wound a man's real manhood and immortality flow out, and he bleeds to an everlasting death. I see this blood flowing now.

I have contemplated the imprisonment of the offender, rather than the seizure of his goods—though both will serve the same purpose— because they who assert the purest right, and consequently are most dangerous to a corrupt State, commonly have not spent much time in accumulating property. To such the State renders comparatively small service, and a slight tax is wont to appear exorbitant, particularly if they are obliged to earn it by special labor with their hands. If there were one who lived wholly without the use of money, the State itself would hesitate to demand it of him. But the rich man— not to make any invidious comparison—is always sold to the institution which makes him rich. Absolutely speaking, the more money, the less virtue; for money comes between a man and his objects, and obtains them for him; and it was certainly no great virtue to obtain it. It puts to rest many questions which he would otherwise be taxed to answer; while the only new question which it puts is the hard but superfluous one, how to spend it. Thus his moral ground is taken from under his feet. The opportunities of living are diminished in proportion as what are called the "means" are increased. The best thing a man can do for his culture when he is rich is to endeavor to carry out those schemes which he entertained when he was poor. . . .

When I converse with the freest of my neighbors, I perceive that, whatever they may say about the magnitude and seriousness of the question, and their regard for the public tranquillity, the long and the short of the matter is, that they cannot spare the protection of the existing government, and they dread the consequences to their property and families of disobedience to it. For my own part, I should not like to think that I ever rely on the protection of the State. But, if I deny the authority of the State when it presents its tax-bill, it will soon take and waste all my property, and so harass me and my children without end. This is hard. This makes it impossible for a man to live honestly, and at the same time comfortably, in outward respects. It will not be worth the while to accumulate property; that would be sure to go again. You must hire or squat somewhere, and raise but a small crop, and eat that soon. You must live within yourself, and depend upon yourself always tucked up and ready for a start, and not have many affairs. . . . It costs me less in every sense to incur the penalty of disobedience to the State, than it would to obey. I should feel as if I were worth less in that case. . . .

I have paid no poll-tax for six years. I was put into a jail once on this account, for one night; and, as I stood considering the walls of solid stone, two or three feet thick, the door of wood and iron, a foot thick, and the iron grating which strained the light, I could not help being struck with the foolishness of that institution which treated me as if I were mere flesh and blood and bones, to be locked up. I wondered that it should have concluded at length that this was the best use it could put me to, and had never thought to avail itself of my services in some way. I saw that, if there was a wall of stone between me and my townsmen, there was a still more difficult one to climb or break through, before they could get to be as free as I was. I did not for a moment feel confined, and the walls seemed a great waste of stone and mortar. I felt as if I alone of all my townsmen had paid my tax. They plainly did not know how to treat me, but behaved like persons who are underbred. In every threat and in every compliment there was a blunder; for they thought that my chief desire was to stand the other side of that stone wall. I could not but smile to see how industriously they locked the door on my meditations, which followed them out again without let or hindrance, and *they* were really all that was dangerous. As they could not reach me, they had resolved to punish my body; just as boys, if they cannot come at some person against whom they have a spite, will abuse his dog. I saw that the State was half-witted, that it was timid as a lone woman with her silver spoons, and that it did not know its friends from its foes, and I lost all my remaining respect for it, and pitied it.

Thus the State never intentionally confronts a man's sense, intellectual or moral, but only his body, his senses. It is not armed with superior wit or honesty, but with superior physical strength. I was not born to be forced. I will breathe after my own fashion. Let us see who is the strongest. What force has a multitude? They can only force me who obey a higher law than I. They force me to become like themselves. I do not hear of *men* being *forced* to live this way or that by masses of men. What sort of life were that to live? When I meet a government which says to me, "Your money or your life," why should I be in haste to give it my money? It may be in a great strait, and not know what to do: I cannot help that. It must help itself; do as I do. It is not worth the while to snivel about it. I am not responsible for the successful working of the machinery of society. I am not the son of the engineer. I perceive that, when an acorn and a chestnut fall side by side, the one does not remain inert to make way for the other, but both obey their own laws, and spring and grow and flourish as best they can, till one, perchance, overshadows and destroys the other. If a plant cannot live according to its nature, it dies; and so a man. . . .

I have never declined paying the highway tax, because I am as desirous of being a good neighbor as I am of being a bad subject; and, as for supporting schools, I am doing my part to educate my fellow-countrymen now. It is for no particular item in the tax-bill that I refuse to pay it. I simply wish to refuse allegiance to the State, to withdraw and stand aloof from it effectually. I do not care to trace the course of my dollar, if I could, till it buys a man or a musket to shoot one with—the dollar is innocent—but I am concerned to trace the effects of my allegiance. In fact, I quietly declare war with the State, after my fashion, though I will still make what use and get what advantage of her I can, as is usual in such cases.

If others pay the tax which is demanded of me, from a sympathy with the State, they do but what they have already done in their own case, or rather they abet injustice to a greater extent than the State requires. If they pay the tax from a mistaken interest in the individual taxed, to save his property, or prevent his going to jail, it is because they have not considered wisely how far they let their private feelings interfere with the public good. . . .

I do not wish to quarrel with any man or nation. I do not wish to split hairs, to make fine distinctions, or set myself up as better than my neighbors. I seek rather, I may say, even an excuse for conforming to the laws of the land. I am but too ready to conform to them. Indeed, I have reason to suspect myself on this head; and each year, as the tax-gatherer comes round, I find myself disposed to review the acts and position of the general and State governments, and the spirit of the people, to discover a pretext for conformity.

> "We must affect our country as our parents;
> And if at any time we alienate
> Our love or industry from doing it honor,
> We must respect effects and teach the soul
> Matter of conscience and religion,
> And not desire of rule or benefit."
>
> . . .

I know that most men think differently from myself; but those whose lives are by profession devoted to the study of these or kindred subjects, content me as little as any. Statesmen and legislators, standing so completely within the institution, never distinctly and nakedly behold it. They speak of moving society, but have no resting-place without it. They may be men of a certain experience and discrimination, and have no doubt invented ingenious and even useful systems, for which we sincerely thank them; but all their wit and usefulness lie within certain not very wide limits. They are wont to forget that the world is not governed by policy and expediency. Webster never goes behind government, and so cannot speak with authority about it. His words are wisdom to those legislators who contemplate no essential reform in the existing government; but for thinkers, and those who legislate for all time, he never once glances at the subject. I know of those whose serene and wise speculations on this theme would soon reveal the limits of his mind's range and hospitality. Yet, compared with the cheap professions of most reformers, and the still cheaper wisdom and eloquence of politicians in general, his are almost the only sensible and valuable words, and we thank Heaven for him. Comparatively, he is always strong, original, and, above all, practical. Still his quality is not wisdom, but prudence. The lawyer's truth is not Truth, but consistency, or a consistent expediency. Truth is always in harmony with herself, and is not concerned chiefly to reveal the justice that may consist with wrong-doing. He well deserves to be called, as he has been called, the Defender of the Constitution. There are really no blows to be given by him but defensive ones. He is not a leader, but a follower. His leaders are the men of '87. "I have never made an effort," he says, "and never propose to make an effort; I have never countenanced an effort, and never mean to countenance an effort, to disturb the arrangement as originally made, by which the various States came into the Union." Still thinking of the sanction which the Constitution gives to slavery, he says, "Because it was a part of the original compact—let it stand." Notwithstanding his special acuteness and ability, he is unable to take a fact out of its merely political relations, and behold it as it lies absolutely to be disposed of by the intellect—what, for instance, it behooves a man to do here in America today with regard to slavery, but ventures, or is driven, to make some such desperate answer as the following, while professing to speak absolutely, and as a private man—from which what new and singular code of social duties might be inferred? "The manner," says he, "in which the governments of those States where slavery exists are to regulate it, is for their own consideration, under their responsibility to their constituents, to the general laws of propriety, humanity, and justice, and to God. Associations formed elsewhere, springing from a feeling of humanity, or any other cause, have nothing whatever to do with it. They have never received any encouragement from me, and they never will."

They who know of no purer sources of truth, who have traced up its stream no higher, stand, and wisely stand, by the Bible and the Constitution, and drink at it there with reverence and humility; But they who behold where it comes trickling into this lake or that pool, gird up their loins once more, and continue their pilgrimage towards its fountain-head.

No man with a genius for legislation has appeared in America. They are rare in the history of the world. There are orators, politicians, and eloquent men, by the thousand; but the speaker has not yet opened his mouth to speak, who is capable of settling the much-vexed questions of the day. We love eloquence for its own sake, and not for any truth which it may utter, or any heroism it may inspire. Our legislators have not yet learned the comparative value of free-trade and of freedom, of union, and of rectitude, to a nation. They have no genius or talent for comparatively humble questions of taxation and finance, commerce and manufactures and agriculture. If we were left solely to the wordy wit of legislators in Congress for our guidance, uncorrected by the seasonable experience and the effectual complaints of the people, America would not long retain her rank among the nations. For eighteen hundred years, though perchance I have no right to say it, the New Testament has been written, yet where is the legislator who has wisdom and practical talent enough to avail himself of the light which it sheds on the science of legislation?

The authority of government, even such as I am willing to submit to—for I will cheerfully obey those who know and can do better than I, and in many things even those who neither know nor can do so well—is still an impure one: to be strictly just, it must have the sanction and consent of the governed. It can have no pure right over my person and property but what I concede to it. The progress from an absolute to a limited monarchy, from a limited monarchy to a democracy, is a progress toward a true respect for the individual. Even the Chinese philosopher was wise enough to regard the individual as the basis of the empire. Is a democracy, such as we know it, the last improvement possible in government? Is it not possible to take a step further toward recognizing and organizing the rights of man? There will never be a really free and enlightened State, until the State comes to recognize the individual as a higher and independent power, from which all its own power and authority are derived, and treats him accordingly. I please myself with imagining a State at last which can afford to be just to all men, and to treat the individual with respect as a neighbor; which even would not think it inconsistent with its own repose, if a few were to live aloof from it, not meddling with it, nor embraced by it, who fulfilled all the duties of neighbors and fellow-men. A State which bore this kind of fruit, and suffered it to drop off as fast as it ripened, would prepare the way for a still more perfect and glorious State, which also I have imagined, but not yet anywhere seen.

15 / Relation to the Government and the Existing Order

LEO TOLSTOY

FROM A PRIVATE LETTER, 1896

The existing order of life is subject to destruction. This is admitted both by those who strive to destroy it and those who defend it.

The competitive order is to be destroyed and to give way to the communistic; the capitalistic order is to be destroyed and to give way to the socialistic; the order of militarism is to be destroyed and to give way to disarmament and arbitration; the separatism of the narrow nationality is to be destroyed and to give way to cosmopolitism and a universal brotherhood; all religious superstitions are to be destroyed and to give way to a rational religious, moral consciousness; every kind of despotism is to be destroyed and to give way to liberty; in short, violence is to be destroyed and to give way to a free and loving union of men.

So far two means have been employed for the attainment of all these ends,—the first, the violent revolutions, the overthrow of the men who supported the undesirable order, and the substitution of others, who were to establish a new, desirable order of life; and the other, which, without destroying the existing order, and entering into the ranks of the government, consists in slowly and by degrees obtaining that change of the existing order which is demanded by the human consciousness of our time.

The first method does not attain its end, because, in the first place, every violent destruction of the existing order evokes in the majority of indifferent people a reaction, a desire at all costs to retain the existing order, and even the one which existed before, when there were no perturbations, and so it calls forth a reaction, which only removes the attainment of the end. In the second place, because the men who enter into the power, while retaining the old governmental machine of violence, very soon become just as despotic, sometimes even more despotic than those which are overthrown. (The reaction of the great French Revolution against the despotism of the royal power, the Na-

SOURCE: *Miscellaneous Letters and Essays*, edited and translated by Leo Wiener (Boston: Dana Estes, 1905), pp. 409–413.

poleonic reaction and that of the year '15, the reactions after the years '30, '48, and '81 in Russia, and now the reaction after the anarchistic explosions and murders in France.)

The second method, which consists in changing the government, by taking part in it and improving it, still less attains its end, because not only the men who enter into the ranks of the government without the aim of a gradual improvement of the existing order, but also those who recognize the government and enjoy the advantages of the government only in order to be able to modify and improve it, imperceptibly to themselves, very soon and inevitably (because their whole life is based on governmental violence) become, not only no correctors and changers of the government's violence, but even the most ardent defenders of the same. It is the same as though a man who undertakes to mend a boat should sit down in it and row.

In the course of several generations men, having come to see the falseness of their situation, have been trying to change it, now with one means, and now with another, but neither means produces any effect, and the situation is growing worse and worse.

There exists one means for the attainment of this end,—a very simple and natural means, which consists in leaving the state and the government alone and not thinking of them, but in thinking only of our life, in elucidating to ourselves the end and significance of our life, and in leading our life in conformity with the elucidated consciousness. And, strange to say, this means—which entirely leaves out the questions about state, government, society—is the only one which solves (and in the most incontestable manner at that) all the political, governmental, and social questions.

This means, in relation to the political, governmental, and social questions, consists, instead of forcibly destroying the existing order of life, or, with the desire to destroy or change it, building our life upon it, in the simplest kind of a method, which, it would seem, would be the first to occur to people,—namely, in taking no part in that violence-using structure of life which we deny and wish to change.

In order not to take part in this violence-using and false structure of life, we must (1) clearly understand the meaning and destiny of our life, (2) clearly understand what in our life corresponds to the destiny of our life, and (3) know those means with which it is possible for us to harmonize our life with the demands of our consciousness.

FROM THE DIARY OF 1895

The situation of the majority of men, enlightened with a true enlightenment of brotherly love, who are now suppressed by the deceit and cunning of the violators, through their compelling this majority to ruin itself, is terrible and seems hopeless.

Only two ways out present themselves, and both are closed: one consists in rending violence by means of violence, terrorism, dynamite bombs, daggers, as did our nihilists and anarchists,—outside of us to break up that plot of the governments against the nations; or to enter into a concerted action with the government, making concessions to it, and, taking part in it, slowly to disentangle the net which binds the nation, and to free it. Both ways out are closed.

Dynamite and the dagger, as experience shows us, only provoke reaction, impair the most precious force,—the only one which is in our power,—public opinion.

The other way out is closed because the governments have already found out to what extent the participation of people wishing to transform it should be admitted. They allow only that which does not impair the essentials, and are very sensitive in regard to what is detrimental for them,—they are sensitive, because their existence is at stake. They admit people who do not agree with them and who wish to reform the governments, not only in order to satisfy the demands of these people, but for their own sakes, for the sake of the governments. These people would be dangerous to the governments if they were left outside the governments and rose against them, by influencing the only, most powerful governmental instrument,—public opinion,—and so they have to make these men harmless, attract them by means of concessions, made by the government,—they must make them harmless, something like the microbe cultures,—and then only use them for the purpose of serving the government's ends, that is, for the purpose of oppressing and exploiting the masses.

Both ways out are solidly and impermeably closed. What is left?

It is impossible to break open a way with violence,—you only increase the reaction; equally impossible it is to enter the ranks of the government,—one becomes a tool of the government. One thing is left,—to struggle against the government with the instrument of thought, of words, of acts,—of life, without making any concessions to it, without entering its ranks, without increasing its force through us.

This one thing is necessary and will certainly be successful. And God wants it, and Christ taught it.

FROM THE DIARY OF 1895

We have come to such a pass that a simply good and sensible man cannot be a partaker in the government, that is, cannot be one—I am not speaking of Russia—cannot in England be one with the land-ownership, the exploitation of the factories and capitalists, the orders in India, the flogging, the opium trade, the annihilation of nationalities in Africa, the preparations for war, and the wars themselves.

And the point of support, when a man says, "I do not know anything about the government, and I do not care to know; but I know that I cannot live contrary to my conscience,"—that point of view is imperturbable, and upon it ought all the men of our time to stand, in order to move life forward. "I know what my conscience commands me to do, but you, people who are busy with the government, arrange the government as you wish, so that it may correspond to the demands of the conscience of the people of our time."

Meanwhile the people occupy the standpoint of the correction and improvement of the governmental forms, and thus, by recognizing the necessity of the government, lose their imperturbable point of support.

16/ Toward a New Understanding of Anarchism

WILLIAM O. REICHERT

It is generally maintained that there are two anarchist traditions in America, not one. Toward the end of the first quarter of the present century it became accepted practice for political scientists to draw a hard and fast distinction between philosophical anarchism and anarchist communism or collectivism on the grounds that the former did not embrace violence whereas the later did. Thus in 1926 Charles E. Merriam maintained that anarchist groups in the United States may be divided into the "philosophical and the fighting anarchists, one believing in the attainment of anarchy by the peaceful processes of evolution and the other by the employment of force and by revolution."[1] A few years later Westel W. Willoughby gave support to Merriam's definition when he maintained that the philosophical anarchist is to be distinguished from the anarchist of deed or of action on the grounds that the

SOURCE: *Western Political Quarterly*, XX (December 1967), 856–865. Reprinted by permission of the author and the University of Utah, copyright holder.

[1] *American Political Ideas* (New York: Macmillan, 1926), p. 349.

former believes that anarchism must be established by the peaceful processes of persuasion and enlightenment, whereas the latter does not believe that society will naturally evolve toward its perfection without the assistance of the revolutionary act.[2] This neat but misleading dichotomy has dogged the anarchist movement ever since with the persistence of a shadow. But a careful study of anarchist theory reveals that the division of anarchist ideas into two separate categories on the basis of whether or not violence is considered a legitimate social means is not a valid distinction.

In constructing a rigid dichotomy which placed philosophical anarchism in opposition to revolutionary anarchism, political scientists greatly oversimplified the theory, thereby causing it to appear uninviting in the eyes of succeeding generations of Americans. But the anarchist movement in America, like its counterpart in other countries, is not given to simplicity of classification and analysis. Wherever this has been attempted, anarchism has been portrayed in a false manner. This, perhaps, is forgivable in the practicing politician or popular journalist. But it is unforgivable in the political scientist. It is to be noted, however, that the facts which surrounded the anarchist movement in the days of Merriam and Willoughby suggested the interpretation they gave it. Given the ideological climate of their period of history, the conclusions they reached were honest and made perfect sense. With the passage of time, these same facts have taken on new significance, which undoubtedly accounts for the numerous books which have recently attempted to reinterpret the meaning of the anarchist idea. This paper will attempt to put the theory of anarchism in a perspective which is more in keeping with its true nature as its advocates on the contemporary social scene see it.[3] Turning to the history of the anarchist idea in America, an attempt will be made to demonstrate that the conviction that violence must be deliberately created in order to carry off a successful social revolution was not a necessary principle in the mind of any reputable American anarchist, whether he be classified as an individualist or communist collectivist.

[2] *The Ethical Basis of Political Authority* (New York: Macmillan, 1930), p. 43.
[3] One of the difficulties of any attempt to study the theory of anarchism is the impossibility of arriving at any exact breakdown of the idea. Paul Eltzbacher in his notable work *Anarchism*, first published in German in 1900, focused upon the writings of seven leading representatives of the idea and was personally satisfied that he had cleared away the confusion of interpretation and analysis which had previously prevented its scientific definition. But it is now clear that Eltzbacher's study, while full of valuable insights and suggestions, is by no means a definitive work. The edition I have used here is the English translation by Steven T. Byington which was first published by Benjamin Tucker in 1907 and which was reissued by the Libertarian Book Club in 1960.

I

The movement of philosophical anarchism, or native American anarchism as it is often called, developed spontaneously out of American culture and never established formal contact of any kind with anarchist movements in other parts of the world. The first anarchists in this country might be said to be the Antinomians, Quakers, and other left-wing religious groups who found the authority, dogma, and formalism of the conventional churches intolerable. Given to a pacifist approach to war, these groups eschewed formal organization as much as possible, only permitting themselves to join with other like-minded individuals in very loosely constructed anti-war federations such as the American Peace Society (founded in 1828), the New England Non-Resistance Society (founded in 1838), and the Universal Peace Union (founded in 1866).[4] Most of these early American anarchists arrived at their political convictions as a reaction to the hypocrisy and social irresponsibility which they felt characterized the organized church movement. Starting as members of one conventional church or another, the native American anarchists, while perhaps continuing to refer to themselves as Christians, developed a political outlook which emphasized the anti-libertarian nature of the state and government. Adin Ballou, founder of the Hopedale Community, was perhaps typical of those who embraced philosophical anarchism as the result of meandering along the byways of Christian unorthodoxy and dissent.[5] Referring back to the early centuries of Christian communism as the source of his authority, Ballou stoutly maintained that the essence of Christian morality is the rejection of force, compromise, and the very institution of government itself. Ballou, unlike many of his contemporaries, did not define pacifism as a passive act but one which may well involve the individual in an active opposition to his government when it engages itself in the business of war. A Christian is not merely to refrain from committing personal acts of violence but is to take positive steps to prevent the state from carrying out its warlike ambitions. Ballou's attitude in this regard, according to Roy Finch, "represents a change from a conservative, individually-oriented pacifism to a radical, social action pacifism," making him one of the early

[4] For details of the American peace movement, see Merle Curti, *Peace or War: The American Struggle 1636–1936* (New York: Norton, 1936).
[5] For a discussion of Ballou's philosophical outlook, see my article "The Philosophical Anarchism of Adin Ballou," *Huntington Library Quarterly*, Vol. 27 (1964).

theorists of the nonviolent movement in this country.[6] Obviously in this phase of its development, philosophical anarchism was indeed indigenous to America, a natural outgrowth of its religious ethos.[7] But the development of anarchism in America was by no means confined to those who had been inspired by a religious idea, as Ballou had been. In fact the greater part of its impetus was derived from non-religious sources which owed almost nothing, excepting the force of reaction, to Christianity.

In the second phase of its development, philosophical anarchism was inspired by the idea of individualism. Arising spontaneously in a number of different places throughout the country, the adherents of the individualist idea gradually came together in a loose movement. Josiah Warren, the "first American anarchist," also had the distinction of publishing the first anarchist periodical in America, the *Peaceful Revolutionist*, which was founded in 1833. Other Americans joined with Warren in proclaiming the state the enemy rather than the friend of the individual. Lysander Spooner, Stephen Pearl Andrews, Ezra Heywood, and William B. Greene all concurred in maintaining that the only legitimate form of social control is self-discipline which the individual must impose upon himself without the aid of government. Where the state imposes its force upon the individual, society is bound to suffer. This is as true in the area of economics as it is in regard to the restraint and punishment of crime. Having been inspired by the writings of Warren, philosophical anarchists formed together in the 1860's into two loose federations, the New England Labor Reform League and the American Labor Reform League. Essentially anarchist in outlook, these two leagues were the source of radical vitality in America for several decades.

An interesting aspect of this period of American history is that many native American anarchists apparently anticipated the essentials of the philosophical viewpoint Pierre-Joseph Proudhon was developing independently at the same time in France and Belgium. The writings of Proudhon, therefore, were quickly assimilated by American anarchists when they began to appear on the bookshelves in this country. The outstanding figure among the native American anarchists was Benjamin Tucker who first gained prominence in radical circles for his translation of Proudhon's *What Is Property?* Starting in 1875 as associate editor of Ezra Heywood's *Word*, the unofficial mouthpiece of the labor reform leagues, Tucker soon established a journal of his own, *The Radical Review*, and later his famous *Liberty*.

[6] "The New Peace Movement—I," *Dissent*, 10 (1963), 90.

[7] A general treatment of the movement is found in Eunice Minette Schuster, "Native American Anarchism: A Study of Left-Wing American Individualism," *Smith College Studies in History*, Vol. 17 (1931–1932).

Tucker is generally acknowledged as the chief political theorist of philosophical anarchism in America despite the fact that almost all his writing was confined to his duties as editor of *Liberty*. Drawing heavily upon the writings of Americans such as Spooner, Greene, and Heywood, and Europeans such as Spencer, Stirner, Bakunin, and Proudhon, Tucker worked out a synthesis of anarchist theory which quickly became a vital source of inspiration and enlightenment for other Americans who were searching for a radical social perspective.[8] No American anarchist before or since, with the exception of Thoreau, has enjoyed the popularity that Tucker did.

Anarchism, as Tucker defined it, was essentially a rejection of all formalism, authority, and force in the interest of liberating the creative capacities of the individual. Reflecting the philosophical assumptions that characterized the viewpoint of Proudhon, Tucker took the difficult position that the anarchist must remove himself from the arena of politics, refusing to implicate himself in groups or associations which have as their end the control or manipulation of political power. For political power not only corrupts but it completely destroys all efforts to create a meaningful social world when it encourages the individual to rely heavily upon the guiding hand of government. Like Proudhon, then, Tucker ruled out the concepts of parliamentary and constitutional government and in general placed himself and the anarchist movement outside the tradition of democracy as it had developed in America. For Tucker no less than for Proudhon, the state was the source of the evil within society. It should, therefore, be abjured and eventually abolished. That it purported to be a democratic state did not alter the case one bit, since democracy, in the anarchist view, is little more than a succession of high-sounding phrases which ultimately prove to be without real significance. From Proudhon, Tucker had learned that the state is a myth, an idea, a conception, which obtains its power to the extent that the individual, acting as mass man, acknowledges it and obeys its commands. When we recognize the state and its ends as legitimate, we become guilty of providing it with power and substance. Many people find it difficult to understand the anarchist's position in this regard. What the anarchist believes, in essence, is that the state, rather than being a real structure or entity, is nothing more than a conception. To destroy the state then, is to remove this conception from the mind of the individual.

The individualist anarchists generally took the position, following Proudhon, that the act of revolution is not political at all and has

[8] The best study of Tucker, as well as the whole movement of native American Anarchism, is found in James J. Martin, *Men Against the State* (New York: Libertarian Book Club, 1957).

nothing whatever to do with the actual overthrow of the existing governmental machinery. Reflecting the nineteenth-century idea of progress, Proudhon maintained that a true revolution can only take place as mankind becomes enlightened. Revolution is not imminent, therefore, although it may well be inevitable. The one thing that is certain is that revolution takes place not by a concerted uprising of the masses but through a process of individual social reformation or awakening. Proudhon, like Tucker and the native American anarchists, believed that the function of anarchism is essentially educational. When enough people are convinced that it is futile to seek the reformation of society through the employment of political power, the actual machinery of government will be destroyed through atrophy. But since it is unlikely that the general enlightenment of mankind will take place any time soon, philosophical anarchists would not and could not discuss the idea of revolution in anything but the most general terms. It was this that was responsible for the charge of quietism that was often directed at them. But while Tucker drew heavily upon Proudhon in regard to theory, he leaned upon Thoreau and the American tradition of nonviolent resistance when it came to the question of strategy, although Proudhon, to be sure, might well be said to belong within this tradition too.[9]

Obviously influenced by Thoreau's example, Tucker refused to pay the taxes the state attempted to levy on his personal property on the grounds that to pay them would make the idea of taxation appear legitimate in the minds of other citizens. Taxation is not legitimate, according to Tucker, for it robs the individual of self-sufficiency and self-determination, not to speak of the fact that government inevitably uses a great part of the revenue it collects for the purpose of waging war and other immoral acts. In the matter of taxation as well as in every other instance in which the state attempts to impose its will upon its subjects, the individual ought to fight it with acts of "propaganda by deed." [10] Tucker, a convinced pacifist, held that all resort to the manipulation of political power and force is ruled out as a possible means of action. The anarchist must never employ violence or any other means which hints of compulsion or coercion. A true act of "propaganda by deed," according to Tucker, is always characterized

---

[9] For a description of Proudhon's theory which emphasizes its nonviolent undertones, see my article "Pierre-Joseph Proudhon: One of the Fathers of Philosophical Anarchism," *Journal of Human Relations*, Vol. 13 (1965).

[10] See Victor S. Yarros, "Philosophical Anarchism (1880–1910)," *Journal of Social Philosophy*, 6 (1941), 251. See also Yarros, "Philosophical Anarchism: Its Rise, Decline, and Eclipse," *America Journal of Sociology*, Vol. 41 (1936); and "Individualist or Philosophical Anarchism," *The New Encyclopedia of Social Reform*, ed. William D. P. Bliss and Rudolph M. Binder (New York: Funk, 1908).

by a sincere, nonviolent attitude on the part of the resistant. Like all anarchists, ethical considerations were always uppermost in Tucker's mind. Although a self-professed atheist, there was, according to one of his disciples, a touch of high moral fervor which hints of Quakerism running throughout his teachings regarding politics.[11] When one places his will against that of the state, Tucker argued, the principles which determine one's action ought to be derived from considerations of moral beauty and truth. For it is the individual, and not the state, who is capable of developing a capacity for moral and social life. The state will be abolished at the point at which people in general have become convinced of its unsocial nature. In the meantime the compelling duty of the anarchist is to bear witness through his personal actions to the futility of attempting to build a meaningful society through cooperation with government. Only the free individual, cooperating with other free individuals, can hope to be successful in building a better world. The courageous individual performs an act of "propaganda by deed" every time he personally resists the enticements of Leviathan. When enough people resist it to the point of ignoring it altogether, the state will have been destroyed as completely as a scrap of paper is when it is tossed into a roaring fire. Obviously Tucker was a direct descendant of Jefferson as well as Proudhon and had much in common with the viewpoints worked out independently by Emerson, Thoreau, and Walt Whitman. Those who argue that the anarchist idea has never had any appeal for Americans have not taken this aspect of American history into consideration. As Herbert L. Osgood, one of the first political scientists to address himself to the problem of interpreting American anarchism, wrote: "Anarchism . . . is, like socialism, a natural product of our economic and political conditions. It is to be treated as such, both theoretically and practically. Anarchism is a product of democracy. It is as much at home on American soil as on European." [12]

II

Much of the confusion surrounding the history of anarchism in the United States initially stems from the stormy figure of Johann Most, who dominated the movement for a decade starting in 1882. Most, who never succeeded in overcoming the appearance and mannerisms of his Germanic origins, was greatly misunderstood by Americans. It

---

[11] Yarros, "Philosophical Anarchism (1880–1910)," p. 251.
[12] Herbert L. Osgood, *Socialism and Anarchism* (Boston, 1889), pp. 30–31. Originally published under the title "Scientific Anarchism," *Political Science Quarterly,* Vol. 4 (1889).

was indeed difficult for many Americans to know what he really believed, for his writing was mainly confined to *Freiheit* which was printed in German. Most toured the country, speaking before many different groups, and this was widely reported in the press. But being an immigrant, Most never succeeded in overcoming the suspicion and hostility of the public in his adopted land. How could he when his following was largely recruited from the waves of European immigrants who descended upon our shores during the years when our doors were opened wide? When the bomb exploded in Haymarket Square, it was a foregone conclusion that the tide of public sentiment would run against the anarchist movement, for its American origins had by this time been obscured by the foreign appearance of the European radicals and syndicalists who now formed its majority. We may quickly dismiss Most, for not only did he fail to contribute anything significant to the theory of anarchism but his many inconsistencies make it questionable whether he was really an anarchist at all in any real sense of the term. At any rate, he had little real influence upon the development of the anarchist idea in America other than being the cause of much of the opprobrium which was brought down on the movement at this time.

A disciple for a time of Johann Most and destined to succeed him as the recognized leader of American anarchism, Emma Goldman came to anarchism because of her inability to compromise with social injustice. Yet as Richard Drinnon has clearly shown, Emma Goldman, like all anarchists around the turn of the century, was a victim of the ideological distortion which characterized the times.[13] A Russian Jew by birth, she was portrayed by the popular press as a vile and unsavory devotee of revolutionary violence. But a sober reading of her utterances in *Mother Earth* reveals her to be anything but an advocate of nihilistic terrorism.

A highly sensitive individual whose interests in philosophical questions stemmed from a refined social consciousness, Emma Goldman, like all anarchists, was a staunch foe of the idea of militarism and the primitive notion that justice is nothing more than a reflection of the will of the strongest amongst us. In her youth, to be sure, she allowed her enthusiasm for social justice to lead her into collaboration with Alexander Berkman in an attempt to assassinate Henry C. Frick, whom she viewed as the personification of all the evils of industrial capitalism. But as Drinnon points out in his magnificent biography, Emma Goldman was later to realize that this act was a youthful indiscretion completely out of tune with the principles of anarchism. She could not, of course, completely wave aside the blot on her early

[13] *Rebel in Paradise* (Chicago: U. of Chicago Press, 1961).

record. But in her maturity her life and action reveal her as being a spiritual descendant of the American tradition of nonviolence.

Perhaps what was mainly responsible for the misunderstanding which came to attach itself to her image was her adamant refusal to consider social violence as an unnatural phenomenon. Like Kropotkin, Emma Goldman believed that violence is the natural consequence of repression and force. The state, in her opinion, sows the seeds of violence when it lends its authority and force to the retardation of social change, thereby creating deep-seated feelings of injustice and desperation in the collective unconscious. "I do not advocate violence, government does this, and force begets force," Emma Goldman proclaimed. "It is a fact which cannot be done away with through the prosecution of a few men and women, or by more stringent laws. . . ." [14] The individual does not freely will to commit an act of retribution against the social system but is forced into it by a conspiracy upon the part of those whose interests lead them to preserve the existing order against all change. In defense of McKinley's assassin, Leon Czolgosz, Emma Goldman took issue with all those, including some radicals, who condemned his action on the argument that it was a useless act. We can no more measure an act of social violence by its practical utility, she argued, than we can understand the usefulness of a tornado or cyclone. In each instance nature has a logic of its own which is not immediately apparent to the observer. Czolgosz's deed resists all understanding unless we view it against the total social context of which it was a part.[15] Were we able to take an objective view of what Czolgosz has done, she argued, we would probably find that his act was as much a reaction to social events he experienced as lightning and thunder are a direct consequence of atmospheric conditions. It is not the instinct of cruelty or any other criminal tendency that causes an individual such as Czolgosz to strike down the highest public official he can get at. On the contrary, Emma Goldman maintained, too often it is a strong social instinct and a desire to express a deep love of mankind that lies behind an act of assassination. Social violence is never arbitrary and meaningless. There is always a deep-seated cause standing behind every deed. However much sympathy we may have for the victim of an assassina-

[14] "The Tragedy of Buffalo," *The Revolutionary Almanac*, p. 56.
[15] Richard Drinnon makes out a good case for the view that Czolgosz was actually a demented youth who had only a vague idea of what anarchism was all about. Drinnon also points out that in her speech at Cleveland, which was used to prove that she had incited Czolgosz to violent action, Emma Goldman ". . . took occasion to attack the popular misconception that anarchism meant bomb throwing and general violence. She for one, she declared, did not believe in violence; she added that anarchism in any case had no necessary connection with violence," *op. cit.*, p. 68.

tion, we must nevertheless see that its perpetrator is never fully in control of his own actions but is merely a small cog in a vast social machine. Social violence, she argued, will naturally disappear at the point at which men have learned to understand and accommodate themselves to one another within a dynamic society which truly values human freedom. Until then we can expect to see the pent-up hostility and frustration of certain individuals and groups explode from time to time with the spontaneity and violence of a volcano. We will be the wiser, according to Emma Goldman, when we learn to look on such cataclysms with the detachment of a geologist viewing an eruption of the earth's crust. To judge Czolgosz in terms of theological or conventional moral presuppositions is both primitive and unscientific.

But it is misleading to dwell too long upon Emma Goldman's theory of social violence to the exclusion of the other significant events of her fruitful life. This, in fact, is the very reason why she has been so completely misunderstood. When we view her life in total perspective we discover that she was dedicated to the cause of peace and was an unyielding enemy of the institution of war. Like the native American anarchists of her adopted land, Emma Goldman believed that the only practical way to eliminate war was to educate men to reject it as incompatible with their basic social and ethical convictions. And thus it was that she lectured all over the United States in denunciation of the Spanish-American War and later throughout England and Scotland against the Boer War. It was for her opposition to America's entry into World War I and her organization of the No-Conscription League that she was arrested, sentenced to two years in prison, and later deported under the terms of the Espionage Act of 1917. What is of interest here is that Emma Goldman, whatever the political labels that became attached to her may have been, was an ardent and dedicated opponent of organized violence and bloodshed. Had she been born a few years sooner, and in the United States instead of Russia, she would undoubtedly have found herself welcomed with open arms into the ranks of the native American anarchists. It should also be kept in mind that Emma Goldman's interests were never political but always social and literary. As a consequence she was in the vanguard of every libertarian movement of her time, indefatigably laboring to effect the enlightenment and betterment of mankind. It was as editor of *Mother Earth* that she collected funds to defend the Sangers in their efforts to disseminate information on birth control, and she herself served fifteen days in the workhouse for lecturing on the subject. Nor is it usually remembered that Emma Goldman's anarchist activity was largely confined to such pursuits as lecturing on modern drama and aesthetics. Completely unpolitical in character, she refused to lead men by their noses, persisting to the end in the belief that reason and goodwill will eventually triumph. At no time in her life did she advocate the legitimacy of political parties. Her sympathies for the poor and the working class were enormous, as was her capacity to love and comfort her friends and lovers. Yet she never allowed her frustrations to lead her to the barricades. It is true that toward the end of her life she supported the Spanish anarchists in their fight against fascism, visiting Barcelona and even making a journey to the front where she watched the anarchist troops trade shots with Franco's snipers. But she did not exult in this violence but rather deplored it, even though she recognized the situation as being inevitable under the given circumstances. If this makes her an advocate of the principle of violence, then the vast majority of men throughout the world who fail to take action to stop a war once it has started must also be called advocates of the principle of violence. The most that can be said against Emma Goldman was that she was not an absolute pacifist and that she would not equivocate with injustice or falsehood. To her credit it must be acknowledged that her battlefield was the lecture hall and the weapon of her choice her rapier-like logic. If she was guilty of violence it was the same kind of violence for which Socrates was put to death. It was not the actual machinery of government which Emma Goldman labored to tear down, but the myth and illusion which trick men into supporting their governments when there is a conflict between moral and political obligation. As more and more historians are coming to see, the caricature of Emma Goldman as an irresponsible malcontent is a distortion wholly out of keeping with the facts. Blinded by its own ideology, America for many years could not bring itself to understand one of its most precocious adopted children. And when it had succeeded in convincing itself that the *enfant terrible* it had created was the prototype of all anarchists, it became inevitable that the philosophy of anarchism should become impervious to our understanding.

III

When one turns to the more recent literature of anarchism in America, the supposed antithesis regarding violence and revolution between philosophical and collectivist anarchists becomes even more blurred and indistinct. According to anarchists themselves, it is misleading to dwell too much on the distinction between the philosophical and collectivist viewpoints. One of the dangers here, according to

David Thoreau Wieck, editor of the now defunct anarchist journal *Resistance*,[16] is that some people desire to portray philosophical anarchism as an integral part of the liberal tradition in America, emphasizing its basic compatibility with the principle of laissez faire. But it is a form of "propagandistic opportunism" to portray philosophical anarchism as American, whereupon by implication anarchist communism must become un-American.[17] In the first place, this makes it appear that liberalism and philosophical anarchism are compatible philosophies, whereas the truth is that they hold radically different theories concerning the nature and the function of the state. And secondly, but even more important, such a distinction leads the unsuspecting to conclude that there are fundamental differences within the anarchist movement regarding the feasibility of violent revolution, whereas the truth is that there is no essential difference between them in this regard.

It can not be stated too emphatically that all anarchists, whether they be called individualists or collectivists, are as one in regard to the conviction that a revolution is a social and not a political phenomenon. Russell Blackwell, one of the foremost American anarchists today, points out that the nature of the revolution advocated by anarchism does not in any instance rely upon force or violence. ". . . the old order is seldom 'overthrown' but collapses of its own weight in the crises. . . ."[18] The crucial distinction between the nature of the revolution advocated by anarchists and that of other political ideologies, according to Blackwell, is that the anarchist revolution must in no instance utilize the antisocial principles of hierarchy, bureaucracy, and authoritarian discipline. Anarchists recognize, of course, that order is essential to social life and that some form of social organization is necessary if chaos is to be avoided. But this order must come from the people and not from organized government. For where the people fail to develop self-discipline, resort is inevitably made to the police powers, the courts, and penal institutions. Such formal methods of social control, however, are antithetical to the goal of human freedom. As Blackwell puts it in his own words:

> Any society to function requires order, and the libertarians must see that this order is imposed from below in response to the popular will, and not institutionalized along dictatorial lines. No State forms must be allowed to coalesce, no regular police force must be permitted since every State, with its police and armed forces is in essence dictatorial

---

[16] There seems to be a move underway to publish *Resistance* again, although it may appear under a new title.

[17] Review of Rudolph Rocker's *Pioneers of American Freedom*, in *Resistance*, Vol. 8 (1949).

[18] "Autonomy and Responsibility," *Towards Anarchism*, No. 50 (1965), 9.

and therefore counter-revolutionary. Control of the revolution must be in the hands of the autonomous groups in the social base. As the conquests of the revolution become solidified, the danger of authoritarian influence for a time will increase. This can be combatted by constant vigilance, and above all by activity involving ever more people in roles of social responsibility. The preservation of maximum autonomy is of the essence for without it the fundamental revolutionary values are lost.[19]

As Blackwell's words make clear, anarchism is unalterably opposed to the creation of artificial social control through conventional political means. Unlike conservatives and liberals who rely heavily upon government to regulate the affairs of people, anarchists are extremely suspicious of any organized agencies of coercion. As Sam Weiner, one of the founders of the Libertarian League has written: "We have nothing to fear so long as no group in society is given political power to rule over others; no one, and no one group must have coercive, police power. This is why anarchists are AT ALL TIMES, for the abolition of the state and centralized control." [20] Anarchists reject the institution of organized police power because it violates the basic principle of individual freedom. Where government imposes order upon society through the employment of techniques of coercion and force, the individual is denied the right to regulate and discipline himself. And even more important, people who have been coerced into order over any appreciable period of time become habituated to force and soon forget how to discipline themselves.

When the anarchist speaks of revolution, then, he makes no reference to the political act of acquiring power through a coup. The anarchist, in fact, is totally opposed to the very idea of political change by means of the revolutionary act. For as Bertrand de Jouvenal has written, "the true historical function of revolutions is to renovate and strengthen Power." [21] The ostensible purpose of any revolution is always said to be the advancement of social progress and humanity. But as Jouvenal points out, the ultimate effect of revolution is always to free power of the restraints which previously limited it, thereby giving it new vigor and prestige. When the anarchist speaks of revolution and the overthrow of the state, what he calls for is not a political act but one that is purely social. The state is not a physical entity which can be destroyed by dynamite or gunpowder. The English anarchist Nicolas Walter, quoting from Landauer's *Die Revolution,* points out that the state is a mode of human behavior and a type of

[19] "Resolution of the Italian Anarchist Federation," *Towards Anarchism,* No. 50 (1965), 25.
[20] "Direct Action and the New Pacifism," *Anarchy,* No. 13 (March 1962), 74.
[21] *On Power* (Boston: Beacon Press, 1962), p. 218.

relationship between people rather than an institution of physical form or substance.[22] We overthrow the state when we withdraw our support from it, refusing any longer to obey its commands. But in order to do this, we must first enter into a new social relationship with our fellowmen, thereby making the existence of the state superfluous. When men decide to live together in the spirit of mutual aid that Kropotkin described as natural to them, the state, according to the anarchist, will turn to dust and ashes of its own accord and not because men have physically destroyed it. In America today, all anarchists, from the collectivists represented by the Libertarian League and Dorothy Day's Catholic Worker movement to the individualists of Mildred Loomis' Green Revolution, are in essential agreement that the social revolution must be nonviolent and unpolitical in character. When we view anarchist theory in this way, it is not incorrect to say that all anarchists are "philosophical," whether they are classified as individualists or collectivists. Conversely, it is incorrect to conclude that *all* anarchist communists or collectivists favor the employment of violence, or that anarchism, as a political theory, supports the principle that violence as a means is justifiable if its end is revolutionary. To be clear on this point is to view anarchism from an entirely different perspective.

[22] "Direct Action and the New Pacifism," *loc. cit.*

EXISTENTIALISM

Rebellion . . . [is] the secular will not to
surrender . . . it keeps us erect in the savage
formless movement of history.
—ALBERT CAMUS, *The Rebel*

Albert Camus is the prototype of
the artist who refuses to ignore the pressing issues of his age. In
"Albert Camus' Politics of Rebellion," Fred H. Willhoite analyzes
the scope and value of personal rebellion in Camus' thought. For
Camus, persistent rebellion against acts of inhumanity just might lead
mankind to the construction of a civilization in which individual
needs will be cultivated.

Marjorie Grene, in her chapter "French Existentialism and Politics:
The New Revolutionary," depicts Jean-Paul Sartre's version of existentialism as an attempt to demonstrate that revolutionary philosophy
is a philosophy of freedom—a philosophy of the very free act itself.
The revolutionary, by his very *choice* of revolution, becomes the autonomous self who wishes "that man freely and totally assume his
destiny."

Existentialism has had an enormous psychological appeal in an age
of growing fragmentation, depersonalization, and estrangement. However, the Sartrean imperative—choose and stick by your convictions
whatever the cost—does create some perplexing political problems.
The imperative is essentially *contentless,* for it deliberately ignores
any attempt to establish priorities among the *ends* toward which ethical and political choices are directed. Indeed, by viewing the world
outside as basically absurd, the Sartrean existentialist reduces the
whole question of priorities to the level of irrelevant metaphysical
speculation. What is to be done when the existential folk hero pursues an authentic commitment to chaos and the mass destruction of
human life? The theme of "standing alone" can easily be turned into
a kind of rugged individualism that disregards any and all social responsibility.

Perhaps in this respect other Existentialists, such as Martin Buber
and Gabriel Marcel, offer a valid response by placing the authentic
life in the service of specific ends. In the place of estranged individuals they substitute the deeply personal "I–Thou" relationship. Their
philosophy is more hopeful than that of Sartre. They see room for
hope in the authentic pursuit of fraternity. Thus, for example, in pro-

testing the Nazi-inspired Vichy regime, Marcel was able to distinguish between mere *obedience* extracted by fear and authentic *fidelity* emerging from sentiments of hope and love. Existential rebellion is thereby placed in a framework rather than valued for its own sake alone.

17 / Albert Camus' Politics of Rebellion

FRED H. WILLHOITE, JR.

"Probably every generation sees itself as charged with remaking the world. Mine, however, knows that it will not remake the world. But its task is perhaps even greater, for it consists in keeping the world from destroying itself." [1] What is the role of the literary artist in the defense of human dignity against forces which threaten the existence of humanity itself? This is the question which the second youngest recipient of the Nobel Prize for Literature, until his tragic accidental death early in 1960, sought to answer through his life and art. Despite his often-expressed desire to be a writer in the same sense that Mozart was a composer, Albert Camus never attempted to place an "aesthetic distance" between himself and the major political issues of his time. Without becoming identified with any party or rigidly defined doctrinal position, he endeavored to become a witness on behalf of concrete, living, powerless human beings in an age which he saw dominated by social and political depersonalization in general and by totalitarianism in particular.

Although Camus was not a political philosopher by profession, his work has considerable value for the student of political ideas, or more generally, of the political culture of post-World War II France. Camus stands in that great line of French *savants* and literary artists who have decisively echoed and influenced the convictions of many of their compatriots: in this sense he is akin to Voltaire, Rousseau, and Victor Hugo. Although it is difficult to estimate very precisely the impact of Camus' writings on French public opinion, Professor

SOURCE: *Western Political Quarterly*, XIV (June 1961), 400–414. Reprinted by permission of the author and the University of Utah, copyright holder.

[1] Albert Camus, "Camus at Stockholm: The Acceptance of the Nobel Prize," translated by Justin O'Brien, *Atlantic Monthly*, CCI (May 1958), 34.

William May seems justified in declaring that "Camus has had a decisive influence on the political convictions of young Frenchmen. . . . (Apparently no book has been as effective as 'The Rebel' in persuading young Frenchmen to reject Marxism.)" [2]

Camus was deeply involved—in deeds as well as in words—in some of the major conflicts through which his generation has passed. The political ferment of the Popular Front era, the Resistance movement, the reshaping of French democratic institutions after World War II, the response to the challenge of totalitarian communism—all these crises elicited his participation and comment. He did not commit himself to any organized political party but stood out as an individualistic champion of decency, modesty, honesty, and compassion in politics. Within the American context, his basically rather simple position might seem unimportant, but in a Europe torn by decades of violent revolution and conflicting ideologies, his attempt to get at and remain faithful to the concrete human foundations of all social policy makes him a significant figure in contemporary political thought.

In order to explicate Camus' basic political ideas, it is necessary first to delineate his vision of the human situation—the meaning, purpose, and pattern of man's life. From his relatively uncomplicated view of the human condition, centering upon a few fundamental themes, emerges the key concept of rebellion, central to his interpretation of and prescriptions for politics. The most significant and searching of Camus' political writing consists of a sustained and reasoned analysis of and attack upon totalitarianism, and the discussion of his specifically political ideas will deal primarily with this aspect of his thought. Some attention will be given, however, to the more constructive aspects of Camus' political thought, an area in which, for the most part, he wrote only sketchily and in very general terms.

THE HUMAN CONDITION

Camus' fundamental perspective was set forth almost in its entirety in the four lyrical essays of *Noces*, written when he was only twenty-three to record his own most intimate experiences and his impressions of the natural world. Obviously, intense personal crises rather than philosophical reading and speculation stimulated the formulation of his basic ideas, which may be summarized under the headings of man's joy in nature, the total this-worldliness of life, happiness conjoined with absurdity, complete honesty to oneself, and—the concept central to his political thought proper—rebellion.

[2] Letter to the author, March 3, 1959.

Camus' viewpoint in *Noces* is radically earth-bound—and so it always remained. His youthful experience of physical nature resulted in a simple and immediate joy so intense that speculation about or belief in otherworldly life seemed irrelevant. He concluded that it is man's role in nature to be a happy creature, but this does not imply that it is possible to overlook the fact of mortality. Life is so good that we desire its eternal continuance. Because the fulfillment of this longing is impossible, we must surmount our trepidation at the prospect of death and, fully cognizant of our fate, affirm the happiness that we can know. The keenness and poignancy of this joy will sustain and enrich our lives if we do not delude ourselves by seeking to transcend the limits of mortality.

Camus' passionate affirmation of the happy life has the effect of intensifying for him a feeling of the absurdity of human existence. If life is joyous, good, and infinitely desirable, it is for man the ultimate absurdity that he should be fully aware of its inevitable extinction. In *Le Mythe de Sisyphe,* a more philosophical work written a few years subsequent to *Noces,* Camus seeks to explicate more fully the meaning of absurdity and discovers that it is essentially the product of the incommensurability of man—who desires total comprehension and eternal life—and the universe—which continually offers new mysteries to man's reason and brings about his inescapable death.

But Camus' belief that life is absurd did not imply for him weary resignation to the whims of an inscrutable fate. For a final significant motif plainly expressed in *Noces* is man's rebellion against whatever oppresses his mind and body—in particular the ultimate oppressor, death. The first clear expression of this theme in Camus' work resulted from an intensely personal experience undergone by the young writer when, faced with the imminent possibility of his own death from tuberculosis, he traveled through Italy attempting to recover from the dread disease.

In Florence he strolled through the graveyard of the Santissima Annunziata, observing that, from the tenor of the epitaphs, it appeared that all those buried there had willingly accepted death. Suddenly he experienced a moment of fierce rebellion against such placid resignation:

> Everything within me protested against this kind of resignation. "One must," said the inscriptions. But I said no, and my revolt was true. That joy which goes about the earth, indifferent and absorbed in itself like a pilgrim—I had to follow it step by step. And as for the rest, I said no. I said no with all my strength. These slabs taught me that this was futile. . . . But today I still do not see what futility takes away from my rebellion, and I feel keenly what is thereby added to it.[3]

[3] "Le désert," *Noces* (Paris: Charlot, 1947), pp. 88–89.

In this moment of instinctive rebellion Camus discovered that his love for the earth, for life in its mingled joy and hopelessness, was so powerful that he could not resign himself to the death which his lucidity would not permit him to overlook. The movement of rebellion surged up within him, and he discovered that all the forces of the world which aim at the obliteration of human life must be resisted. His experiential sequence: life is very good though mortal and therefore absurd; yet when the joy of living overwhelms us, we rebel against death and all death-bringers; because our revolt is in the name of life, it leads us to a keener awareness of the poignant happiness that can be ours if we affirm our allegiance to the earth.

This distinctively individual experience of rebellion, later conceptualized by Camus in his attempt to delineate its nature and significance, became in his writings the existential standard by which political ideas and empirical polities are to be evaluated. Whatever of value we may discover in Camus' conception of politics springs ultimately from his own intensely personal reaction to human mortality.

But Camus could not speak meaningfully to the life of man in society until he had passed beyond his own immediate experience of and reaction to the world to arrive at serious consideration of the corporate dimension of man's life. Although his early works contain intimations of such a concern,[4] on the whole it seems true that the chaotic circumstances of the war years provided the matrix for and a stimulus to Camus' development beyond the delineation of personal experience toward the construction of a positive morality for the individual and humane political principles for society.

Camus' experiential approach to the formulation of personal ideas and convictions leads to the conclusion that his active participation in the Resistance (as editor of the clandestine newspaper *Combat*) must certainly have affected his point of view. A profound sense of human solidarity in the struggle against evil and oppression, a visceral contempt for totalitarianism and its treatment of persons, an upsurging faith in the potentialities of human feeling and intelligence— these were some of Camus' attitudes that were either born or reached maturity during the difficult years of the Occupation.

The most moving and effective expression of Camus' newly articulated political humanism is his great novel *La Peste* (published in 1947) which tells of the ravages of a bubonic plague epidemic in an Algerian city and of the reactions to this crisis of various groups

---

[4] For example, the "Conqueror," an exemplary person sketched in *Le Mythe de Sisyphe*, is neither tyrant nor totalitarian. Fully conscious of the ultimate absurdity of life, he has chosen to defend the poor and helpless against oppression as his way of rebelling against evil and death, the handmaidens of absurdity. See "The Myth of Sisyphus," *The Myth of Sisyphus and Other Essays*, translated by Justin O'Brien (New York: Knopf, 1955), pp. 85–90.

and individuals. Camus indicates on the title page that this book is allegorical, but it contains several levels of meaning. In the first place it is an allegory on contemporary events, such as the German Occupation and the totalitarian world of concentration camps, terror, and wholly depersonalized bureaucracy. But even more significantly, the characters and events of *La Peste* give evidence of the development and enrichment of Camus' conception of the human condition.

In particular, the necessity and efficacy of action in the social sphere are affirmed, in the guise of a patient and determined emergency public health team led by a stoical young doctor. Rebellion against the plague—death, suffering, and injustice—is presented as the pathway to genuine humanity. The moral solipsism of the absurd man is somehow broken into by a feeling that his personal revolt is grounded in an experience common to his fellows. Happiness remains of central value, but in the sense that furthering the happiness of others becomes a duty for the rebel.

Camus attempted elsewhere to reason out the motivations for the plague-fighters'—and his own—service to humanity, but these intellectual efforts were not in themselves very persuasive. The way that Camus felt toward his fellow men was infinitely more important to him than the way he thought about them. To give hope to the humiliated and the debased was his aim, but—"Not through virtue . . . but through a sort of almost organic intolerance, which you feel or do not feel. Indeed, I see many who fail to feel it, but I cannot envy their sleep." [5] Camus' compelling personal vision of the human condition thus traverses a difficult route—from its starting-point of life's absurdity to a radically earth-bound and tough-minded humanism, in which instinctive rebellion against suffering, oppression, and death leads to involvement in the problems of human society.

From this standpoint Camus interprets modern totalitarianism as the tragically corrupted offspring of the rebellion of men against their condition—rebellion which is itself essential for the realization of true human dignity. The experience of rebellion holds the center of the stage in Camus' reflections on political life and thought, as he seeks to show how it has gone awry in modern times and calls for renewed fidelity to true rebellion as the only hope for a just and humane social order.

REBELLION AND REVOLUTION

In *L'Homme révolté* Camus attempts to go to the experiential root of that kind of rebellion which is especially relevant to politics. Initially

[5] "The Artist and His Time," *The Myth of Sisyphus and Other Essays,* p. 211.

he seeks to answer the question, how does rebellion, insofar as its corporate implications are concerned, originate and become actualized in the individual life? It first occurs when some oppressed individual, for example a slave, finally utters an instinctive "no" to a demand made upon him which he feels simply goes too far in debasing his person. In this act, which may well precede conscious formulation of values applicable to the situation, the oppressed one, in his negation of the command addressed to him, tacitly affirms certain human rights and values. There springs up in his consciousness the awareness that within his very being as a living person there is something "with which man can identify himself, if only for a time." [6] In effect, the human conscience comes to light in the experience of rebellion, which in itself proclaims that there are certain limits to the ways in which human beings may legitimately be treated. If the rebel becomes willing to die for the sake of the values implicit in his revolt, this indicates that these values transcend the individual; thereby the rebel emerges from his solitude and is given a reason to act.

Camus' analysis of revolt suggests to him that there is in fact a common human nature: "Why rebel if there is in oneself nothing permanent to conserve?" [7] The slave who adjudges a command to deny something fundamental in him feels in the same moment that this something is of genuine significance because it is common to all men. Rebellion, although it originates in individual experience, is not essentially an egoistic movement; individuals will rebel against falsehood and the oppression of others as well as against personal suffering. Rebellion stakes everything on the degree in which it invokes that which is common to the community of men. The rebel who defends the oppressed does not so act because he identifies himself with them either in a psychological or in a calculating manner: "There is only the identifying of destinies and the taking of sides." [8]

Human solidarity is founded upon this positive kind of rebellion and the values which it discloses as applicable to all persons. Rebellion which goes beyond the limitations within human nature which it reveals becomes untrue to its own experience, destroys human solidarity, and thereby becomes itself pretentious and oppressive. This latter variety of rebellion has forgotten that when one revolts against suffering, injustice or absurdity, the resultant experience of human solidarity is best expressed in a neo-Cartesian postulate, "I rebel, therefore *we* are." [9]

For Camus, rebellion means not only an individual and collective refusal of death and absurdity in the name of nature and happiness; it comes to imply resistance to physical or political oppression as well

[6] *L'Homme révolté* (Paris: Gallimard, 1951), p. 26.   [7] *Ibid.*, p. 28.
[8] *Ibid.*, p. 29.   [9] *Ibid.*, p. 36.

—for such oppression is on the side of death and misery in negating men's freedom and happiness. Camus' basic intent at this point is to establish that there are intrinsic limits to the kind of treatment which may be meted out to human beings, if their essential humanity is to be preserved.

In his attempt to understand the political situation of our time, Camus seeks to trace the history of rebellion during the past century and a half. Reinforcing and often equivalent to the fundamental level of personal experience of rebellion shared by many individuals in modern times are what he terms metaphysical and historical revolt. The former evolves into the latter, as the World of revolt becomes the Flesh of history.

Metaphysical rebellion is "the movement in which a man sets himself against his condition and the whole of creation." [10] It is a Western phenomenon, for it could occur only in conjunction with Christianity. It is in fact a rebellion against the image in much of Christian history of the authoritarian God who metes out rewards and punishments, despite what Camus sees as His own guilt in allowing injustice, cruelty, and death to reign in the world. Metaphysical rebellion is not essentially atheistic; rather it is blasphemous in its denunciation in the name of unity and justice of the God who is the father of death and the supreme scandal.

But as this explication implies, a frontal attack upon the absolute God was not possible so long as Christian faith remained dominant in the West. Medieval Christendom believed that it was only just that some men should be masters and others servants, that man's lot was by nature and by right not an easy one on this earth; for God Himself had come into history and suffered as a man, showing that man was created to suffer: "If everything, without exception, from heaven to earth, is bound up in sorrow, then a strange kind of happiness is possible." [11] But as soon as the Age of Reason had for many undermined the validity of Christian theology, religious faith could no longer justify the master-slave relationship. If Christ were believed to be merely human, God was in fact responsible for suffering and injustice without Himself participating in these woes. Such a God, to men who rebelled against oppression and falsehood, was an abomination; hence they denied Him.

In Camus' eyes, the central philosophical figure in the rebellion of modern men against God and the human condition is Friedrich Nietzsche, in whose thought the nihilistic elements latent in metaphysical revolt are clearly articulated for the first time. For Nietzsche the death of God means that there is no law superior to or apart from

---

[10] *Ibid.*, p. 39.   [11] *Ibid.*, p. 53.

man nor any lawgiver but man—no external standards transcend human values. But this very absence of eternal law does not mean solely that "everything is permitted"; it means that nothing is allowed apart from human denial or permission. No liberty is possible except in a world where both the permitted and the prohibited are delimited. Since man must create his own values, Nietzsche proposes to replace all value judgments with "a single yes, a total and exalted adherence to this world. . . . Total adherence to total necessity, this is his paradoxical definition of freedom." [12] In effect, fate becomes divine and the world, as the ultimate, is god. As part of the world, men, by wholeheartedly accepting and affirming its reality partake of the divinity: "To say yes to the world repeatedly is to re-create the world and oneself at the same time, to become the great artist, the creator. . . . Divinity without immortality defines the freedom of the creator." [13]

Camus indicates that Nietzsche's nihilism implies that man lives without restraints, except for those he places upon himself; that he can re-create the world in whatever image he desires. And though Nietzsche did not so conclude, it is possible to use his ideas to justify, as did the Nazis, the conclusion that to say yes, unqualifiedly, to the world, includes affirming the legitimacy of murder. Nietzsche goes beyond nihilism in leaping from the negation of the ideal to its secularization: he concludes that since men cannot attain to salvation through God, their salvation must come through their own efforts on earth: "Philosophy secularizes the idea. But tyrants come, and soon they secularize philosophies which put them in the right." [14] This was the fate of Nietzsche's thought at the hands of National Socialism.

As Camus views the recent past, metaphysical rebellion and nihilism have continually revealed the visage of human protest against the injustice and absurdity of Creation and the human condition. Nihilism concludes in declaring the solitude of all earthly creatures and the nothingness of all morality. But few have been able to live with these conclusions; most rebels have sought to re-create the world and its values in their own image, often by unleashing personal desire and the will to power, ending in suicide, madness, murder, and destruction.

But in its essence, Camus asserts, true rebellion can never be other than a protracted protest against death, the fact of man's mortality, which seems to deprive life of all significance: "Rebellion demands, not life, but a meaning for life." [15] Rebellion that remains faithful to its inspiration seeks to create this *raison d'être* for humanity by struggling against evil in the form of unjust suffering.

[12] *Ibid.*, p. 96.   [13] *Ibid.*, p. 98.   [14] *Ibid.*, p. 104.   [15] *Ibid.*, p. 129.

The rebellion against God as the creator and preserver of an evil and absurd world is, as Camus sees it, the beginning of both tragedy and triumph for modern man. In his revolt man pledges himself to build the only kingdom—that of Justice—which can replace the realm of Grace, to reunite the human community upon the debris of the divine community: "Kill God and build a Church—this is the constant and contradictory movement of rebellion." [16] The tragic side of this effort to build the Church of Rebellion is contemporary totalitarianism, the joint product of metaphysical revolt and political revolution. It is the totalitarians who have carried into effect the dictum of the nihilistic rebel, who adds to the "I rebel, therefore we are" of the original experience of revolt a second postulate, "And we are alone." [17]

The principles of metaphysical rebellion were first actualized in historical form, Camus contends, in the events of the French Revolution. The year 1789 saw more than a revolt against tyranny; the principle of divine right and the legitimacy of the Kingdom of Grace were attacked in the name of absolute Justice. A civil religion was established by Jacobins who believed themselves to be disciples of Rousseau. All were required to worship at the altar of Truth, Justice, and Reason, the new triune godhead. But abstract principles are inherently of feeble attractive powers, and "to worship a theorem for a very long time faith is insufficient; thus a police force becomes necessary." [18] The Reign of Terror was employed in a quest for the total realization of a virtuous national unity.

In Camus' view, the most important thinker in the onward march of historical rebellion is Hegel, in whose thought all values, even the shadowy Jacobin triumvirate, lose their transcendent status and become wholly incorporated into the flux of history. But inasmuch as Hegel asserts that certain values are capable of full realization in the course of the historical process, they become absolute ends or goals and no longer serve as landmarks or guides for the regulation of means. The good and true become that which survives the inexorable process of the historical dialectic; in other words the successful, the efficacious. The only ethical guide to the choice of means is then a purely pragmatic criterion, as the end of history becomes an all-consuming passion, justifying any means that will lead to its realization: "One must act and live in terms of the future. All morality becomes provisional." [19]

Hegel's only suggestion for a provisional ethic was conformance with the customs and spirit of the times. Camus points out that more revolutionary spirits than Hegel were to accept his basic premises but

[16] *Ibid.*, p. 131.   [17] *Ibid.*, p. 132.   [18] *Ibid.*, p. 155.   [19] *Ibid.*, pp. 179–80.

reject his conformism in the name of a more "active fatalism" which sought to help along at break-neck speed the "inevitable" movement of history toward its sublime consummation. To the Jacobin legacy to totalitarianism—the principle that the state as the incarnation of virtue may be protected and aggrandized by terror—Hegel adds immeasurably by reinforcing the principle that the end justifies the means. If no values transcend the flux of history, and if one knows that history is proceeding tortuously but inexorably toward a future incarnation of virtue perfected in all mankind, who can adjudge one guilty if he employs any means—murder, concentration camps, total regimentation of human lives—in passionate dedication to the consummation of the glorious future?

Camus states, however, that before such immanent ends could inspire the totalitarian spirit, Hegel's philosophical idealism had to be materialized, conjoined with rebellion against immediate injustice, and rationalized in terms of the revolutionary aspirations of an age. For contemporary "rationalized" totalitarianism, therefore, Karl Marx is the prophet of truth. But in addition to his heavy reliance upon Hegel, Marx is also greatly indebted to Christianity and to the bourgeois spirit of his time, as well as to the scientific way of thinking.

Initially, Camus asserts, Marx rebelled against the way in which nineteenth-century capitalists treated their workers—as sub-human implements rather than men. This was the genuinely human impulse of the true rebel. But when Marx attempted to rationalize and systematize his rebellion, philosophic, religious, and environmental influences turned his thinking into a prophetic ideology; and his role as a realistic social critic gradually receded in importance as prophecy became a consuming passion.

From Christianity Marx appropriates both the idea of linear history progressing toward a goal and a spirit of totality. From the first of these concepts, Camus avers, Christians had deduced that nature was but the raw material of history, to be worked upon, transformed, and mastered by men in the course of human endeavor. Marx secularizes this idea so that man in his thought becomes not only the master of nature but also the lord of history.

The Christian belief that God is totally sovereign over human life is also secularized by Marx, in whose thought revolutionary ideology claims omniscience and omnipotence. Camus declares that this Christian idea, cut loose from its religious moorings, has become murderous: "Those who claim to know and regulate everything end up by killing everything." [20] This secularized spirit of totality, incorporated into contemporary dictatorships in large measure because of Marx's

[20] "Deux réponses à Emmanuel d'Astier de la Vigerie," *Actuelles: Chroniques, 1944–1948* (Paris: Gallimard, 1950), p. 198.

influence, has been of crucial significance in the development of the institutions of the totalitarian state—for example organized terror, concentration camps, and all-pervasive multi-tiered bureaucracy.

Camus points to the bourgeois ideas of inevitable scientific progress and direct correlation between the course of industrial production and the development of human nature as influencing crucially Marx's thought. This resulted in his retaining what Camus considers the basic error of modern industrial society—to regard human beings as expendable commodities in the onward march of economic and political "progress." This tendency has been most fully realized by the totalitarian regimes which justify themselves as champions of true humanity. Such was not Marx's real intent; Camus indicates that part of the ethical grandeur of Marxism consists in its creator's vehement protest against the indignity and meaninglessness of work in modern society, against the treatment of persons as things.

But Marx shares the fate common to most prophets: his message is modified or ignored by his ostensible followers when it conflicts with their fundamental intentions. And Camus declares that in fact a basic premise of Marx's thought does justify the totalitarians as his heirs. For Marx the single overriding value is absolute justice, and this can be realized only in the classless society—which would come into existence only at the conclusion of violent and bitter class warfare. One does not become overly concerned about the morality of one's tactics when engaged in mortal combat; the end of the classless society justifies any means necessary to its attainment.

Camus indicates that Marxian socialism has become a religion of history—a faith with an immanent *parousia* and a provisional ethic consisting of nothing but the doctrine of success in its most unvarnished form. The victory of Bolshevism in Russia gave the Marxists their opportunity, and Lenin represents a crucial turning-point. In his writings and his active leadership during the formative years of the Soviet Union he showed an overriding concern for the attainment of goals. Forced by circumstances to be more practical than Marx, he formulated the conception of an elite guard of dedicated professional revolutionaries, who would plan the insurrection and govern thereafter—as long as necessary—as representatives of the true will of the proletariat. The result has been governance by a self-perpetuating oligarchy or a dictator—the authority theoretically charged with the obligation to determine what means are most efficacious under given conditions for the final realization of revolutionary aspirations. These rulers have not hesitated to avail themselves of such techniques as mass murder and systematic injustice, perpetrated in the name of justice and humanity.

In contrast to this "rational" or ultimate goal-directed terror of the historically actualized Marxian state, Camus discusses the "irrational" terrorism of the fascist (including German National Socialist) state, indicating however that the two types of totalitarianism spring from the same philosophic and spiritual roots. German Nazism was a horrendous vulgarization of certain ideas of Hegel and Nietzsche, but despite (or perhaps because of) its philosophic degeneracy, it was none the less deadly in effecting the premise that the death of God and the impossibility of transcendent values mean in practice that might makes right. Hitler and Mussolini were the first to build "a State on the idea that nothing has meaning and that history is nothing but chance and force." [21]

The fascists did not attempt to escape nihilism by positing an absolute and rational end to history as had Marx, but as in communist theory and practice, so for the fascists, any means is justified, because "the success of an action is set up as an absolute goal." [22] Therefore terrorism and force came to be the accepted modes for achieving any particular end in the fascist states; the application of these means was not justified by any ultimate goal, hence was more "irrational" than the program of communist totalitarianism. Action, force, strength, militancy—these were the genuinely meaningful facts of history from the fascist perspective. Camus believed that this form of totalitarianism also represents a betrayal of man's rebellion. Both the true rebel and the nihilist have been overwhelmed by their experience of the world's injustice and absurdity, but the faithful rebel has continued to struggle against these forces, whereas the nihilistic fascists cooperate with them.

To recapitulate Camus' view of the roots and essential nature of totalitarianism: this diabolical form of society, whether "rational" or "irrational," has come to exist because of the failure of men to be true to their rebellion against absurdity and injustice. In his initial experience of revolt the rebel senses values common to man *qua* man. The primary datum given in this experience is an intuitive awareness of human solidarity—"I rebel, therefore we are." From this knowledge ought to spring a profound respect for the dignity of all individuals, with whom the rebel shares a common fate. All abstract and futurized ideals must be subordinated to a concern for concrete and immediate human needs, to the struggle against present injustice and oppression. Man in his rebellion against an unjust sovereign God should not invest himself with an illusory pseudo-divinity. To be true to himself and to his fellows man must remain fully human, taking into account the limitations placed upon his vision and efforts by finitude and ignorance, employing none but just and humanitarian means in his in-

[21] *L'Homme révolté*, p. 222.
[22] "Le socialisme mystifié," *Actuelles*, p. 150.

cessant struggle against present evil. Camus finds totalitarian "revolutions" intolerable on the basis of values which continually oriented his thought: happiness as man's highest good, fidelity to the earth and to concrete persons, and rebellion in the name of life and happiness against death and its cohorts.

REBELLION AND POLITICAL MODESTY

As a champion of threatened human values, Camus did not give as high a priority to the elaboration of his political aspirations as to his denunciations of the forces which he feared might obliterate all possibility of a sanely human society. Thus much of what might be termed his political "prescription" consists simply of admonitions to rebel against particular forces of inhumanity. The basic political values that he espoused were rather clearly delineated in his various writings (most of an *ad hoc* nature), but his ideas for incorporating these values into political structures were set forth, on the whole, in general and nebulous terms.

Camus' trenchant critique of totalitarianism does not mean that he was perfectly content with contemporary non-totalitarian society. In fact he consistently attacked the social and economic injustices, conformism, and sterile ideologies of bourgeois society. At the heart of Camus' dissatisfaction with his own society was rebellion against what he considered to be the ultimate injustice—the death penalty. As one who loved and affirmed life and its joys as man's highest good, Camus was implacably opposed to man's taking the side of death. One of the few political "causes" with which he persistently identified himself was the abolition of capital punishment, and he directed his keen intelligence and moral vigor to a rigorous analysis and condemnation of the death penalty as maintained in France.[23]

Camus employs many telling arguments in his demonstration of the evils of the guillotine. But from the explicit perspective of his own presuppositions, Camus' principal objection to the death penalty is its totality and irreparability. No one is wise or good enough to be justified in making ultimate claims upon the lives of others. Society, which claims the right to administer the death penalty to murderers, must itself assume much of the responsibility for their crimes. Camus clearly recognizes that individuals must be held responsible for their acts if social cohesion is to be maintained at all. But the influences of environment make it impossible for anyone to be totally responsible for what he does, and total punishment cannot be justified: "The

[23] See "Réflexions sur la guillotine," Albert Camus and Arthur Koestler, *Réflexions sur la peine capitale* (Paris: Calmann-Lévy, 1957).

death penalty, which is satisfactory neither as an example nor as an instrument of distributive justice, usurps in addition an exorbitant privilege in claiming the right to punish a guilt that is always relative with a definitive and irreparable punishment." [24]

Camus argues that justice must become modest if it is to be effectively just. The very finality of total punishment constitutes a pretension to omnipotence on the part of society; there is no assurance that those who are executed are the unredeemable or even the guilty—"justice" has been know to err. Punishment as such should not be abolished but only irreparable punishment; its ultimacy is unfitting to man, a finite and imperfect creature. Sparing a murderer's life makes it at least possible for the most hideous criminal to do some good which may partially offset the evil for which he is responsible. Capital punishment is simply inconsonant with the human condition as Camus envisions it: "Capital judgment breaks up the only undeniable human solidarity, solidarity against death. . . ." [25]

A basic reason, Camus believes, that capital punishment is retained is that political society itself has been inflated to become the end and purpose of human existence, that its conservation and historical success have become overriding values. The state has become the most pretentious of murderers—actually in certain countries and potentially in all that retain the death penalty. No longer is it men's primary need that society defend itself against uncooperative individuals; rather individuals must now ward off the secularized religious claims of the state: "How can mid-century European society survive without deciding to defend persons, in every way possible, against statist oppression? To prohibit putting men to death would be to proclaim publicly that society and the State are not absolute values, to decree that nothing authorizes them to legislate definitely or to produce the irreparable." [26] The abolition of the death penalty should be the first article in the legal code of a United Europe. This provision would be the first—and most important—step toward a moderate, rational, and genuinely human society.

Camus' opposition to capital punishment was clearly derived from his rebellion against the forces of death. He did not believe that men are justified in shattering intentionally the complicity that exists among them by virtue of their sharing a common fate. The simple existence of physical life was in his view unquestionably good; in fact it is the ultimate of human knowledge and experience. He found himself highly critical of his own society as well as totalitarian ones, because they share a common pretension to a degree of wisdom and virtue sufficient to justify the negation of human life. Camus believed that

[24] *Ibid.*, p. 158.   [25] *Ibid.*, p. 169.   [26] *Ibid.*, p. 175.

the first requirement of a society which will cease to create despair in men's hearts is to restrict justice to the modesty and earthly character which epitomize the true rebel—the man who is fully aware of and responsive to the limitations and potentialities of the human condition.

At the heart of Camus' constructive political thought is not a program or a doctrine, but certain values, and above all a spirit of "measure"—a determination to remain faithful to the limits of human nature. The rebel realizes that a quest for total justice inevitably debases men and altogether negates justice. But as a combatant against unhappiness and oppression the rebel cannot resign himself simply to ignoring and living with the injustices of society. The true rebel undertakes the difficult task of finding a middle way between amoral revolutionism and passively immoral quietism. He remains acutely aware that as a finite being located within the historical process he cannot transcend its fluxes and relativities so as to comprehend its total meaning and thereby be justified in attempting to force his fellows into the mold of a universal pattern. Man's enterprises are at best calculated risks, for even the best of intentions are sometimes betrayed into the commission of gross injustice.

Political action that truly seeks to realize a greater degree of justice for men in history will be true to the human condition and to the limitations of history if it proceeds in a spirit of consent to relativity, if it seeks only proximate ends. Camus in effect desires a transvaluation of historicist (Marxist or nihilist) values: "The end justifies the means? Possibly. But what justifies the end? To this question, which historical thought leaves hanging, revolt replies: the means." [27] Although the rebel seeks to make society more nearly just by working for human happiness, these ends cannot be attained through the use of means which utilize injustice and increase men's unhappiness.

His values and approach led Camus to the espousal of liberal democracy as the most desirable form of government. He believed that within his experience of revolt the rebel catches a glimpse of human solidarity in a complicity against death and will therefore seek to nurture this complicity by keeping open the channels of communication between human beings. This makes the liberal democratic value of free speech extremely significant, for it alone enables men to realize their common destiny and engage in mutual effort in accordance with their essential solidarity. Camus called for the creation and maintenance of a *civilisation du dialogue,* in which each man would be free to express his views in the common struggle against the injustice of man's lot. But the building of this civilization can only be

---

[27] *L'Homme révolté,* p. 361.

gradual and painstaking; every democratic freedom realized in practice thus far must be protected to prevent recurrent attacks upon human dignity in the name of absolute justice.

Camus purported to derive from the passionate experience of rebellion such values as empiricism and modesty in politics, the relativity of ends and the inviolability of means, as he sought to bridge the gap between the European revolutionary tradition of the past two centuries (epitomized for him by Marx and Nietzsche) and parliamentary democracy which operates on the common-sense level, such as (proverbially at least) that of Great Britain. Camus was both opposed to political messianisms and distrustful of a bourgeois order which he believed showed little concern for the advancement of authentic social justice.

CONCLUSION

Albert Camus' contribution to political understanding consists in large part of his quite individual attempt to interpret the origins of totalitarianism. He approached this extremely involved historical and theoretical problem from the perspective of a sensitive and philosophically knowledgeable literary artist, seeking to communicate to intelligent and morally concerned persons the meaning and potentialities —for good and for evil—of the European revolutionary tradition.

Camus' emphasis on the ideological roots of totalitarian society is scarcely unique, but his approach is highly personal and reveals something of the nature of the individual and social tensions that characterize the life of "post-Christian man." For Camus contends that rebellion by rationalists, romanticists, and moralists against the Christian tradition has been the crucial shaping force in the development of a philosophical and literary climate in which communist and fascist ideas could emerge.[28] But unlike theorists such as Jacques Maritain and Emil Brunner, Camus does not regret the rebellion against God but concurs in it, seeking only to limit its claims and objectives wholly to the sphere of human knowledge and action. Thus he rejects both the trans-historical messianism of communism and fascistic nihilism as creators of new gods to oppress mankind.

---

[28] Cf. Carl J. Friedrich and Zbigniew K. Brzezinski, *Totalitarian Dictatorship and Autocracy* (Cambridge: Harvard University Press, 1956), pp. 87–88: ". . . in spite of these sharp conflicts between totalitarian ideologies on one hand and the Christian and Democratic heritage on the other, it is only within the context of this heritage that the ideologies can be fully understood. . . . There is . . . a style of living involved that calls for transcendent explanations of what is right. When the theological explanations become untenable as a result of the decline of religious faith, these 'secular religions' then fill the vacuum."

Camus, in his personal rebellion against injustice and death, hovered at times on the fringes of contemporary revolutionary movements. His preoccupation with the absurdity of life clearly marked him, in his earlier years, as a potential nihilist. And for a brief period during his youth he was a member of the Algerian Communist party —but commenting on this experience he said, "If I was once a communist, I have never been a Marxist." [29]

Not only do Camus' personal history and tortuously constructed philosophical viewpoint make for a note of peculiar authenticity in his treatment of totalitarian ideology, but his widespread literary interests bring to the attention of political theorists and historians of ideas the illustrative significance of such artists as the Marquis de Sade, Lautréamont, Dostoevski, and Rimbaud, as publicists of blasphemous rebellion and/or nihilism—creators, in part, of the moral vacuum in which new messianisms could flourish.

In addition to his broad-ranging approach to crucial questions of political development, Camus presented certain quite specific critiques and proposals, for example in his essay opposing capital punishment. In that instance he produced one of the most logical, trenchant, and convincing contributions to the steadily growing controversy surrounding the death penalty. This brief work illustrates his great talent and sensitivity as a social and political moralist, and in particular it points up the relevance to non-totalitarian societies of his denial of the validity of totality as a category for political thought and action.

As repeatedly pointed out in this article, Camus bases his denial of totality, and in fact almost the entirety of both his critical and constructive political thought, on the notion of rebellion against absurdity, injustice, and death. The question which must be asked is whether values may be validly derived from this phenomenon of experience. Rebellion—because it is primarily existential, not conceptual in nature—is an ambiguous term in Camus' writings. But he clearly sought to extend its significance beyond the individual's experience to make of it a social imperative, in order that nihilism might be transcended.

However, in attempting to vindicate rebellion as the source of knowledge of the commonness of human nature and of genuinely humane values, Camus seemed in fact to postulate an unempirical kind of "pure" revolt; in effect he implicitly affirmed certain standards prior to revolt itself by which rebellion and the acts in which it results are to be evaluated. Despite Camus' contention to the contrary, rebellion alone cannot furnish us with values—the rebel acts for the

[29] Quoted by Pierre Aubery, "Albert Camus et la classe ouvrière," *French Review*, XXXIII (October 1958), 20.

sake of pre-existent norms, though they may be implicit rather than overtly acknowledged. Even Camus' youthful rebellion against mortality was motivated by the love of life and joy in nature that he knew and treasured as the good prior to the poignant moment of metaphysical revolt he experienced in Florence. A particularly discerning critic points up the shakiness of Camus' position:

> Certainly, as Camus thinks, all revolt entails a value, but actually values of different kinds: pleasure, excitement, freedom, etc. By choosing the master-slave relationship as the prototype of revolt, Camus can indirectly call upon a long tradition which does not find the justification of revolt in the act itself but in principles of another order which precede it. . . . Camus minimizes the role of egoism in revolt. If revolt, however, is conceived in all its variety, egoism, with its companion miscalculation, is often at the root of it. The purity of revolt is a fiction.[30]

But although Camus' method may not be entirely faithful to the canons of logic—or indeed to empirical reality—he believed that he had succeeded in authenticating certain basic values by building upon the sole foundation of personal experience. And despite the philosophic weaknesses of his approach, his political legacy includes a compelling and relevant justification of liberal democracy, a proximate perspective on political justice, and a quietly authoritative defense of concrete persons against the de-humanizing effects of totalitarian ideology and practice. He sought to demonstrate to his compatriots that their revolutionary tradition has been partially responsible for the betrayal of man in the contemporary world but that it contains resources which, if combined with their own instinctive rebellion against inhumanity, can lead modern Europe to the construction of a civilization in which human nature will be cultivated rather than controlled.

[30] Kermit Lansner, "Albert Camus," *Kenyon Review*, XIV (Autumn 1952), 575.

18/ Jean-Paul Sartre: French Existentialism and Politics— The New Revolutionary

MARJORIE GRENE

. . . In looking at the political theory of French existentialism, one is continually faced with the question. . . . *How,* in this highly individualistic theory of human nature, does the liberty of one involve the liberty of all? Or, in the light of our examination of *L'Être et le néant,* how does one reconcile a principle of the mutual respect of free beings for one another's freedom with the principle that each man's freedom reciprocally implies the repression of every other?

Quite apart from logic and philosophy, the first answer to that question is a historical one. French existentialism did not begin with the Resistance. Sartre's pre-war publications, like *Le Mur* and the *Esquisse d'une théorie des émotions,* differ in no fundamental way from the later developments of his theory. But existentialism as a popular movement in French philosophy and, in particular, existentialism as a political philosophy did grow into their present prominence out of the peculiar stresses of the Occupation and the peculiar pattern of life —that is, of torture and death—in the Underground. That pattern illuminated, more dramatically and more insistently and on a national scale, what the inner self-torment of a Kierkegaard had revealed a century earlier: the utter loneliness of each of us in moral crisis and the essential union, almost the identity, of that loneliness and the freedom that we find in it. Man makes himself, but only in secrecy and solitude—publicity is betrayal or illusion. This contrast, in the Occupation, takes the extremer shape of paradox: the more oppressed we are externally, the freer we can be in our own decisions, in our single lives. . . .

Whatever one may think of the theoretical correctness of the existentialists' view of the individual and of its consistency or otherwise with their political philosophy, one must qualify such criticism . . . by conceding that those of us who have not known the daily threat of

SOURCE: Marjorie Grene, *Introduction to Existentialism* (Chicago: The University of Chicago Press, 1968), pp. 96, 98–101, 110–119. Copyright 1948,© 1959 by The University of Chicago. Reprinted by permission of the author and the publisher. This book was first published under the title *Dreadful Freedom.*

death or torture have ultimately no right to speak against it. "It is characteristic of the French," Edmund Wilson wrote in his otherwise excellent review of Sartre in the *New Yorker*,[1] "that the destruction of French institutions should have seemed to them a catastrophe as complete as the Flood and caused them to evolve a philosophy which assumes that the predicament of the patriotic Frenchman oppressed by the German occupation represented the situation of all mankind." Perhaps so; it may be that French existentialism more than other philosophies expands a unique situation into a universal theory. But Wilson would scarcely be the last to admit that something similar is true of philosophers generally, as it is of artists, and that for each philosophy the unique experience from which the resultant system has grown as much confirms as invalidates the theory itself. And in this case our fortunate ignorance of the situation must make us, at any rate, hesitant in our judgment of the consequent theory. Perhaps it was unique only in the sense of historical accident; perhaps it was unique, rather, as the existentialists believe, in its revelation of the very limits of human liberty. Thucydides, too, saw the effect of one war on one people and saw in it the situation of all mankind; that is, at least, good precedent for the existentialists' procedure.

What makes the Resistance most significant for the politics of the French school, however, is not simply the secret, yet dramatic, loneliness of each Underground worker, but the conjunction of solitude with solidarity in this invisible army. In the Resistance it was true, undeniably, that each man, deciding alone and of himself, did decide for all. . . .

Like the experience of liberty in enslavement, the experience of "total responsibility in total solitude" is here undeniably genuine. In the resistance the freedom of one *did* involve, immediately and heroically, the freedom of many. It was as himself *and* as a Frenchman that each man had to ask, "If they torture me, shall I be able to keep silent?"—just as, conversely, it was himself as much as France that each collaborator betrayed. But it is here, too, that the theoretical question becomes insistent. The situation of the Resistance, in which each man does indeed decide for everyone, was made a consistent whole by the dramatic force of its actual existence. But when this situation is elevated to the status of an abstract system, what link is there to bind, theoretically, the solitude with the responsibility, the one with the all? The picture of the individual vis-à-vis his torturer remains as the human, historical foundation of Sartre's theory of the relation to another as conflict. But what conception of community, country, or humanity provides, in existential theory, the logical equiv-

[1] Edmund Wilson, "Jean-Paul Sartre, the Novelist and the Existentialist," *New Yorker*, August 2, 1947, p. 61.

alent for the other side of the Resistant's solitary and dangerous decision?

The problem of connecting logically, the private and public aspects of existentialism becomes acute . . . if we look at its supporters' explicit statements of political and social theory. The *locus classicus* for this theory, at present writing, is Sartre's pair of articles on materialism and revolution in *Les Temps modernes*.[2] The first essay considers a series of contradictions in materialism, notably, in dialectical materialism, the contradiction, as Sartre sees it, between the unique concrete wholes envisaged by dialectic and the abstract, quantitative relations with which scientific materialism is bound to deal. So, for example, Engels is incorrect, he says, in his assertion that physics moves from quantitative to qualitative concepts: it moves only from quantity to quantity. Even Einsteinian physics deals wholly in external and quantitative relationships; and, what is most essential, even Einsteinian physics, like all science, deals with the abstract conditions of the universe in general, not, like dialectic, with the growth of a living concrete totality. Sartre admits freely the usefulness, for revolutionary purposes, of the materialist myth—or at least its usefulness in the past. Yet both as philosopher and as revolutionary he questions the long-term efficacy of such a "monster" and proceeds, in the second essay, to construct an alternative theory of revolution with, in his view, a sounder, nonmaterialistic basis.

The revolutionary, according to Sartre, must be oppressed, but essentially oppressed, that is, oppressed in such a way that only a radical change in the structure of the society can relieve his oppression:

> What the American Negroes and the bourgeois Jews want is an equality of rights, which does not in any way imply a change of structure in the regime of property; they simply want to be assimilated to the privileges of their oppressors, that is, at bottom they seek a more complete integration.
>
> The revolutionary is in a situation such that he can in no way share those privileges; it is by the destruction of the class that is oppressing him that he can obtain what he demands. That means that the oppression is not, like that of the Jews or Negroes, considered as a secondary and, as it were, lateral characteristic of the social regime but that it is, on the contrary, constitutive. The revolutionary is, then, at once a victim of oppression and a keystone of the society which oppresses him; more precisely, it is in so far as he is oppressed that he is indispensable to that society.[3]

[2] Sartre, "Matérialisme et révolution," *Les Temps modernes*, I, Nos. 9 and 10 (June and July, 1946). Selections from these two essays also appeared in translation in the July–August, 1947, *Politics*.

[3] *Les Temps modernes*, No. 10, p. 2.

That means, secondly, that he is a worker: it is those who "work for the ruling class" who are indispensable to the society in their very oppression. Such is his situation; the third characteristic of the man, according to Sartre, is that he goes beyond his situation—*il la dépasse* —toward a radically different situation, which it is his aim to create. A philosophy of revolution, then, will be a philosophy "in situation" but also a program of action beyond that situation. In particular, it will substitute a new conception of value for that of the ruling class; and, since this ruling class founds its domination on its conception of the rights of man, that is of the divine right of the bourgeois ruler to oppress the proletarian worker, it will be not an assertion of rights but a denial of them. Hence, presumably, the appeal of materialism, since it substitutes a natural conception of the human species for the bourgeois pretense of human dignity, which is only the dignity of ruler-person against worker-thing. But, by so doing, it negates all values, whereas what the revolutionary seeks is a new conception of values, one which goes beyond the present situation, which envisages goods to be created in revolution rather than imposed by reaction.

To describe adequately the revolutionary attitude, then, Sartre says, four points are needed:

> (1) that man is unjustifiable, that his existence is contingent in that neither he nor any Providence has produced it; (2) as a consequence, that every collective order established by men can be transcended [*dépassé*] in the direction of other orders; (3) that the system of values current in a society reflects the structure of that society and tends to preserve it; (4) that it can, therefore, always be transcended toward other systems, which are not clearly perceived because the society which they express does not yet exist but which are anticipated and, in one word, invented by the very effort of the members of the society to transcend it.[4]

These points, he continues, neither materialism nor idealism provide. Materialism with its rigid causality leaves no room for freedom—and the transcendence of one value-situation toward another, which is essential to the revolutionary, *is* freedom: "This possibility of moving away from a situation [*décoller*] to take a point of view on it (point of view which is not pure knowledge but indissolubly understanding and action)—this is precisely what we call 'freedom.' "[5] Idealism does no better, he believes, since, while recognizing subjectivity, it fails to acknowledge, what is equally important, the hardness of fact —the stubbornly existent obstacles which the revolutionary, in his very freedom, has set himself to overcome. Moreover, idealism is, for Sartre as clearly as for the orthodox Marxist, merely the attempt of

[4] *Ibid.*, p. 12.   [5] *Ibid.*, p. 13.

the ruling class to cloak its self-interest in grand phrases. The correct account is one different from either of these:

> A being contingent, unjustifiable, but free, completely plunged into a society which oppresses him but capable of transcending that society by his efforts to change it, that is what the revolutionary man claims to be. Idealism mystifies him in that it binds him with its already given rights and values; it masks his power of inventing his own paths. But materialism also mystifies him, by robbing him of his freedom. The revolutionary philosophy must be a philosophy of transcendence [*une philosophie de la transcendence*].[6]

So the revolutionary philosophy turns out to be the philosophy of freedom—not just the philosophy of those who seek freedom but the philosophy of the very free act itself, the philosophy of transcendence; that is, though Sartre does not here call it so, it turns out to be existentialism. And what is more, as *the* philosophy of freedom, it turns out, according to Sartre, to be *the* philosophy of man in general. It starts, indeed, in one class, that of the workers—but a bourgeois doubtful of his own class values may come to accept it; and, besides, it seeks, despite the probable need of bloodshed, not so much to destroy the ruling class as to join workers and former rulers in a community of men, to make them equally free. So it is not, like either materialism or idealism, a myth used by one faction or another but a statement of the nature and action of the free man as such: the revolutionary, by his very choice of revolution, becomes "the man who wishes that man freely and totally assume his destiny." [7]

Such, in brief outline, is Sartre's philosophy of revolution. There is, of course, an obvious plausibility in the equation of the free act with the revolutionary act—there is a striking parallel, if not a logical equivalence, between the existential concept of transcendence, of choice in, but beyond, a concrete situation, and the revolutionary's transcendence of his social and political situation in his very grasp of it. But, despite the striking rightness of some of Sartre's incidental observations . . . , the theory as a whole has a certain artificiality about it: it is, again, somehow too logical in the wrong places. The philosopher's love of a neat logical construct has several times led to a failure of Sartre the artist: as in *The Flies*, which is topheavy with existential theory, or even in *The Unburied Dead*, where the possible variants on the genuinely moving theme of death and torture are so exhaustively and conscientiously explored that the result is something

---

[6] *Ibid.*, pp. 13–14. I have translated *dépasser* by "transcend." The French term *transcendence* occurs only in the final phrase "philosophy of transcendence."
[7] *Ibid.*, p. 30.

more like a psychologist's card-index than a tragedy.[8] But here it is the philosopher himself who is guilty of too much neatness with too little reality or, in the jargon of the trade, too much coherence with too little adequacy.

This is apparent at several points. In the first place, one is likely to ask one's self, as Sartre himself asks of the Communist: What of the revolutionary after the revolution? The philosophy of the free man in its political aspect is the philosophy of transcendence as such, of going beyond the present society to create a new one. At present, in Sartre's picture, it is the dichotomy of oppressor and oppressed that motivates such transcendence. But what of the free man in the free society? If he is still free, he still transcends his situation to a new one; he is still, by definition, a revolutionary, but against what? Against freedom itself? That is absurd. The reply might be, I suppose, that revolutionary philosophy is, as Sartre says, "in situation": it is thought *now* directed to a currently pressing and significant end. But Sartre has insisted, against the Communists, that a *philosophy* of revolution must be at once immediately practical and universally true; otherwise it is not a philosophy but a mere myth, a myth which may by its falsity ultimately stifle revolution itself. Sartre's philosophy, by contrast, must be not a lie however noble, but *the* truth of *la condition humaine*. In that case one is bound to try at any rate to envisage his free man in settings beyond the present one, to imagine him *in* the future that alone gives substance and significance to his freedom. And there one can see him only as a lost revolutionary: as one who *has* created by his free act the society embodying, as far as a society can, the values in which he has chosen to believe, yet whose very nature as free demands that he once more deny *these* values in his transcendence, that he go beyond the very liberty for which he has lived his life and risked his death to something beyond liberty itself—and beyond that again, and so forever. In endless regress as such there is no contradiction, but there is in this one; for here revolution for free-

---

[8] Cf. Edmund Wilson's comparison of Sartre with Steinbeck in the review already quoted (p. 58): "Like Steinbeck, Sartre is a writer of undeniably exceptional gifts: on the one hand, a fluent inventor, who can always make something interesting happen, and, on the other, a serious student of life, with a good deal of spirit. Yet he somehow does not seem quite first-rate. A play of Sartre's, for example, such as his recent 'The Unburied Dead'—which is, I suppose, his best play—affects me rather like 'The Grapes of Wrath.' Here he has exploited with both cleverness and conviction the ordeal of the French Resistance, as Steinbeck has done that of the sharecroppers; but what you get are a virtuosity of realism and a rhetoric of moral passion which make you feel not merely that the fiction is a dramatic heightening of life but that the literary fantasy takes place on a plane which does not have any real connection with the actual human experience which it is pretending to represent."

dom implies revolution against freedom. And back of that logical impasse there is a hint at least of a much profounder difficulty in existential theory—liberty as such, in its bare logical essence, does not appear an adequate replacement for more substantive conceptions of value.

In the description of the present, prerevolutionary situation, moreover, there are, for the American reader at least, equally disquieting limitations. Sartre's sketch of the oppressed worker's situation is an account of a capitalist society in which an acute and well-defined class-consciousness is much more highly developed than it is with us. *If* one is already a Marxist and has already interpreted the legend of American democracy in terms of its economic origins, one can satisfactorily explain the lack of a stable class-consciousness out of those same economic conditions—and proceed to try to create one. But Sartre's description is, presumably, not deduced from any theory; and, as a straightforward "phenomenological" account, it simply does not fit our case. The *fact* of oppression and exploitation exists, of course—it is probably just about as hard for a West Virginia miner's son to grow up to anything but the mines—where he works hard and dangerously for other men's profits—as it is for Sartre's French laborer to be anything but the victim of exploitation that his father was before him. But if the American worker sometimes feels himself cheated, it is only because, as Sartre says of the Forty-eighters, he wants particular conditions bettered within the society: here, however—and this is the important point—not because he accepts oppression but because he cannot seriously conceive of himself as oppressed at all; because he feels that by some absurd accident he has been, for the moment, deprived of the privilege which must and shall accrue to *all* Americans—the right to possess, to raise further and further the famous standard of living that distinguishes us among the peoples of the earth. Sartre is probably quite right in saying, in his editorial on America, that the American myth is not so much lived by as lived under, that every American tries constantly, with an odd insecurity, to re-win and reassert its efficacy for himself. Yet, despite this relation of distance between the people and their faith, it is still, for most of them, the only faith they know or can imagine; and for such a faith (as several contributors to *Temps modernes's* United States issue have stressed) a rigid division of classes, clearly recognizable from both sides of the cleavage, can hardly be said to exist. Here, it seems to me, much more than in the relation of his thought to the French Resistance, Sartre has indeed tried to build a general theory upon a situation whose geographical and historical limits seriously impair its universal validity.

These are both disturbing limitations in the Sartrean theory; but

there is a more serious and more sweeping objection, which we anticipated at the outset of this chapter. Sartre's political theory and his
analysis of the individual, using as they do the same central concepts
—situation, freedom, transcendence—form an interesting pair of parallels. Is there, or is there needed, any bridge, any logical connection,
between the two, or can the parallelism stand as such? That there is
need for such a connection can, I suppose, hardly be questioned; for
any theory of the state and society, no matter how wide its field of
reference, rests ultimately on and follows from some theory of the nature of the individual, if only on a denial that there *is* an individual.
That Sartre tries, in his own case, to make such a connection is also
clear; and it is, I am afraid, equally evident that he fails to make it
with cogency or conviction.

The crux of the matter lies in the concept of *solidarity*. The revolutionary must be distinguished from the rebel. He does not seek liberation for himself alone, for that would involve only absorption into the
ruling class. He seeks it for his whole class, even, at last, for all mankind. In his description of class-consciousness in *L'Être et le néant*
Sartre has represented the oppressed group as united, indirectly, for
such joint action, by their awareness of the oppressor as onlooker.[9]
Directly, however, they are still bound by the ties of conflict only,
which alone forms the dynamic of one individual's relation to another, whether within or beyond his class. The conception of the oppressor as onlooker and therefore as destroyer of subjectivity is likewise involved, in part, in the *Temps modernes* essays. But there are
at least strong hints that this alone is not enough: that something
more than an indirect *nous-objet* is needed *within* the oppressed class
itself if one is to achieve solidarity rather than anarchy, a common
revolution for freedom rather than the sporadic rebellion of the individual against his individual tyrant. Look at two passages in the second essay:

> We have seen . . . that the revolutionary act is the free act *par
> excellence*. Not at all of an anarchist and individualist freedom; in that
> case, as a matter of fact, the revolutionary, by his very situation, could
> only claim more or less explicitly the rights of the privileged class, that
> is, his integration to the higher social strata. But since he claims at the
> heart of the oppressed class and for all the oppressed class a more ra-
> tional social status, his freedom resides in the act by which he de-
> mands the liberation of all his class and, more generally, of all men. It
> is, at its source, recognition of other liberties, and it demands to be
> recognized by them. Thus it places itself from the beginning on the
> plane of solidarity.[10]

[9] See p. 91.   [10] Sartre, "Matérialisme et révolution" (second half), p. 26.

This is, at first sight, a clear and logical statement of the revolutionary position; but its Achilles' heel appears in the sentence: "It is, at its source, recognition of other liberties, and it demands to be recognized by them." Whence this recognition of other "liberties"? From where in the circle of conflicts can it spring? The threat of the oppressor and the stand of the oppressed against him one can see as a variant on the basic pattern of the subject-object conflict. But a tie of mutual recognition, first among the oppressed and ultimately among all mankind—that one finds one's self, within the framework of Sartre's existentialism, unable to conceive. Within that framework, as Sartre himself has said, "respect for another's freedom is an empty phrase" (*le respect de la liberté d'autrui est un vain mot*).[11]

The second passage is, if anything, more weasel-worded:

> A revolutionary philosophy must take account of the plurality of liberties and show how each one, even while being liberty for itself, can be object for the other. It is only this double character of freedom and objectivity that can explain the complex notions of oppression, of struggle, of frustration, and of violence. For one never oppresses but one freedom; but one cannot oppress it unless, in some respect, it lends itself, that is, unless, for the Other, it presents the exterior of a thing. Thus one will understand the revolutionary movement and its project, which is to make society pass by violence from a state wherein liberties are alienated to another state founded on their reciprocal recognition.[12]

Here we have the explicit statement of the oppressor-oppressed/subject-object equation. It is in terms of conflict and, as far as one can see, conflict only that the revolutionary recognizes the "plurality of liberties." But suddenly out of this grim picture "one understands the revolutionary movement and its project, which is to make society pass by violence from a state wherein liberties are alienated to another state founded on their reciprocal recognition." From what human situation, from what new and marvelous source in the depths of a subjectivity otherwise so lonely, so closely and so constantly endangered, does this balm of reciprocal recognition flow? Without it the whole theory of revolution as *the* philosophy of human liberty, as man's call "to his total destiny," collapses into unreality. Yet in the existential view of the individual there is no place for such recognition and therefore, one is bound to conclude, no foundation on which to build the political theory which Sartre himself has sketched.

[11] Sartre, *L'Être et le néant*, p. 480.
[12] Sartre, *Matérialisme et révolution* (second half), p. 28.

III/Civil
Disobedience and
Democracy

CIVIL DISOBEDIENCE
AND DEMOCRACY

> . . . where intelligent men of good will and
> character differ on large and complex moral is-
> sues, discussion and agitation are more appro-
> priate than civilly disobedient action.
>
> — SIDNEY HOOK

> I believe that there is a "natural right" of re-
> sistance . . . to use extralegal means if the
> legal ones have proved inadequate. Law and
> order are always and everywhere the law and
> order which protect the established hierarchy.
> It is nonsensical to invoke the absolute author-
> ity of this law and this order against those
> who suffer from it and struggle against it. . . .
> If they use violence, they do not start a new
> chain of violence, but they break an estab-
> lished one.
>
> —HERBERT MARCUSE

Frequently it is argued that civil
disobedience is not a justifiable political strategy for change in a
democratic society where civil rights and set procedures for change
exist. The democrat is asked to weigh carefully the "cumulative consequences" of his actions, lest his civilly disobedient acts encourage
general disorder and the destruction of established democratic procedures. In effect, this formulation raises the following question: Must
an individual member of a democratic society give up his right to
judge the wisdom and justice of public policy made in the name of
the majority?

In his article "Is It Ever Right to Break the Law?" one of America's
leading contemporary social philosophers, Charles Frankel, argues
that even in an ideal democracy those who practice civil disobedience perform a very important service. The civilly disobedient remind the majority that even those who obey the law have as much a
moral obligation to investigate the morality of their actions and the
justice of their society as do those who disobey. If this argument is
valid in the abstract, it is even more germane in a less-than-perfect
democracy where police may be hostile, elections rigged, courts

biased, and individuals otherwise politically powerless. Disobedience, in brief, can sometimes "shame a majority" into changing the status quo. Yet Frankel believes that disobedience is a grave enterprise to be justified only if provocation is intense, if basic moral principles are at stake, and if all legal methods of recourse have been exhausted.

American democratic thought is replete with discussions of the role of civil disobedience. Paul F. Power's article "On Civil Disobedience in Recent American Democratic Thought" not only ably summarizes the issues raised by these discussions but also focuses on the question, Is there any service that "carefully defined" civil disobedience might perform in democratic theory and practice? For Power, civil disobedience might serve as a buffer for civil rights and liberties and act as a check or a challenge to representative democracy. Like Frankel, he argues that disobedience also might function as an "educational strategy" that forces a society to reflect continually on the persistent questions of political obligation. Power's arguments are examined in the context of the positions of such contemporary social critics as Herbert Marcuse, Howard Zinn, Christian Bay, and David Spitz.

The questions of the legitimate scope of civil disobedience in American society and the relationship between disobedience and violence form one of the chief concerns of the Eisenhower Commission on the Causes and Prevention of Violence. The wide division of opinion reflected in the Commission's statement "Civil Disobedience" is testimony to the complexity of the issues involved. Opinions were so divided that the Commission was forced to present its report in three sections that came down on different sides of the issues. The seven conservative members of the Commission endorsed Section I, a short statement decrying "a climate of lawlessness" that they believed to be an "inevitable consequence" of widespread acts of civil disobedience in America. Chairman Milton Eisenhower and five other Commission members refused to endorse Section I, but joined the majority in support of the less categorical conclusions of Section II. This section asks the potential disobedient to reflect carefully on the probable short- and long-term consequences of his acts of disobedience, lest the hopes for a just society be extinguished in a wave of repression.

Several of the Commissioners who dissented from Section I also filed individual reports that comprise Section III. The most eloquent defense of nonviolent civil disobedience is embodied in the statement filed by Judge Higginbotham. Responding to the majority's attempt to link civil disobedience to lawlessness, Judge Higginbotham replies: "It is not non-violent civil disobedience which causes millions to go to bed ill-housed, ill-fed, and too often with too little hope." In this spirit, he calls for a rebirth of the political climate of the early 1960's when the country was beginning to face *its* obligations to blacks who had systematically been denied basic civil and human rights.

The pluralist theorists of democracy believe that political freedom can be measured by counting the available alternatives within a political system for individual political participation through group activity. Hence, they define a democratic political system as one in which a wide range of choice exists for the organized political consumer. Recently, the practice of political pluralism has come under attack on two grounds. First, critics argue that contemporary American "pluralist democracy" does not fulfill its theoretical promise to offer the rank-and-file citizen meaningful political choices. In addition, it is argued that political resources are unevenly distributed among the population, thus producing biased channels of access to the levers of political power that create and define political choices. In effect, recent critics have attacked democratic pluralism less for its normative or theoretical shortcomings than for its failure to live up to its promise of widespread citizen control of public policy leading to an open, responsive, and participatory political order.

Speaking in this context, Christian Bay recommends civil disobedience as an essential prerequisite for individual freedom and democratic control in a mass society. If we are to move toward an open democracy as against one dominated by elites concerned with preserving the status quo, Bay foresees the need for model citizens who behave less like Adolph Eichmann and more like Camus' rebel. Bay advocates a redefinition of the concept of "citizenship" away from a model extolling uncritical loyalty and docile legal obedience and toward a model of the conscientious citizen who feels personally responsible for the acts of his government.

19 / Is It Ever Right to Break the Law?

CHARLES FRANKEL

During recent months, public events have repeatedly dramatized an old and troublesome problem. A group of students defies the State Department's ban on travel to

SOURCE: *The New York Times Magazine* (Jan. 12, 1964). © 1964 by The New York Times Company. Reprinted by permission.

Cuba; a teachers' union threatens a strike even though a state law prohibits strikes by public employes; advocates of civil rights employ mass demonstrations of disobedience to the law to advance their cause; the Governor of a Southern state deliberately obstructs the enforcement of Federal laws, and declares himself thoroughly within his rights in doing so.

An observer can approve the motives that lead to some of these actions and disapprove others. All, nevertheless, raise the same fundamental question: Does the individual have the right—or perhaps the duty—to disobey the law when his mind, his conscience or his religious faith tells him that the law is unjust?

The question is as old as Socrates. It has regularly propelled men into radical examination of the premises of personal morality and civic obligation and, indeed, of government itself. And it is an interesting question not only for its philosophical implications but because it has always been a painfully practical question as well, and never more so than today.

Our period in history is frequently described as "materialistic" and "conformist," an age in which governments have enormous powers to crush the bodies and anesthetize the minds of their subjects, and in which the great masses of men and women—presumably in contrast with men and women of other times—prefer to play it safe rather than raise questions of basic moral principle. It is to the point to note, however, that massive resistance to law, justified in the name of higher moral principles like "freedom," "equality," and "national independence," has been a conspicuous feature of our period, and one of its most effective techniques of social action. Millions of ordinary people with no pretensions to being either heroes or saints have employed it in India, in South Africa, in the resistance movements against the Nazis, and in the struggle for equality for Negroes in the United States.

Moreover, such massive resistance to law is by no means confined only to supremely glorious or dangerous causes; nor is it used only by revolutionaries, underdogs, or outsiders. During Prohibition, a large number of respectable, conservative Americans dutifully broke the law in defense of what they regarded as an inalienable human right. In this case, doing one's duty happened also to be agreeable and even fashionable, but this does not change the fact that many right-thinking citizens, who today condemn pacifists or integrationists for using illegal methods to advance their cause, have themselves used such methods happily and unashamedly.

When is it justified for the citizen to act as his own legislator, and to decide that he will or will not obey a given law?

An answer that covers all the issues this question raises cannot be given here, nor can a set of principles be proposed that will allow anyone to make automatic and infallible judgments concerning the legitimacy or illegitimacy of specific acts of civil disobedience. Such judgments require detailed knowledge of the facts of specific cases, and such knowledge is often unavailable to the outsider. Nevertheless, it is possible to indicate some of the principal issues that are raised by civil disobedience, some of the more common mistakes that are made in thinking about these issues, and, at least in outline, the approach that one man would take toward such issues.

We can begin, it seems to me, by rejecting one extreme position. This is the view that disobedience to the law can never be justified in any circumstances. To take this position is to say one of two things: either every law that exists is a just law, or a greater wrong is always done by breaking the law. The first statement is plainly false. The second is highly doubtful. If it is true, then the signers of the Declaration of Independence, and those Germans who refused to carry out Hitler's orders, committed acts of injustice.

It is possible, however, to take a much more moderate and plausible version of this position, and many quite reasonable people do. Such people concede that disobedience to the law can sometimes be legitimate and necessary under a despotic regime. They argue, however, that civil disobedience can never be justified in a democratic society, because such a society provides its members with legal instruments for the redress of their grievances.

This is one of the standard arguments that is made, often quite sincerely, against the activities of people like supporters of the Congress of Racial Equality, who set about changing laws they find objectionable by dramatically breaking them. Such groups are often condemned for risking disorder and for spreading disrespect for the law when, so it is maintained, they could accomplish their goals a great deal more fairly and patriotically by staying within the law, and confining themselves to the courts and to methods of peaceful persuasion.

Now it is perfectly true, I believe, that there is a stronger case for obedience to the law, including bad law, in a democracy than in a dictatorship. The people who must abide by the law have presumably been consulted, and they have legal channels through which to express their protests and to work for reform. One way to define democracy is to say that it is a system whose aim is to provide alternatives to civil disobedience. Nevertheless, when applied to the kind of situation faced, say, by CORE, these generalizations, it seems to me, become cruelly abstract.

The basic fallacy in the proposition that, in a democracy, civil disobedience can never be justified, is that it confuses the *ideals* or *aims* of democracy with the inevitably less than perfect accomplishments of democracy at any given moment. In accordance with democratic ideals, the laws of a democracy may give rights and powers to individuals which, in theory, enable them to work legally for the elimination of injustices.

In actual fact, however, these rights and powers may be empty. The police may be hostile, the courts biased, the elections rigged— and the legal remedies available to the individual may be unavailing against these evils.

Worse still, the majority may have demonstrated, in a series of free and honest elections, that it is unwavering in its support of what the minority regards as an unspeakable evil. This is obviously the case today in many parts of the South, where the white majority is either opposed to desegregation or not so impatient to get on with it as is the Negro minority. Are we prepared to say that majorities never err? If not, there is no absolutely conclusive reason why we must invariably give the results of an election greater weight than considerations of elementary justice.

It is true, of course, that one swallow does not make a summer, and that the test of legal democratic processes is not this or that particular success or failure, but rather the general direction in which these processes move over the long run. Still, the position that violation of the law is never justifiable so long as there are legal alternatives overstates this important truth. It fails to face at least three important exceptions to it.

In the first place, dramatic disobedience to the law by a minority may be the only effective way of catching the attention or winning the support of the majority. Most classic cases of civil disobedience, from the early Christians to Gandhi and his supporters, exemplify this truth. Civil disobedience, like almost no other technique, can shame a majority and make it ask itself just how far it is willing to go, just how seriously it really is committed to defending the status quo.

Second, there is the simple but painful factor of time. If a man is holding you down on a bed of nails, it is all very well for a bystander to say that you live in a great country in which there are legal remedies for your condition, and that you ought, therefore, to be patient and wait for these remedies to take effect. But your willingness to listen to this counsel will depend, quite properly, on the nature of the injury you are suffering.

Third, it is baseless prejudice to assume that observance of the law is *always* conducive to strengthening a democratic system while disobedience to the law can never have a salutary effect. A majority's complacent acquiescence in bad laws can undermine the faith of a minority in the power of democratic methods to rectify manifest evils; yet a vigorous democracy depends on the existence of minorities holding just such a faith.

Disobedience to bad laws can sometimes jolt democratic processes into motion. Which strengthens one's hope for democracy more—the behavior of the Negroes in Birmingham who broke municipal ordinances when they staged their protest marches, or the behavior of the police, using dogs and fire hoses to assert their legal authority?

Another factor should also be taken into account. In our Federal system, there are often legitimate doubts concerning the legal validity, under our Constitution, of various state or local ordinances. Disobedience to these laws is in many cases simply a practical, though painful, way of testing their legality. But even where no thought of such a test is involved, there is often present a moral issue which no one can easily dodge—least of all the man whose personal dignity and self-respect are caught up in the issue.

A citizen caught in a conflict between local laws and what he thinks will be upheld as the superior Federal law can sometimes afford to wait until the courts have determined the issue for him. But often he cannot afford to wait, or must take a stand in order to force a decision. This is the situation of many Negro citizens in Southern states as they confront the conflict between local and Federal laws.

Yet there is another side to the story. It would be a mistake to conclude from what has been said that civil disobedience is justified, provided only that it is disobedience in the name of higher principles. Strong moral conviction is not all that is required to turn breaking the law into service to society.

Civil disobedience is not simply like other acts in which men stand up courageously for their principles. It involves violation of the law. And the law can make no provision for its violation except to hold the offender liable to punishment. This is why President Kennedy was in such a delicate position last spring at the time of the Negro demonstrations in Birmingham. He gave many signs that, as an individual, he was in sympathy with the goals of the demonstrators. As a political leader, he probably realized that these goals could not be attained without dramatic actions that crossed the line into illegality. But as Chief Executive he could not give permission or approval to such actions.

We may admire a man like Martin Luther King, who is prepared to defy the authorities in the name of a principle, and we may think that he is entirely in the right; just the same, his right to break the law cannot be officially recognized. No society, whether free or tyrannical, can give its citizens the right to break its laws: To ask it to do so is to ask it to proclaim, as a matter of law, that its laws are not laws.

In short, if anybody ever has a right to break the law, this cannot be a legal right under the law. It has to be a moral right against the law. And this moral right is not an unlimited right to disobey any law which one regards as unjust. It is a right that is hedged about, it seems to me, with important restrictions.

First of all, the exercise of this right is subject to standards of just and fair behavior. I may be correct, for example, in thinking that an ordinance against jaywalking is an unnecessary infringement of my rights. This does not make it reasonable, however, for me to organize a giant sit-down strike in the streets which holds up traffic for a week. Conformity to the concept of justice requires that there be some *proportion* between the importance of the end one desires to attain and the power of the means one employs to attain it.

When applied to civil disobedience, this principle constitutes a very large restriction. Civil disobedience is an effort to change the law by making it impossible to enforce the law, or by making the price of such enforcement extremely high. It is a case, as it were, of holding the legal system to ransom. It can arouse extreme passions on one side or the other, excite and provoke the unbalanced, and make disrespect for the law a commonplace and popular attitude.

Although violence may be no part of the intention of those who practice civil disobedience, the risks of violence are present, and are part of what must be taken into account when a program of civil disobedience is being contemplated.

In short, civil disobedience is a grave enterprise. It may sometimes be justified, but the provocation for it has to be equally grave. Basic principles have to be at issue. The evils being combated have to be serious evils that are likely to endure unless they are fought. There should be reasonable grounds to believe that legal methods of fighting them are likely to be insufficient by themselves.

Nor is this the only limitation on the individual's moral right to disobey the law. The most important limitation is that his cause must be a just one. It was right for General de Gaulle to disobey Marshal Pétain; it was wrong for the commanders of the French Army in Algeria, 20 years later, to disobey General de Gaulle.

Similarly, if it is absolutely necessary, and if the consequences have been properly weighed, then it is right to break the law in order to eliminate inequalities based on race. But it can never be necessary, and no weighing of consequences can ever make it right, to break the law in the name of Nazi principles.

In sum, the goals of those who disobey the law have to lie at the very heart of what we regard as morality before we can say that they have a moral right to do what they are doing.

But who is to make these difficult decisions? Who is to say that one man's moral principles are right and another man's wrong? We come here to the special function that civil disobedience serves in a society. The man who breaks the law on the ground that the law is immoral asks the rest of us, in effect, to trust him, or to trust those he trusts, in preference to the established conventions and authorities of our society.

He has taken a large and visible chance, and implicitly asked us to join him in taking that chance, on the probity of his personal moral judgment. In doing so, he has put it to us whether we are willing to take a similar chance on the probity of our own judgment.

Thomas Hobbes, who knew the trouble that rebels and dissenters convinced of their rectitude can cause, once remarked that a man may be convinced that God has commanded him to act as he has, but that God, after all, does not command other men to believe that this is so. The man who chooses to disobey the law on grounds of principle may be a saint, but he may also be a madman. He may be a courageous and lonely individualist, but he may also merely be taking orders and following his own crowd. Whatever he may be, however, his existence tends to make us painfully aware that we too are implicitly making choices, and must bear responsibility for the ones we make.

This, indeed, may be the most important function of those who practice civil disobedience. They remind us that the man who obeys the law has as much of an obligation to look into the morality of his acts and the rationality of his society as does the man who breaks the law. The occurrence of civil disobedience can never be a happy phenomenon; when it is justified, something is seriously wrong with the society in which it takes place.

But the man who puts his conscience above the law, though he may be right or he may be wrong, does take personal moral responsibility for the social arrangements under which he lives. And so he dramatizes the fascinating and fearful possibility that those who obey the law might do the same. They might obey the law and support what exists, not out of habit or fear, but because they have freely chosen to do so, and are prepared to live with their consciences after having made that choice.

20/On Civil Disobedience in Recent American Democratic Thought*

PAUL F. POWER

Theoretical discussions of civil disobedience on ethical and political grounds received special attention in this country during the Nuremberg trials, the security and loyalty controversies of the 1950's and the pre-arms control years of nuclear power. A fourth wave of interest formed after the early civil rights protests and a fifth is appearing to consider dissent from national policies on the Vietnam War. In this paper civil disobedience is viewed from a trough between the fourth and most recent wave. The phenomenon is interpreted with selected ideas from the study of political obligation [1] and unconventional dissent. The essay first assesses recent American analysis of civil disobedience to determine what the criteria should be to distinguish it from other forms of political action and to discover its political ethics. Secondly, there is an attempt to answer the question: Is there any appreciable service that carefully defined civil disobedience might perform in American democratic thought? The complete enterprise is provoked by a need to examine new strategies for democratic citizenship in a time when the deficien-

* Research for this project was supported by a summer faculty fellowship of the University of Cincinnati. I wish to thank John T. Bookman for helpful criticisms of an earlier version of my paper.

[1] Prominent commentary on political obligation was offered by Thomas Aquinas, Locke, Rousseau, and notably T. H. Green, who may have been the first to use the term. A study of Green's thought and environment is Melvin Richter, *The Politics of Conscience: T. H. Green and His Age* (Cambridge, Mass.: Harvard University Press, 1964). Reassessments include John R. Carnes, "Why Should I Obey the Law?," *Ethics*, 71 (1960), 14–26; Hanna Pitkin, "Obligation and Consent," *American Political Science Review*, 59 (1965), 990–1000, and 60 (1966), 39–52; John Plamenatz, *Consent, Freedom and Political Obligation*, 2nd ed. (New York: Oxford University Press, 1968); T. C. Pocklington, "Protest, Resistance, and Political Obligation," a paper presented at the 1969 Annual Meeting of the American Political Science Association, New York, September 3–6, 1969; and Joseph Tussman, *Political Obligation and the Body Politic* (New York: Oxford University Press, 1960).

SOURCE: *American Political Science Review*, LXIV (March 1970), 35–47. Reprinted by permission of the author and the publisher.

cies of American political life are becoming known to increasing numbers and varieties of people instead of remaining the preserve of enlightened elites.

CURRENTS OF THOUGHT

The rule-breaking aspect of "civil disobedience," a term usually credited to Thoreau, offers fewer difficulties for an examination of the topic than the "civil" feature. Typically, "disobedience" is breaking a legal norm that has authoritative sanction. The norm does not have to be a state law but might be a rule of a subsidiary group, such as the university, which in American constitutional theory and practice has the right to make and enforce internal regulations, subject to the state's writ and charter. Although this discussion has implications for disobedience within subsidiary groups, in the main it revolves around citizen resistance to the laws and policies of the state. "Civil" is open to several interpretations. These five meanings cover most possibilities: [2] 1) recognition of citizen obligations for the existing legal order; 2) the opposite of military; 3) civilized or moral; 4) public instead of private; and 5) affecting the political society. All of these, but especially 1), 3) and 5), are directly pertinent for the objectives of this paper. The meanings of both parts of the term become clarified when criteria are examined.

Many of the suggestions for the criteria of "responsible" civil disobedience can be identified with one or the other of two currents of thought and sometimes with both. One will be called "neo-conservative." [3] It views political obligation from a stress on the rule of law as the balance-wheel between majority will and minority rights. The rule of law includes the judicial development of civil liberties and the legislative protection of civil rights. The pattern has no internal agreement about rates and kinds of innovations required to strengthen democracy. Yet, it sets a premium on acceptance of the out-put of the historical constitutional system as the hallmark of the good citizen. Reflecting more than a trace of positivism, the neo-conservative tendency sharply distinguishes between private motives and

---

[2] Christian Bay, "Civil Disobedience," *International Encyclopedia of the Social Sciences*, Vol. II, pp. 473–486, at pp. 473–474.

[3] Representative statements are Francis A. Allen, "Civil Disobedience and the Legal Order," *University of Cincinnati Law Review*, 36 (1967), 1–38, 175–195; Abe Fortas, *Concerning Dissent and Civil Disobedience* (New York: The New American Library, 1968); Erwin N. Griswold, "Dissent—1968," *Tulane Law Review*, 42 (1968), 726–739; and Sidney Hook, "Social Protest and Civil Disobedience," *The Humanist*, 27 (Sept.–Dec., 1967), 157–159, 192–193.

legal behavior. The current is unlikely to give any significant aid to an interpretation of sovereignty whereby the citizen realizes his true morality through conformity to the state's determination of right in the tradition of Bosanquet. Lacking dedication to this notion, the neo-conservative current participates in discussions of the special conditions under which civil disobedience might take place without endangering a democratic system.[4] Its outlook, however, is often negative, aligning easily with the Kerner Report's finding that in the recent past "uncivil" disobedience shared with white terrorism and defiant officials the responsibility for creating a climate that encouraged and approved violent protest.[5]

The neo-conservative current sometimes approves or condones civil disobedience, especially to test the constitutionality of statutes, but it contrasts with a second current which welcomes the incorporation of responsible law-breaking into democratic theory as a beneficial, though rarely used, mechanism. This second alignment will be called "institutional libertarian" or simply "libertarian." [6] Ranging from the idioms of welfare capitalism to social democracy, it combines a defense of a legal democratic order with sponsorship of evolutionary changes in the distribution and uses of power to better meet human needs. Divided about a number of issues, the current has yet to show if its future lies with those concerned with perpetuating the due process tradition who attempt to define civil disobedience, such as Morris Keeton, or with "radical liberals" who are more interested in urging newer versions of democracy than in explaining how to achieve

---

[4] There are commentators whose alarm about civil disobedience suggests that there is a fully conservative category. See Morris I. Liebman, "Civil Disobedience—A Threat to Our Law Society," John W. Riehm, "Civil Disobedience—A Definition," *American Criminal Law Quarterly*, 3 (1964), 21–26, 11–15; and former Justice Whittaker's remarks in Charles E. Whittaker and William Sloane Coffin, Jr., *Law, Order and Civil Disobedience* (Washington: American Enterprise Institute for Public Policy Research, 1967), pp. 1–25. A majority of the National Commission on the Causes and Prevention of Violence held that civil disobedience, including non-violent action, is potential anarchy: *New York Times*, Dec. 9, 1969, pp. 1, 44.

[5] *Report of the National Advisory Commission on Civil Disorder* (Washington: Government Printing Office, 1968), p. 92.

[6] Internal agreements on justification, and means and ends of ethical resistance provide considerable diversity to the current. But consult Hugo A. Bedau, "On Civil Disobedience," *The Journal of Philosophy*, 58 (1961), 653–665; Harrop A. Freeman and Bayard Rustin in Harrop A. Freeman, ed., *Civil Disobedience* (Santa Barbara: Center for the Study of Democratic Institutions, 1966), pp. 2–10, 10–13; Morris Keeton, "The Morality of Civil Disobedience," *Texas Law Review*, 43 (1965), 507–525; and Michael Walzer, "The Obligation to Disobey," *Ethics*, 77 (1967), 163–175.

them.[7] The libertarian persuasion often serves as an infrequently acknowledged ally of black power and radical New Left groups in their "anti-oligarchy" struggles. The relationship is not one whereby these groups offer substantial analysis of civil disobedience. For the black power advocates this condition may stem from an emphasis within the early civil rights movement, and certainly from without, on its obligation to use non-violent means. The older stress invalidates discussion of civil disobedience for newer black leaders who believe, as academicians came to believe about the anti-communist provision of the National Defense Act, that a minority community had been affronted, and it would no longer tolerate the condition.[8] An explanation of why the radical New Left has not contributed to discussion of civil disobedience is that it tends to consider the phenomenon as little more than a mechanical strategy in the struggle against the alleged evils of the American and associated systems, causing a dearth of analysis according to values other than those of the crucible. The relative silence of the radical New Left about the philosophical significance of civil disobedience may be valid testimony that the subject is indeed worthless.[9] But since this paper's presumption is that the topic deserves study, it will have to proceed. Because black power and the radical New Left are not substantively concerned with civil disobedience, non-conservatives and libertarians are challenged to demonstrate that it is significantly involved in those broad issues of defining and reaching a better political life that energize non-debaters as well as many discussants.

[7] Civil disobedience is one, undefined form among many "disorderly surrogates" for socially acceptable types of protest in the stockpile of the "politics of radical pressure," recommended in Arnold S. Kaufman, The Radical Liberal (New York: Atherton Press, 1968), pp. 56–75, at 70.

[8] The anti-patrician and self-determinist spirit is evident in Floyd B. Barbour (ed.), The Black Power Revolt (Boston: Sargent, 1968), and Nathan Wright, Jr., Black Power and Urban Unrest (New York: Hawthorn Books, 1967).

[9] It is true that Herbert Marcuse has referred to "uncivil" disobedience. See An Essay on Liberation (Boston: Beacon Press, 1969), pp. 68–69. But his view of the phenomenon is controlled by beliefs that capitalist "pseudo-democracy" eventually absorbs any kind of non-mass opposition and hypocritically distracts attention from its own brutality through discovery of "illegitimate" resistance. Ibid., pp. 64–65, 76–77. A radical New Left view of the national and world scene is Carl Oglesby's section in Carl Oglesby and Richard .Schaull, Containment and Change (London: Collier-Macmillan, 1967), pp. 3–176. For a glimpse of strategy in Students for a Democratic Society targeting, see "The Rudd October Proposals," in Cox Commission Report, Crisis at Columbia (New York: Random House, 1968), Appendix B. The sources, ideas and literature of the New Left in Europe and the United States are reviewed in Rosemary Ruether, "The New Left: Revolutionaries After the Fall of the Revolution," Soundings, 51 (1969), 245–263.

Without pausing here to identify the specific points where the neo-conservative and libertarian currents agree or differ on the standards for "responsible" civil disobedience, I find that together they suggest the following criteria: 1) The act must be performed openly—secrecy is prohibited. 2) It must be a deliberate, not an accidental step. 3) The action is clearly unlawful, i.e., not permissible under existing laws and court interpretations of civil rights and liberties. 4) The illegal act is voluntary, not induced by others. 5) The conduct proceeds from "conscientious" dissent, inspired by moral or religious beliefs. 6) The objective sought is a concrete, public reform. 7) Legal remedies must be exhausted before disobedience is undertaken. 8) The disobedient is obligated to use "non-violent" means. 9) Throughout his challenge he demonstrates concern for the rights of others. 10) A proximate relation exists between the rule under attack and the reasons for dissent. 11) The disobedient must submit to the legal consequences of his act. This is not an exhaustive list, but it is suggestive of numerous criteria.

One can immediately comment on 1), 2) and 3). Meant to exclude subversion or evasion of law, the public test is open to a claim of exemption for some who violated the Fugitive Slave Law of 1850, the 18th Amendment and current state laws on abortions. If clandestine infractions are acceptable, perhaps only retrospective sorting by disinterested or "winning" historians can judge the disobedients. Meanwhile, one can reasonably expect that generally the public test must be met. The criterion of deliberate infraction is troublesome when the public standard is forgiven, thus making proof difficult. To consider an act eligible for "responsible" civil disobedience in the absence of evidence of advertancy, one may have to assume, intending no entrapment, its deliberate commission. On the test of illegality, there would seem to be no great difficulty in accepting the standard. A problem is how to treat the opinion that civil disobedience is not involved when the breaking of a law is subsequently found to be no violation because the "law" was invalid under superior legislation or a constitutional ruling.[10] To accept this view narrowly limits "civil disobedience" to unsuccessful, legal challenges and denigrates political

---

[10] Legalists associated with federal civil rights activities have argued that civil disobedience is not present when rule-breaking is later held legal under existing Congressional legislation or Constitutional principles: William L. Taylor, "Civil Disobedience," in Donald B. King and Charles W. Quick (eds.), *Legal Aspects of the Civil Rights Movement* (Detroit: Wayne State University Press, 1965), pp. 227–235, at 228–229; and Burke Marshall, "The Protest Movement and the Law," *Virginia Law Review*, 51 (1965), 785–803, at 795–796. The focus of Taylor and Marshall is on the sit-ins in the early 1960's and the arrests that followed but never received Supreme Court approval.

and ethical justification of disobedience. This is an inhibiting prospect for political philosophy.

THE ISSUE OF "CONSCIENTIOUS" OBJECTION

On the assumption that the disobedient act must be public, deliberate and illegal, this paper will examine four tests of civil disobedience which are crucial for distinguishing it from other kinds of political action and exploring its political ethics. They are the criteria of "conscientious" objection, willingness to accept the legal consequences of disobedience, "non-violent" means, and a proximate relation between the target and the grievance. To take the first, the stipulation that the infraction must be based on moral or religious conviction, i.e., the dictates of one's conscience, is found among both neo-conservatives and libertarians. Although definitions are seldom offered, both groups tend to consider "conscience" as a sacred and sovereign monitor, operating as if in the presence of God, rather than to imply Freud's super-ego, a product of fear and guilt. Moreover, they tend to think of conscience responding to significant, public challenges.[11] Neo-conservatives and libertarians are not alike on exemplification. Libertarians pay tribute to such exemplars as Gandhi and Thomas More. These men, it is held, demonstrated the qualities of mind and spirit and the political ethics which all potential rule-breakers should emulate. The neo-conservatives do not take this tack usually. A representative outlook is that of Erwin N. Griswold, who, instead of valuing famous disobedients, gives recognition to the "forum of conscience" described in Chief Justice Hughes' dissent in *U.S. v. MacIntosh* as an area where "duty to a moral power higher than the state has always been maintained." [12] Having done this and acknowledged a moral right to commit civil disobedience when there is a conflict of loyalties, Griswold stresses that the act is a rare event never to be cloaked with the legitimacy of civil liberties as construed by the Supreme Court and seldom to be tolerated by the majority's legislative will. Although this rendering does not rule out innovative rule-breaking, the outlook implies that conscientious disobedience has few contributions to offer democratic theory.

In contrast, institutional libertarians find civil disobedience a potential resource. Frequently they show the influence of liberal theology and resistance ideas indebted to Roger Williams, the *Vindiciae*

[11] On the possibly quandary of the nuclear commander, see Guenter Lewy, "Superior Orders, Nuclear Warfare, and the Dictates of Conscience in the Atomic Age," *American Political Science Review*, 55 (1961), pp. 2–23.

[12] 283 U.S., 605, 633 (1931); Griswold, *op. cit.*, 728–738.

Contra Tyrannos and John Knox. Of special interest, these commentators provide for individual civil disobedience which the elitism of Reformation traditions normally would have excluded. The method is to interpret St. Peter's "Obey God rather than men" dictum (Acts 5:29) to deny the state's absolutism and to permit citizen disobedience by divine authority without reference to human institutions.[13] The Petrine injunction has two weaknesses which are illuminated by Leslie W. Dunbar's criticism of natural law renditions for failing to require that the disobedient must always take the burden of justifying his act. He objects to a special defect:

> This comes about when the tradition asserts that the right of conscientious disobedience represents obedience to God rather than man; thus "God justifies." That this borders on blasphemy is a truth which at least two millennia have conspired in suppressing. It is of a piece with the other too numerous manifestations of western civilization's pathetic repudiation of its own responsibility for its moral values. When we take the step of civil disobedience no presumptuous claim that "God justifies me" must be on our lips; only a plea that he do so. It is not God rather than man that we obey, but God rather than man that we seek to please, and therein lies a tremendous difference. We cannot explore this matter here, other than to note that what one *offers* to God cannot be logically evaluated.[14]

While Dunbar's larger finding is that mass black protest in the South was genuine disobedience and that it was justified, not by conscience or natural law, but by its political ends and non-violent means, his unhappiness with God's "validation" is an instructive reminder that some "conscience" justifications of disobedience raise the issue of self-certification through rationally unreachable claims, and they manipulate theological ideas. The first problem complicates the task of determining constructive rebels from their opposites. Dunbar offers an appealing solution: After the mystical disobedient offers up his act, he must appeal to men for secular judgment. Thereby two courts will have the benefit of review. On manipulating theological notions, one could say that this condition is difficult to avoid in an age when

---

[13] A leading statement of this view which rests its certainty in Christ is John C. Bennett, "The Place of Civil Disobedience," *Christianity and Crisis*, 27 (Dec. 25, 1967), 299–302. Religious institutions, it has been urged, have a duty to speak and act corporately on the great issues of conscience and not limit themselves to urging individual members to speak and act: Robert McAfee Brown, *et al., Vietnam: Crisis of Conscience* (New York: Association Press, 1967), pp. 62–106, at 63.

[14] "Sources of Political Rights," paper read to Southern Political Science Association, Durham, N.C., November 13, 1964. Mimeo., p. 7. Italics in the original.

inner direction is widely respected or tolerated and those who believe in extra-human causes are experiencing revolutions. A more critical response is to suggest that Dunbar's point about pleasing instead of appealing to God implies a significant part of the "Obey God rather than man" directive that is often omitted—the possibility of God's punishment if the disobedient is acting contrary to divine will and law.[15] In *Antigone* the heroine pitted her understanding of higher law against Creon's state command, but although she perished, in an ultimate sense the Gods vindicated her and punished him. Is it unfair to argue that when a disobedient invokes the Petrine doctrine, he ought to admit that he is in principle subject to the risk that God's penalties may be visited on him, not as testimony to state sovereignty, but because the law was more in tune with God's justice than his act? I think not. For without the corollary of God's justice, the "obey God rather than men" formula allows rule-breakers who invoke it to try to have the best of the subjective world in which they presumably believe. This is a questionable procedure in terms of limiting self-certification.[16]

A comment should be made here about recent developments in non-selective conscientious objection to compulsory military service which reveal a conflict between public policy and claimed moral impulse. Applying the protection of due process, but denying that Congress had violated the First Amendment by requiring belief in a Supreme Being, the Supreme Court in *U. S. v. Seeger* held that an objector, not an atheist, with sincere and meaningful beliefs parallel to the convictions of theists who is conscientiously opposed to participation in war in any form is qualified for exemption from combatant training and service.[17] In the 1967 Selective Service Act, Congress responded to *Seeger* by removing the Supreme Being test; but, intending to exclude Seeger-type beliefs, it retained religious training and belief as the origin of conscientious objection and kept a ban on exemption based on essentially political, sociological or philosophical views, or a personal moral code. In 1968 the Selective Service introduced a form to review Seeger-type beliefs. *Seeger* and the changes are only slight adjustments in the government's effort to determine sincerity and uphold equity. Together with the premises of the Universal Military Training and Service Act, they do not contribute to a common understanding of "conscience," and they raise questions

---

[15] There is also the possibility that the Devil rather than God is the source of inspiration. The perplexing implications of this option for actor and authorities were found at least as recently as John Brown of Harpers Ferry.

[16] An example of the self-protecting formula is found in William Sloane Coffin, Jr.'s comments in Whittaker and Coffin, *op. cit.*, pp. 29–41.

[17] 380 U.S., 163 (1965).

about the government's right to define and apply tests about highest convictions.[18]

Political obedience and the issue of conscience are joined especially in controversies about *selective* objection to military service, for which there is no statutory provision in the United States. For present purposes the importance of the controversies lies in their debate of the question: do convictions that a particular war is immoral and unjust meet the test of conscientious objection? The neo-conservative is likely to hold that selective objection is judgmental, i.e., "political," and should not be confused with traditional, i.e., "religious," conscientious objection which is a fundamental and rare phenomenon that government can and should legally tolerate. To this view sincere claims of selective objection to particular wars are worthy of respect. But they cannot be honored because they do not have the requisite "religious" quality and they clash with the idea that the government's will is paramount until changed by the representative machinery or public opinion.[19] The libertarian, however, is apt to be sympathetic to a temporal faith interpretation of conscientiousness and willing to consider selective objection as potentially legitimate and not an indefensible challenge to national defense or democratic theory.[20] The difference between the two currents on the issue of selective objection focuses attention on how far each will permit legal exemptions from the requirements of citizenship to be extended in the name of conviction. Essentially the neo-conservative will allow non-performance that

[18] See Christopher H. Clancy and Jonathan A. Weiss, "The Conscientious Objector Exemption: Problems in Conceptual Clarity and Constitutional Considerations," *Maine Law Review*, 17 (1963), 143–160. If upheld, the Federal District Court ruling in *U. S. v. Sisson* (297 F. Supp. 902, 1969), which found that the 1967 law unconstitutionally discriminates against non-theists, religious or not, with profound moral convictions, will move the C. O. issue closer, either to the opening of Pandora's box or the victory of the inner light, depending on one's view. Ending compulsory military service would retire the question, unless there is another major war.

[19] Fortas, *op. cit.*, pp. 51–52.

[20] On selective objection to military service, the American Civil Liberties Union has equated the genuine objector's belief with conscience that is entitled to First Amendment protection whether or not he claims to be "religious." Although no testing formula was suggested, it has held that administrative scrutiny of the objector will detect the unconscientious and discourage this means to avoid the draft. *Civil Liberties* (March, 1966). Without plebiscites, church elites have endorsed selective objection. A statement upholding conscientious resistance to military service in particular wars received the approval of most American delegates to the Fourth (1968) Assembly of the World Council of Churches. The selective objection issue is a new and ambivalent question for historical critics of all wars. See American Friends Service Committee, *The Draft?* (New York: A.F.S.C., 1968), esp. Chap 3, "From Witness to Resistance: The New CO."

does not injure the rights of others or public safety, as with the constitutional refusal of Jehovah Witnesses to salute the flag, or that does not seriously affect a public mission, as in the instance of traditional conscientious objection to bearing arms at any time. In contrast to the neo-conservative, the libertarian will take greater risks in exempting non-conformists from public affirmation of national loyalty and performance of citizen duty. The former moves with court and legislative answers, the latter anticipates favorable responses from them, making their agreement on a conscience test of civil disobedience an unlikely prospect.

WHAT OBLIGATIONS DOES THE DISOBEDIENT ASSUME?

To leave the criterion of conscientious dissent suspended between two schools is not a happy condition. However, I will let it remain there until later to consider other evidence of good will, asking about civil disobedience what T. H. Green asked of the legal obligation to obey—what external things should be expected? [21] For this purpose two standards are useful—the disobedient's willing acceptance of legal penalties and his use of "non-violent" means. For the rule-breaker to voluntarily submit to the legal consequences of his act is held, especially by neo-conservatives, to be a central proof of one's good faith and lack of criminal or revolutionary intentions.[22] It is conceded that voluntary submission obliges the state to consider that the disobedient, not the rule, should be vindicated. For many neo-conservatives the test of full submission is for the disobedient to willingly plead guilty. Even though on moral and constitutional grounds he usually opposed his own formal guilt, the example of Martin Luther King, Jr. is valued by neo-conservatives because of his sacrificial style and testimony to the ideal of law expressed in this way: "And I submit that the individual who disobeys the law, whose conscience

21 Thomas Hill Green, *Lectures on the Principles of Political Obligation* (London: Longmans, Green and Co., 1921), pp. 35–38.
22 Sidney Hook, *The Paradoxes of Freedom* (Berkeley and Los Angeles, University of California Press, 1967), pp. 116–118; Allen, *op. cit.,* 10–11; Fortas, *op. cit.,* p. 34. See also "A Declaration of Confidence in Columbia's Future," signed by faculty members of the Columbia Law School, *New York Times,* May 17, 1968, p. 41. Neo-conservatives honor Socrates as the Responsible Disobedient, holding that he drank the hemlock to testify to the state's integrity and the rule of law even as he believed that he had been unjustly accused and convicted. A variation is that the Gadfly's submission proved that he would let others disobey laws if they would assume the risk he had assumed: Charles Fried, "Moral Causation," *Harvard Law Review,* 77 (1964), 1258–1270, at 1269.

tells him it is unjust and who is willing to accept the penalty by staying in jail until that law is altered, is expressing at the moment the
very highest respect for the law." [23]

On the question of submission, libertarians are likely to refer to the
varieties of legal situations under which civil disobedience might take
place and to the possible weakening of protections for the accused
through guilty pleas. The two patterns agree on minimum requirements that the disobedient should not become a fugitive from justice
and after arrest should use conventional, legal means.

Protest circles have produced criticisms or rejections of the submission criterion, especially the neo-conservative version. Notable arguments hold that only obscurantist or craven men accept the requirement; by their courageous disobedience to reform democracy for
philosophical reasons, a few men have prepaid society for any inconvenience they may have caused; acceptance of punishment encourages the state to keep and enforce the law or policy under attack; not
to resist imprisonment or other penalty is to discredit the logic of disobedience; the law disobeyed is clearly unjust or unconstitutional so
that acceptance of punishment is testimony to moral or legal falsehood. Howard Zinn's censure of neo-conservative submission covers
some of these notions and adds others:

> If a specific act of civil disobedience is a morally justifiable act of
> protest, then the jailing of those engaged in that act is immoral and
> should be opposed, contested to the very end. The protestor need be
> no more willing to accept the rule of punishment than to accept the
> rule he broke. There may be many times when protestors *choose* to go
> to jail, as a way of continuing their protest, as a way of reminding
> their countrymen of injustice. But that is different than the notion that
> they *must* go to jail as part of a rule connected with civil disobedience.
> The key point is that the spirit of protest should be maintained all the
> way, whether it is done by remaining in jail, or by evading it. To ac-
> cept jail penitently as an accession to "the rules" is to switch suddenly
> to a spirit of subservience, to demean the seriousness of the protest.[24]

A radicalization of protest idiom is clearly evident in many of these
ideas. Conceivably they suggest an understanding of civil disobedience that calls into doubt the foundations of the democratic state, as
known to date. But even granting the presence of revolutionary ideas,
the disciplined observer should not be hasty to conclude that conspir-

---

[23] Martin Luther King, Jr., "Love, Law and Civil Disobedience," *New South*, 16
(1961), 3–11, at 8. It is less clear that King's adherence to the edifice of the
law prevailed in his last few years when war policies and the maldistribution
of wealth became his targets.
[24] Howard Zinn, *Disobedience and Disorder: Nine Fallacies on Law and Order*
(New York: Vintage Books, 1968), pp. 120–121. Italics in the original.

acy is at work and the commonwealth is imperiled. On the grounds that civil disobedience is a relief valve for an uncertain mixture of insurgent thought and non-revolutionary opinion, some concessions to the criticisms of the submission test should be made. In particular, the neo-conservative insistence on a guilty plea should be eliminated. The result would be to make the submission criterion no more and no less than the requirement of a *legal* struggle *within* the state's jurisdiction. A search for "sanctuary" or flight to avoid prosecution would be evidence of something other than civil disobedience.

There is a close relationship between the submission test and the question of "non-violent" means. Christian Bay's encyclopedia article states that civil disobedience requires "carefully chosen and legitimate means," but holds that they do not have to be "non-violent." [25] Yet, neo-conservatives and institutional libertarians usually agree on the need for this criterion which is meant to certify the actor's acceptance of the legal structure and to help the act's efficacy by avoiding society's fear of violence and preventing counter-force. There are vexing problems of definition. Criteria-makers have come to no agreement as they face "non-violent" conduct ranging from Mennonite non-resistance through attempts to block a submarine launching to self-immolation. A main source of difficulty is the fact that efforts to expound on the moral or practical value of non-violence, efforts which have a permanent place in American social and intellectual history, have not completed the task of developing a theory of political institutions based on the norm.[26]

The problems of defining and institutionalizing "non-violence" imply a discussion of its opposite. The key question here is who may use violence legitimately? Drawing on traditional political obligation, the neo-conservative has answered with a moderate but explicit doctrine of state sovereignty. The libertarian is not greatly different, holding that the state alone has a legitimate monopoly over violence. While one could reasonably argue that the state has only a *de facto*

---

[25] Bay, *op. cit.*, p. 474.

[26] Commenting from within the peace movement on the division between the non-violent ethic and politics, A. J. Muste observed: "And since, in itself pacifism does not provide criteria for political discrimination, these criteria must be found elsewhere. In their search for sound criteria not all pacifists mine the same political quarry." Quoted in James A. Finn, *Protest: Pacifism and Politics* (New York: Random House, 1968), p. 200. Pacifist and related writings from William Penn to Bayard Rustin are collected in Staughton Lynd (ed.), *Nonviolence in America* (Indianapolis: Bobbs Merrill, 1966). Gandhian resistance to reform the law is urged in Harris Wofford, Jr., "Non-Violence and The Law," *Journal of Religious Thought*, 15 (1957), 25–36. *Satyagraha* is appraised in my "Toward a Reassessment of Gandhi's Political Thought," *Western Political Quarterly*, 16 (1963), 99–108.

and not a *de jure* monopoly over violence until the principle of consent is more fully realized, I see no viable alternative to retaining the neo-conservative, and by and large the libertarian insistence, that violence is rightly employed only by legal authorities who through legislative and judicial means determine what is and what is not anti-social behavior. In the crucible, public executives and their agents may equate illegality with violence and anarchism and act repressively on the confusion. The disobedient can help to prevent these defects by his peaceful conduct. More explicitly, the disobedient should be governed by the moral conviction that he is a witness to charity that he finds lacking in the state, obligating him to abstain from physical injury to persons and things. To hold that there ought to be a distinction between the lesser evil of violence to things and the greater evil of injury to persons is to invite a further debate about arson and theft, a process that will undermine the original ethic that was invoked.[27] "No contusions or breakage" may have little claim as a sophisticated rule for civil disobedience, but it is readily comprehensible and testifies to a prime democratic value, peaceful change.

A discussion of civil disobedience as potential revolution is suggested by the last criterion to be examined, a proximate relation between the violated rule and the cause for grievance. The neo-conservative tendency interprets the standard as insisting on a cause and effect bond. It is unsettled about any other understanding. Francis A. Allen writes:

> But dilemmas arise when the object of protest is a condition that does not result from the enforcement of any particular law or from the conduct of any readily identifiable person or group, but which, on the contrary, is the consequence of a whole complex of social, cultural, and historical factors. . . . Direct action that assumes the characteristics of a secondary or tertiary boycott is not well calculated to a call for the moral response from the larger community upon which the classic theory of civil disobedience largely relies. Moreover, such programs contain a large and unmistakable ingredient of irrationality. . . . Such forms of protest, whatever the provocations that induced them, represent a retreat from reason and ultimately threaten the nonviolent character of the present movement.[28]

[27] Contrast Zinn, *op. cit.*, p. 46. For a dualistic thesis that when avenues for peaceful change have been closed, exhausted or found ineffective, violence is needed as much as peaceful civil disobedience as a mechanism to advance democratic values, subject to the government's enforcement of order and its removal of the causes of the outbursts, see Ralph W. Conant, "Rioting, Insurrection and Civil Disobedience," *The American Scholar*, 37 (1968), 420–433, at 433.

[28] Allen, *op. cit.*, 12–13.

Although Allen's illustration of a non-proximate condition is Negro disobedience for the proclaimed goal of increased economic opportunities, his comment is representative of neo-conservative concern about civil disobedience launched recently against national military policies. The libertarian tendency, which is equally devoted to rationality and peaceful means, does not share the neo-conservative objections to secondary and thus "political" relationships. To this view, Thoreau's refusal to pay his poll tax to draw attention to his objections to the Mexican War and slavery had no logical defects. Similarly, it is unlikely to fault the logic of the 1967 March on the Pentagon to publicize and alter Vietnam policies, however the means and the grievance are themselves judged.[29] Unlike the neo-conservative pattern, the libertarian outlook construes broadly the relevancy of a disobedient act for the rule broken. Although not all libertarians may object to *U. S. v. O'Brien's* denial of immunity for acts of "symbolic speech" which protested the wisdom of distant governmental decisions by challenging their legal armor,[30] the tendency they represent is fundamentally tolerant about the secondary character of rule-breaking which aims at the Leviathan through one of its peripheral laws.

Civil disobedience should not have to meet the neo-conservative exclusion of a secondary relationship between the violated law and the basic grievance. The breaking of a marginal, innocuous statute to communicate protest about a legally distant wrong is either individual witnessing or interest group behavior that a self-confident democracy can withstand without serious injury, especially in view of the public obloquy visited by majority opinion on non-conformists. If civil disobedience is restricted to the testing of rules believed unjust or unconstitutional—as the neo-conservative test of proximate relation between object and complaint requires—civil disobedience would be confined to an essentially quasi-legal function when it may have a legitimate, politicized role as a "Question Time" for the majority will transcribed through the existing representative system. Under the heading of proximate relationship, it would seem sufficient to ask and expect an affirmative answer to the question, "Is the protest di-

[29] The preparations and conduct of the October, 1967 demonstrations at the Pentagon had factors of interest to the student of civil disobedience. One participant-observer finds the criteria of advance notice, "non-violence," and appeal to the public conscience. He also suggests as the claim that the government was obliged to negotiate on how it would be disobeyed. See Norman Mailer, *The Armies of the Night* (New York: New American Library, 1968). A situational description of the Pentagon events as a mixture of Gandhian and insurgency tactics is reported in *Liberation*, 12 (November, 1967) 3–7 (David Dellinger), 26–28 (Arthur Waskow).

[30] *U.S. v. O'Brien*, 88 S. Ct. 1673 (1968).

rected toward a specific need or wrong, clearly identified among the protesters; and has care been exercised to communicate its nature to bystanders and opponents?" [31] An "immoral" war or "retrogressive" tax policy would seem to be sufficiently specific; "poverty" or "racism" would probably be too general to qualify.

It would be premature to conclude that the norms of concreteness and honest publicity are enough to convince those who ask for a proximate relationship between the infraction and the grievance that the prospect of revolution is thereby significantly lessened. Indeed, the question whether revolution is or is not immediately beyond the threshold of civil disobedience can be raised at several turns in the discussion of standards for acceptable rule-breaking. Opinion falls between two limits. One is identifiable with conservativism and holds that civil disobedience is incipient rebellion.[32] The other is on the outer frontier of institutional libertarianism and asks that civil disobedience as "non-violent revolution" should be given legal immunity.[33] Although the bulk of the commentators are willing to avoid bracketing civil disobedience with revolution, neo-conservatives are apt to entertain and answer forebodingly the question: "Is there an attack on the system?" This phenomenon implies their general misgiving about allowing any rule-breaking in an operating, if imperfect, pluralist democracy. Libertarians are less fearful about civil disobedience being or becoming an attempt to displace the current regime. They depend on the standards of disclosure and "non-violence" to build a wall around the disobedient to tell him from the insurgent.

The neo-conservative fear that rebellion is inherent in rule-breaking is especially troublesome for the task of establishing criteria for civil disobedience. If the concern becomes overriding there is a risk that under its weight other criteria will fall. To avoid this contingency the discerning student will have to do one of two things. Either he will try to work out his own set of answers to show that there is no insuperable logical difficulty in viewing civil disobedience as a non-revolutionary question.[34] The other option is for him to rely on a belief that in a democratic context "principled" lawbreaking is worthy of ethical examination regardless of the risk that it may produce, intentionally or otherwise, the reality of political violence. I would recommend the second alternative, and support it with the addition of

---

[31] Keeton, *op. cit.*, 515. Italics of the original removed.

[32] Riehm, *op. cit.*, 14. See also Lewis H. Van Dusen, Jr., "Civil Disobedience: Destroyer of Democracy," *American Bar Association Journal*, 55 (Feb., 1969), 123–126.

[33] Freeman, *op. cit.*, pp. 5–6.

[34] For this position, see Richard Wasserstrom, "Disobeying the Law," *The Journal of Philosophy*, 58 (1961), 641–653.

two widely-proposed criteria—the exhaustion of legal remedies before disobedience is undertaken and demonstrated care for substantial rights of others, e.g., First Amendment rights. The former helps to maintain the validity of redress procedures, which if discredited by non-use, may not provide adequate justice for anyone. The latter requires the disobedient to show non-ideological evidence of the humanism which he has proclaimed as his *weltanschauung*.

Civil disobedience therefore emerges as rule-breaking which meets certain standards. Assuming the act to be deliberate, it should be an articulated, public deed, aimed at a specific wrong and conducted peacefully with concern for others inside the state's jurisdiction after completing legal, remedial action. Selective borrowing from neo-conservative and libertarian norms opens the way to a discussion of whether there are significant tasks in democratic theory which might be performed through civil disobedience. Before that enterprise is undertaken some settlement must be made of the test of conscientious dissent.[35]

WHAT IS "CONSCIENTIOUSNESS"?

Because of the centrality of "conscientiousness" for many definitions of civil disobedience, it deserves the most careful evaluation as a possible source for justification of rule-breaking in a democratic context. The standard is open to two defective understandings. On the neo-conservative side there is the risk of sacrificing the possibly creative voice to the rule of law. Among libertarians there is the chance of the absolutism of individual conscience overcoming civic virtue and order. Even if a balance were struck between the tendencies, application would be a basic problem of the test. "There cannot be," Franz Neumann wrote, "a universally valid statement telling us when man's

[35] Appeals to Nuremberg principles to justify disobedience have a close affinity to conscientious dissent. The focus of the relevant passages of the 1945 London Agreement on moral choice in the face of immoral state orders tends to assign the principles to a category of inner judgment. [The Agreement is in *Journal of International Law*, 39 (1945), Supp., 257–264.]. It is debatable whether that judgment is "only" *entitled* to decide for disobedience or is *obligated* to so decide. The latter interpretation has been influential in popular resistance ideas. See Benjamin Spock, "Vietnam and Civil Disobedience," *The Humanist*, 28 (1968), 3–7, at 6. This stand was also adopted by Capt. Howard B. Levy in his military trial. *United States v. Levy*, CM416463 (Army Bd. of Rev. Aug. 29, 1968), *et cetera*. His view was an interpretation of Army Field Manual 27–10, *The Law of Land Warfare* (1965). Yet, this document, which outlines legal responsibility for war crimes, stipulates neither entitlement nor obligation to disobey.

conscience may legitimately absolve him from obedience to the laws of the state." [36] Neumann may have been premature in closing the door on scientific determination of conscientiousness, but his comment recalls the near inscrutability of the inner light and the extreme difficulty of giving it consensual recognition. An amendment may be in order to require an affirmative response from the "conscience" of others as evidence of the disobedient's own credentials. The implications of this qualification include the transference of the testing process from the actor to his audience. This amendment has the drawbacks of opening the question of how significant followership or its absence is to judging the disobedient and recalling Rousseau's general will as a "conscience" for the whole community. The former leads to a discourse on effective leadership, not valid rule-breaking; and the latter leads to controversies about the meanings of the *Social Contract* that are unsettled two centuries after its publication. Because of these problems, the amendment does not offer a reliable way to determine the individual's merit.

Given the diversity of meanings and the many questions about recognition and application which spring up around "conscientiousness" as a guide to identifying disobedience which a more perfect democracy would permit, one is left with the choice of either eliminating the criterion from consideration as Sidney Hook has done in the name of secular humanism [37] or relying on an interdependency of the disobedient and the state that will salvage some acts of conscience from its power.[38] Recognizing significant problems in either direction that require further exploration, I would choose the second course, endorsing Professor Dworkin's thesis that the regime's discretionary authority not to prosecute is the least unsatisfactory device to recog-

---

[36] Franz L. Neuman, *The Democratic and the Authoritarian State* (Glencoe: The Free Press, 1957), p. 158.

[37] Hook contends that "conscience" is a dangerous guide for principled action, which if accepted, opens the way for totalitarians along with peace workers. See especially *Paradoxes of Freedom*, Chapter 3. His thesis is overly dependent on viewing conscience as a basis for *political theory*, whereas many who claim its guidance are no more or less than moralists who may be correct or mistaken in their judgments but who seldom offer political theories. I agree with Hook's evaluation that individual conscience alone is an untrustworthy basis for consent to law. Contrast Harold J. Laski, *Authority in the Modern State* (New Haven: Yale University Press, 1927), pp. 32–47. Recent controversies have caused constitutional libertarians to attempt to combine political respect for and legal skepticism about disobedience based on highest principle: "The American Civil Liberties Union Statement on Civil Disobedience," February 1, 1969, mimeo.

[38] A third way is possible if one believes that the entire question of civil disobedience is based on what may be *owed to others* through shared values and associations. For this approach, which differs from mine, see Walzer, *op. cit.*, *passim*.

nize the existence and condone the public results of the dictates of private conscience.[39] Some will object that the solution leaves conscience the prisoner of state theory—any state theory. The complaint has reasonable grounds, but it overestimates the achievements of those who wish to realize the ideal in which no man is ever forced to act in a manner contrary to his conscience.[40] Another objection is that anti-populist favoritism is practiced through forgiveness of "principled" rule-breaking, an indulgence not to be extended to the "generality" of men—a term used by Judge Charles Wyzanski, Jr. when he accepted a man's refusal on non-theistic, conscientious grounds to be inducted for combat service in Vietnam.[41] The criticism is especially difficult to answer because it exposes the elitist character of civil disobedience to which so little attention has been paid.[42]

The main problem, however, is to avoid two extremes. To ignore individual conscience as a guide to state response to disobedience is an undesirable concession to legal positivism and philosophical relativism. To elevate conscience as a self-determined yardstick is an unwelcome step toward political atomism. A balance is possible when the non-prosecution option is accepted. It depends on the forbearing character of the American state. Less than optimal, the quality ought to be refined and strengthened; but its present condition is intrinsically valuable to help recognize and respect the dictates of private conscience.

CIVIL DISOBEDIENCE
AND DEMOCRATIC GOVERNMENT

With the completion of the foregoing sketch of criteria for civil disobedience that reveals certain political ethics and distinguishes it from

[39] Ronald Dworkin, "On Not Prosecuting Civil Disobedience," *New York Review of Books,* 10 (1968), 14–21.

[40] The ideal has received notable support from the Roman Catholic Church in Vatican Council II's "Declaration on Religious Freedom." A state, even one that is democratic, can make a declaration of this kind only at its peril. No longer a state, but still a government, the Church faces numerous dilemmas in combining the "no-coercion-toward-conscience-even-when-wrong" ideal with Apostolic and Papal theories. As discussed in the Encyclical *Humane Vitae,* the birth control issue is one controversy in which the difficulties are revealed. For the American Catholic Bishops' 1968 statement on the issue in which on net balance conscience "as a law unto itself" is subordinated to the Church's teaching authority, see "Human Life in Our Day," *Catholic Mind,* 66 (1968), 1–28.

[41] *U. S. v. Sisson,* 297 F. Supp. 902 (1969).

[42] For the caution that in a democratic context civil disobedience is minority rule, see John H. Schaar, *Loyalty in America* (Berkeley: University of California Press, 1957), p. 52.

political revolution and conventional dissent, a provisional response can now be made to the question whether resistance of this kind contributes a service to American democratic thought. A subsidiary issue deals with the possible defects of the current. From the standpoint of American political obligation the area that is most pertinent is the Lockean dispensation. According to this theory, primordial consent established a political society out of which a state emerged, probably through a second contract, as Althusius had argued more clearly than Locke. In any event, original consent entitles the state to a basic loyalty. The citizens retain a portion of their pre-civil authority to self-government through the persistence of inviolable rights and a representative system operating through majority will. It is the delegational machinery which normally keeps the state accountable to its citizens who give a few men a fiduciary power to govern. *In extremo,* citizens may legitimately use violence to remake the state when it violates the terms of its mandate. Minority discontent is no proof that the mandate is broken. Only majority sanction can legitimize the claim. Private conscience is recognized by the Lockean tradition, but it is not the basis for a right to rule-breaking.[43]

The Lockean view of obedience and dissent has two main weaknesses. The fiction of voluntary membership in a political community is at best a literary metaphor or at worst a device for assuring the state consensualist value under the guise of a myth. For civil disobedience a result of the fault is to assign an awesome burden of moral justification for any illegal act to the disobedient, even when the law violated is patently inequitable. The civil disobedient learns what other law-breakers have found, that he faces not only the immediate legal network, but a surrogate to which presumably he had consented in a primeval cavern. Not all evidence of this problem in American political thought lies with Lockean theory, Hobbes' single contract and Leviathan having made themselves felt despite the stronger current of the former. Still, Lockean explanation about the genesis of political obligation gives the state an unearned title to expect and exact obedience even before the stuff of the second contract, the representative system, comes into focus.

The second weakness of Lockean theory lies in its anti-individualist and conformist bent that contrasts with Locke's natural rights and social ideas. The bias shows in his insistence that majority will is needed to begin the valid overthrow of unjust rulers and in the politically undernourished place given to conscience. The influence of these beliefs on any kind of dissent is especially revealed in a condi-

---

[43] A similar understanding of Lockean obligation and dissent is Harry Prosch, "Toward an Ethics of Civil Disobedience," *Ethics,* 77 (1967), 176–191, at 178–179.

tion Robert A. Dahl calls a "J-Curve" situation where the bulk of the citizens agree on many political issues. Relating this condition to political philosophy, he writes:

> A vast number of questions that might be of abstract interest to philosophers, moralists, theologians, or others who specialize in posing difficult and troublesome questions are, in any stable political system, irrelevant to politics because nearly everyone is agreed and no one can stir up much of a controversy. If a controversy does arise because of the persistence of a tiny dissenting minority, in a republic the chances are overwhelming that it will soon be settled in a way that corresponds with the view of the preponderant majority.[44]

The condition described is precisely the kind where there ought to be an opportunity to ask troublesome questions and to demand answers from public authorities that are innovative. In an unstable system many voices are heard and the democratic state is apt to change its policies and laws. Sympathetic to Dahl's "others," I detect a need to keep open the possibility of challenges to laws and policies, regardless of the opinion of the "preponderant majority." That this can be allowed in terms of Lockean understandings of dissent is doubtful.

It would be unwise to conclude that because Lockean ideas about obedience and dissent have drawbacks their framework should be discarded. Not only are alternatives, e.g., Hobbesian or Marcusian theories, antithetical to such democratic values as privacy and self-fulfillment, but the Lockean tradition has developed intellectual commitments to civil liberties and participatory government that are crucial for the protection and advancement of human rights and regime accountability. What might be done profitably is to adopt an idea of "justice" to link, without confusing, the rulers and the governed. Skeptical of founding "justice" on the mythical soil of contract, I agree, nonetheless, that some understanding of the notion might overcome the weaknesses of Lockean theory.[45] Understood as a trans-political, moral ideal rooted in the nature and destiny of man, "justice" partakes of T. H. Green's "common good," [46] despite the reservations that can be introduced about his statism and unclear teleology. For civil disobedience an eclectic conception of "justice" which is not mortgaged to primordial contract or state "ends" provides a shared

[44] Robert A. Dahl, *Pluralist Democracy in the United States: Conflict and Consent* (Chicago: Rand McNally and Co., 1967), pp. 272–273.

[45] Justice and contract are joined in John Rawls, "The Justification of Civil Disobedience," in *Civil Disobedience: Theory and Practice,* Hugo Adam Bedau, ed. (New York: Pegasus, 1969), pp. 240–255.

[46] On Green's "common good," suggesting that its social context is true but because of faulty use of words he failed to distinguish different goods, see Plamenatz, *op. cit.,* pp. 62–81.

field for presumptions about obedience to compete with disciplined challenges. The competition is on terms which do not preordain the outcome, although they unapologetically respect systemic legitimacy.

To proceed this far is to go beyond the matter of imperfections in the predominant stream of American democratic thought and to enter a discussion of whether civil disobedience is well qualified to guard and further democratic ideals. On this question, Bay is a prominent spokesman for the affirmative. He suggests that civil disobedience can be a new and vital way to realize human values no longer served by majoritarianism because of the inroads of modern knowledge and the distortion of the rule of law and representative machinery into ultimate goods. Visualizing a non-elitist polity with a reallocation of power that lessens poverty and violence and expands human rights, he wishes to substitute for the classic justification of democracy through political obligation an ethic of individual responsibility for the likely results of one's political conduct, including obedience to law.[47] This proposal is valuable to the degree that it reminds conservatives and neo-conservatives of Bracton's dictum that the king is *sub deo et lege,* and how in our time the rule of law means that "the law itself is based on respect for the supreme value of human personality." [48] Bay's reliance on individual rectitude is more controversial, for although he denies that Thoreau is the model for civil disobedience, his ideas align with the New Englander's thesis that the free man defines his own responsibility.[49] The realization of Bay's goals, which others seek, requires limits. I contend that the limits mean that the free and responsible man operates *within* a community that develops his rectitude and the state's. Is this stand close to that of David Spitz who refers to the foundation of the problem of political obligation in the Aristotelian question about whether a good man can always be a good citizen? He argues that it is possible to be true to both through the loyalty of the citizen to the principles of democracy, despite the presence of unjust laws. In the last analysis, Spitz re-

---

[47] Bay, *op. cit.,* pp. 484–485. The populism inherent in Bay's ideas is more apparent than real, for he would trade the elitism behind liberal democracy for a new elitism of radicals who would produce bold policies.

[48] International Commission of Jurists, *The Rule of Law in a Free Society: A Report on the International Congress of Jurists, New Delhi: 1959* (Geneva: International Commission of Jurists, 1960), p. 196. Bay criticizes the dogma of the rule of law in pluralist democratic theory in "Civil Disobedience: Prerequisite for Democracy in Mass Society," in *Political Theory and Social Change,* David Spitz, ed. (New York: Atherton Press, 1967), pp. 163–183.

[49] "The only obligation which I have a right to assume," Thoreau said, "is to do at any time what I think right." "Civil Disobedience," *The Works of Thoreau,* Henry S. Canby, ed. (Boston: Houghton Mifflin Co., 1937), pp. 789–808, at 790–791.

lies on the goodness and honesty of man operating from moral principles to judge rationally the likely results of his disobedience, and to
bring his pressure to bear on the state to try to produce a greater
benefit than what is apt to come from obedience.[50] As an amendment,
I would suggest that, in addition to combining the good man's work
for the development of the state, the state must be allowed to help
him. This is not testimony to the sanctity of the state.[51] As in classical
liberalism, he will control the moral balance, but there is or there
ought to be a mutuality between man and the state.[52] For state power
can help to liberate him from deprivations. Existentialism to the contrary, he cannot perform the task alone.

Applied to responsible civil disobedience, mutuality does not mean
that legal immunity ought to be extended to it. This would be to legitimize and normalize civil protest into a formal, remedial institution
that the democratic system already provides in other ways. Routiniza-
tion would also destroy the logic and spontaneity of disobedience.
Yet, civil disobedience can aid, as it has in the past, the selective incorporation into civil rights and liberties of public speech and behavior previously denied to citizens. While some attempts fail and may
deserve to fail in such marshy areas of criminal law as conspiracy and
trespass, disobedience of the law, as the neo-conservative admits, is
sometimes a useful tool to expand the arena of liberty. Moreover, responsible civil disobedience can continue to aid social changes that
are beyond the capacity or will of representative institutions. Although civil rights disobedience within individual states had their approval, this is a basic frontier neo-conservatives would rather not
pass. They can be answered with the reply that civil rule-breaking
can energize the political system to take additional steps to advance
social progress, provided it is understood that the criteria suggested
in this paper or similar tests are developed as insurance that principled disobedience is not a threat to the constitutional order, but an
effort to retain it because of its demonstrated values.[53]

---

[50] David Spitz, "Democracy and the Problem of Civil Disobedience," *American
Political Science Review*, 48 (1954), 386–403, at 401–403.

[51] On some dangers of civil religion, see Lewis Lipsitz, "If as Verba Says, the
State Functions as a Religion, What Are We to Do to Save Our Souls?",
American Political Science Review, 62 (1968), 527–535. A vineyard note is
Barbara Deming, "Desanctifying Authority," *Liberation*, 12 (November, 1967),
32–33.

[52] "Mutuality" between citizen and state is explored in Robert J. Pranger, *Action,
Symbolism, and Order: The Existential Dimensions of Politics in Modern Citizenship* (Nashville: Vanderbilt University Press, 1968), pp. 54–57.

[53] For this point, see Wilson Carey McWilliams, "Civil Disobedience and Contemporary Constitutionalism: the American Case," *Comparative Politics*, I
(1969), 211–227, at 221.

Those who believe that the representative model, operating fundamentally by "majority" will, coalition leadership and a developing system of rights and liberties, is the best arrangement to be expected in an imperfect world, are unlikely to invite civil disobedience into the house of Madison and Lincoln. Essentially, this is the neo-conservative current. Some, but perhaps not all, libertarians are open to the prospect of legitimizing civil disobedience as a genuinely democratic method. They believe, and I would agree, that civil disobedience can provide a theoretical service in a democracy through the reform of the delegational pyramid. For without contending that Rousseau's city-state ought to be the paradigm for democracy, I suggest that the representative structure which welfare democracy inherited from last century's liberalism and improved in this century has not been so administratively effective or so politically virtuous that it cannot be improved by new arrangements for combining obedience and consent. To experiment is a risk for democratic political obligation. But is there not an equally serious risk if stability is valued ahead of the expansion of accountability?[54] Distinguished from the use of force to impose decisions and from the existing regime of rights and liberties, disciplined civil disobedience is possibly a creative way to ask the citizens of the state if they are satisfied with other aspects of the delegational model that has served well but which may not have produced the most equitable and efficient allocation of power and resources to deal with emergent disaffection and unmet needs in the national polity.

But how *necessary* is civil disobedience, given the availability of many legal forms of political opposition and reform? To face this question is to appeal for empirical studies of the benefits or costs of civil disobedience undertaken in our time, measured against the reasonably well-known strengths and drawbacks of conventional forms of political opposition. Recent studies of violence in the United States are of no great value because they have proceeded almost without the aid of ethical distinctions about various kinds of disorder.[55] The distinctions, as I have tried to show, can be made. The task is to use some set to isolate *civil* disobedience from other forms of unconventional dissent and after empirical analysis to declare whether there is a *need* for this special form of opposition in terms other than the ones that are used frequently to justify it.

[54] Political obligation rests on a narrow interpretation of order and stability in Charles S. Hyneman with Charles E. Gilbert, *Popular Government in America: Foundations and Principles* (New York: Atherton Press, 1968), pp. 274–275.

[55] A minority of the Eisenhower Commission on Violence cited ethical criteria in its dissent from the majority's faulting of civil disobedience: n. 4, *supra*.

Meanwhile, three compelling reasons support the incorporation into American democratic philosophy of *civil* disobedience. As a buffer between civil liberties and rights, and direct action and Communardist ideas, having kinship with both, it provides a testing zone for challenges to representative democracy without complete submission to either established or new rules of the game. Civil disobedience takes soundings for the operative formulas of democracy, not the least of which is how to probe for a conception of justice held by dissidents and state alike. Finally, the phenomenon is an educational strategy to rethink persistent questions of political obligation. For all three reasons incentives are supplied, not only by intellectual curiosity, but also by the power, merits and inadequacies of discontent itself.

21/*From* Final Report of the National Commission on the Causes and Prevention of Violence: Civil Disobedience*

(Section I is adopted by a majority of the Commission: Commissioners Boggs, Hoffer, Hruska, Jaworski, Jenner, McCulloch and McFarland. Commissioners Eisenhower, Harris, Hart, Higginbotham and Menninger do not adopt Section I, but instead believe that such relationship as may exist between disobedience to law and the contemporary forms of violence occurring in the United States is more adequately and accurately discussed in Chapter 2 of the Task Force Report, *Law and Order Reconsidered*, which is incorporated herein as Section II. Cardinal Cooke does not join the majority statement in Section I but does approve of Section II. Thus, all Commissioners approve of Section II.

(Four Commissioners have filed additional statements, appearing in section III as follows: (A) additional statement of Cardinal Cooke, (B) additional statement of Ambassador Harris, (C) additional statement of Senator Hart, and (D) additional statement of Judge Higginbotham.)

* An edited version of statement issued December 8, 1969.

SOURCE: *Final Report of the National Commission on the Causes and Prevention of Violence* (Washington, D.C.: G.P.O., 1969).

I

In a Task Force Report, *Law and Order Reconsidered,* presented to our Commission, the authors found it impossible to present a discourse on law and law enforcement without including a discussion of civil disobedience as contemporarily practiced. We, too, regard the impact of civil disobedience practices as so relevant to the problem of maintaining our society obedient to law that, in addition to endorsing the Staff Report,[1] we feel impelled to add comments of our own.

Our concern with civil disobediences is not that they may involve acts of violence *per se.* Most of them do not. Rather, our concern is that erosion of the law is an inevitable consequence of widespread civil disobediences.

> As observed by a legal scholar, . . . it is necessary to persuade those bent on civil disobedience that their conduct is fraught with danger, that violation of one law leads to violation of other laws, and eventually to a climate of lawlessness that by easy stages leads to violence.[2]

Our Commission heard the testimony of a number of noted educators who described their experiences with and causes of campus disruptions. The head of one of the nation's largest universities summed up his views with this comment: "I think that civil disobediences are mainly responsible for the present lawbreaking on university campuses."

An analysis of widely publicized defiances of law antecedent to the eruption of campus disorders supports that conclusion. For several years, our youth has been exposed to dramatic demonstrations of disdain for law by persons from whom exemplary conduct was to be expected. Segregationist governors had disobeyed court orders and had proclaimed their defiance of judicial institutions; civil rights leaders had openly disobeyed court injunctions and had urged their followers to do likewise; striking teachers' union members had contemptuously ignored judicial decrees. It was not surprising that college students, following adult example, destroyed scientific equipment and research data, interfered with the rights of others by occupying laboratories and classrooms, and in several instances temporarily closed their colleges.

---

[1] Incorporated herein as Section II.

[2] Norman Dorsen, Professor of Law and Director of the Arthur Garfield Hays Liberties Program, New York University School of Law.

The cancerous growth of disobediences has now reached many high schools and junior high schools of the nation.

Pointing out that force and repression are not the only threats to the rule of law, the dean of one of the nation's largest law schools observed:

> The danger also arises from those groups whose commitments to social reform and the eradication of injustices lead to the defiance of law and the creation of disorder. We are learning that the rule of law can be destroyed through lack of fidelity to the law by large numbers of citizens as well as through abuses of authority by governmental officials.[3]

In our democratic society, lawlessness cannot be justified on the grounds of individual belief. The spectrum of individual consciences encompasses social and political beliefs replete with discordant views. If, for example, the civil libertarian in good conscience becomes a disobeyer of law, the segregationist is endowed with the same choice of conscience, or vice versa. If this reasoning is carried to its logical conclusion, we must also make allowance for the grievances of numerous groups of citizens who regard themselves shackled by laws in which they do not believe. Is each group to be free to disregard due process and to violate laws considered objectionable? If personal or group selectivity of laws to be obeyed is to be the yardstick, we shall face nationwide disobedience of many laws and thus anarchy.

We regard the right of peaceful dissent to be fundamental, not only to the individual freedoms we enjoy, but to the social progress so essential to our nation. Yet, just as fundamental are the disciplines that must control our individual and group actions, without which individual freedoms would be threatened and social progress retarded.

The United States Supreme Court, in upholding convictions for contempt of court of civil rights leaders, admonished all our citizens in these words:

> . . . no man can be judge in his own case, however exalted his station, however righteous his motives, and irrespective of his race, color, politics or religion. . . . One may sympathize with the petitioners' impatient commitment to their cause. But respect for judicial process is a small price to pay for the civilizing hand of law, which alone can give abiding meaning to constitutional freedom.[4]

[3] Francis A. Allen, Dean of the Law School and Professor of Law, University of Michigan.
[4] *Walker v. City of Birmingham*, U.S. 307, 320–321.

Every time a court order is disobeyed, each time an injunction is violated, each occasion on which a court decision is flouted, the effectiveness of our judicial system is eroded. How much erosion can it tolerate? It takes no prophet to know that our judicial system cannot face wholesale violations of its orders and still retain its efficacy. Violators must ponder the fact that once they have weakened the judicial system, the very ends they sought to attain—and may have attained—cannot then be preserved. For the antagonist of the disobeyer's attained objectives most likely will proceed viciously to violate them and since judicial institutions would no longer possess essential authority and power, the "rights" initially gained could be quickly lost.

It is argued that in instances where disobeyers seek to test the constitutionality of a legislative enactment or a court decree, and are willing to accept punishment, their acts should be condoned. We suggest that if in good faith the constitutionality of a statute, ordinance or a court decree is to be challenged, it can be done effectively by one individual or a small group. While the judicial test is in progress, all other dissenters should abide by the law involved until it is declared unconstitutional.

We commend to our fellow citizens the words of Richard Cardinal Cushing:

> . . . observance of law is the eternal safeguard of liberty, and defiance of law is the surest road to tyranny. . . . Even among lawabiding men, few laws are loved, but they are uniformly respected and not resisted.

If we are to maintain and improve our democratic society, the government, including the judiciary, must have the respect and the loyalty of its citizens.

II *

Disobedience to Law

Over the past two decades increasing numbers of people seem to have embraced the idea that active disobedience to valid law—

---

* This section reproduces Chapter 2 of the Report of our staff Task Force on Law and Law Enforcement, *Law and Order Reconsidered* (U.S. Government Printing Office: Washington, D.C., 1969). The chapter was prepared by the Directors of the Task Force, based in part on contributions by Francis A. Allen, Dean of the Law School, University of Michigan; Charles Monson, Associate Academic Vice President, University of Utah; and Eugene V. Rostow, Professor of Law, Yale University.

perhaps even violent disobedience—is justified for the purpose of achieving a desirable political goal. This idea found widespread support in the South as the white majority in that region resisted enforcement of the constitutionally defined rights of Negroes, and some such notion was probably not far from the minds of the Alabama State Troopers when they attacked Dr. King's peaceful demonstration at Selma in 1965. No doubt it was also prominent in the thinking of the Chicago policemen who administered punishment to the demonstrators in Chicago during the Democratic Convention of 1968.

The same idea—that disobedience to law is justified in a good cause which can be furthered in no other way—is also widely held by many students, black citizens and other groups pressing for social change in America today. It is the illegal and sometimes violent activities of these groups that have been most perplexing and disturbing to the great majority of Americans. Their actions have prompted the most intense interest in the ancient philosophical question of man's duty of obedience to the state. Business lunches and suburban cocktail parties have come to sound like freshman seminars in philosophy, as an older generation has argued back and forth over the rightness and the wrongness of "what the kids and the Negroes are doing."

When deliberate, active disobedience to duly enacted, constitutionally valid law is widely engaged in as a political tactic, and when "civil disobedience" is a topic hotly debated on every side, it is impossible for a Task Force on Law and Law Enforcement to file a report that does not discuss this age-old subject, however briefly.

THE AMERICAN IDEAL. In a democratic society, dissent is the catalyst of progress. The ultimate viability of the system depends upon its ability to accommodate dissent; to provide an orderly process by which disagreements can be adjudicated, wrongs righted, and the structure of the system modified in the face of changing conditions. No society meets all these needs perfectly. Moreover, political and social organizations are, by their nature, resistant to change. This is as it should be, because stability —order—is a fundamental aim of social organization. Yet stability must not become atrophy, and the problem is to strike the proper balance between amenability to change and social stability.

Every society represents a style of living. The style is represented by the way in which people relate to the social structure, the way in which social decisions are made, the procedures which govern the ways people in the society relate to each other. In a democratic society such as ours, the governing ideals are government by the rule of law, equality before the law, and ultimate control of the law-making process by the people. We depend upon these principles both to accommodate and to limit change, and to insure the style of living we prefer.

As Tocqueville observed, America is peculiarly a society of law. The law has played a greater part among us than is the case in any other social system—in our restless and jealous insistence on the utmost range of freedom for the individual; in our zeal to confine the authority of the state within constitutional dikes; and in our use of law as a major instrument of social change. The practice of judicial review in the United States has had an extraordinary development, with no real parallels elsewhere. It has kept the law a powerful and persistent influence in every aspect of our public life.

We believe with Jefferson that the just powers of government are derived—and can only be derived—from the consent of the governed. We are an independent, stiff-necked people, suspicious of power, and hardly docile before authority. We never hesitate to challenge the justness and the constitutional propriety of the powers our governments and other social institutions assert. In the robust and sinewy debates of our democracy, law is never taken for granted simply because it has been properly enacted.

Our public life is organized under the explicit social compact of the Constitution, ratified directly by the people, not the states, and designed to be enforced by the courts and by the political process as an instrument to establish and at the same time to limit the powers of government. As Justice Brandeis once observed, "[t]he doctrine of the separation of powers was adopted by the Convention of 1787, not to promote efficiency but to preclude the exercise of arbitrary power. The purpose was, not to avoid friction, but, by means of the inevitable friction incident to the distribution of the governmental powers among three departments, to save the people from autocracy. . . . And protection of the individual . . . from the arbitrary or capricious exercise of power . . . was believed to be an essential of free government."

The social contract of our Constitution goes beyond the idea of the separation of powers, and of enforceable limits on the competence of government. The governments established by the national and state constitutions of the United States are not omnipotent. A basic feature of the Constitution, made explicit in the Ninth and Tenth Amendments, is that rights not delegated to governments are reserved to the people. The Amendments may not be directly enforceable in the courts, but the idea they represent animates many judicial decisions, and influences the course of legislation and other public action.

In a multitude of ways, the Constitution assures the individual a wide zone of privacy and of freedom. It protects him when accused of crime. It asserts his political rights—his right to speak, to vote, and to assemble peaceably with his fellows to petition the government for a redress of his grievances. Freedom of speech and of the press are guaranteed. Religious liberty is proclaimed, and an official establishment of religion proscribed. And the Constitution seeks assurance that society will remain open and diverse, hospitable to freedom, and organized around many centers of power and influence, by making the rules of federalism and of liberty enforceable in the courts.

The unwritten constitution of our habits is dominated by the same concern for preserving individual freedom against encroachment by the state or by social groups. The anti-trust laws; the rights of labor; the growing modern use of state power to assure the equality of the Negro; the wide dispersal of power, authority, and opportunity in the hands of autonomous institutions of business, labor, and education— all bespeak a characteristic insistence that our social arrangements protect liberty, and rest on the legitimacy of consent, either through the Constitution itself, made by the people, and capable of change only by their will, or through legislation and other established methods of social action.

In broad outline, such is the pluralist social compact which has evolved out of our shared experience as a people. It has its roots in our history. And it grows and changes, in accordance with its own rules and aspirations, as every generation reassesses its meaning and its ideals.

OUR CONTEMPORARY DISCONTENTS. Today there are many who maintain that these ideals, and the institutions established to maintain them, no longer operate properly. In recent years, increasing numbers of Americans have taken to the streets to express their views on basic issues. Some come to exercise their right to dissent by parades and picketing. Some dramatize their causes by violating laws they feel to be wrong. Some use the issues being protested as drums to beat in a larger parade. For example, the Vietnam war has been used on one side as a dramatic moment in the ubiquitous, always-evil Communist conspiracy; on the other as an exemplar of the fundamental diabolism of western capitalist nations. Some take to the streets in the belief that the public, if made aware of their grievances, will institute the necessary processes to correct them. Others come in anger; not hopeful, but insistent; serving notice, not seeking audience. Finally, there are even a few who take to the streets to tear at the fabric of society; to confront, to commit acts of violence, to create conditions under which the present system can be swept away.

Out of the widening protest, one disturbing theme has repeatedly appeared. Increasingly, those who protest speak of civil disobedience or even revolution as necessary instruments of effecting needed social change, charging that the processes of lawful change built into the system are inadequate to the task.

The American response to this disobedience to law—to events which are contrary to our fundamental beliefs about the mode of social and political change—has been ambivalent. The reason lies in the fact that the American people are going through a crisis of conscience. The issues in whose name violence has been committed have deeply disturbed and divided the American people. The tactics of the demonstrators have encountered angry opposition, but many Americans continue to sympathize with some or all of the goals sought by the demonstrators. After all, although one might argue that the Negro has advanced in the last ten years, few would maintain he has attained full first-class citizenship. And who would say the ghettos are not an agonizing disgrace? Similarly, Vietnam is hardly an open-and-shut case. The only point of view from which it is clearly praiseworthy is the self-interest of ourselves and our allies. The draft, another key issue, is at best a regrettable and clumsily administered system. Finally, when the young charge that our system—political and social—is shot through with hypocrisy, only the most fanatic feels no twinge.

We must, of course, realize that civil rights demonstrations arise from great suffering, disappointment and yearning. We must recognize the importance to the democratic process, and to the ultimate well-being of our nation, of young people combatting hypocrisy and indifference. But when these emotions become a basis for action and when that action creates social disorder, even the most sympathetic are forced to judge whether and to what extent the ends sought justify the means that are being used.

The difficult problem in this endeavor is to maintain perspective. The issues have reached a stage of polarization. Partisans on each side constantly escalate the rhetorical savagery of their positions, adding nothing but volume and abuse. There is a great temptation to take sides without thoughtful inquiry—if for no other reason than because it is simpler. What are some of the considerations which should guide us in this inquiry?

MORAL JUSTIFICATIONS FOR DISOBE-
DIENCE TO LAW: THE NEEDS OF THE INDIVIDUAL. The idea that men have the right to violate the law under certain circumstances is not new. The oldest justification for such action seems to have been through appeal to a higher "natural law" which is the only proper basis of human law. This theory, which dates at least as far back as

Plato, and which is in our own Declaration of Independence,[5] has recently found expression in the thought of Martin Luther King:

> A just law is a man-made law of God. An unjust law is a code that is out of harmony with the moral law. To put it in the terms of Saint Thomas Aquinas, an unjust law is a human law that is not rooted in eternal and natural law.[6]

For St. Thomas political authority was derived from God and hence binding in conscience, but where authority was defective in title or exercise, there was no obligation of conscience.[7] Such a condition arose in the case of a ruler who had either usurped power or who, though legitimate, was abusing his authority by ruling unjustly. Indeed, when the ruler contravened the very purpose of his authority by ordering a sinful action, the subject was under an obligation *not* to obey. In the case of abuse of authority, St. Thomas apparently endorsed nothing more than passive resistance by the citizen; but where the ruler illegitimately possessed himself of power through violence, and there was no other recourse for the citizen, then St. Thomas allowed active resistance and even tyrannicide.

Later Catholic thinkers, such as the Jesuit, Francis Suarez, denied the divine right of kings, holding that the ruler derives his authority immediately from the people and only ultimately from God. These doctrines led logically to the conclusion that in any circumstances in which a ruler turns into a tyrant, whether originally a legitimate ruler or not, he may be deposed by the people, by force if necessary. This conclusion became, of course, the generally accepted view in the secular world, with the theories of Locke and Jefferson and the American and French Revolutions in the eighteenth century and the rise of liberal democracy in the nineteenth.

The notion of a "social compact" was always closely bound up with the emerging ideas of popular sovereignty.[8] This theory, especially prominent in John Locke, expresses the view that governments evolve by the consent of the governed and that the constitution establishing a government is a contract or agreement which, once it is established, is binding upon all men, both those opposed to it and those who favor it. When government's laws are consistent with terms of

5 "We hold these truths to be self-evident, that all men are created equal, that they are endowed by their Creator with certain unalienable Rights, that among these are Life, Liberty and the pursuit of Happiness."

6 King, "Letter from the Birmingham Jail" (1963).

7 See generally the illuminating article by MacGuigan, "Civil Disobedience and Natural Law," 11 *Catholic Lawyer* 118 (1965).

8 See Copleston, *History of Philosophy*, vol. 3 (Westminster, Md., 1953), pp. 348–49.

the covenant, then the people must obey them. But the people "are absolved from obedience when illegal attempts are made upon their liberties or properties, and may oppose the unlawful violence of those who were their magistrates when they invade their properties contrary to the trust put in them. . . ." [9]

Most of the unlawful opposition today to the Vietnam war is justified on the ground that the war is itself immoral and "unlawful" in various respects. Since it is immoral, the argument goes, there is no moral duty to obey those laws which are in the aid of the conduct of the war. Indeed, the argument continues, one's true moral duty is to resist the war and to take affirmative action to impede its prosecution. On theories of this kind, Americans have refused to be drafted; they have disrupted Selective Service facilities and destroyed Selective Service records; they have vilified the President, the Secretary of State and the Secretary of Defense and attempted to disrupt their public speeches; they have attempted to bar companies and governmental agencies participating in the war effort from university campuses and to disrupt the universities that refused to accede to that demand.

At the level of individual morality, the problem of disobedience to law is wholly intractable. One is tempted to suggest that even if the war is immoral, the general level of morality of the country is not much improved by the conduct described above. Moreover, if we allow individual conscience to guide obedience to the law, we must take all consciences. The law cannot distinguish between the consciences of saints and sinners. As Burke Marshall has said:

> If the decision to break the law really turned on individual conscience, it is hard to see in law how Dr. King is better off than Governor Ross Barnett of Mississippi, who also believed deeply in his cause and was willing to go to jail.[10]

Where issues are framed in purely moral terms, they are usually incapable of resolution by substantially unanimous agreement. Moral decisions are reached by "individual prudential application of principle, with the principles so general as to be only of minimal assistance and with almost the whole field thus left to prudence." [11] This fact is illustrated by the story of the exchange that occurred between Emerson and Thoreau, the latter of whom had in 1845 personally seceded from the United States in protest against slavery. As part of his anti-

[9] Locke, *Second Treatise on Civil Government,* ch. 19, "Of the Dissolution of Government," sec. 228.

[10] Burke Marshall, "The Protest Movement and the Law," 51 U. Va. L. Rev. 785, 800 (1965).

[11] MacGuigan, *op. cit.,* p. 125.

slavery campaign, Thoreau was spending a night in jail. Emerson paid him a visit, greeting him by saying, "What are you doing in there, Henry?" Thoreau looked at him through the bars and replied, "What are you doing out there, Ralph?" [12]

But the issue raised by conscientious disobedience to law also has some more tractable social dimensions. What is the effect upon our society of this kind of conduct? For instance, how does it affect the people who engage in the disobedience? Does it have an effect upon other people? What does it do to our system of laws?

THE PROBLEM OF CONTAGION: THE NEEDS OF SOCIETY. Although there are some who argue that tolerating any form of law violation serves as an encouragement of other forms of anti-social or criminal behavior by the violators, some research in this area suggests precisely the opposite. A series of studies of approximately 300 young black people who engaged in a series of acts of civil disobedience were undertaken in a western city. On the basis of their observations, the authors concluded: "[T]here have been virtually no manifestations of delinquency or anti-social behavior, no school drop-outs, and no known illegitimate pregnancies. This is a remarkable record for any group of teen-age children of any color in any community in 1964." [13]

In any event, the evidence is insufficient to demonstrate that acts of civil disobedience of the more limited kind inevitably lead to an increased disrespect for law or propensity toward crime. In fact, some experts have argued that engaging in disciplined civil disobedience allows people to channel resentment into constructive paths, thereby reducing the propensity for engaging in antisocial behavior.

But the fact that disobedience to law does not appear adversely to affect the attitudes of the people who emerge in it is only one small part of the problem. For such conduct does have a serious adverse effect both upon other people in the society, and, most importantly of all, upon the system of laws upon which society must inevitably depend.

The effect of civil disobedience upon others in the community is clear. Except in the case of those acts designed solely to appeal to the conscience of the community, the purpose of much contemporary disobedience to law is to influence community action by harassing or intimidating the members of the community into making concessions to a particular point of view. In the case of the opposition to the Vietnam war, for example, those engaged in acts of disobedience are

[12] *Ibid.*

[13] Pierce and West, "Six Years of Sit-Ins: Psychodynamics Causes and Effects," 12 *International Journal of Social Psychiatry* 30 (Winter 1966).

largely bent upon making miserable the lives of public officials who support the war, upon bringing economic pressure to bear on commercial enterprises participating in the war effort, and upon generally inconveniencing the public to dramatize a disaffection for war and convince others that the war is not worth the trouble it is causing. To the extent that these efforts succeed, others are obviously adversely affected.[14] But the most serious effect of all is suggested in the following question:

> [W]hat lesson is being taught to the wider community by the precept and example of civil disobedience? Is it tutelage in nonviolence or in defiance of authority, in rational confrontation of social ills or in undisciplined activism? [15]

There is every reason to believe that the lesson taught by much of the current disobedience to law is disastrous from the standpoint of the maintenance of a democratic society.

The experience of India in this regard is instructive because that country has had such a long and widespread familiarity with the practice of civil disobedience:

> The fact is that the effect of protest behavior on the functioning of the political system has been palpable. We have already seen that Indians compel official attention and constrain decision-making by deliberately engaging in activities that threaten public order. Violence or the threat of violence has become an important instrument in Indian politics. Public protests involving a threat to public order and nonviolent civil disobedience have become habitual responses to alleged failures by government to do what a group of people want. While it is true that political accommodation is real in India, it is achieved at a higher level of political disorder than in any other of the world's democracies.[16]

The experience of India seems to indicate that civil disobedience has a strong tendency to become a pattern of conduct which soon replaces normal legal processes as the usual way in which society functions. Put in American terms, this would mean, once the pattern is established, that the accepted method of getting a new traffic light might be to disrupt traffic by blocking intersections, that complaints

---

[14] Even in the narrowly defined situation of acts designed solely to appeal to the conscience of the community, adverse effects frequently flow to others. Thus a refusal to accept induction into the armed services means that someone else must serve.

[15] Allen, "Civil Disobedience and the Legal Order," Part 1, 36 *University of Cincinnati Law Review* 1, 30 (1967).

[16] Bayley, *Non-violent Civil Disobedience and the Police: Lesson to be Learned from India* (consultant paper submitted to the Task Force), p. 15.

against businessmen might result in massive sit-ins, that improper garbage service might result in a campaign of simply dumping garbage into the street, and so on. Of course, these kinds of actions are not unknown in America today, but in India they have become a necessary part of the political system. Without a massive demonstration to support it, a grievance simply is not taken seriously because everyone knows that if the grievance were serious, there would be a demonstration to support it.

The adverse effect upon normal democratic processes is obvious. Though not intended to destroy democratic processes, civil disobedience tends plainly to impair their operation. This is a fact to which those who engage in civil disobedience should give consideration lest, in seeking to improve society, they may well seriously injure it.

This observation, however, will not answer the arguments of those who believe that the urgency of their message is so strong that illegal tactics are weapons that must be used—whatever the risks that such use may entail. But even urgent messages too frequently repeated lose their appeal. Where once people at least listened patiently, now only deaf ears are turned. Moreover, as Martin Luther King recognized, violence against an oppressor only tends in the long run to justify the oppression. Repeatedly putting one's body "on the line" does not enhance, but diminishes, the worth of that body to the dominant society. Those militants who now advocate revolution as the only alternative have recognized this truth.

The belief that a violent revolution is necessary to achieve social justice depends on the assumption that certain injustices are intrinsic to our system and therefore not amenable to change within the system. For revolution is justified only as a last resort, when justice is achievable by no other means.

We agree with the overwhelming majority of the people in this country that our problems, serious as they are, are not of the kind that make revolution even thinkable, let alone justifiable. We believe that political and social mechanisms do exist and have produced significant change in recent years. The remedy for the discontented, we believe, is to seek change through lawful mechanisms, changes of the kind that other chapters of the Task Force report suggest.

But our beliefs and our words are really beside the point. What is important is rather the beliefs of those diverse, alienated groups in our society for whom the political and social mechanisms do not seem to work. We can only hope that the majority will respond convincingly to the needs of the discontented, and that the discontented will remain open to the possibility of achieving this response through peaceful means.

CONCLUSION. Official lawlessness —by some southern governors, by some policemen, by corrupt individuals in positions of public trust—is widely recognized as intolerable in a society of law, even if this recognition is too infrequently translated into the effective action to do something about the problem. We believe that the time has also come for those participating today in the various protest movements, on and off the college campuses, to subject their disobedience to law to realistic appraisal. The question that needs to be put to young people of generous impulses all over the country is whether tactics relying on deliberate, symbolic and sometimes violent lawbreaking are in fact contributing to the emergency of a society that will show enhanced regard for human values—for equality, decency, and individual volition.

For some in the protest movement, this is not a relevant inquiry; their motivations are essentially illiberal and destructive. But this is not descriptive of most of those engaged today in social protest, including most who have violated the law in the course of their protest; their intention is to recall America to the ideals upon which she is founded.

We believe, however, that candid examination of what is occurring in the United States today will lead to the conclusion that disobedience to valid law as a tactic of protest by discontented groups is *not* contributing to the emergence of a more liberal and humane society, but is, on the contrary, producing an opposite tendency. The fears and resentments created by symbolic law violation have strengthened the political power of some of the most destructive elements in American society. Only naive and willful blindness can obscure the strength of these dark forces, which, but for the loosening of the bonds of law, might otherwise lie quiescent beneath the surface of our national life. An almost Newtonian process of action and reaction is at work, and fanaticism even for laudable goals breeds fanaticism in opposition. Just as "extremism in defense of liberty" does not promote liberty, so extremism in the cause of justice will extinguish hopes for a just society.

III

A. Additional Statement of Cardinal Cooke

Our democratic society is based on the concept and common agreement that civil law deserves the respect and obedience of every citizen. Civil disobedience as an act of conscience expressed by public acts of defiance is permissible only as a last resort to obtain justice when all the other remedies available in our system of representation and checks and balances have been exhausted. Civil disobedience can only be justified when a civil law is conscientiously regarded as being clearly in conflict with a higher law—namely our Constitution, the natural law or divine law. In this extreme case, non-violent forms of civil disobedience, accompanied by willing acceptance of any penalty the law provides, are the only means that can be justified in our democratic society. These principles are not only the foundation of an ordered society under law, but they guarantee our freedom and our social progress as well.

B. Additional Statement of Ambassador Harris

I must take exception to Section I of this chapter. No data developed by or presented to this Commission show a significant relationship between civil disobedience based upon conscience and violence, as the statement itself admits when it says that most civil disobedience does not involve acts of violence *per se*. Furthermore, governmental commissions should tread very lightly, if at all, in fields where individuals make claims of conscience. Those who have urged civil disobedience, from Gandhi to Martin Luther King, and including those who supported the trials of Nazi leaders at Nuremberg, have asserted that there are some laws so repugnant to the dignity of man that regardless of the concurrence of the majority, the law must not be obeyed. A nation whose history enshrines the civil disobedience of the Boston Tea Party cannot fail to recognize at least the symbolic merit of demonstrated hostility to unjust laws.

I am not nearly so certain as are the supporters of Section I that the legal process will always respond effectively to those who resort only to petition and lawsuit. Perhaps my uncertainty is due to the fact that I see a relationship between the civil disobedience of anti-segregation sit-ins and the eventual elimination of laws requiring segregation of the races. Certainly, black Americans had used legal process at least as early as the Dred Scott case. Yet, despite a Civil War, constitutional amendments and court decisions, black Americans at the beginning of this decade were still faced with laws and practices treating them as second-class citizens. Section I condemns acts such as the sit-ins if they were not for the purpose of instituting a specific test case.

Section I lumps together refusals to obey a law because of the fundamental demands of conscience, on the one hand, and the simple refusal to obey a law because one disagrees with a particular law, on the other. Although I agree that both law violators are to be punished, I believe there is a difference in incidental willful violation of the law, and carefully considered violation based upon clearly stated objections that have been brought to the attention of government through traditional legislative-legal process and have nonetheless been ignored.

It should be clear that extensive acts of civil disobedience based upon the demands of conscience are a symptom, and not a cause of societal ills. When otherwise law-abiding citizens claim that conscience will not permit them to obey laws supported by the majority, that majority must, if the society is to remain healthy, examine the laws to ascertain whether they are fair and just, and change them if they are not. This is the process followed in reacting to the civil disobedience of black Americans, and it is a process no less necessary in dealing with others who resort to civil disobedience because of a claim that their conscience will not permit obedience of the law.

I believe, as stated in Chapter 6, that "every society, including our own, must have effective means of enforcing its laws, whatever may be the claims of conscience of individuals." But law enforcement, without continuing review and modification of law, is not the hallmark of a democratic society.

Those who adopted Section I have never belonged to a group required to sit in the back of the bus, or excluded from restaurants because of race, with the approval of legislatures, courts and administrators. I am a member of such a group, and I refused to obey those segregation laws, even though I knew they had been approved by the Supreme Court in *Plessy* v. *Ferguson* and affirmed by decades of acceptance by the majority. It seems unlikely that the segregation law would have been changed had only one person or a small group indicated opposition to it.

It is not inconceivable to me that other persons may feel as deeply about other subjects as I did about racial segregation, and with equal justification. Such well-founded opposition, even if expressed through the ultimate recourse to civil disobedience, is a reflection of the highest respect and hope for a democratic society. It manifests a faith that if the majority understand the real consequences of its intransigence, the majority will change.

Willingness to incur the wrath and punishment of government can represent the highest loyalty and respect for a democratic society. Such respect and self-sacrifice may well prevent, rather than cause, violence.[17]

---

[17] "In fact, some experts have argued that engaging in disciplined civil disobedience allows people to channel resentment into constructive paths, thereby reducing the propensity for engaging in antisocial behavior." *Law and Order Reconsidered*, ch. 2, "Disobedience to Law," p. 19 (incorporated as Section II).

C. Additional Statement of Senator Hart

Despite the compelling logic of the majority opinion on civil disobedience, I feel that history will continue to note circumstances when it is not immoral to be illegal.

Certainly, it is risky for a society to tolerate the concept of civil disobedience, however non-violent it may be. The British governors of India will testify to that. But my faith in the flexibility of the American democratic system just will not allow me to get terribly "up tight" about the prospect of massive disobedience.

We all revere the rule of law. Yet, legal absolutism is as hard to swallow as straight whiskey. A drop of water not only improves the flavor of the grain but diminishes the strain on the system that must absorb it.

Perhaps unfortunately, this issue of unquestioning respect for law arises at a moment of history when the civil rights movement has proven the social efficacy of occasional, selective civil disobedience.

As Ambassador Harris points out in her views, legal absolutism would have had an equally difficult time achieving full consensus after the Boston Tea Party.

If an American citizen honestly feels his conscience to be offended by a law, I would have difficulty disputing his right to dramatize his dissent through disobedience provided that:

a. His disobedience is absent violence on his part, and

b. He is willing to submit to the sanctions that disobedience may visit upon him.

Understand, any tolerance that I might feel toward the disobeyer is dependent on his willingness to accept whatever punishment the law may impose. This willingness provides the test of moral conviction and is the safeguard against capricious lawlessness.

If the dramatic act attracts no sympathy from the public that is its audience, if it raises no issue that evokes mass response, if it makes no constitutional point that the courts can agree with, then little harm is done to the fabric of society.

And if the act illuminates a wrong, some good could come of it. My experience in Congress tells me that remedial legislation is not always enacted in response to the cool logic and moral concepts of the legislators.

Reputable scholars tell us that there are indeed occasions when public "heat" has prodded leadership bodies into actions they may otherwise have avoided—a theory I find difficult to dispute.

My faith in the Constitution is great. And our constitutional system will certainly admit of fewer Joans of Arc than less enlightened structures.

Still, a close scrutiny of my own failings—at the risk of unfairly projecting a generalization from a single specific case—leads me to have some doubts about the infallibility of Congress.

It is even conceivable that I might concur in a bill that history comes to regard as an immoral measure. And if one or several citizens truly feel their consciences so offended by that law that they are willing to accept punishment rather than obey it, then I find it difficult to condemn them in advance.

D. Additional Statement of Judge Higginbotham

1. WHEN THIS COMMISSION has been unanimous on so many matters of fundamental importance, it is indeed unfortunate that a majority of seven has caused a minority of six to get involved in an extended debate on the tangential issue of non-violent civil disobedience.[18] The Task Force chapter on "Disobedience to Law," [19] which apparently all of the Commissioners today adopt, clearly states: "In any event the evidence is insufficient to demonstrate that acts of civil disobedience of the more limited kind lead to an increased disrespect for law or propensity toward crime."

Of course, it is always easier to blame the failures of our society on those who protest than it is to accept our responsibility to create a just society.

Is non-violent civil disobedience, as the majority suggests, the major factor to single out as leading inevitably to the erosion of law and the onset of violence? It was not non-violent civil disobedience which caused the death of the Kennedys and Dr. King. It is not non-violent civil disobedience which causes millions to go to bed ill-housed, ill-fed, and too often with too little hope.

---

[18] There is no disagreement among any of the Commissioners in our unanimous condemnation of civil disobedience accompanied by violence. I sincerely regret that, due to the pressure of our adjournment time, we were not able to have an additional Commission meeting wherein my present separate statement could be presented and considered. For I know that by their *deeds,* some members of this Commission's majority, such as Congressman William M. McCulloch, have been great profiles in courage to all men interested in equal justice under the law. Congressman McCulloch, one of the most distinguished members of the United States House of Representatives, was a member of the Kerner Commission, and for decades he has been a champion for the human rights of all.

[19] This chapter is a portion of the extraordinarily excellent and well-balanced report of the Task Force on Law and Law Enforcement under the superb leadership of James S. Campbell, Esquire.

Only last month in their superb report on *Poverty Amid Plenty: The American Paradox,* the President's Commission on Income Maintenance Programs found that in 1968, twenty-five million Americans were living in poverty as measured by the federal government's own poverty index. The Commission further found:

". . . severe poverty and its effects throughout the nation and among all ethnic groups. This poverty is not only relative to rising American living standards, but is often stark and absolute. There are too many American families with inadequate shelter, inadequate clothing, absolute hunger, and unhealthy living conditions. Millions of persons in our society do not have a sufficient share of America's affluence to live decently. They eke out a bare existence under deplorable conditions." [20]

The major problem in our country thus is not non-violent civil disobedience; rather, as the National Advisory Commission on Civil Disorders (the Kerner Commission) noted, it has been our failure to have "a realization of common opportunities for all within a single society," and the failure to have a "commitment to national action" which is ". . . compassionate, massive and sustained, backed by the resources of the most powerful and the richest nation on this earth. From every American it will require new attitudes, new understandings and, above all, new will." [21]

2. DURING THE EARLY 1960's, John Fitzgerald Kennedy, Martin Luther King, Robert Francis Kennedy and Lyndon Baines Johnson gave great hope to many who were weak, or poor, and particularly to those who were non-white.
As I read one portion of Section I, there appears to be an implicit call for a retreat from the spirit of the early 1960s when our country was finally starting to face up to its obligation to right the wrongs which had been imposed on black Americans for more than three centuries. Nowhere is that retreat more evident than in the majority statement that:

We suggest that if in good faith the constitutionality of a statute, ordinance or a court decree is to be challenged, it could be done effectively by *one* individual or a small group. While the judicial test is in progress, all other dissenters should abide by the law involved until it is declared unconstitutional.

[20] Report of the President's Commission on Income Maintenance Programs, *Poverty Amid Plenty: The American Paradox* (Prelim. Ed. November 12, 1969), p. 1.
[21] *Report of the National Advisory Commission on Civil Disorders* (U.S. Government Printing Office: Washington, D.C., 1968), p. 1.

Is it the majority's position that while Rosa Parks litigated her refusal to take a back seat in 1955 on the Montgomery, Alabama, bus, all other Negroes were obligated to continue to accept the degradation of the rear seats assigned them?

Is the majority suggesting that when the first Negroes sat in at a lunch counter in Greensboro, North Carolina, all other Negroes were forbidden to seek an integrated lunch until the issue reached the Supreme Court? Does the majority suggest that there is no correlation between the march in Selma, Alabama, and the ultimate passage of the 1965 Civil Rights Act?

So that no one will misunderstand me, let me make clear my concern about the outbreak of riots and other violent public disorders. I do not urge, I do not sanction, I do not suggest violence—spontaneous or planned—as a way to correct injustices in our system. Moreover, I believe that all those adjudicated guilty under constitutionally valid laws, whether for conscientious civil disobedience or for some other violation of law, must bear the penalties.

Of course, a willingness to accept such penalties was an outstanding characteristic of the leaders of the civil rights movement during the last two decades (particularly Dr. King)—unlike many of those who unlawfully sought to frustrate the goals of the civil rights movement. The majority statement ignores the many critical distinctions —of which this is just one—between the actions of the civil rights leaders and their powerful opponents in the South who often used violence or who persistently violated their oath of office to uphold the law of the land.

If the majority's doctrine of "everyone wait until the outcome of the one individual test case" had been applied by black Americans in the 1960s, probably not one present major civil rights statute would have been enacted. I fear that the majority's position ignores the sad actual history of some of the most tragic "legal" repression of the civil rights of Negroes in this country.

Burke Marshall, "one of the late President Kennedy's most valued advisors," [22] set a standard of commitment to human rights which should be a model for our country during its present troubled times. In 1964, in his illuminating book *Federalism and Civil Rights*, Mr. Marshall, then Assistant Attorney General of the Civil Rights Division, discussed the Mississippi experience on the right to vote:

> For significant portions of a few states, and for most of Mississippi, Negro disenfranchisement is still a current practice, almost ninety-five

---

[22] Foreword by the then Attorney General Robert F. Kennedy, July 15, 1964, to Marshall, *Federalism and Civil Rights* (New York: Columbia University Press, 1964), p. x.

years after the enactment of the Fifteenth Amendment. This has been true since the removal of direct (meaning, in this case, military) federal control over the voting and registration processes, and the return of those processes to the states.

This year [in 1964] we have seen the Governor of one state interfere with a local registration board because too many Negroes were being registered. It was only two years ago that another state passed a whole new set of laws aimed at restricting Negro registration, and last year that a third issued new instructions for the strict use of the registration form as a kind of aptitude test.

When the will to keep Negro registration to a minimum is strong, and the routine of determining whose applications are acceptable is within the discretion of local officials, the latitude for discrimination is almost endless. The practices that can be used are virtually infinite.

In Mississippi then, the statistics alone are illuminating. In 1899, twenty-five years after the armed maneuvering of 1874 and nine years after the 1890 convention, the number of Negroes of voting age who were registered was down to 9 percent. By 1955, the gap had widened. In only eleven counties were over 10 percent registered (and in one of those counties the figure was to fall to less than 2 percent the following year); in eight counties, the figure was between 5 and 10 percent: in twenty counties it was from 1 to 5 percent; and in forty-three counties less than 1 percent of Negroes of voting age were registered. The total Negro registration in the state was slightly over 4 percent. These figures are approximately accurate today.

After the invalidation of the white primary, Negroes were prevented, until 1955, from registering by repeated uses of devices so absurd as to be drearily cynical. They were asked to define, for county registrars themselves without training or education, terms such as ex post facto, habeas corpus, due process of law, impeachment, and to interpret the preamble to the Mississippi Constitution. Some were told that they could not register until they could repeat the entire Mississippi Constitution by heart. In one county, Negro applicants were invariably informed that the registrar was not in. In another they were simply refused permission to apply at all.

The pattern of such practices had its inevitable effect. Except in a handful of counties, Negroes could not register to vote, and they did not try.

Following the school decisions of 1954, Mississippi changed its voting laws to meet the expected onslaught of federal law. These became effective on March 24, 1955. As of March, 1964, . . . data . . . taken from records analysis in seventy-two of the eighty-two counties in the state, describe individual incidents and designs of behavior that resulted in continued Negro disenfranchisement under the new laws.

The records show . . . a wide variation in the comprehensibility of the sections of the Mississippi Constitution chosen to test applicants, a matter within the complete discretion of the registrar. For example, the simplest section used is the one stating that there shall be no imprisonment for debt. In one county, this was given often to whites, but never to Negroes. On the other hand, Negroes have been given most complex sections to explain, such as Section 236, describing in detail the levee taxes for the state.

Where the same section is used to test members of both races, the results are not fairly judged. The records disclosed repeated examples where Negroes were turned down for having given inadequate answers even though their answers were better than those given by whites who were accepted.

There were many instances, throughout the counties, of assistance being given to whites, but not to Negroes. In some counties, application forms filled out by whites consistently showed, beyond any possibility of coincidence, almost identical answers on the constitutional interpretation test. In addition, on many occasions, illiterate whites who could not read or answer the questions on the application form without help were registered after being coached by the registrar. At the same time, well-educated Negroes were turned down.[23]

I have cited the Mississippi voting experience in some detail because it demonstrates the tenacity with which injustice can cling to an oppressed group for more than one hundred years when legislative and judicial branches lack the will to destroy injustice.

Recent advances in the field of civil rights have not come about—and could never have come about—solely through judicial tests made "by one individual" while all others in the silent black majority waited for the ultimate constitutional determination.

Rather, the major impetus for the Civil Rights Acts of 1957, 1960, 1964 and 1965, which promised more equal access to the opportunities of our society, resulted from the determination, the spirit, and the non-violent commitment of the many who continually challenged the constitutionality of racial discrimination and awakened the national conscience.[24]

3. A DEBATE ON CIVIL DISOBEDI-ENCE is inexpensive and undemanding. It requires no regeneration of our political and social institutions, no effort to open the doors of opportunity to the disadvantaged, no acts of courage and compassion by dedicated individuals seeking to heal the divisions in our society. It requires neither a reordering of national priorities, nor a reallocation of our immense financial resources.

A debate on civil disobedience can be costly in one sense, however:

---

[23] *Ibid.*, pp. 15–19. See also the perceptive statement of Stephen J. Pollak, the able Assistant Attorney General in charge of the Civil Rights Division in 1968, in his Emancipation Day speech at Mobile, Alabama, Jan. 5, 1969.

[24] I do not, of course, suggest that such protests alone produced the important civil rights legislation of the recent decade, for the support was multi-faceted.

it can distract attention from the real work and the real contributions of this Commission. When legislators and future historians appraise the work of our Commission, I hope that they will remember, not this minor skirmish over a secondary issue, but rather the important recommendations we have made under the unending dedication and great leadership of Dr. Eisenhower.[25] Most fervently of all, I further hope that our nation will find the resolve to support, with decisive action, some of the significant programs which we and other national commissions have recommended, and particularly those of sufficient scope and importance to require a reordering of our nation's priorities and a reallocation of our financial resources.

Despite significant contributions which I think this Commission has made, I must confess to a personal sense of increasing "commission frustration." From having served on three previous national fact-finding commissions, I fear that as some of the conditions in America get worse and worse, our reports about these conditions get better and better. There is too little implementation of the rational solutions proposed, and too often the follow-up is only additional studies.

In the last 25 years our country has been deluged with significant Presidential and national fact-finding commissions, starting with President Truman's Commission to Secure These Rights in 1947. Some of the other great commissions have included the Crime Commission (President's Commission on Law Enforcement and Administration of Justice), The Council to the White House Conference to Fulfill These Rights, the Kerner Commission (National Advisory Commission on Civil Disorders), the Kaiser Commission (President's Committee on Urban Housing) and the Douglas Commission (National Commission on Urban Problems). Thus the problems of poverty, racism and crime have been emphasized and re-emphasized, studied and re-studied, probed and re-probed.

Surveying this landscape, littered with the unimplemented recommendations of so many previous commissions, I am compelled to propose a national moratorium on any additional temporary study commissions to probe the causes of racism, or poverty, or crime, or the urban crisis. The rational response to the work of the great commissions of recent years is not the appointment of still more commissions to study the same problems—but rather the prompt implementation of their many valuable recommendations.

The Kerner Commission concluded its report as follows:

[25] Dr. Milton S. Eisenhower has been the president of three great American universities. He has been the perfect model of an effective and impartial chairman. He has devoted hundreds of hours to the Commission's task, and, in addition, he has the extraordinary virtue of being able to listen both intently and patiently.

One of the first witnesses to be invited to appear before this commission was Dr. Kenneth B. Clark, a distinguished and perceptive scholar. Referring to the reports of earlier riot commissions, he said:

"I read that report . . . of the 1919 riot in Chicago, and it is as if I were reading the report of the investigating committee on the Harlem riot of '35, the report of the investigating committee on the Harlem riot of '43, the report of the McCone Commission on the Watts riot.

"I must again in candor say to you members of this commission—it is a kind of Alice in Wonderland—with the same moving picture re-shown over and over again, the same analysis, the same recommendations, the same inaction." [26]

And I must also conclude my comments with the perceptive statement of a distinguished psychiatrist, Price M. Cobbs, who testified before our Commission. In a foreword to one of the Task Force reports submitted to us, Dr. Cobbs and his colleague, Dr. Grier, note:

The National Commission on the Causes and Prevention of Violence has a grave task. If violence continues at its present pace, we may well witness the end of the grand experiment of democracy. The unheeded report of the Kerner Commission pinpointed the cause of our urban violence, and this report presents the tragic consequences when those in power fail to act on behalf of the weak as well as the powerful.

This country can no longer tolerate the divisions of black and white, haves and have-nots. The pace of events has quickened and dissatisfactions no longer wait for a remedy.

There are fewer great men among us to counsel patience. Their voices have been stilled by the very violence they sought to prevent. Martin Luther King, Jr., the noble advocate of non-violence, may have been the last great voice warning the country to cancel its rendezvous with violence before it is too late.

The truth is plain to see. If the racial situation remains inflammatory and the conditions perpetuating poverty remain unchanged, and if vast numbers of our young see small hope for improvement in the quality of their lives, then this country will remain in danger. Violence will not go away because we will it, and any superficial whitewash will sooner or later be recognized.[27]

---

[26] *Report of the National Advisory Commission on Civil Disorders, op. cit.*, p. 265.

[27] *The Politics of Protest* (New York: Simon and Schuster, 1969), pp. ix, x. Drs. Cobbs and Grier are the authors of *Black Rage*.

22 / Civil Disobedience: Prerequisite for Democracy in Mass Society

CHRISTIAN BAY

I

During a recent debate on the war in Vietnam an irate member of the audience demanded to know if I was in favor of civil disobedience. My reply was "Yes, on some occasions." He sat down in silence, with a broad grin. Nothing else that I said from then on was worth taking seriously, so far as he was concerned. I might as well have come out in favor of arson. And I am sure many in the audience felt as he did.

This widespread tendency to recoil from the very concept of disobedience, even passive and presumably nonviolent disobedience, in a society priding itself on its liberties, is a measure of the degree of stability, if not immunity to real social change, that has been achieved by the present socioeconomic and political system in the United States.

To the spiritual fathers of the American democracy, most notably John Locke and Thomas Jefferson, it seemed evident that any liberty-loving people should have the right to stage even a bloody revolution against a tyrannical government; by comparison, the remedy of nonviolent civil disobedience would seem a mild brew indeed.

Among the most forceful counter-norms, or norms tending to lead many of us to reject *a priori* the very thought of civil disobedience, is another Lockean principle: the sanctity of the rule of law. Spokesmen for our academic as well as our political and economic establishments are for obvious reasons far happier with this part of Locke's theory of civil government.

Now, the classical writings of our democratic heritage, not unlike the Bible or the classical Marxist literature, can be used to prove the legitimacy of almost anything, and therefore, more critically viewed, of almost nothing. This point should be particularly poignant for those who have followed, during the last decades, developments in research and theory in the field of political behavior. For reasons of conveni-

SOURCE: David Spitz, ed., *Political Theory and Social Change* (New York: Atherton Press, 1967), pp. 163–183. Copyright © 1967 by Atherton Press. Reprinted by permission of the author and the publisher.

ence and perhaps of habit as well, it has remained orthodox for our colleagues to proclaim their fealty to our democratic way of life (some, indeed, seem to feel that we are entitled to force other nations, too, to be guided by our example); and this fealty has remained unshaken, by and large, by the wealth of data that have come forth to demonstrate the wide and growing gulf between most of the classical ideals of democracy and what goes on in its name in today's mass societies.

Let us return to the part of our democratic heritage of particular concern here: the insistence on the sanctity of the rule of law. Now, a strong case for exalting the law (and indirectly, the lawyer) can be made from my own political ground of commitment to no system but to the sanctity of life, and the freedoms necessary for living,[1] *insofar as* laws (and lawyers) are to operate to protect all human lives, with priority for those most badly in need of protection. But to claim a corresponding sanctity for the laws that we have today, which as in *every* state to a considerable extent, operate in the service of those who are privileged and influential in our socioeconomic order, seems to me to constitute an outright fraud at the expense of all the political innocents, unless one can claim for oneself, too, the innocence of not knowing any significant part of our modern behavioral literature.

At best a claim can be made that general obedience to the law is a lesser evil than general disobedience, which could well lead to much violence and conceivably even to a return to a Hobbesian state of nature. But this surely is a false issue, for no society has ever known either general obedience or general anarchy. Most of us have become trained, as generations of our ancestors have before us, to obey almost all laws almost by instinct, and certainly by habit if not by conviction. Others have become conditioned to breaking laws, frequently for reasons of stunted growth on account of emotional as well as socioeconomic deprivation.

Democracy has not yet been achieved, at least not in any real sense, as we shall see, in the modern world. If so, then the most familiar justifications demanding obedience to "democratically enacted" laws would seem to have no firm foundation. For the argument that every law represents the will of all, or the will of the majority, is empirically false; so is the argument that all laws aim at serving the common good. So is, as we have seen, the argument that disobedience to *any* law will promote anarchy.

Yet it obviously will not do, either, to assert that all laws can be ignored, or that any particular law can be obeyed or disobeyed as a matter of convenience. Nobody in his right mind will support all dis-

---

[1] See below, section III. This position is developed at greater length in my *The Structure of Freedom* (New York, 1964, 1958).

obedience, however "civil," regardless of the issues involved. The question to be tackled, then, is not whether but when and on what grounds civil disobedience can be justified.

My point of departure is essentially Locke's: Respect for the rule of law, or for the democratic processes that produce our laws, clearly must be contingent on and limited by standards for judging either the caliber of these processes or the purposes they promote; or, more precisely, by standards for judging how well these processes promote the purposes of politics. The *fundamental* purpose of politics, as I see it, is not to perpetuate a given political order but to protect human life and basic human rights. It cannot, if I may rub the point in, be the legitimizing purpose of politics or of government to perpetuate a political order that is democratic in name but in fact serves primarily to bolster privileges, not to equalize rights—as does our and surely every other political order achieved till now.

The course of my argument in the remainder of this chapter will be as follows: first (II) comes a definition and a discussion of the concept of civil disobedience; next (III) a very brief statement of my own normative position, affirming the value of freedom and, only secondarily, of democracy as an aim; and then (IV) a discussion of the increasing chasm between current realities and the classical aims of democracy. I shall next (V) try to show how an expansion of the role of civil disobedience would, if anything could, turn the trend around, so that we might hope to move toward rather than away from democracy; and, finally (VI), I shall argue how essential civil disobedience is for the liberation of the individual as a political citizen—as a man and as a sharer of the burdens and benefits of politics. Since "real" democracy would require "real" citizens, this argument, too, will support the case for civil disobedience as a prerequisite for achieving something approximating democracy in modern societies.

II

"Civil disobedience" will here refer to any act or process of public defiance of a law or policy enforced by established governmental authorities, insofar as the action is premeditated, understood by the actors(s) to be illegal or of contested legality, carried out and persisted in for limited public ends, and by way of carefully chosen and limited means.

The notion of *disobedience* presupposes the concept of a norm to be disobeyed; typically a legal norm, but in any event a norm which is assumed by *some* people in power to be authoritative in the sense that transgressions would be expected to lead to punishment in one form or another. Disobedience can be active or passive; it can be a matter of doing what is prohibited or of failing to do what is required. But mere noncompliance is not enough; the action or nonaction must be openly insisted on if it is to qualify as civil disobedience, as the concept is interpreted here. For example, failure to vote in a country in which there is a legal obligation to vote does not in itself constitute civil disobedience; one would have to state in public that one does not intend to comply with the particular law; typically but not necessarily, one would publicly encourage others, too, to disobey.

The act of disobedience must be illegal, or at least be deemed illegal by powerful adversaries, and the actor must know this, if it is to be considered an act of civil disobedience.[2] Note the distinction between *conscientious objection* to military service and civil disobedience in countries that permit exemptions from otherwise obligatory service for reasons of conscience. The conscientious objector engages in civil disobedience only if he knowingly and explicitly objects to military service on grounds not recognized by the law, or in a country that makes no exceptions for reasons of conscience.

"Civil" is the more ambiguous of the two terms. At least five different meanings would appear plausible, and in this area it would seem reasonable to cast the net wide and consider each of the following meanings equally legitimate:

1. The reference can be to a recognition of general obligations of citizenship and thus to the legitimacy of the existing legal order as a whole; pains taken to limit defiance to a particular legal clause or policy, and/or to avoid violence, may (but need not) be construed as an affirmation of general citizenship duties.

2. "Civil" can be taken to refer to the opposite of "military," in a broad sense. The customary stress on nonviolence may be construed to signify either (a) a recognition of the state's claim to monopoly with respect to legitimate use of physical violence, or (b) a rejection of all physical violence as illegitimate or morally wrong under all circumstances regardless of purpose.

3. "Civil" can refer to the opposite of "uncivil" or "uncivilized"; acts of civil disobedience may seek to embody ideals of citizenship or morality that will inspire adversaries and/or onlookers, hopefully, toward more civilized behavior, or behavior more in harmony with the ideals that inspire a given campaign of civil disobedience.

4. "Civil" can also be taken to refer to public as distinct from private: as citizens we act in public. Acts of civil disobedience seek not only to affirm a principle in private, but to call public attention to the

[2] See Harrop A. Freeman, "Civil Disobedience," in *Civil Disobedience*, Harrop A. Freeman *et al.* (Santa Barbara, 1966).

view that a principle of moral importance is held to be violated by a law or a policy sanctioned by public authorities.

5. "Civil" can suggest that the objective of obedience is to institute changes in the political system, affecting not only one individual's or group's liberties but the liberties of all citizens. A religious sect persisting in outlawed practices of worship (say, the Peyote cult among western American Indians, before the U.S. Supreme Court came to its rescue) may insist only on being left alone, or may at the same time consciously assert a principle to the effect that other sects, too, should enjoy the equivalent rights. Degrees of consciousness about the wider implications of disobedient behavior are not well suited as conceptual demarcation lines, however, and it would seem most practical to include even very parochially motivated acts of disobedience within the scope of the concept of civil disobedience.

The ambiguities of the term "civil" are far from exhausted by this brief list, but the five meanings presented are probably among the more common. The chances are that most of those who practice civil disobedience think of their behavior as "civil" in a sense, whether articulated or not, which embraces more than one of these associations, and perhaps others as well.

Returning now to the definition with which we began, let us note, first, that acts of civil disobedience may be illegal and legal at the same time, in cases of conflict of laws. For example, disobedience campaigns have been conducted against state segregation laws in the American South, in the belief that under the Federal Constitution such acts of disobedience will *eventually* be deemed legal in the Federal courts.

The ends of civil disobedience must be public and limited, it is suggested. The ostensible aim cannot, within the reference proposed, be a private or business advantage; it must have *some* reference to a conception of justice or the common good. (This is not to deny, of course, that individual motives for engaging in civil disobedience at times may be neurotic or narrowly self-seeking, consciously or subconsciously.) The proclaimed ends must be limited, too; they must fall short of seeking the complete abolition of the existing legal system; those who want a "nonviolent revolution" may engage in civil disobedience, but they, too, proclaim specific, limited ends each time. Also, according to the usage recommended here, the proclaimed aims must fall short of intending the physical or moral destruction of adversaries, even if at times a calculable risk of casualties may be tolerated. The ends of civil disobedience must be potentially acceptable to those in the *role* of adversaries even if to current adversaries they may be anathema on psychological grounds.

Above all, the proclaimed ends of civil disobedience, as the concept is understood here, must be formulated with a view to making them appear morally legitimate to onlookers and to the public. Educational objectives prompt most civil disobedience campaigns, and are never wholly absent. If a trade union violates the law to gain equality or justice, in some sense, for their members, we may speak of civil disobedience, but not if a key position in the economic system tempts a union to violate the law for the purpose of extorting unreasonable privileges in return for obeying the law. A civil disobedience campaign can aim at destroying privileges considered unjust, but not at abolishing the right to equal protection of an already underprivileged minority group.

The "carefully chosen and limited means" of civil disobedience are calculated to achieve maximum efficiency in promoting the ends and also maximum economy in seeking to reduce as much as possible the cost of the struggle in terms of suffering and deprivation. True, Gandhi at times stressed the value of bearing or even seeking suffering, but he always wanted to avoid inflicting suffering on his adversaries or on third parties.

"Civil disobedience" should be kept apart from "nonviolent action." The latter concept by definition rules out violent acts while the former does not, as defined here.[3] Among some pacifist believers in civil disobedience it seems to be assumed that a complete commitment to nonviolence, even in the sense of avoiding the provocation of violence on the part of adversaries, is ethically superior to a more pragmatic attitude toward the possible use of violence. No such assumption is made here. "Carefully chosen and limited means" in the definition at the outset refers to choice of means rationally calculated to promote the limited ends. For many reasons it seems plausible that such rational calculation normally will suggest strenuous efforts toward either avoidance or reduction of violence. Civil disobedience activists and social scientists ought to be equally interested in research on the causation and consequences of violence and nonviolence under conditions of social conflict; the expansion of this type of knowledge would seem of crucial importance for achieving increasingly realistic calculations of the most effective and economic means toward the chosen ends of civil disobedience campaigns, and also toward determining when such campaigns are and when they are not likely to be successful.[4]

[3] An opposite view is adopted by Hugo A. Bedau, "On Civil Disobedience," *Journal of Philosophy*, LVIII (1961), 653–665; by Carl Cohen, "Essence and Ethics of Civil Disobedience," *The Nation*, CXCVIII (March 16, 1964), 257–262; and by Freeman, *op. cit.*

[4] My discussion in section II is adapted from my forthcoming article "Civil Disobedience," in the *International Encyclopedia of the Social Sciences* (in press).

III

My normative position is essentially a simple one, even if it, like any other normative position, raises complex issues in application. Man and his world are, after all, almost infinitely complex.

The primary purpose of politics and of government, I hold, is to protect human life, and to expand the sphere of freedoms securely enjoyed by the individual—all individuals, mind you, on an equal basis. If all are equally entitled to grow and live in freedom, then those currently most deprived, in every unequal society, must have the highest priority claim on protection by the state.

A different way of stating the same fundamental commitment is to say that governmental coercion—and governments are by their nature coercive—can be justified only to the extent that it in fact serves to reduce coercion; and physical violence and oppressive economic deprivation prior to other, less debilitating restraints.

If I may anticipate for a moment my argument in the next section, no political order achieved so far, and that goes for our western ways of government, too, has been justifiable in these terms, if reasonably strictly construed. Demands on government arising from the lesser pains and frustrations suffered by influentials have generally taken precedence over demands arising, or demands that *should* arise, from the more debilitating indignities suffered by the poor and the inarticulate—whose very deprivation (with its cultural and psychological aspects) in fact prevents them, except in exceedingly rare revolutionary situations, almost unthinkable in the privilege-entrenched North American political order, from playing any political role at all.

According to the classical ideals, democracy should be a commonwealth of political equals, who are free to advance the common good and also their own good by constitutional means—that is, by legislation, brought about by processes designed to make sure that the laws express the well-deliberated desires *and* needs of the people. I feel committed to the aim of achieving democracy in this ideal sense because such a system would, to the extent that it could be brought about, be hospitable to respect for life and for human rights on the basis of equality. It would be easy to obey, presumably, the laws enacted in an ideal democracy. I shall argue, however, that this ideal cannot be realized, or even appreciably advanced, without a much expanded role for civil disobedience, given our present political order.

IV

Many leading political theorists would have us believe that western democracy as we know it in the United States and Britain today comes about as close to perfection as can any political order that fallible human beings can hope to attain. Some would have us dismiss as senseless "extremism" any radical questioning of the merits of our political *status quo,* and have even proclaimed an "end of ideology."

The classical ideals of democracy (excepting, most notably, the rule of law) have been all but abandoned by some of these theorists, or at any rate have been restructured so that their commitment to democracy has become a commitment to uphold what essentially amounts to the *status quo.*[5] Now, Bertrand Russell has remarked somewhere that the ruler of Hobbes's state would be far worse than Hobbes himself imagined if the citizens were to be as meek and submissive as Hobbes wanted. It is a fundamental part of my own thesis that every political order tends to become more tyrannical the more submissive its citizens are. Western democracies probably form no exception to this rule. In fact, as de Tocqueville saw, a peculiar hazard of democracies is that citizens are brought not only to comply with authority edicts but to regard them as binding morally as well, since they claim to represent the people's will.[6]

Democratic governments, like all others, seek to isolate and emasculate radical dissenters. If the domestic methods of democratic governments have been less extreme and less brutal than those of most dictator regimes, this probably reflects the usual stability of established democratic regimes, more so than any real appreciation of the value of dissent and dialogue about political fundamentals. True, the right to dissent is proclaimed as one of the many political virtues of our system, so that radical dissenters must be tolerated to a considerable extent, but there are many safeguards against permitting a fair hearing for their views. States and indeed all large organizations, as numerous studies from Michels'[7] on have shown, tend toward oligarchy and toward becoming instruments in the service of their respective oligarchies, at the expense of rank-and-file members.

[5] See, most notably, the last chapter in each of the following volumes: Bernard R. Berelson, Paul F. Lazarsfeld, and William N. McPhee, *Voting* (Chicago, 1954); Seymour Martin Lipset, *Political Man* (Garden City, 1960); and Gabriel A. Almond and Sidney Verba, *The Civic Culture* (Princeton, 1963).

[6] See Alexis de Tocqueville, *Democracy in America* (New York, 1954), Vintage Books ed., especially Vol. I, Chap. XV.

[7] Robert Michels, *Political Parties* (Glencoe, 1949, 1915).

The fact that the Anglo-Saxon democracies at most times have been able to dispense with the coarser methods of political repression, which in itself should be valued and indeed welcomed as a major achievement of our species, is at the same time a testimonial to the unlikelihood of any real changes taking place within the framework of established democracies. It is argued in our civics texts that the governing political parties in democracies tend to accept defeat at the polls gracefully because they know they may have a chance to come back to power again another time, if the rules of the democratic game are maintained. A fuller explanation of this willingness to abide by election results surely should include, however, especially in the United States but in most other democracies as well, the fact that not much is really at stake in elections, generally speaking, for the major interests. The tradition of "negative government" prior to Franklin Roosevelt made the United States government unable, even if it had been willing, to reduce the amount of socioeconomic injustice; and even after Roosevelt, though a trend toward "positive government" has been growing, and perhaps culminating with the early years of Lyndon Johnson, the division of powers, the conservatism of the mass media, the enormity of the economic power of the privileged strata, and a host of other circumstances have made it virtually impossible to expect government to become an instrument, even in part, for the interests of the downtrodden, or for the enlargement of human rights at the expense of privileges.

True, there have been proclaimed programs of Square Deal, New Freedom, New Deal, Fair Deal, New Frontier, and more recently, the Great Society. In its affluence America has been able to keep most of its underprivileged from actual starvation and has increased the opportunities for gifted or energetic young people of all classes and races. This has been done perhaps in part with lofty motives but probably also in part to attract votes and also, especially in recent decades, out of concern for America's image abroad; surely also in part as a means to forestall or reduce the incidence of acts of desperation like race riots, industrial violence, and the like.

As Dahl has observed, democratic government, even an ideal democratic government, has no ready way of registering the intensity of feeling about public issues.[8] "One man, one vote" means equal weight for the concerned vote and the indifferent vote; for the intelligent and the foolish vote; for the vote in defense of elemental dignities of life and the vote in pursuit of added privileges for groups already favored. As David Truman has observed, however, in our democracy the potential existence of new groups and new coalitions does put

[8] Robert A. Dahl, A Preface to Democratic Theory (Chicago, 1963), Phoenix Books ed., especially pp. 48–50, 90 ff., and 134–135.

some limits on what a government will do, even if elected by a wide margin.[9] But the trouble is, as most of our civic culture-championing pluralists fail to acknowledge, that the potential groups and coalitions a president or governor or mayor needs to worry about are rarely made up of the underprivileged—except, perhaps, if they are desperate to the point of being riot-prone, or intelligently led to the point of being prone to engage in civil disobedience. Normally, except in countries with strong political labor movements, the underprivileged have been made politically ineffective to the point of emasculation by their circumstances of life; coalitions of influentials and privileged are usually the only effective potential groups, and theirs are the interests that most executives prefer to appease rather than confront. As Murray Edelman puts it, in every conflict of interest between the many and the few, the many tend to be given symbolic gratification by way of democratic rhetoric and nice-sounding laws, while the few are given the tangible benefits, including a way of enforcing or not enforcing the laws that suit them.[10]

As Kolko and others have documented, the structure of economic wealth and power in this country has not been changed at all for the last half-century.[11] For all the slogans, Square Deal to Great Society, political influence remains in the hands of the economically strong while the poor remain inarticulate and largely without influence. Even the trade unions, though in the past they have served the economic interests of some categories of poor, are politically irrelevant today, having become guilds for the protection of their own shrinking number of members only, and uninterested in general issues of social justice, either domestically or internationally.

I am not out to castigate United States democracy as distinct from other democracies. My point is that the realities of western democracies keep stacking the cards in favor of the influentials and the privileged, who are therefore in a position to keep expanding their power and influence, while the underprivileged are becoming less and less able even to *think* and much less to act politically. The United States is merely the society in which this development has come the farthest, perhaps because the accumulation of private wealth has been and is larger than anywhere else. Ironically and significantly, the United States is also the modern nation most explicitly committed to the political principles of democracy, and has been for the longest time.

Democracy as we know it in the West has become, it would seem, an almost foolproof instrumentality to preserve the political and socioeconomic *status quo*. Orderly political change has become imprac-

---

[9] David B. Truman, *The Governmental Process* (New York, 1951), *passim*.
[10] Murray Edelman, *The Symbolic Uses of Politics* (Urbana, 1964).
[11] Gabriel Kolko, *Wealth and Power in America* (New York, 1962).

ticable, I submit, except to the extent that citizens free themselves from their prevailing belief that democracy has already been achieved, and that the laws enacted in their society therefore must be obeyed.

Under conditions of democratic pluralism, an uncritical submission to the rule of law means not only the shunning of violence but also, in effect, the abandonment of all intelligent effort to work effectively for changing the system. For it means agreeing in advance to live by rules in fact operating to forestall the development of democracy in any real sense. These are the rules by which the powerful have become more powerful, and the powerless more emasculated, while only the appearances of democracy have been maintained—an ever more challenging task, incidentally, but a task to which our media of communication and indoctrination so far have proved equal. Thus the discrepancies between our rose-colored perceptions of a government "by the people" and the stark realities of poverty and oppression have kept on growing.

Apparently, stability has kept growing, too. But for the human factors of alienation and desperation, this process might continue indefinitely. But social pathologies were bound to grow below the surface. Not only common crimes but also disorderly attacks against "the system" are likely to occur to an increasing extent. They will be destructive of lives and property but will fail to promote more democratic realities. They may well tempt the present and future American governments to engage in increasingly reckless violence abroad, as a means of seeking to recover national unity, to avoid the alternative of reducing the domestic socioeconomic injustice at the root of national disunity.

V

All organizational leaders are troubled by the fact that, as Philip Selznick has put it, human beings can be recalcitrant rather than pliant instruments in their designs.[12] This goes for statesmen and political leaders as well. Dictators may have to rely on secret police and recurrent terror to prevent revolutions and *coups d'état*. Democratic statesmen in some ways have an easier time of it, as we have seen, as they normally can rely on a broad consensus affirming not only a faith in democracy as an ideal but a belief that democracy has been achieved and that all democratically enacted laws must be obeyed, and that whatever is done by democratically elected statesmen is le-

[12] Philip Selznick, *TVA and the Grass Roots* (Berkeley, 1949), pp. 252–253.

gitimate. If Texas oilmen in effect are subsidized by all consumers of gasoline; if wars are fought to install aggressive satellite regimes on unwilling foreign nations; and so on: To the extent that people believe democracy has been achieved in their country, they tend to become pliant rather than recalcitrant; they can be "managed."

Yet degrees of and extent of pliancy vary with issues and with events. Generally speaking, it is greater the less immediately the individual is affected by particular laws and policies—or rather, the less he is aware of being affected. A policy of supplying faraway foreign dictators with napalm and other achievements of American know-how for use against their rebellious compatriots is readily accepted as being in the national interest on the say-so of a president; it is only when sons and brothers and boy friends and husbands are sent off to kill and to risk their own lives far away that a policy may be questioned or even resisted.

On the other hand, these are precisely the situations in which strong feelings about the inherently superior righteousness of the "democratic cause" are most easily developed, and an intelligent dialogue made most difficult.[13] At such times public witness by way of disobedient acts may be the only way to convey to the average citizen even an *awareness* of the existence of strongly felt dissent. In times of hero-worship, resistance to jingo sentiments must perhaps be heroically bold in order to become visible, lest the average citizen either remain unaware of the existence of dissent or else confuse opposition to a war with cowardice.

Ironically, the most striking example of bold and also effective resistance to legislation in recent American history had little to do with heroism. I refer to our experiment with Prohibition during the twenties. Let me stress that this is not an example of civil disobedience as defined in this paper, for the Volstead Act was usually evaded in secret, even if Clarence Darrow is said to have referred to bootleggers as fighters for American liberties and to have predicted the erection of statues to Al Capone in many a public park.[14] My point is simply that our own recent history testifies to the power of popular defiance to change a law.[15] This result is more likely to come about, presumably, the more widespread and determined the defiance, civil or not, of a particular law.

[13] "The first casualty in every shooting war is common sense, and the second is free and open discussion," wrote James Reston in *The New York Times* of February 12, 1965, five days after the beginning of the United States bombing of North Vietnam.

[14] See Harry Elmer Barnes, *Prohibition Versus Civilization* (New York, 1932), pp. 71–72.

[15] In fact, Mr. Darrow is quoted as claiming that this "nullification," as he calls it, is a traditional American way of changing the law, *ibid.* See also Clarence Darrow and Victor S. Yerros, *The Prohibition Mania* (New York, 1927).

But there is little prospect, alas, that laws and policies supported by far more powerful economic interests—say the Vietnam war, or the continuing inequities in our school systems—can be changed by way of disobedience, civil or not. It takes knowledge, independence of livelihood, and certain skills in interpersonal relations to engage in civil disobedience. True, something has been and more will perhaps be accomplished in race relations, a field in which some acts of disobedience against some southern state laws have become almost respectable elsewhere in the nation, under the impact of a growing concern for America's image abroad in its confrontation with communist nations. But issues of war and peace are beyond the reach of most people, as are even more the underlying issues of an economic system which depends on preparations for war and serves to bolster and expand privileges instead of rights.

Our only hope, as I see it, is in education—that is, education toward intellectual and political independence for the individual. We badly need an education that enables and encourages each young citizen to think for himself about the proper aims of government, or the state, and to judge by his own standards to what extent the government of his own nation pursues those aims. Only to that extent should it have his support. To the extent that his government pursues illegitimate aims, in his judgment, or employs means subversive of and menacing to the values a just government must uphold, civil disobedience may well be the right response if acts of protest within the framework of existing legislation would be ineffective or take too long a time.[16] Or it may be the wrong response. My point is that a man is not educated to the point of political responsibility unless he can and will make this decision for himself.

And the most elementary requirement of political education, thus conceived, is liberation from the prevailing pluralist democratic myth, which claims a reverence for the Majesty of the Law—all laws!—on the ground that they have been democratically enacted. It is about time, I think, that political theorists, at least, free themselves from the stultifying grip of this myth, however convenient it may be as a rationalization for political inaction and, in my terms, political irresponsibility.

[16] "What I have to do is see, at any rate, that I do not lend myself to the wrong which I condemn. As for adopting the ways which the state has provided for remedying the evil, I know not of such ways. They take too much time, and a man's life will be gone." Henry David Thoreau, "Civil Disobedience," in his *Walden and Other Writings* (New York, 1950), Modern Library ed., pp. 644–645.

VI

In psychological terms, attention to the functions of political opinions for the individual provides an additional ground for arguing that the individual should strive to become sovereign in the choice of his fundamental political commitments.

We are aware today of the wide extent to which government policies as well as public opinion are the outcome of neurotic anxieties and fears, which are difficult to diagnose with exactitude and are more difficult still to cure. Modern psychologists and political scientists have established in a general way how political opinions are developed to meet personality needs, and how the individual's ability to cope with anxieties at various levels determines his capacity for rationality and a realistic long-term assessment of his own good as well as the common good.[17] Most people are neurotic and conformist as well as rational, in varying mixtures; enlightened, civilized policies are unlikely to emanate from democratic processes except to the extent that influential leaders become capable of farsighted rationality. Yet democratic competition for office and power almost invariably strengthens the neurotic aspects and lessens the rational aspects of political behavior; most electoral appeals, especially in times of crises when cool rationality is most needed, are directed to anxieties and paranoid sentiments rather than to reason or enlightened hopes.

The conscientious dissenter who cannot opt out of this system has no easy guide available for determining when to obey and when to disobey the law. There is no general solution to his dilemma, except to urge that he insist on protecting his own sanity and powers of reason, the autonomy of his own social conscience, and his own right to grow toward whatever moral stature or humanity he is capable of achieving. The criteria for concrete decisions to obey or disobey must depend on the nature of each situation, anticipating by careful inquiry and reflection the consequences of either obeying or disobeying; but they must also depend on each moral dissenter's personality and beliefs, especially his beliefs concerning priorities among evils or among good causes.

This open-endedness of the modern dilemma of civil disobedience fits well with Albert Camus's theory of rebellion as an individual re-

---

[17] See especially Daniel Katz, "The Functional Approach to the Study of Attitudes," *Public Opinion Quarterly*, XXIV (1960), 163–204; and M. Brewster Smith, Jerome S. Bruner, and Robert W. White, *Opinions and Personality* (New York, 1964). In this section, too, several paragraphs are adapted from my forthcoming article for the *International Encyclopedia, op. cit.*

sponsibility: While only an active and pressing social conscience can bring an individual to full life as a human being, his responsibility for action or inaction as a social being is strictly individual and lonesome. What is given, according to Camus, is only the immorality or inhumanity of a life of acquiescence in evil; he goes even further and argues that a commitment never to resist violence with violence amounts to such acquiescence, or "bourgeois nihilism." But he offers no guidelines for concrete political decisions.[18]

It is worth noting that legislation to legitimize certain grounds for conscientious objection to military service has tended to excuse only those who could prove they had no rational, politically articulate basis for objecting to becoming soldiers. In the United States as in other western democracies, only a religious basis for objection was recognized at the outset. To the extent that the courts or subsequent legislation have attempted to liberalize the rules, as has happened in the States and in other western nations, the tendency has been to lower the demand for evidence of church membership or religious orthodoxy of some kind, but to keep insisting that objection is no longer legitimate unless it remains apolitical, and condemns all past and future warfare indiscriminately.

For contrast, take Bertrand Russell's response when he was once chided on a British "Brain Trust" program over the BBC for having gone to jail for resisting World War I as a pacifist, while he had supported World War II, and now once again seemed prepared to object to the point of civil disobedience against preparations for a third world war. He said, "I want to pick my wars." This, in my view, is a simple but profound statement of responsible citizenship. What other human right can be more basic than the right to choose what cause, if any, to kill for and to die for?

Yet this, of course, is precisely the kind of human right that no government, dictatorial or democratic, wishes to grant. Legal recognition of politically motivated conscientious objection would hamper the pursuit of "tough" foreign policies in a way that religiously or pacifistically motivated objection will not. Any government can limit the influence of saints; far more dangerous to established privileges and policies are citizens who combine radical dissent with political know-how, or saintly aims like social justice, freedom, or peace with flexible tactics of protest inside and outside the law.

It seems to me that Camus's theory of rebellion has contributed at least two important thoughts toward a modern theory of civil disobedience. One, which has been touched on already, is his view that a rigid adherence to nonviolent means of protest in some situations may

[18] Albert Camus, *The Rebel* (New York, 1958), especially Part V.

amount to acquiescence in continued violence and oppression. For him as for the orthodox pacifists, violence is always the supreme evil; but to him it is in part an empirical question whether violence in given situations can be overcome or reduced by entirely nonviolent means (or, of course, by any combination of violent and nonviolent means). In my view and in Max Weber's terminology, he argues that an ethics of *a priori* duty must be supplanted by an ethics of responsibility, a responsibility for anticipating as full a range of consequences of alternative means of action as experience and research can establish, if there is time, before deciding on a course of action, nonviolent or in part violent.

It is precisely because the consequences of revolutionary activity are likely to be both violent and to a large extent unpredictable (especially with respect to the extent and duration of acts of violence) that Camus is so strongly in favor of rebellion, in his sense, as an alternative to revolution. His rebel is the piecemeal revolutionary—the politically responsible citizen who is committed to fight violence and oppression by the most *economic* means, i.e., he seeks to avoid the use of violence whenever possible, and above all to avoid the use of remedies that could be worse than the present evil—worse in terms of degrees and extent of violence suffered. With respect to his aims, Camus's rebel is related to the revolutionary in that he will be satisfied with nothing less than complete justice or a complete end to oppression, but he is apt to be less confident that this utopia can ever be fully realized. When it comes to his choice of means, Camus's rebel is identical with the type of responsible citizen extolled in these pages: the person who honors not the Rule of Law so much as the Rule of Justice, and who is prepared to support or commit civil disobedience against oppressive government or legislation.

If Camus has helped draw the demarcation line and develop the rationale for modern civil disobedience, as distinguished from revolutionary activity, [19] he has also, as a second contribution to a modern theory of civil disobedience, been the first to articulate the psychological necessity of being a rebel, or a citizen in principle prepared to commit civil disobedience against oppressive laws and policies, if one is to achieve one's full human stature. Rebellion, as a manifestation of revulsion against injustice, is to Camus an essential dimension of the free man's life; only men who remain too neurotic, too stymied to develop a consciousness of their own humanity, their own solidarity

---

[19] To distinguish the two concepts is not to say that the same person or movement cannot at the same time believe in civil disobedience and in revolution. For example, one may have proximate or short-range aims to be served by civil disobedience and yet believe in eventual revolution; or one may believe in revolution as an ultimate resort if results of civil disobedience are too limited or too slow.

with all men, can remain indifferent and passive when confronted with victims or perpetrators of injustice. In a cruelly competitive society, perhaps most men remain stymied, or in Camus's sense less than fully human; yet at all times there have been rebels, believers in obedience to their own principles as a higher necessity than obedience to the powers that be, or the laws with which these powers guard their interests. I have argued in this chapter that only a good supply of such individuals can help us come closer to the achievement of democracy; Camus argues that only such qualities in a man can help him achieve his own individuality as well as his own humanity.

But in our time, with its unprecedented technology, capable of bureaucratizing acts of murder, and of dehumanizing men who may make decisions about life or death for millions of fellow human beings, the more effective education of an expanding supply of rebels may well be our civilization's last hope of survival. Without thousands of young men able and willing to disobey calls to contribute to moral monstrosities like, for example, American warfare in Vietnam, where is there hope that the bureaucratized, consensus-manufacturing forces of destruction of the modern super-powers—the Leviathans of our time—can be checked before our civilization becomes engulfed in a third world war?

In the name of democracy a new kind of servitude has developed in the West. Witness the hundreds of thousands of men who, educationally unequipped to judge for themselves, have been shipped to a far-off land to kill and perhaps die for what they cheerfully believe is the cause of democracy, or at any rate their own nation's best interests. And witness the many admonitions to dissenters against the war policy that they limit their protests to legal channels, again in the name of democracy, lest its rules of order be violated. Naturally, only harmless, easily manageable forms of protest are desired; violence in contests for power at home is inveighed against with democratic moral fervor by the same leaders who look to violence as almost the only way to engage in contests for power abroad. Advocacy of force and violence at home is condemned, and so is advocacy *against* use of force and violence abroad, for both kinds of advocacy could menace the *status quo*.

Let me conclude by returning to the most fundamental argument of this essay: Governments exist for the purpose of establishing and defending human rights, with the most basic rights, like protection against violence and starvation, taking precedence over less basic rights. The common good, according to this view, hinges on the good of the least favored individuals, taking into account also the prospects for those not yet born.

This or any similar type of basis for political obligation directed to the ends of politics, which relegates not only democracy but also respect for the law in all its alleged majesty to the status of means, takes the vestiges of the role of subject out of the role of citizen. It substitutes an ethics of individual responsibility for the probable results of one's political behavior, including law-abiding as well as legally obligated behavior, for an ethics of duty to subordinate conscience, knowledge, and individual judgment to existing legal norms, government directives, or a majority vote.

The judgments at Nuremberg and the wide attention given to the Eichmann trial in Jerusalem have increased acceptance for the view that the autonomy of the individual conscience is a vital resource in our modern technological and bureaucratized civilization. The "essence of totalitarian government, and perhaps the nature of every bureaucracy," writes Hannah Arendt, "is to make functionaries and mere cogs in the administrative machinery out of men, and thus to dehumanize them." [20] "Each time we obey an order from higher up, without evaluating and judging it in moral terms, there is the Eichmann within ourselves bending his neck," writes a reviewer of Arendt's book, and further observes: "Eichmann was neither intellectually nor morally worse equipped than most people . . . his fault was that he did not feel personally responsible for what his government did. In this respect he is not unique." [21]

The human race may never fully achieve democracy; no large nation is likely to come very close to this exacting ideal, although I believe it can be approximated in the foreseeable future in university communities and perhaps in some other local communities. What is important, if we value freedom for all on the basis of justice, is that we move toward rather than away from democracy. For this purpose our educational institutions must try to produce, I submit, men and women less like Eichmann, and more like his opposite, more like Camus's rebel. The rebel, or the believer in civil disobedience in the fight against oppression, is to this writer the model of the responsible citizen who wishes to promote democracy. What we don't need, in my view, and what we are now oversupplied with, is the cheerful, loyal, pliable, law-abiding, basically privatist type of citizen extolled not only in our high school civics texts but in our professional civic culture and end of ideology literature as well.

[20] *Eichmann in Jerusalem* (New York, 1963), p. 289.
[21] Jens Bjorneboe, "Eichmann i vaare hjerter" ("Eichmann in our hearts"), *Orientering*, Oslo (December 18, 1965).

IV/ Contemporary Applications

CONTEMPORARY APPLICATIONS

> The danger of the past was that men became slaves. The danger of the future is that men may become robots. True enough, robots do not rebel. But given man's nature, robots cannot live and remain sane, . . . they will destroy their world and themselves because they cannot stand any longer the boredom of a meaningless life.
>
> —ERICH FROMM

The scope of the problem of political obligation in mass technological societies is wider than the question of obedience or resistance to governmental authority. Often the individual must decide whether or not to submit to decisions made by a host of giant corporate bureaucracies. Indeed, because of their substantial impact on the individual and society, such institutions have acquired the label "private governments." In "Civil Disobedience and Corporate Authority," Michael Walzer is concerned with the hurdles the American legal system places in the way of politically powerless and economically disadvantaged groups when they attempt to articulate interests and fulfill economic needs in the face of powerful corporate bureaucracies that lack democratic controls. Walzer discusses the sit-down strikes against General Motors in 1936–1937 as an example of justified forceful resistance to corporate authority. He rejects the Lockean notion that an organization's members have given "tacit consent" to authoritarian rule during working hours. He opposes making "property rights" sacrosanct. Yet, ironically, in certain respects, such as his emphasis on individual political rights and on the need for those resisting authoritarian rule to acquire majority support, he rather closely resembles Locke. In discussing forceful activities aimed at "shutting down" an institution, his central concern is to broaden the concept of civil disobedience by expanding its legitimate methods and targets.

In his essay "Injustice and Bureaucracy," Lewis C. Mainzer addresses the problem of unjust bureaucratic rule from the perspective of the isolated individual employee. Mainzer warns the individual that hierarchical authority is often used personally and not merely of-

313

ficially because bureaucracy lacks both the assumption of popular sovereignty and the mechanisms for holding rulers accountable. Exploring various alternatives open to bureaucratic subordinates faced with perceived injustice, Mainzer discusses the merits and probable costs of such individual choices as disobedience, nihilistic rebellion, various forms of "resignation," and stoic *incivisme*. In focusing on the need for human choice in an inevitably unjust and often absurd world, Mainzer's discussion most closely resembles the contemporary existentialist approach to obligation and disobedience.

Herbert Marcuse's analysis of modern society has become a primary source for student revolutionary ideas and rhetoric. His goal is a society without conditioned consumption, without repression, and without irresponsible uses of technology—a social order that will foster the emergence of a new type of man seeking the maximum development of rationality and happiness. Although Marcuse's philosophical apparatus is dominated by the theories and jargon of Hegel, Freud, and Marx, his goal of personal autonomy does not differ radically from the philosophical anarchist ideal. Marcuse's normative preferences are succinctly stated in his interview with three French journalists: "Marcuse Defines His New Left Line." In this dialogue Marcuse expresses the desire for a revolutionary new beginning and offers a political strategy to achieve this goal. He invokes a "natural law" right of resistance to tyranny to justify rejection of established law and the contemporary "destructive" social order.

Despite his sympathy for the spontaneity found in student movements, Marcuse argues that effective opposition to the concentrated power of repressive establishments requires organization sufficient to bring about "progressive" restraints against "reactionary" forces, whether capitalist or Stalinist. His restraints range from preventing air pollution to denying free speech to groups designated "reactionary" by the New Left revolutionary. His concept of "progressive restraint" clearly resembles the Hegelian organic view that delimits individual freedom for the sake of the common good or historical "progress." There appears to be a distinct tension between Marcuse's ultimate goal of spontaneity and autonomy and his strategy of coercion by a "progressive" elite.

In "Black Power," Stokely Carmichael and Charles V. Hamilton argue that black liberation in American society is unlikely to occur in a "politics as usual" climate. White racism, both individual and institutional, is incompatible with black political influence. Black powerlessness makes it necessary for blacks to organize indigenous political structures to make effective demands on the political system. Black power, in effect, means racial pride, self-development, and a new political militancy. Carmichael and Hamilton reject the passive rhetoric of "love, suffering, and nonviolence" employed by the civil rights movement of the early 1960's. Their perspective on obligation and disobedience may be summed up in the sentence "There can be no social order without social justice." Their strategy includes an attempt to brandish the potential for violence by reminding the white majority that if it remains indifferent to the social and economic conditions of blacks in the South and in the ghettos, it must share full responsibility for the violence that may follow.

The legal philosopher Ronald Dworkin has developed a strong case against prosecuting the civilly disobedient. In his article "On Not Prosecuting Civil Disobedience," Dworkin argues that although a society cannot survive if it tolerates all forms of disobedience, it does not follow that it will crumble if it tolerates some. Certainly, for example, a prosecutor may decide that it is not prudent to press charges if the disobedient is young, if the law is unpopular, unworkable, or generally disobeyed or for other reasons. Dworkin is especially interested in providing "good reasons" to avoid prosecuting those who disobey draft laws out of conscience. He is concerned with the role of *intention* in civil disobedience cases, and, like Thoreau, he elevates individual reason and conscience to a primary position. He also opposes the prosecution of conscientious objectors on prudential grounds, pointing out that jailing such men will only reinforce their estrangement from the political order. It is Dworkin's hope that the Draconian notion that "lawbreakers must be punished" will loosen its hold on the legal profession and the general population. In its place he seeks an appreciation for the complexity of the rule of law and its prudential requirements if it is to survive.

Harmon Zeigler's "Group Theory and Political Obligation" is empirical in approach and resembles some of the concerns of Benthamite utilitarianism. Both are concerned with motivation—that is to say, with isolating determinants of political behavior. Specifically, Zeigler discusses the factors other than group activity that influence the individual's perception of his political environment and that, in turn, serve to rationalize or undermine obedience to constituted authority. In addressing the question "Why do men obey laws?" Zeigler criticizes the group theory assumption that *tangible* rewards and sanctions are the sole motive for individual political obedience. He attempts to assess the importance of intangible, *symbolic* manipulation by political elites in generating protest or political quiescence. At the empirical level, his discussion offers convincing evidence that psychopathology and politics often are closely linked. At the normative level, it should serve as a warning to the individual to be on his guard against political elites who respond to concrete political grievances by merely manipulating symbols to relieve anxieties while failing to alter the distribution of tangible values significantly. Yet Zeigler himself fails to draw this conclusion. He argues only that symbolic rewards can generate the sense of obligation needed for "the survival and stability" of the political system.

If the Nuremberg judgment of 1946 meant anything, it meant that the soldier and even the civilian must decide for himself whether or not he should obey a superior's official orders, because he might be held responsible for his acts even to the extent of the death penalty. At Nuremberg, four victorious nations—the United States, Russia, Great Britain, and France—prescribed the right and duty of military disobedience to superior orders to commit war crimes, crimes against peace, and crimes against humanity. Nonetheless, none of the four states that imposed this moral standard on the defeated Nazi officials has adopted it for its own military establishment in any consistent manner. The recent tragedy at My Lai and the consequent military court proceedings against Lieutenant William Calley and others have vividly dramatized for this nation the moral question of conscientious objection vs. blind obedience to superior military orders.

The final selection, by Guenter Lewy, is concerned with the hypothetical moral dilemma of the military subordinate commanded to use nuclear weapons—facing a situation in which he may be punished if he disobeys and prosecuted for crimes against humanity if he obeys. Lewy's article, "Superior Orders, Nuclear Warfare, and the Dictates of Conscience," sets forth a discussion that examines three key questions—the validity of "superior orders" as a legal defense, the legality of using nuclear weapons, and the dictates of conscience in such situations. Lewy confronts a perennial problem of political obligation—the relationship between individual conscience, the laws of war, and the requirements of national security—in an age when the destructive process has become ever more depersonalized by the growing physical, psychological, and technological distance between the soldier and his victims. In the context of modern warfare it has thus become more important than ever for conscientious citizens to give serious weight to Thoreau's counsel to "be men first, and subjects afterwards."

23/ Civil Disobedience and Corporate Authority

MICHAEL WALZER

Civil disobedience is generally described as a nonrevolutionary encounter with the state. A man breaks the law, but does so in ways that do not challenge the legitimacy of the legal or political systems. He feels morally bound to disobey; he also recognizes the moral value of the state; civil disobedience is his way of maneuvering between these conflicting moralities. The precise requirements of civility have been specified by a number of writers, and while the specifications vary, they tend to impose a similar discipline on the disobedient persons. Above all, they impose the discipline of nonviolence. Civility, it is generally said, requires first the adoption of methods that do not directly coerce or oppress other members of society and, second, it requires nonresistance to state officials enforcing the law. I want to argue that there is a kind of disobedience that does not meet either of these requirements, and yet sometimes falls within the range of civility.

Perhaps the actions I am going to describe should not be called civil disobedience at all; I don't want to quarrel about names. But it is arguable, I think, that narrow definitions of civil disobedience rule out certain sorts of unconventional yet nonrevolutionary politics which should not be regarded as attacks on civil order. These may well involve both coercion and violence, though always in severely limited ways. It is important to recognize the significance of such limits when making judgments about civility. The insistence on the absolute nonviolence of civil disobedience is, in any case, a little disingenuous, since it disregards, first, the coercive impact disobedience often has on innocent bystanders and, second, the actual violence it provokes and sometimes is intended to provoke, especially from the police. I don't doubt that it is preferable that no one be coerced and that police violence be met with passive resistance, but there may be occasions when neither of these is politically possible, and there may also be occasions, not necessarily the same ones, when they are not morally required. Such occasions, if they exist, would have to be de-

SOURCE: Philip Green and Sanford Levinson, eds. *Power and Community: Dissenting Essays in Political Science* (New York: Pantheon Books, 1970), Ch. 8. Copyright © by Random House, Inc. Reprinted by permission of the author and the publisher.

scribed and delimited precisely. One of the dangers of a narrow definition of civil disobedience is that it simply rules out the effort to do
this. By setting rigid limits to civil conduct, it virtually invites militants of various sorts to move beyond the bounds of civility
altogether—and it invites the police to respond always as if they
were confronting criminals. (Sometimes, of course, the police are confronting criminals, but it is important that we know, and that they
know, when this is so and when not.)

The limits of civility are a matter of academic interest in more than
the usual sense just now, and I do want to speak to the problems of
student radicalism. But my more immediate focus will be on the past
—for the sake of clarity and dispassion. There are historical cases in
which the coercion of innocent bystanders and resistance to police
authority have in fact proven compatible, or so it seems to me, with a
kind of civility. The sit-down strikes against General Motors in
1936–37 provide a classic example, to which I will later refer in some
detail. For now it is enough to indicate the general principles under
which such cases may be justified. They *may* be justified when the initial disobedience is directed against corporate bodies other than the
state; when the encounter with these corporations, though not with
the state that protects them, is revolutionary or quasi-revolutionary in
character; and when the revolution is made in good faith. I'll suggest
later on just what these principles involve, and I'll also argue very
briefly that some (at least) of the recent student sit-ins, though they
have been defended by reference to the 1936 strikes, cannot be justified in the same way.

Americans today probably have a greater number of direct contacts
with state officials than ever before. We continue, however, to have
many contacts, perhaps more, that are mediated by corporate bodies.
These corporations collect taxes on behalf of the state, maintain standards required by the state, spend state money and, above all, enforce a great variety of rules and regulations with the silent acquiescence and ultimate support of the state. Commercial, industrial,
professional, and educational organizations and, to a lesser degree,
religious organizations and trade unions, all play these parts—and
yet very few of these reproduce the democratic politics of the state.
They have official or semiofficial functions; they are enormously active and powerful in the day-to-day government of society, but the
authority of their officers is rarely legitimized in any democratic fashion. These officers preside over what are essentially authoritarian regimes, with no internal electoral system, no opposition parties, no
free press or open communications network, no established judicial
procedures, no channels for rank-and-file participation in decision-

making.[1] When the state acts to protect their authority, it does so through the property system, that is, it recognizes the corporation as the private property of some determinate group of men, and it protects their right to do, within legal limits, what they please with their property. When corporate officials defend themselves, they often invoke functional arguments. They claim that the parts they play in society can only be played by such men as they, with their legally confirmed power, their control of resources, their freedom from internal challenge, and their ability to call on the police.[2]

Neither of these arguments justifies or requires absolute power, and some of the subjects of corporate authority have managed to win rights against it, rights that generally come to them as citizens and are also protected by the state. I am thinking of such things as the right to work no more than a specified number of hours, the right to work in at least minimally safe surroundings, and so on. The right to strike is of the same sort, though it was for a longer time unprotected. The claim of workers to shut down a factory they did not own was once widely regarded as a denial of property rights and a threat to the efficient running of the economy. For years the strike was the most common form of working-class civil disobedience, but it has long since been allowed by the state. I should note that the right of students to strike is not similarly allowed, since students cannot, so far as I know, claim state protection against expulsion after an unsuccessful strike. In any case, such rights, even if securely held, would still not be comparable to the rights a citizen has in a democratic state, and just how far they can or ought to be extended remains unclear, a matter of continuing public debate. By and large, the subjects of corporate authority are . . . subjects, and state citizenship does not generate corporate citizenship even when it guards against the worst forms of corporate tyranny.

There is one argument in support of this subjection that at least falls within the realm of democratic theory. This is the argument from

---

[1] The list is adapted from Robert Pranger, *The Eclipse of Citizenship: Power and Participation in Contemporary Politics* (New York, 1968); see especially pp. 73–76. See also the excellent discussion in Grant McConnell, *Private Power and American Democracy* (New York, 1966), Chapter 5. I should say at this point that I am not considering public corporations and civil services in this essay, though their employees may also be deprived of the benefits of internal democracy. Many of the arguments that I make later on may well apply to them, but their special position vis-à-vis a democratic government raises problems I cannot cope with here.

[2] These are the implicit assumptions, for example, of Peter Drucker's *The Concept of the Corporation* (New York, 1946). In Chapter 3, Drucker describes the suggestion box as a crucial channel for worker participation in corporate management.

tacit consent, which holds that corporate subjects are, in some morally significant sense, voluntarily subjects. By their willing entry into, and acceptance of the jurisdiction of, one or another corporate body, they commit themselves, on this view, to obey rules and regulations they have no part in making. They join the firm, go to work in the factory, enter the university, knowing in advance the nondemocratic character of all these organizations, knowing also who runs them and for what purposes. They are not deceived, at least no one is trying to deceive them, and so they are morally bound for the duration of their stay. And however subject they may be during that time to authoritarian pettiness and to oppressive rules and regulations, they are never the captives of the authorities. Their citizenship guarantees their ultimate recourse: if they don't like it where they are, they can leave.

This is a serious argument and deserves some attention. Residence in a democratic state does, I think, generate a *prima facie* obligation to obey the laws of that state—in part because of the benefits that are necessarily accepted along with residence, in part because of the expectations aroused among one's fellow residents, and finally because of the universality of obligation in a democracy, from which no resident can easily exclude himself. But the effects of residence in a nondemocratic state are surely very different. There the right of resistance and revolution may well be widely shared, and there is no reason why a new resident should not associate himself with the rebels rather than with the authorities. It is not obvious that the same distinction applies to the corporation, since the strict forms of political democracy are often said to be impractical in corporate bodies organized for industrial or educational purposes. But this is precisely what is at issue in most cases of corporate disobedience, and I see no reason to prejudge the issue by agreeing that tacit consent to nondemocratic corporations establishes any greater degree of obligation than tacit consent to nondemocratic states. In any case, arguments about the possible reaches of democracy are carried on almost continuously within both the corporation and the state; surely no one can bind himself not to join them; and it is one of the characteristics of political arguments in nondemocratic organizations that they will often take "illegal" forms. Such forms may even be necessary if the arguments are to be carried on at all. So there can be no binding commitment not to break corporate rules and regulations or, at least, there can be no binding commitment until the best possible democratic procedure for establishing rules has been adopted.

There is another reason for rejecting the argument from tacit consent: corporate bodies do not offer anything like the same range of benefits that the state provides. Membership in them in no sense replaces citizenship in the state. A man may well provide himself with new benefits and even incur powerful, perhaps overriding obligations by joining a corporate body, but he cannot be conceived as having yielded any of the legal rights he has as a citizen. Corporate officials may offer him a trade: we will pay you so much money, they may say, if you surrender the right to strike. That agreement, whatever its moral force, is not legally binding so long as the right to strike is recognized by the state. But the legal rights of a citizen are also matters of dispute, and so it is always possible for a corporate subject to break the rules and regulations, appealing to the laws of the state or to the established rights of citizenship as his authority for doing so.[3]

It is when such an appeal is not recognized by state officials that civil disobedience may begin. But for the moment, I want only to suggest that disobedience to corporate rules is probably justified whenever it is undertaken in good faith as part of a struggle for democratization or for socially recognized rights. By the phrase "in good faith," I mean to limit the occasions of justifiable disobedience to cases in which four conditions hold: when the oppressiveness of the corporate authorities can be specified in some rational way; when the social functions of the corporation have been taken into account in judging the rights its participants might enjoy; when concrete proposals for corporate reorganization have been brought forward; and when a serious effort has been made to win massive support for these proposals.

I would assume also that whatever channels for "legal" reform are available within the corporation have been tried. But it is important to stress the fact that such channels don't always exist in the sorts of bodies I am considering here. Indeed, in many of them any serious demand for democratization may plausibly be called revolutionary, for it involves an attack upon the established authority system of the corporation. This was certainly true, for example, of the demands of the labor movement, as one of its historians has noted: "If revolution is defined as a transfer of power from one social group to another, all forms of union activity which involve a challenge to the power of owners and managers are revolutionary." [4]

If this is so, then all the forms of revolutionary politics that we know from the history of authoritarian states may now be reenacted

---

[3] Perhaps there is a moral as well as a legal basis for such appeals: it can be argued, I think, that in discussing rights and obligations, one can always appeal from less to more democratic bodies. Obviously, this can work against the state as well as in its favor; for some examples, see my "Obligation to Disobey," in David Spitz, editor, *Political Theory and Social Change* (New York, 1967).

[4] Robert Brooks, *When Labor Organizes* (New Haven, 1937), p. 112.

on a smaller stage. In such situations we ought to anticipate this kind of politics and not be shocked or surprised when it comes. Thus the presence of corporate police and spies (as in the auto plants before 1936) and the pervasive atmosphere of fearfulness generated by unlimited power will often impose secrecy and a severe discipline upon the revolutionary organization. At critical moments, initiatives may be seized by small minorities of militants, who claim to represent their fellow subjects but who also force them to make choices they did not anticipate and might well prefer not to make. Those who refuse to join the revolution may be threatened, mocked, perhaps beaten, their right to work systematically denied. Finally, the militants and their new supporters, now embattled and exposed, will often resist corporate countermoves, and may do so even if these countermoves have state support. All this, secrecy, discipline, coercion, and resistance, still falls or may fall, I want to argue, within the limits of civility—so long as the revolution is not aimed at the state itself and so long as the corporate authorities really are as oppressive as the rebels claim.

There is another condition, of course: that the corporate revolution not take the form of a violent coup, an attempt to blow up the central offices of the corporation, or to murder or terrorize its personnel. It is crucial that violence on this scale, if it occurs, does not occur at the initiative of the rebels. And in fact it rarely does occur at their initiative; in almost all the cases I can think of (there may have been some recent exceptions), the rebels have followed a different course. Their strategy is almost always to shut down the corporation, to curtail its operations or to stop them altogether, until some new distribution of power is worked out. It is important to note that this first shut-down is different from all those that come later. Once the authority and cohesion of the corporate subjects have been recognized, strikes may become a permanent feature of the power system. The simple withdrawal of workers from their routine activities will then be sufficient to close the corporation, and even the threat to strike will be a valuable bargaining point in its ongoing politics. But this was not so earlier, and the first strikes may have to take direct and coercive forms. Generally, they involve the physical occupation of the corporate plant and the expulsion of nonstrikers. Occupation is preferable to withdrawal, because it can be achieved successfully without majority support, and majorities are not readily organized under authoritarian conditions. Occupation is also preferable because it precludes, at least for a time, the effective dismissal of the strikers and the resumption of corporate activity with new subjects. For these reasons, the sit-down or sit-in is the typical form of revolutionary activity in nondemocratic corporations.

The state then comes into the picture not to enforce the laws against assault and murder but to enforce the property laws. This is the paradox of corporate revolution: the revolutionaries encounter the state as trespassers. However serious their attack on corporate authority, they are guilty only of minor crimes in the eyes of the state, though one would not always guess this from the response of state officials. In fact, violence often, perhaps most often, begins with law enforcement.

In suggesting how disobedience to corporate rules and regulations might be justified, I have treated the corporation as a political community within the larger community of the state. I have discussed its government and the rights of its subject population. This is obviously not the way, or not the only way, the officials of the corporation and the state regard the matter. They see the corporation also as a piece of property, protected as property by the law. When corporate officials find "their" buildings occupied, their first response is to call on the police to clear them. The police sometimes come and sometimes do not. They are pledged to enforce the law, but they also take orders from the political leaders of the state, who may (and, I would suggest, ought to) see in the corporate revolution something more than a mere violation of the property laws. What is at issue here is not who owns the corporation, but what such ownership entails and, above all, what, if any, governmental powers it entails. It is one of the characteristic features of feudal regimes that the ownership of property always entails governmental powers (and responsibilities): public functions such as war-making, tax-collecting, and adjudication are dispersed among a class of landlords, and the right to carry out such functions is literally owned along with the land. Clearly no modern state, even more clearly no democratic state, can permit or tolerate such a dispersal of powers. Corporate officials who carry out governmental or quasi-governmental functions (even the simple maintenance of social order within the corporation) must be responsible to the larger community, whose citizens they and their subjects are. But this means that the state has an interest in the internal politics of the corporation, an interest that may or may not be served by police intervention on behalf of private property. It is not far-fetched, I think, to suggest that the interests of a democratic state are best served by corporate democratization—at least so long as this process does not seriously interfere with the social functions of the corporation, in which the larger community also has an interest.

It is important, in any case, for state officials to realize that when they enforce the trespass laws against strikers, they are also acting to restore not merely the "law and order" of the state but that of the corporation as well. They are enforcing another set of rules in addition to their own. And while they can argue that the strikers have every right and opportunity to work in public and try to change the first set of rules, they must recognize that the second set can, perhaps, only be changed by the very revolutionary action they are repressing. When police resist efforts to overthrow the state, they are behaving in a perfectly straightforward way. But the case is not straightforward when police resist efforts to overthrow corporate authority. Corporate authority is not the same as the authority of the property laws—it does not have their democratic legitimacy—and the difference between the two may require the police to use some discretion in moving against men who violate the laws of the state solely in order to challenge the authority of the corporation. The corporate rebels may, for example, be defending rights they actually have as citizens. Their violation of the law may be a means of bringing to the attention of their fellow citizens other, more important violations of the law.[5] And then the police must choose the laws they will enforce, and may reasonably choose to do as little as possible for the time being. Police inaction may even be justified if the rebels are wrong, or if the courts hold that they are wrong, about their rights as citizens, for the size and scope of the strike may suggest changing communal values which the political leaders who command the police may choose to respect if only in order to avoid violence.

The rebels may, of course, be wrong in other ways: the militant minority may not have even the silent and fearful sympathy of the others; its demands may be inconsistent with the continued fulfillment of important social functions. But corporate authorities always claim that these two conditions hold, and they have done so in many cases where they clearly didn't. Since the truth is often difficult to discover, especially in the early hours or days of a rebellion, state officials must keep an open mind as long as they can. Police action may be necessary, but it is rarely necessary immediately. It is, however, almost always upon the demand of the corporate authorities that the police act quickly. If there is any hesitation their subjects, they think, will rally around the militants—though it is obviously also possible that they will desert the militants, leaving them helpless and isolated. Time is the best test of the support the strikers actually have among the passive majority but, historically, this has not been a test the authorities are willing to risk. Delay, moreover, pushes them toward negotiations with the strikers, and the beginning of talks is itself a victory for democratization even if no other demands are allowed. Hence any refusal to enforce the law probably constitutes a kind of indirect inter-

[5] Joel Seidman, *Sit-Down* (League for Industrial Democracy pamphlet, New York, 1937), p. 38.

vention by the state against the corporation. It would be naive to deny this; I can only suggest that the interests of a democratic state are sometimes served in this way.

If the police do enforce the law, then they must expect that the strikers will respond in the context of their own revolutionary situation. They are not at war with the state but are caught up in a political struggle of the most serious sort; and direct police intervention, whatever its supposedly limited purposes, brings the police into that struggle and into what may appear as the closed circle of its strategic necessities. The more desperate the struggle, the less likely they are to meet with either obedience or a merely passive resistance. Even active resistance in such circumstances, however, does not necessarily constitute an attack upon the law and order that the state represents. It may do so, of course, if state officials are totally committed to the maintenance of corporate authority in its established forms and if their interference on behalf of that authority is not merely occasional but systematic. Clearly there have been governments so committed, and to their officials corporate revolution must look like (and may actually be) revolution *tout court*. But the history of liberal government is a history of retreat from such commitments, retreat from the total support, for example, of church prelates (ecclesiastical authority, and above all the right to collect tithes, was once protected by the property laws), of industrial magnates, and so on. The occasion for such retreats has generally been an act or a series of acts of corporate rebellion which state officials decided they could not or discovered they need not repress.

Continuous repression, if it were possible, would virtually force the rebels to expand their activity and challenge the state directly. And there are always some militants among the rebels who assume that such repression is inevitable. Like the corporate authorities, they see civil order and corporate authority inextricably intertwined. But this is rarely, if ever, the case. Law and order is indeed always law and order of a particular sort; it necessarily has a specific social content. But law and order is also a universal myth; the liberal state is at least potentially a universal organization; and in the name of its myths its leaders can always or almost always dissociate themselves from some particular piece of social oppression. For this reason, corporate rebellion is potentially a limited form of political action and potentially a kind of civil disobedience. The violation of property laws is not in itself an act of revolution against the state, and state officials acknowledge this and confirm it when they give up on such things as collecting tithes or clearing the factories. If they do intend to be civil and hope to be treated civilly, the rebellious subjects of corporate authority must in turn be careful not to make revolutionary claims against the state. Doubtless the occasion calls for a certain rhetorical extravagance, but that can be ignored so long as the actions of the rebels bespeak a concern for the appropriate limits. In general, this is the case: the rebels argue by their very actions that the commitments which they have made to one another (their new-found solidarity) establish an obligation to disobey not all laws but only *these* laws, for example, the trespass laws. They claim for their revolutionary organization not that it replaces the state or is a law unto itself, but only that it wins primacy in this or that limited area of social life. It requires its members to violate state laws *here*, not everywhere, and insofar as it justifies the use of violence against state officials, it does so only if they intervene against the revolution. The justification is local and temporary and does not challenge the general authority of the police to enforce the law. In fact, the rebels will often demand law enforcement—against the corporation—and explicitly pledge themselves to obedience, as they should do, whenever obedience is compatible with corporate democracy.

All these arguments are illustrated by the auto workers' sit-down strikes of 1936–37, and I think the illustration is worth presenting in some detail since so little has been written about this form of civil disobedience. The right of workers to strike has come to be so widely accepted that its illegal and semilegal history and all the philosophical issues raised by that history have been forgotten. The sit-down, moreover, was not only called illegal by the local courts in 1937, it eventually was called illegal by the Supreme Court. And the strike that went so far to establish the right of corporate subjects to organize and defend themselves remains illegal today. Yet it is, not the case that all corporate systems have been democratized, nor do all corporate subjects have the same rights. The questions raised in 1936–37 still have to be answered.

I don't think I need to describe at length the kind of oppression that existed in General Motors plants before the victory of the auto workers. Corporate officials possessed absolute authority over hiring and firing, the conditions of work, the pace of work, and the rates of pay. They used this power not only to maximize production and profit, but also to maintain the established authority system. In effect, they ran a miniature police state in the factories, and the organization of the workers, their incipient union, took on in response the features of an underground movement.[6] This movement claimed a kind

[6] See Henry Kraus, *The Many and the Few: A Chronicle of the Dynamic Auto Workers* (Los Angeles, 1947), Chapter 1, for an account of what organizing was like before the sit-downs. Kraus was editor of the *Flint Auto Worker*, the local union newspaper, during 1936–37.

of legality not within the corporation but within the state: its spokesmen insisted that they were acting in accordance with the National Labor Relations Act, which made the encouragement of union organization a matter of public policy, and in defense of those legal rights that workers were said to have in regard to their jobs.[7] But though union workers might argue that their activity was democratically authorized outside the factories, inside it necessarily took revolutionary and sometimes nondemocratic forms.

There can be no doubt that the union enjoyed widespread sympathy among the workers. But union members did not make up anything like a majority at any of the struck plants, and in some of them this was true not only of members but also of supporters. Majority rule does not operate very well in the early stages of the struggle for democracy, when the majority is likely to be both passive and frightened, justifiably anxious for its jobs, and often resentful of militants who don't share that anxiety or repress it in the name of possibly distant goals. Hence the way is always open for vanguard initiatives which are dangerous both practically and morally. Militants who seize the initiative always run the risk of finding themselves alone, deprived not only of effective support but of moral justification. In 1936, the risks paid off; the basis of a democratic movement did in fact exist, though this could not be known, and was not known with any certainty, in advance.

It is important to stress the risks the strikers accepted and had to accept if they were to undertake any political action at all. But it is also important to stress all they did to minimize those risks. A long history of struggle and failure precedes the dramatic victory of 1936. The commitment of the union militants to corporate democracy is best evidenced by their months and years of work in the factories, building support, searching for activists, adjusting their own proposals to meet the interests of the men on the job. A strike might have been attempted without all that. Angry men were never lacking in the auto plants. But there is a kind of legitimacy that can only be won by hard work. Without a disciplined base the civility of the strike would have been precarious at best, and it is not difficult to imagine isolated militants, faced with certain defeat, setting fire to a factory or shooting at the police.

But a successful strike requires not only that the militants find majority support, it also requires that they coerce minorities, and often that they begin to do so before they have demonstrated the extent of

---

[7] Solomon Barkin, "Labor Unions and Workers' Rights in Jobs" in Arthur Kornhauser, et al., editors, Industrial Conflict (New York, 1954), p. 127. These claims were eventually rejected by the courts. Cf. Leon Green, "Sit-Down Strikes are Legal," New Republic, March 24, 1937.

their support. This is not a usual feature of civil disobedience against the state, but it has to be remembered that what is going on in the corporation is not civil disobedience at all but revolution. Exactly what this involves can be seen most clearly in the seizure of Chevrolet Plant No. 4, the turning point of the General Motors strike. The union was relatively weak in Plant No. 4, and its seizure required careful planning. Company police were lured away by a demonstration in another factory; several hundred union militants from Plant No. 6 were brought in during a change of shifts; and these men together with union supporters already inside succeeded in forcing the shutdown of No. 4. Before the strikers carried the day, however, there was a time when uncommitted workers were attacked from both sides. Here is the account of a union official:

> A few of the staunchest unionists got into the aisles and began marching around shouting . . . "Strike is on! Come on and help us!" Many of the workers stood waveringly at their posts. . . . And meanwhile the superintendents and foremen . . . tore about, starting the conveyors up again, yelling to the men to "get back to work or you're fired." . . . Some of the men began working again or at least made a desperate effort to do so under the tumultuous circumstances as they were still anxious to differentiate themselves from the strikers. But the ranks of the latter grew inexorably. . . . There was practically no physical violence. The men would merely act fierce and holler threats. There was huge Kenny Malone with wrench in hand tearing down the lines and yelling: "Get off your job, you dirty scab!" Yet he never touched a man. . . .[8]

This is a graphic description of a revolutionary moment, the decisive overthrow of the absolutism of superintendents and foremen, and it is clear, I think, that one can justify the coercion of the "wavering" workers only by reference to that end and to the legitimate expectation that it was widely shared. For the moment, however, the militants could only assume that the end was widely shared, and such assumptions may have to be sustained without proof for some time. In Plant No. 4 the political battle was won, but the moral outcome, so to speak, remained inconclusive:

> The fight was over; the enormous plant was dead. . . . The unionists were in complete control. Everywhere they were speaking to groups of undecided workers. "We want you boys to stay with us. It won't be long and everything will be settled. Then we'll have a union and things will be different." Many of the workers reached their decision (for the union) in this moment. Others went home, undeterred by the strikers. About two thousand remained and an equal number went off.[9]

[8] Kraus, pp. 214–215.   [9] Kraus, p. 216.

I don't mean to suggest that *any* degree of coercion of undecided or neutral persons can be defended by reference to the end of corporate democracy. But it is likely that, given the limits I have already sketched, virtually any degree of necessary coercion can be defended. Surely it would be dishonest for those of us who value democracy in corporations as well as in states to pretend that we would judge the GM strike differently if Kenny Malone had actually hit somebody with his wrench—though we are certainly glad (and should be glad) to be told that he didn't. But in discussing violence against state officials, somewhat different standards apply, at least they apply if we believe the state to be so constituted that attempts on its authority are not easily justified. Within the corporation, revolutionary initiatives may well be appropriate; within the larger democratic community, they are inappropriate, and the corporate rebels demonstrate their civility only insofar as they make clear, as the auto workers did, that they intend no such initiatives. During the GM strike, for example, a number of workers were arrested, and the union leaders ordered mass demonstrations in front of the local police station. They thus used against the police legal forms of protest that they had declined to use against the corporation.

On the day after the seizure of Plant No. 4, a Michigan court issued an injunction against the strike, and the strikers began discussing among themselves what they would do if confronted by police or National Guardsmen. There were a few men in the factories and among the union's leaders who urged passive resistance. They thought the workers should allow themselves to be carried out of the factories. But a much larger group favored active resistance, on the pragmatic grounds that there was no working-class tradition of passivity and no religious or ideological foundation for a politics of nonviolence. The spectacle of strikers being carried, limp and unresisting, in the hands of the hated police would have, they argued, a profoundly disillusioning effect on the families of the strikers and on all the men who had so far refused to join the revolution. It would seem a terrible defeat rather than a moral victory, an incongruous and humiliating end to a period of heroic action. This argument carried the day, and the strikers publicly committed themselves to fight back against any effort to use force to clear the factories.[10]

At the same time, they did everything they could do, short of leaving the factories, to avoid such an outcome. They established their own law and order, a strikers' discipline far stricter than that of the foremen; they banned liquor from the occupied plants, worked out informal agreements with the police which permitted workers to come

[10] In a letter to Governor Murphy; on the arguments within the union, see Kraus, pp. 220, 231–233.

and go and food to be brought in, and carried out all necessary repair and maintenance work on factory machinery.[11] Above all, they repeatedly stressed their willingness to negotiate a settlement. This last is a crucial token of civility. However radical their demands, and even if those demands imply that the corporate authorities ought not to be authorities at all, the rebels can never deny to their opponents the recognition they themselves seek. The call for unconditional surrender may sometimes be appropriate in time of war and civil war, but it is never a political demand, nor is it compatible with civil peace.

The argument in the factories indicates some of the problems of any absolute commitment to nonviolence. Men who live in a democratic state can plausibly be said to be obligated to preserve its peace, to accept the forms of its law and order. But the strikers did not live only in the state. They were members, as all of us are, of overlapping social circles, and within the spheres specific to them—General Motors, the auto industry, the capitalist industrial system generally—they did not enjoy the benefits usually associated with the words law and order. These were worlds of oppression and struggle, in which the mutual forbearance necessary to civil disobedience did not exist. And in those worlds, state police had all too frequently played a role no different from that of company police, implicating themselves in the oppression and compromising their own authority. The point where the two circles overlapped had thus been dominated by the violence of the corporate world. It was only the refusal of Michigan's Governor Frank Murphy to enforce the court injunction —his own civil disobedience—that reestablished the state as a universal organization and a sphere of nonviolence, within which auto workers could conceivably incur serious obligations to the public peace.

Most of the criticisms of the strikers were simply refusals to recognize the pluralism of their lives and the possible pluralism of their commitments. When A. Lawrence Lowell, President-Emeritus of Harvard University, said that the sit-downs constituted "an armed insurrection . . . defiance of law, order, and duly elected authorities," he was suggesting that the spheres of corporate and state authority coincided perfectly.[12] I have already argued that this is sometimes true, and when it is civility on the part of corporate rebels it is almost impossible. But it was not true in Michigan in 1937. Governor Murphy, who had only a few months before become a "duly elected authority" with the support of the auto workers, symbolized this fact.

[11] Seidman, pp. 32–36.

[12] Quoted in J. Raymond Walsh, *C.I.O.: Industrial Unionism in Action* (New York, 1937), p. 182.

His affirmation of the independence of the state recognized that the primary focus of the strike was on General Motors and not on Michigan or the United States, and so ended the threat to civil order. By forcing negotiations between the corporate authorities and the union leadership, he began the long (and as yet incomplete) process of bringing some kind of legitimacy into General Motors. Until that process is well begun, I see no reason to deny the workers the right to use (limited) force within the corporate world, against their oppressors and against any allies their oppressors might call in. But I don't mean to state a general rule; the argument depends upon the specific character of the overlapping social circles.

Even if the police had gone in, the resistance of the workers would not have constituted an "armed insurrection," though it is not difficult to imagine an insurrection growing out of such an encounter. Particular, limited acts of resistance, coupled with appeals to community laws and values, do not necessarily break through the bounds of civil order. There was, in fact, an action of this sort early in the strike, a short, sharp battle between police and strikers (known, among the strikers at least, as the Battle of Bull Run) which took place at the initiative of the police.[13] I don't believe that incidents of this sort detract in any serious way from the double description of the strike that I have attempted to sketch: revolution in the corporate world, civil disobedience in the state. Obviously that dualism breeds difficulty; neither label is precise. Together, I think, they capture something of the social and moral reality of the sit-down.

Civil disobedience has often been divided into two types: direct disobedience, in which state laws thought to be unjust are openly defied; and indirect disobedience, in which state policies thought to be unjust are challenged by the violation of incidental laws, most often trespass laws. I have tried to describe a third type, more indirect than the second, in which the state is not challenged at all, but only those corporate authorities that the state (sometimes) protects. Here the disobedience takes place simultaneously in two different social arenas, the corporation and the state, and in judging that disobedience different criteria must be applied to the two, though I have tried to show that the two sets of criteria are not entirely unrelated. When revolution is justified in the corporation, then certain limited kinds of coercion and violence may be justified against state officials protecting corporate property. I assume a strong presumption against such violence, however, and I would want to justify it only when the oppression of the corporate subjects is palpable and severe and the in-

[13] Kraus, pp. 125 ff.

terference of the police of such a kind that leaves the rebels no alternative but resistance or defeat. At the same time, it seems to me that state officials, recognizing the oppression, ought not to interfere, ought to refrain, that is, from enforcing the property laws, and so avoid even limited violence.

The character of private governments obviously varies a great deal, and so the argument I have developed on the basis of the General Motors strikes will not apply in any neat and precise way to all other sit-downs. The student rebellions of the sixties, for example, are very different from the labor rebellions of the thirties. But I do believe that the same criteria can be used in framing our judgments in these two, and in many other, cases. This suggests the sort of questions we must ask the student militants: what is the nature of the oppression you experience? have you worked seriously among your fellow students (and among your teachers) to build support for your new politics? do you have, or potentially have, majority support? what are your specific proposals for university reform? and so on. By and large, I think, these questions have not been adequately answered—chiefly for two reasons that I can only mention briefly here. First of all, contemporary universities are very different from the GM plants of 1936 (or even of 1969). However authoritarian their administrations, their students enjoy personal and civil liberties undreamt of in the factories, and these liberties open the way for a great variety of political activities short of sitting-in. And yet, second, contemporary student movements have rarely been able, in fact, they have rarely attempted, to win and hold majority support. Their militants have too often rushed into adventures that cannot hope to win such support, in part because they have nothing to do with corporate democratization, in part because they call into question the very functions of the university the militants profess to value.

It is, nevertheless, not difficult to imagine universities so rigidly authoritarian and student movements so committed as to justify the sorts of politics I have been examining. There have certainly been justified sit-ins during the past several years, sit-ins that actually moved this or that university closer to whatever form of democracy is appropriate to the academic community. There have also been sit-ins justified in part, open at the same time to severe criticism, that resulted or might have resulted in similar movements. The theoretical model I have tried to elaborate permits us, I think, to defend such movements and their necessary methods—but always in a manner that reveals to the participants themselves the nature and limits of their action.

The problems of university government indicate clearly the great importance of arguing about the possibilities of democracy in every institutional order and not only in the state. I don't mean to prejudge these arguments, at any rate, I don't mean to prejudge them absolutely. A government of equals may be possible in one setting; weighted voting, or some such recognition of inequality, may be necessary in another; collective bargaining between employees and managers may be appropriate in a third. The range of political decision-making or of bargaining may have to be limited in this way or that, or it may not be limited at all. There is no single desirable system of internal adjudication. But I think it can be said flatly that some kind of democratic legitimacy is always necessary to corporate authority. Insofar as corporations lack this legitimacy, their very existence breeds revolt, and the more private and autocratic their government is, the more angry, perhaps violent, the revolt will be. If democratic states choose to shelter corporate autocrats, then they must learn to shelter corporate rebels as well. And if rebels are asked, as they should be, to maintain civility, then the authorities must see to it that civility is a genuine option for them, and not merely a convenience for the autocrats.

24 / Injustice and Bureaucracy

Lewis C. Mainzer

Man seems impelled to expect justice, despite his continuing experience of injustice. We judge the world and people, if not God, by the standard of justice. We have a deep expectation, echoing Job, that our adversaries should not be immeasurably stronger than we and that someone should appoint us a time to secure justice. In Kafka's modern parable of man's search for justice, the instrument which no man can comprehend or master is not the God who speaks to Job, but a bureaucracy which men create. Man alone is the victim of man organized. The form of association typical of our time, bureaucracy, is indelibly identified with the perpetration of injustice.

Bureaucracy pervades modern life. Bureaucratic organizations, more or less fully developed, conduct the activities of the civil service, the army, large business, churches, charities, schools, and the like. Government bureaucracy is widely considered a threat to the freedom of citizens, but the bureaucratic official in and out of govern-

Source: *The Yale Review* (Summer 1962), 559–573. Copyright Yale University.

ment exercises a more immediate and continuous power over subordinates within his organization than over outsiders. Even in a constitutionally governed nation, a subordinate may feel that he suffers a
lifetime of oppression under unjust superiors. Because justice is a
basic standard for all human relationships, when men live so largely
within bureaucracies two questions are fundamental: (1) Is injustice
likely within bureaucracy? (2) How can one respond to injustice
within bureaucracy?

   If one inquires about justice within bureaucracy, one turns to the
relationship between ruler and ruled. Rule by one man over another
is always in need of justification. Anarchists and pluralists, among the
moderns, have felt keenly that political authority and the state cannot
simply be taken for granted, and they are partly right. The bureaucracy, like the state, involves rule. Much "human relations" literature
suggests how power is or should be tempered within organizations,
but some of it glosses over the hard facts of power, that in every bureaucracy men do give or imply orders and are obeyed. Because bureaucracy involves rule, it poses the need to justify the authority of
one man over another.

   Not the existence of authority, an ineradicable condition for human
living together, but the quality of rule needs continuous justification.
The acceptance of authority within the family and the political system, if one stakes out its proper limits, is a reasonable price to pay for
humanness and civilization. Bureaucratic authority no doubt permits
the accomplishment of great tasks. Chester Barnard, in a remarkable
description of bureaucracy, comes in the end to stress the role of the
executive and the need for moral responsibility on the part of the executive. If the executive is weak or foolish or bad, his subordinates
and the organization suffer. The executive is, after all, a man possessed of office and power. A bad ruler can prevent Hobbesian chaos,
assuring men peace but not justice; a bad bureaucratic superior
affords legitimacy but not justice. Accepting the need for authority
within bureaucracy, one must ask about the purposes for which it is
used.

   Whose ends does rule serve within bureaucracy? It was the hope of
Mary Follett that business might so integrate the activities of its employees that each might achieve his important ends and contribute
from his own knowledge and experience. Conflict between worker
and management, between the individual's purposes and those of the
organization, would be ended. The ends sought would include the
ends of all. One may be impressed with the decency of Miss Follett's
vision, but her dream has not come true in any substantial degree.
The individual's aims still count for very little, the organization's aims
for very much.

Indeed, in a recent study Chris Argyris argues that formal organization is not compatible with "mature" behavior. Though his data relate largely to factory workers, his summary of evidence of the disaffection of workers with the regime of the formal organization is impressive. Only by such responses as formation of informal organizations, which restrict output, and apathy respecting one's work is a measure of sanity retained. To the extent that, as Argyris argues, the formal organization degrades the members, especially in the lower reaches, only a formal sort of equalitarian justice is possible. The organization members can be treated with uniformity and paid well to endure the degradation of meaningless, unsatisfying work. Trade unions can assure this; to fight organization, men organize, but their work remains dehumanizing.

One must add that many people, unlike mass production workers, engage in work which is inherently interesting and challenging, though they work within the formal structure of bureaucracy. Their situation is potentially satisfying and worthy of a human being. Much depends on the kind of authority to which they are subject. Under a just superior, the mere fact of bureaucratic organization may not prove degrading. The bureaucratic life may be made worthwhile by the quality of justice in the actions of the administrative superior.

A good many human beings share Lord Acton's assumption that all power tends to corrupt, but it is fair to note the many instances of men who rise to the challenge of office. We credit the United States presidency with qualities which call out virtue in the incumbent, and it is said that power did not corrupt Marcus Aurelius. Obviously power does not always corrupt. And not only power corrupts; impotence may corrupt too. When all is said, however, power does have a tendency to corrupt; it gives the opportunity to do bad things which lack of power denies to a man. Also, one who has power tends not to be too fastidious in choosing means to preserve it. "A man who wishes to make a profession of goodness in everything must necessarily come to grief among so many who are not good," Machiavelli advised a ruler. "Therefore it is necessary for a prince, who wishes to maintain himself, to learn how not to be good, and to use this knowledge and not use it, according to the necessity of the case." If one seeks power, and does it thoroughly, one may have to sacrifice virtue.

What is needed to succeed in a bureaucracy? Obviously qualities differ among different individuals in different positions of power. One may advance as a result of seniority, character, luck, nepotism, popularity, or other qualities. Sheer ability certainly helps, but when one listens to the utterances of such successful organization leaders as heads of great corporations, military leaders, or presidents of universities, one knows that many of these men are not necessarily wise.

We are struck by the number of men, especially in the United States, who rise to high administrative posts from professions other than administration. It is common for engineers to become business leaders and for teachers, scientists, and others to become high administrators in their own realms. They give up, save perhaps for token performance, their engineering, teaching, research, or other original skill or profession. These ambitious men must compensate in some way for the loss of satisfactions involved in sacrificing their professions. In many cases they may turn to administration when they sense their own creative limits within their profession. They may compensate for their sacrifice of professional activity or for their doubt of their own professional creativity by administering up to the hilt. Though they reminisce about "the good old days" and "the old drawing board," they like and need authority over individuals and discretion in significant matters. To turn one's back upon a profession for which one has prepared throughout many valuable years is so serious a decision that we can scarcely expect those who do it not to be men who find real satisfaction, or who will learn to find it, in the use and display of power.

Above all else what is needed to succeed in a bureaucracy is ambition. Mr. Lloyd George observed that there is "no generosity at the top." A kind of toughness and opportunism is as necessary at the top of a bureaucracy as at the top of a political system. Harold Lasswell's psychoanalytic analyses led him to conclude that driving administrators are basically like demagogic politicians. They simply found different career avenues "available for identification at critical phases of growth." The difference in the name of the function—administration or politics—misleads us, and the stereotype of the timid civil servant hides a lot of hard ambition. Only one who really wants to succeed and who will fight for success with all the tools at hand is likely to work his way up. Save in quiet corners where a peaceful seniority system prevails, at every level superiors are likely to be a little tougher than subordinates.

A recent study of American big business leaders by Warner and Abegglen confirms that getting to the top and staying there is highly competitive. Those not born to position who have started at the bottom and worked their way up are marked by a "feeling of loss and deprivation, that the father is withholding something from the son that he might provide." Mobility is partly to be explained as "an effort to gain this withheld support, and to prove oneself a worthy and able figure in the eyes of the father." These vertically mobile men, very often from troubled homes where the father has failed in family responsibilities, do not become deeply involved with people at work or at home; their energy is focused upon one thing—a successful

business career. They are not pictured as moved by a need to domi-
nate other men so much as by vast indifference to the lives of others.
In American large business today, then, the men at the top are under
great pressure; in order to succeed they often treat all other people as
simply means or, at worst, obstacles. They are unsuited to treating all
men as ends or to judging their own acts by the standard of justice.

Attitudes toward authority, whether or not rooted in early relations
with one's father, reflect basic elements of one's personality. In the
use of authority, as in the reaction to it, irrational behavior is intertwined with deliberate calculation of effective means to carefully
evaluated ends. The uses of power reflect the needs of the power-
seeker who has part way succeeded. We are told that Jason said "he
felt hungry when he was not a tyrant." Not every power wielder
within a bureaucracy craves authority or is unjust, but insofar as the
position calls to and molds character, it produces those in whom
burns little passion for justice. Whether control over others or simply
success is a central need of a man's personality, the quest for position
and power may blind him to the ends of others. Friendship or love
might conquer this unconcern for others, but these qualities have
small place in hierarchical relations. To find justice in the family,
where everyone counts, is hard enough; to find it in a bureaucracy,
where no one counts, is infinitely more difficult.

In truth, the subordinate in bureaucracy becomes not a means to
his own ends or even to the ends of the organization, but a means to
the ends of the superior. Because success of the organization is so
closely related to his own success, the superior's motives may seem
identical with the good of the organization. But if we can separate
the good of the organization from the good of the superior, we find
that the superior is really guided mainly by his own good. The only
common form of deliberate executive self-sacrifice to the organization
—hard work—is actually a means to furthering the career and using
the energies of the executive. The executives who say that "work is
my only hobby" are telling the truth. They work for themselves. The
superior, however much given to the language of organizational loyalty, loves himself, not the organization; the organization is the field
within which he operates, not the end itself. Let his rewards be
blocked and his contempt for the organization becomes manifest. In
sum, the subordinate, through the justifying language of the needs of
the organization, is used to meet the superior's need for success—in
terms of expansion of his program, reputation of his agency, high production, and the like. Hierarchical superiors regularly violate what
Tillich calls "the absolutely valid formal principle of justice in every
personal encounter, namely the acknowledgement of the other person
as a person."

Are there not controls to prevent the abuse of authority by bureaucratic superiors? It is tempting to say that those in authority will not
abuse it because of "understandings" or "opinion." We frequently encounter this train of reasoning in analyses of the British constitution,
for this constitution seems to consist so largely of "conventions," often
"unwritten" at that, which are not legally enforceable. A. V. Dicey
found "by far the most perplexing of the speculative questions suggested by a study of constitutional law" to be: "What is the sanction
by which obedience to the conventions of the constitution is at bottom enforced?"

In a brilliant chapter examining the sanctions for these constitutional understandings, Dicey answers his own question by saying that
"the force which in the last resort compels obedience to constitutional
morality is nothing else than the power of the law itself." One who violates the conventions must, ultimately—and before too long—break
the laws, for the two are interwoven. This assumes, of course, an independent body of opinion and an independent set of courts, neither
dependent on Crown or Ministry. Jennings protests that "the real
question which is presented to a Government is not whether a rule is
law or convention, but what the House of Commons will think about
it if a certain action is proposed." Both the legal and the political interpretation agree on the need for an independent body within the
system. Precisely what is lacking in bureaucracy is an independent
group corresponding to the legislature, the parliamentary opposition,
the courts, or a free citizenry. Everyone is "involved" and everyone is
dependent.

For Dicey, the constitutional conventions are maintained to insure
the supremacy of the House of Commons and, ultimately, the "sovereignty of the people"; for Jennings, conventions are obeyed because
of the political power of the electorate. In bureaucracy there is no assumption that ultimately power rests with the majority, nor any machinery by which the majority can turn out those in positions of authority. To rely with confidence on "conventions" of morality and
justice in a bureaucracy is to rely very largely on the sense of justice
and self-restraint—never certain qualities among rulers. There is neither a body independent of the executive nor a majority with effective power.

Within a large organization there are generally many rules with
which the official must comply, however, and which guarantee the
status of the subordinate. The public laws also provide protection
against the misuse of authority. In the bureaucracies of government
there may be the eyes of the legislature and the courts and of interest-group organizations and the press. All these help prevent abuse of
authority. Even in the army the officer or noncommissioned officer

may, as in the United States, be strictly limited in what he may demand and in the punishments he may impose.

Max Weber, impressed by the impersonality of bureaucracy, described bureaucracy in terms of the limitation of authority to official functions. Men occupy positions and obedience is owed to them only as the occupants of superior posts and respecting official matters. The superior can give the subordinate orders only in the realm of business; the personal life of the subordinate is exempt from this limited kind of authority. Compared with total subjection, this is no small gain for the subordinate, but the bureaucracy is not nearly as impersonal as Weber argued. Compared with the family or with feudalism it may well be called impersonal. The willingness to treat members officially as less than whole men is impersonal. But members of a bureaucracy do not interact simply as office holders. Unless their contacts are extremely limited, they interact as whole human beings, including the whole web of being called personality.

Within the limits of what is legally or officially permitted, authority may be abused. The guarantee that authority must be used only respecting official matters breaks down in practice. The salesman who must sell more may, in effect, be subject to pressure to deceive innocent buyers. The worker who must produce shoddy work is required to sacrifice the standard of good work. The person who must handle human cases too quickly or harshly must give to each case less than he would of his wisdom and kindness.

The actions which superiors judge and control often involve moral judgments by the subordinates. In every instance of this sort, some conception of a good and a bad man and a good and a bad life is implicit in the action of the superior, though he is likely to talk in terms of being practical or realistic or of using necessary means toward good ultimate ends. Slyness may be praised, integrity condemned; superiors may reward bad actions and may punish good actions. Official matters are finally only human acts and they carry moral implications. The superior, in rewarding and punishing, may corrupt the subordinate by inducing him to do bad acts and to adopt wrong values; he may subject the subordinate to injustice. Of course the subordinate may impute injustice where it does not exist. Many people feel persecuted when they are being justly treated. This does not, however, diminish the importance of the problem. Who can doubt that the subordinate within bureaucratic organization may suffer injustice at the hands of a superior who does not reward virtue, but praises and rewards bad actions?

What alternatives are open to the hierarchical subordinate within a bureaucracy whose superior is unjust in dealing with him? The individual unjustly treated must choose, deliberately or otherwise, a response. One of the old questions in political philosophy is whether a good man can be a good citizen of a bad state; the question has its analogue in bureaucracy. The obvious and probably most natural alternative for the subordinate is to fight back.

The subordinate is not powerless. In a real sense, authority comes from the subordinate, not from the superior. Thus, if a priest threatens to exclude one from heaven, he who is chastised may laughingly reply that he doubts the existence of heaven and the holiness of the priest. Or, contrariwise, he may beg forgiveness and promise to mend his ways. One decides whether or not the priest has authority over one. The bureaucratic subordinate may successfully engage in a good deal of disobedience. In every organization, many orders are ignored, just as many statutes are not enforced. The superior's lot is not a happy one if his subordinates are contemptuous of his authority. He depends on the subordinates, for if the subordinates do not do their job, the superior's mission is not accomplished. A continuous dose of threats and punishments by the superior is bad for morale and for real cooperation. The superior who cannot get along with his subordinates does not look good to those above and about him in the organization.

There is, of course, another side to authority. If the priest really influences admission to heaven, he may punish. If one defies authority in a bureaucracy, one may be denied advancement or may be discharged. Surely this is the exercise of authority from above. The advantages are by no means all with the subordinate if he fights back. Formal authority, with whatever sanctions the organization possesses, rests in the hands of the superior, not the subordinate. The superior can, perhaps within limits, denounce, penalize, or discharge the subordinate. The whole power of the organization is on his side.

The weight of the bureaucracy is always against a challenge by a subordinate to his superior. The maintenance of the system of authority seems to require that the superior's judgments be upheld, in turn, by his superiors. The decision is less one of whether the superior or the subordinate is right than one of whether the authority of the superior is to be successfully challenged. This means that appeal over the head of the superior is usually unsuccessful. A successful administrator senses that he must ordinarily back those under him, even when they have made a bad decision; this creates confidence and preserves authority.

Appeal is difficult also because the superior can easily stay within the bounds of what is legally or officially permissible. Unless he is very foolish, he will not violate a union contract or the laws of a public jurisdiction. What he can be accused of is injustice, but this is much more difficult to establish than illegality. The superior of the challenged superior official may be willing to act where there has been a violation of the rules, but he does not want to play Solomon.

If one appeals on the basis of justice, the odds are not encouraging. Higher officials are concerned with the success of the organization. The goals they seek are the organization's goals and their own. Subordinate members have personal goals, but these are of only manipulative interest to the managers of the organization, for whom the members are always means. Very few people enjoy digging coal or filing letters or handling complaints, yet people do all these tasks and no one much cares whether it is interesting or enjoyable work. The only appeal that carries weight within bureaucracy is that the superior is failing the organization. But of course the superior is in a much better position to make that very claim against the subordinate than vice versa.

In sum, the subordinate may choose to fight, but he is likely to lose. Whether or not to fight is a practical decision, with moral implications, for the subordinate to make in each case. If injustice involves other victims, one may feel obligated to fight on their behalf, and broader considerations enter. More often than not the subordinate will be defeated by the weight of the organization, which will be mobilized to preserve authority and the fiction of the wisdom which flows from above.

One may rebel against the injustice of authority within bureaucracy by adopting an extreme nihilism. If true values do not guide those with power, one may reason, then values have no real place in this system of living. Readers of Camus' study of the rebel are familiar with the idea that rebellion may lead to denial of values and to crime. The administrative crime is sabotage of the function of the agency and undermining of authority. Self-seeking—that is, personal gain or pleasure—or sheer destruction may be sought. Needless to state, a reaction against injustice which starts from the idea of justice and ends with rejection of all values has little to commend it. It is simply frustration given false philosophic credentials.

There is a second alternative. Rather than fight back, one may resign from the organization. A limited number of people, incapable of living in an unjust world, may choose suicide. Some men may choose to follow Gauguin, but for most people used to industrial civilization there is no real idyllic alternative. More generally, it may be possible for an individual to earn his living and perform his other activities outside bureaucracies; for many people in our age, this is not feasible. If one resigns, one must join another organization. There are circumstances in which this is a satisfactory alternative, for by it one may escape from a bad situation.

Injustice is likely within any bureaucracy. By resigning one escapes from a bad situation but, sooner or later, one is likely to encounter another. There is no safe haven. Even if one finds a just superior, one cannot count on serving under him more or less "permanently." The difficulty with resignation from the organization, then, is that one may have to repeat the act any number of times. After a while not only has one lost one's vested position in successive organizations, one has a reputation for instability. Something must be wrong with someone who moves from organization to organization. Who would believe that the person who is prone to resignation has been seeking justice? Anyway, others would be right to guess that he is a bad risk to remain long with them. If an organization can demand one quality, it is reliability. Resignation, then, is not without its uses, and practical considerations of what is given up and what the alternatives are certainly must be weighed. If it implies, however, that elsewhere justice is likely, it only deceives.

Resignation of a different sort offers a third alternative for one who suffers injustice in bureaucracy. This resignation is, however, not dismissing oneself from the organization but accepting the situation and dismissing its importance. It is apparently a somewhat "unrealistic" solution. Actually it may be quite realistic; it is based upon a true understanding of what the world is like.

Justice is not achieved within bureaucracies any more than within other human relationships. It is not impossible that one will be treated justly, but there is no reason to expect continued and consistently just treatment. Resigning oneself to the fact of injustice frees one from certain compulsions. So long as the rewards of the bureaucracy are the only rewards a man cares for, he is deeply engaged with the bureaucracy. If he is unjustly treated, he must either submit to his superior, in spirit as well as in form, or he must engage in combat or resign from the organization. In any case, he pays tribute to the importance of the bureaucracy and the superior.

No doubt it is difficult to believe that bureaucracy is not important, if one earns a living, and perhaps carries on other activities too, within a large organization. Is it not possible, however, to treat the bureaucracy as a fact of the environment and no more? If one lives in a very hot climate or in the midst of very foolish or bad people, it may be well not to make the climate or the people the center of one's existence. Of course one must continue to earn a living, and in accord with one's skills and training, and this may require working within a bureaucracy. If the bureaucracy is simply a fact of environment, however, praise or blame or reward or punishment from superiors become, if not totally unimportant, certainly a secondary aspect of life. One need simply have no interest in the judgments of superiors.

How can a man who works within a bureaucracy be unconcerned

with the actions of his superior? He must not care too much whether he is praised and whether he is rewarded. If he does not care for praise and rewards, and if he can tolerate some extra burdens and listen with equanimity to foolish things, he can take the sting out of the authority of the superior. Authority met with acceptance serves to get the action commanded but does not touch the spirit of the subordinate.

Either one must be without much ambition or one must adopt the standards expressed by those with authority within the organization or else one must live by other, equally demanding though different, standards. The crux of the possibility of philosophical resignation to the injustice of bureaucracy lies in the belief by the individual in a set of ethical standards not derived from the organization. One must have some firm ideas about what is good if one is to treat with unconcern one's fortune within the bureaucracy. If success is the only goal, one is doomed to worship the bureaucratic gods.

Is the attitude of the man in bureaucracy who is simply being used and knows it comparable to the attitude of *incivisme* attributed to the French? One gives service, but one's heart is never in the collective enterprise and one's confidence is never vested in those who have power. French *incivisme*, Philip Williams argues, does not mean that the French are bad citizens. It is, rather, an attitude of civic indiscipline or individualism, of resistance to power and its holders, a tradition of the negative, hostile response to a governmental demand. The man touched by *incivisme* is the reverse of the "organization man." Each gives service, but only the latter gives his heart and his conscience to the organization. *Incivisme,* the response to a history of the abuse of authority, is the response of a people with a good historical memory and a vigorous sense of individualism. If it saps strength from the collectivity at times, it may also retain vigor in the parts— which are men, the most important units.

Incivisme may be a dangerous analogy because the general attitude toward *incivisme* is scarcely as sympathetic as that suggested above. To Godfrey, a qualified American observer of France, *incivisme* or uncivicness involves a disgust, a dissociation, a "fundamental distrust of the whole business of politics and democracy as it is now constituted." French individualism has become "narrow, self-centered, and inner-directed"; for French democracy, *incivisme* is "catastrophic." *Incivisme*, then, is the policy of the disenchanted, of those who have given up on politics as other than something to watch. As Hannah Arendt writes of France, "the public realm has almost completely receded, so that greatness has given way to charm everywhere." No wonder a French writer recently devoted himself to seeking solutions to *"la crise du civisme."*

Incivisme, then, can be treated as the admirable spirit of individu-alism and revolt against the abuse of authority, against the romanti-cizing of the state, or as the selfish and disenchanted way of the poor, grudging citizen. The concept is ambiguous because the difficult question of proper behavior—of an attitude toward politics and power—is involved. Can a rational man serve the state well and love it? The political problem is analogous to the bureaucratic.

Resignation and detachment runs contrary to the urgings of those who, in some spirit of philosophy or psychology (wishing for us a good life or a healthy one) ask for the reconciliation of man to his work. This reconciliation, for many of those whose work is within a large organization, entails either degradation or ambition to succeed in the terms in which the organization defines success. To be spared the curses of slavery and opportunism of character, one may have to renounce the activities within large organizations as major sources of goals or satisfactions. The most obvious alternatives are the values of family and home and beloved possessions, the appeal to posterity for recognition, and the stoic goal, "the special happiness of the virtuous man in freedom from disturbance, in repose of spirit, and inward in-dependence." Any attempt at philosophical resignation to, and the draining of significance from, the organization entails difficulties.

If one turns to home and family and things, to this shelter and full individuality, one retreats from realms of enterprise and achievement. In the world of business, the rewards are generally money, authority, and a peculiar type of prestige. In other realms, however, lasting honor and a chance to serve public interests may be at stake. Miss Arendt writes, in examining a question larger than bureaucracy, that "to live an entirely private life means above all to be deprived of things essential to a truly human life: to be deprived of the reality that comes from being seen and heard by others, to be deprived of an 'objective' relationship with them that comes from being related to and separated from them through the intermediary of a common world of things, to be deprived of the possibility of achieving some-thing more permanent than life itself." Resignation may entail a lack of courage, the substitution of charm for greatness, the renunciation of the hope of leaving behind attainments which bring immortality. Tillich warns of the "resignation of power"—power in a rather broad sense—as "the attempt to annihilate oneself in order to escape guilt."

One may be able to participate in the "public" realm without doing so within a bureaucracy. The bureaucratic and the public are by no means precisely the same, though the public realm has been heavily bureaucratized. Accepting bureaucratic injustice and seeking to ac-complish in some other sphere, one might perhaps place one's faith in the judgment of posterity. Thus one may attempt to make one's mark in a lasting way in the realm of handicraft or art or letters or the like. Surely he who leaves behind something lasting has a chance, even after death, to be judged fairly respecting at least some of his qualities.

In a more stoical resignation than that which turns to the small world of beloved people and things or to the doing of great actions without immediate honor, the whole world is, as Marcus Aurelius would have it, but a dream. Then, of all things, "we ought to lay them bare and look at their worthlessness and strip them of all the words by which they are exalted." Fame too counts for nothing. One may wonder about the place of vigor and daring and the doing of the world's work, though Roman stoics served the public needs. Can human nature, by dint of the exercise of reason, conquer human nature, subduing so thoroughly the emotions and appetites? Does the stoic doctrine, so bloodless and free of emotion, crumble before vigor, competitiveness, playfulness, before the animality and the glory-seeking of man? How much force is added to the doctrine through joining it to a religious creed which calls for faith in the existence of another world?

Because sensible people often regard themselves as largely determined by their past, unless they turn to religious redemption, we always ask about our children and the paths they may still choose. What shall we tell our children, who will mostly work within large organizations; how can we help them to survive within organizations with their integrity intact? William H. Whyte tells them how to cheat on a personality test, so that they can move ahead in the organization. He would have them take on the "protective coloration" of the organization but secretly fight it. The fight, we should add, is for the good cause of individualism plus success within organizations, for "the bureaucratic way is too much with most of us" to renounce the quest for organizational success. It is an informed and worldly answer.

Any alternative answer requires that we teach virtue and the love for justice, as well as the worldly knowledge of the unlikelihood of justice. To learn how to succeed within organizations at any price is to unlearn justice and integrity. And love for justice without the worldly knowledge that justice is an unlikely quality, that one must be prepared for injustice in oneself and others, leads to inhumane systems and defeated humans. A bureaucratic life requires of a man qualities of character such that "the bureaucratic way" is not too much with him.

Philosophical resignation, which permits one to give honest service to a bureaucracy one does not love, takes different forms. One may turn from bureaucracy to home and possessions. One may seek to create or achieve in other, nonbureaucratic realms, perhaps accepting the judgment of posterity. One may, in fatalistic stoic style, accept everything that is, as according to nature. One may, through an otherworldly religious creed such as Christianity, turn away from this world. It would be absurd to suggest that a specific system of philosophy is the only one which permits philosophical resignation to the injustice of bureaucracy. Any philosophy which affords a man a measure of inward independence, so that he does not care too much for the praise of men with power, may assist him to endure bureaucracy, integrity intact.

25 / Marcuse Defines His New Left Line: A Conversation with Jean-Louis Ferrier, Jacques Boetsch, and Françoise Giroud

In terms of day-to-day effect, Herbert Marcuse may be the most important philosopher alive. For countless young people, discontented, demonstrating or fulminating, on campus or in the streets, here and abroad, this 70-year-old scholar is the angel of the apocalypse. "Away with the world's mess," his message seems to say. "Let us have a clean, revolutionary, new start." Born in Berlin, a Social Democrat in his youth, Marcuse came to the United States in 1934 and has been a citizen since 1940. His writings, particularly "One-Dimensional Man" (1964), have made him a hero of the New Left. Three staff members of the French magazine L'Express, Jean-Louis Ferrier, Jacques Boetsch and Françoise Giroud, found him on holiday on the Riviera. This translation by Helen Weaver of their conversation sets forth the man and his ideas.

Six months ago, sir, your name was almost unknown in France. It came to prominence in connection with the student revolt in Berlin, then in connection with student demonstrations in America. Next it was linked with the May demonstrations here. And now, all of a sudden, your last book has become a best-seller. How do you see your own position in relation to the student uprisings all over the world?

Source: *The New York Times Magazine* (Oct. 27, 1968), 29–31, 87, 89–90, 92, 97, 99–100, 109. Copyright © 1968 by The New York Times Company. Copyright © 1968 l'Express. All rights reserved. Reprinted by permission.

MARCUSE: The answer is very simple. I am deeply committed to the movement of "angry students," but I am certainly not their spokesman. It is the press and publicity that have given me this title and have turned me into a rather salable piece of merchandise. I particularly object to the juxtaposition of my name and photograph with those of Che Guevara, Debray, Rudi Dutschke, etc., because these men have truly risked and are still risking their lives in the battle for a more human society, whereas I participate in this battle only through my words and my ideas. It is a fundamental difference.

Still, your words preceded the student action.

MARCUSE: Oh, there are very few students who have really read me, I think. . . .

No doubt, especially in France; but there are also very few students who have chosen a doctrine for their revolt. Can we say that for these students you are the theorist?

MARCUSE: If that is true, I am very happy to hear it. But it's more a case of encounter than of direct influence. . . . In my books, I have tried to make a critique of society—and not only of capitalist society—in terms that avoid all ideology. Even the Socialist ideology, even the Marxist ideology. I have tried to show that contemporary society is a repressive society in all its aspects, that even the comfort, the prosperity, the alleged political and moral freedom are utilized for oppressive ends.

I have tried to show that any change would require a total rejection or, to speak the language of the students, a perpetual confrontation of this society. And that it is not merely a question of changing the institutions but rather, and this is more important, of totally changing human beings in their attitudes, their instincts, their goals, and their values.

This, I think, is the point of contact between my books and the worldwide student movement.

But you feel that they did not need you to arrive at these ideas, is that right?

MARCUSE: One of the essential characteristics of the student movement is that the students apply to reality what has been taught them in the abstract through the work of the masters who have developed the great values of Western civilization. For example, the primacy of natural law over established law, the inalienable right to resist tyranny and all illegitimate authority. . . . They simply cannot comprehend why these great principles should remain on the level of ideas instead of being put into practice. And that is exactly what they are doing.

Do you mean that fundamentally this is a humanist movement?

MARCUSE: They object to that term because according to them, humanism is a bourgeois, personal value. It is a philosophy which is inseparable from a destructive reality. But in their minds there is no point in worrying about the philosophy of a few persons; the point is to bring about a radical change in the society as a whole. So they want no part of the term "humanist."

You know, of course, that here in France we are very far from that "affluent society" whose destruction you propose and which for the moment exists, for better or worse, only in the United States.
MARCUSE: I have been accused of concentrating my critique on American society, and this is quite true. I have said so myself. But this is not only because I know this country better than any other; it is because I believe or I am afraid that American society may become the model for the other capitalist countries, and maybe even for the Socialist countries. I also believe that this route can be avoided, but again, this would presuppose a fundamental change, a total break with the content of the needs and aspirations of people as they are conditioned today.

A break . . . that is, a revolution.
MARCUSE: Precisely.

Do you believe in the existence of a revolutionary impulse in the industrial societies?
MARCUSE: You know quite well that the student movement contains a very strong element of anarchy. Very strong. And this is really new.

Anarchy—new?
MARCUSE: In the revolutionary movement of the 20th century, I believe it is new. At least on this scale, it is now. This means that the students have perceived the rigidity of the traditional political organizations, their petrification, the fact that they have stifled any revolutionary impulse. So it is outside of these organizations that the revolt spontaneously occurs.

But spontaneity is not enough. It is also necessary to have an organization. But a new, very flexible kind of organization, one that does not impose rigorous principles, one that allows for movement and initiative. An organization without the "bosses" of the old parties or political groups. This point is very important. The leaders of today are the products of publicity. In the actual movement there are no leaders as there were in the Bolshevik Revolution, for example.

In other words, it is anti-Leninist?
MARCUSE: Yes. In fact, Daniel Cohn-Bendit has severely criticized Leninism-Marxism on this ground.

Does this mean that you rely on anarchism to bring about the revolution you desire?

MARCUSE: No. But I do believe that the anarchist element is a very powerful and very progressive force, and that it is necessary to preserve this element as one of the factors in a larger and more structured process.

And yet you yourself are the opposite of an anarchist.

MARCUSE: That may be true, but I wish you'd tell me why.

Isn't it because your work is dialectical? Your work is very carefully constructed. Do you think of yourself as an anarchist?

MARCUSE: No. I am not an anarchist because I cannot imagine how one can combat a society which is mobilized and organized in its totality against any revolutionary movement, against any effective opposition; I do not see how one can combat such a society, such a concentrated force—military force, police force, etc.—without any organization. It won't work.

No, it won't work. The Communists will quote you Lenin's analysis of "leftism" which, according to him, was the manifestation of "petits bourgeois overcome with rage before the horrors of capitalism . . . a revolutionary attitude which is unstable, unproductive, and susceptible of rapidly changing into submission or apathy or going mad over some bourgeois fad or other."

MARCUSE: I do not agree. Today's left is far from the reaction of a *petite bourgeoisie* to a revolutionary party, as in Lenin's day. It is the reaction of a revolutionary minority to the established party which the Communist party has become, which is no longer the party of Lenin, but a social democratic party.

If anarchy doesn't work and if the Communist parties are no longer revolutionary, what do you hope for from the student unrest but a superficial disorder which only serves to stiffen the repression?

MARCUSE: All militant opposition takes the risk of increasing repression. This has never been a reason to stop the opposition. Otherwise, all progress would be impossible.

No doubt. But don't you think the notion of the "progress" that might result from a revolution deserves to be better defined? You denounce the subtle restraints that weigh upon the citizens of modern societies. Wouldn't a revolution result in exchanging one series of restraints for another?

MARCUSE: Of course. But there are progressive restraints and reactionary restraints. For example, restraints imposed upon the elemental aggressiveness of man, upon the instinct of destruction, the death instinct, the transformation of this elemental aggressiveness into an energy that could be used for the improvement and protection of life—such restraints would be necessary in the freest society. For example, industries would not be permitted to pollute the air, nor would the "White Citizens Council" be permitted to disseminate racism or to possess firearms, as they are in the United States today. . . . Of course there would be restraints; but they would be progressive ones.

The ones you mention are commonplace enough. The possession of firearms is forbidden in France, and in America it is a survival, not a creation of the affluent society. Let us consider freedom of expression, which means a great deal to us. In the free society which you advocate this freedom disappears, does it not?

MARCUSE: I have written that I believe it is necessary not to extend freedom of the press to movements which are obviously aggressive and destructive, like the Nazi movement. But with the exception of this special case, I am not against freedom of expression. . . .

Even when this means the propagation of racist, nationalist or colonialist ideas?

MARCUSE: Here my answer is no. I am not in favor of granting free expression to racist, anti-Semitic, neo-Nazi movements. Certainly not; because the interval between the word and the act is too brief today. At least in American society, the one with which I am familiar. You know the famous statement of Justice Holmes, that civil rights can be withdrawn in a single case: the case of immediate danger. Today this immediate danger exists everywhere.

Can't this formula be turned against you in connection with students, revolutionaries, or Communists?

MARCUSE: It always is. And my answer is always the same. I do not believe that the Communism conceived by the great Marxist theorists is, by its very nature, aggressive and destructive; quite the contrary.

But has it not become so under certain historical circumstances? Isn't there something aggressive and destructive about the Soviet policy toward Hungary in 1956, or toward Czechoslovakia today?

MARCUSE: Yes. But that isn't Communism, it is Stalinism. I would certainly use all possible restraints to oppose Stalinism, but that is not Communism.

Why do you criticize America more severely for its deviations from the democratic ideal than you do Communism for its deviations from the Communist ideal?

MARCUSE: I am just as critical of these deviations in Communist countries. However, I believe that the institutions and the whole culture of the capitalism of monopolies militate against the development of a democratic socialism.

And you believe that one day we shall see an ideal Communist society?

MARCUSE: Well, at least there is the theory. There is the whole

Marxist theory. That exists. And there is also Cuba. There is China. There is the Communist policy during the heroic period of the Bolshevik Revolution.

Do you mean that Communist societies do these reprehensible things in spite of themselves? That the Soviet Union invaded Czechoslovakia in spite of herself?

MARCUSE: In spite of the idea of Communism, not in spite of the Soviet Union. The invasion of Czechoslovakia is one of the most reprehensible acts in the history of Socialism. It is a brutal expression of the policy of power that has long been practiced by the Soviet Union in political and economic competition with capitalism. I believe that many of the reprehensible things that happen in the Communist countries are the result of competitive coexistence with capitalism, while poverty continues to reign in the Communist countries.

Here you are touching upon an important point. It does not seem possible to reduce poverty without an extremely coercive organization. So once again we find that restraint is necessary.

MARCUSE: Certainly. But here, too, there can be progressive restraint. Take a country in which poverty coexists with luxury, waste and comfort for the privileged. . . . It is necessary to curb this waste to eliminate poverty, misery and inequality. These are necessary restraints.

Unfortunately, there is no economic correlation. It is not the curbing of waste that eliminates poverty, it is production.

MARCUSE: That's true. But my point is that the restraints that certainly exist in, say, Cuba, are not the same as those that are felt in capitalist economies.

Cuba is perhaps not a very good example of a successful Socialist economy, since the country is totally dependent on daily deliveries of Soviet petroleum. If the Soviet Union were to stop those deliveries for two weeks . . .

MARCUSE: I don't know what would happen. But even under these conditions of dependence on the Soviet Union, Cuba has made tremendous progress.

In comparison with what she was that's certainly true. Have you been there?

MARCUSE: No. I can't get authorization from the Americans.

Why do you despair of all progress within the framework of the American democracy?

MARCUSE: Do you really think that democracy is making progress in the United States?

Compared with the period of "The Grapes of Wrath," yes.

MARCUSE: I disagree. Look at the elections, the candidates for the

Presidency of the United States, fabricated by the huge political machines. And who can find the differences between these candidates? If that's democracy, it's a farce. The people have said nothing and they have been asked nothing.

True. But at the same time thousands of young Americans have shown in recent months that they were against the war in Vietnam, that they were willing to work to eliminate the ghettos, to act in the political sphere.

MARCUSE: This movement is encountering a more and more effective repression.

Do you feel, then, that we are witnessing a definite obstruction of American society?

MARCUSE: The answer is a little more complicated than that. There is a possibility of progress toward democracy in the United States, but only through movements that are increasingly militant and radical. Not at all within the limits of the established process. This process is a game and the American students have not lost interest in playing this game, they have lost confidence in this allegedly democratic process.

Do you believe in the possibility of revolution in the United States?

MARCUSE: Absolutely not. Not at all.

Why not?

MARCUSE: Because there is no collaboration between the students and the workers, not even on the level on which it occurred in France in May and June.

In that case, what role do you attribute to the students?

MARCUSE: They are militant minorities who can articulate the needs and aspirations of the silent masses. But by themselves they are not revolutionaries, and nobody says they are. The students know that very well.

So their only role is to reveal?

MARCUSE: Yes. And this is very interesting. Here as well as in the United States, the students can truly be called spokesmen.

And who will make the revolution in America, in Germany, in France, if the students do not make contact with the working class?

MARCUSE: I cannot imagine. In spite of everything that has been said, I still cannot imagine a revolution without the working class.

The drawback—at least from the viewpoint of revolution—is that the working class is more interested in belonging to the affluent society than in destroying it, although it also hopes to modify certain aspects of it. At least this is the case in France. Is it different in other countries?

MARCUSE: You say that in France the working class is not yet integrated but that it would like to be. . . . In the United States it is integrated and it wants to be. This means that revolution postulates first of all the emergence of a new type of man with needs and aspirations that are qualitatively different from the aggressive and repressive needs and aspirations of established societies. It is true that the working class today shares in large measure the needs and aspirations of the dominant classes, and that without a break with the present content of needs, revolution is inconceivable.

So it will not happen tomorrow, it seems. It is easier to seize power than to change the needs of men. But what do you mean by aggressive needs?

MARCUSE: For example, the need to continue the competitive struggle for existence—the need to buy a new car every two years, the need to buy a new television set, the need to watch television five or six hours a day. This is already a vital need for a very large share of the population, and it is an aggressive and repressive need.

Aggressive to watch television? But it would seem on the face of it to be a passive activity.

MARCUSE: Are you familiar with the programs on American television? Nothing but shooting. And they always stimulate the consumption that subjects people to the capitalist mode of production.

There can be a different use of television.

MARCUSE: Of course. All this is not the fault of television, the fault of the automobile, the fault of technology in general. It is the fault of the miserable use that is made of technological progress. Television could just as well be used to reeducate the population.

In what sense? To persuade people that they do not need cars or television sets or refrigerators or washing machines?

MARCUSE: Yes, if this merchandise prevents the liberation of the serfs from their "voluntary servitude."

Wouldn't this create some problems for the people who work in the factories where they make cars, refrigerators, etc?

MARCUSE: They will shut down for a week or two. Everyone will go to the country. And then the real work will begin, the work of abolishing poverty, the work of abolishing inequality, instead of the work of waste which is performed in the society of consumption. In the United States, for example, General Motors and Ford, instead of producing private cars, will produce cars for public transportation, so that public transportation can become human.

It will take a lot of television programs to persuade the working class to make a revolution that will reduce their wages, do away with their cars and reduce their consumption. And in the meantime there is reason to fear that things may take a different turn, that all the people affected by the economic difficulties may potentially fur-

nish a fascist mass. Doesn't fascism always come out of an economic crisis?

MARCUSE: That's true. The revolutionary process always begins with and in an economic crisis. But this crisis would offer two possibilities: the so-called neo-fascist possibility, in which the masses turn toward a regime that is much more authoritarian and repressive, and the opposite possibility, that the masses may see an opportunity to construct a free society in which such crises would be avoidable. There are always two possibilities. One cannot, for fear of seeing the first materialize, stop hoping and working for the second through the education of the masses. And not only by words, but by actions.

For the present, aren't you afraid that these actions, especially when they are violent, will produce the opposite effect, and that the society will become even more repressive in order to defend itself?

MARCUSE: Unfortunately, that is a very real possibility. But that is not sufficient reason to give up. On the contrary, we must increase the opposition, reinforce it. There will always be privileged classes which will oppose any fundamental change.

It is not the privileged classes which have manifested their opposition in France. It is the middle class and part of the working class. The privileged classes have been content to exploit the dissatisfaction.

MARCUSE: Next you'll tell me that the revolutionary militants are responsible for the reaction. In Germany they are already saying that neo-Nazism is the result of student action.

In France, the result of the elections is incontestably the response of the majority of the country to the May movement, which frightened them.

MARCUSE: Well, we must fight that fear!

Do you think that one can fight fear with violence?

MARCUSE: Violence, I confess, is very dangerous for those who are the weakest. But first we should examine our terminology. People are always talking about violence, but they forget that there are different kinds of violence, with different functions. There is a violence of aggression and a violence of defense. There is a violence of police forces or armed forces or of the Ku Klux Klan, and there is a violence in the opposition to these aggressive manifestations of violence.

The students have said that they are opposing the violence of society, legal violence, institutionalized violence. Their violence is that of defense. They have said this, and I believe it is true.

Thanks to a kind of political linguistics, we never use the word violence to describe the actions of the police, we never use the word violence to describe the actions of the Special Forces in Vietnam. But the word is readily applied to the actions of students who defend themselves from the police, burn cars or chop down trees. This is a typical example of political linguistics, utilized as a weapon by the established society.

There has been a lot of fuss in France over the burned automobiles. But nobody gets at all excited about the enormous number of automobiles destroyed every day on the highways, not only in France but all over the world. The number of deaths in highway accidents in America is 50,000 per year.

And between 13,000 and 14,000 in France.

MARCUSE: But that doesn't count. Whereas one burned automobile is terrible, it is the supreme crime against property. But the other crime doesn't count!

How do you explain this phenomenon?

MARCUSE: Because the other crime has a function in production. It is profitable to society.

But people don't kill themselves to make a profit. How can you separate the society from the people who compose it? Society is not some special tribunal of people who meet in secret and say to each other: we are going to see to it that people kill themselves on the highways so that we can sell a lot of cars! Society is everyone, and everyone consents. You have a car yourself and you drive it. . . .

MARCUSE: But there is a very good reason for all this. It is that this society, at the stage it is at, must mobilize our aggressive instincts to an exorbitant degree to counteract the frustrations imposed by the daily struggle for existence. The little man who works eight hours a day in the factory, who does an inhuman and stupefying work, on the weekend sits behind a huge machine much more powerful than himself, and there he can utilize all his antisocial aggressiveness. And this is absolutely necessary. If this aggressiveness were not sublimated in the speed and power of the automobile, it might be directed against the dominant powers.

This seems to be what is happening in spite of the weekend traffic!

MARCUSE: No. It is only the students who are revolting and crying, "We are all German Jews!" that is, We are all oppressed.

And why do you think this diffuse oppression is more precisely experienced and formulated by the students? Why is it that the torch of revolution which seemed to be wavering, to say the least, in the industrial countries, has passed into their hands?

MARCUSE: It is because they are not integrated. This is a very interesting point. In the United States, for example, there is a vast difference in behavior between the students and teachers in the social sciences and humanities on the one hand and the natural sciences on the other. The majority comes from the first group. In France, I believe it is not the same. . . .

No, it isn't.

MARCUSE: And in the study of these sciences they have learned a great deal. The nature of power, the existence of the forces behind the facts. They have also become very much aware of what goes on in societies. And this awareness is absolutely impossible for the vast majority of the population, which is, in some sense, inside the social machine. If you will, the students are playing the role of the professional members of the intelligentsia before the French Revolution.

You know that Tocqueville denounced the role of writers in the revolution of 1789, precisely because they were on the fringe of political life, lacking experience in public life, constructing arbitrary schemata.

MARCUSE: Magnificent! And here is my answer to Tocqueville. I say that it is precisely *because* the students and intellectuals have no experience in what is today called politics that they are in the avant-garde. Because the political experience today is the experience of a game that is both faked and bloody.

Politics has always been a bloody game which kings and heads of state played among themselves. Do you mean that today it is faked because the people have the illusion of participating in this game?

MARCUSE: Yes. Who really participates in politics? Who takes part in it? Any important decision is always made by a very small minority. Take the war in Vietnam. Who really participated in that decision? A dozen people, I would say. Afterwards the Government solicits and receives the support of the population. But in the case of Vietnam, even Congress did not get a chance to learn the facts. No, the people do not participate in decisions. We do not participate. Only in secondary decisions.

But if the American Government stops the war tomorrow—they certainly will some day—won't it be as a result of public opinion? Of the revolt in public opinion?

MARCUSE: Precisely. And who is responsible for this change in public opinion?

American television.

MARCUSE: No, no! First there were the students. Opposition to the war began in the universities.

There is a slight contradiction in what you say, since you have written that this opposition is tolerated insofar as it has no power.

MARCUSE: It may have the power to alter American policy, but not the system itself. The framework of society will remain the same.

And to try to destroy this society which is guilty of violence, you feel that violence is both legitimate and desirable. Does this mean that you think it impossible to evolve peacefully and within the democratic framework toward a nonrepressive, freer society?

MARCUSE: The students have said it: a revolution is always just as violent as the violence it combats. I believe they are right.

But you still think it is possible, in spite of the judgment of Freud, to whom you refer frequently in "Eros and Civilization," to create a free society. Doesn't this betray a remarkable optimism?

MARCUSE: I am optimistic, because I believe that never in the history of humanity have the resources necessary to create a free society existed to such a degree. I am pessimistic because I believe that the established societies—capitalist society in particular—are totally organized and mobilized against this possibility.

Perhaps because people are afraid of freedom?

MARCUSE: Many people are afraid of freedom, certainly. They are conditioned to be afraid of it. They say to themselves: if people only had to work, say, five hours a week, what would they do with this freedom?

This is a condition which is not related to capitalism. The whole Judeo-Christian civilization is founded on work and is the product of work.

MARCUSE: Yes and no. Look at feudal society. That was truly a Christian society and yet work was not a value in it; on the contrary.

Because there were slaves, villagers. It was very convenient for the feudal lords.

MARCUSE: There were slaves, but the system of values was altogether different. And it was within this system that the culture was created. There is no such thing as bourgeois culture. Every genuine bourgeois culture is against the bourgeoisie.

In other words, we should return to the feudal system, but with machines taking the place of the slaves?

MARCUSE: We must have machines in places of slaves, but without returning to the feudal system. It would be the end of work, and at the same time the end of the capitalist system. Marx saw this in that famous passage where he says that with technological progress and automation, man is separated from the instruments of production, is dissociated from material production, and acts simply as a free subject, experimenting with the material possibilities of the machines, etc. But this would also mean the end of an economy founded on exchange value. Because the product would no longer be worth anything as merchandise. And this is the specter that haunts the established society.

Do you regard work, effort, as a repressive value?

MARCUSE: It all depends on its purpose. Effort is not repressive by itself. Effort in art, in every creative act, in love. . . .

Would you work if you were not obliged to do so?

MARCUSE: Certainly. I work if I am not obliged to do so.

Do you consider yourself a free man?

MARCUSE: Me? I believe that nobody is free in this society. Nobody.

Have you been psychoanalyzed?

MARCUSE: Never. Do you think I need to be?

It's quite possible, but that's beside the point. What seems curious is that you have made such a thorough study of the work of Freud and his views on the inevitably repressive quality of all civilization without asking yourself about your own obstacles to the exercise of your personal freedom.

MARCUSE: I have discussed Freud only on the level of theory, not on the level of therapy.

Don't you give European civilization any credit for being able to create its own values in reaction to American civilization while at the same time appropriating the positive element in that civilization, that is, the technical progress which you yourself have said is absolutely fundamental to the liberation of man?

MARCUSE: It is almost impossible to speak of a European civilization today. Perhaps it is even impossible to speak of a Western civilization. I believe that Eastern civilization and Western civilization are assimilating each other at an ever increasing rate. And the European civilization of today has already absorbed much of American civilization. So it seems impossible to imagine a European civilization separated from the influence of America. Except, perhaps, in a few very isolated sectors of intellectual culture. Poetry, for example.

So you think the battle is lost. That we are Americans?

MARCUSE: We mustn't say it is lost. It is possible to change, to utilize the possibilities of American civilization for the good of humanity. We must utilize everything that enables us to facilitate daily life, to make it more tolerable. . . . We could already, today, end air pollution, for example. The means exist.

What role do you envision for art in the free society of which you dream, since art is by definition denial, challenge?

MARCUSE: I am not a prophet. In the affluent society, art is an interesting phenomenon. On the one hand, it rejects and accuses the established society; on the other hand, it is offered and sold on the market. There is not a single artistic style, however avant-garde, that does not sell. This means that the function of art is problematic, to say the least. There has been talk of the end of art, and there really is among the artists a feeling that art today has no function. There are museums, concerts, paintings in the homes of the rich, but art no longer has a function. So it wants to become an essential part of reality, to change reality.

Look at the graffiti, for example. For me, this is perhaps the most interesting aspect of the events of May, the coming together of Marx and André Breton. Imagination in power: that is truly revolutionary. It is new and revolutionary to try to translate into reality the most advanced ideas and values of the imagination. This proves that people have learned an important lesson: that truth is not only in rationality, but just as much and perhaps more in the imaginary.

The imaginary is above all the only realm where man's freedom has always been complete, where nothing has succeeded in curbing it. Dreams bear witness to this.

MARCUSE: Yes. And this is why I believe that the student rebellion, whatever its immediate results, is a real turning point in the development of contemporary society.

Because the students are reintegrating the imaginary with reality?

MARCUSE: Yes. There is a graffito which I like very much which goes, "Be realists, demand the impossible." That is magnificent. And another: "Watch out, ears have walls." That is realistic!

You have no desire to go back to Germany?

MARCUSE: I don't think so. Only to give lectures. But I like the German students very much, they are terrific!

Have they succeeded any better than the others in making contact with the working class?

MARCUSE: No. Their collaboration has been even more precarious.

Is it true that in the United States you received threats from the Ku Klux Klan?

MARCUSE: They were signed Ku Klux Klan, but I don't think it was they who sent them.

Is it true that you moved out of your house following these threats?

MARCUSE: Yes. Not in a panic, but I did leave. Frankly, I wasn't afraid. My students came and surrounded the house with their cars to protect me. . . . In one sense, they were right in thinking that there was a risk.

And do you feel that your life in the United States can continue, now that your notoriety has put you in the public eye?

MARCUSE: I'm not sure, not at all sure. At the university there's no problem. But universities are always oases.

Do you think that the American university as it is set up now can be a model for the French university, for example?

MARCUSE: One must distinguish among American universities. The

large universities are always sanctuaries for free thought and a
rather solid education. Take mine, for example, the University of
California in San Diego. This is probably the most reactionary area
in the United States—a large military base, a center of so-called
defense industry, retired colonels and admirals. I have no difficulty
with the university, the administration, or my colleagues. But I
have a great deal of difficulty at the hands of the community, the
good middle-class townspeople. No problems with the students. Relations between professors and students are, I think, much more informal than here and in Germany.

In this respect, you know, there really is an egalitarian tradition
in the United States. The sanctity of the professor does not exist. It
is the American materialism that prevents it. The professor is a sal-
aried man who has studied, who has learned certain things, and
who teaches them; he is not at all a mythical personage identified
with the Father, not at all. His political position depends upon his
position in the university hierarchy. If you reach a permanent position it is practically impossible to fire you. My own situation is precarious, and I am very curious to find out whether I will be able to
retain my position at the university.

*What you say is very serious. If freedom of expression no longer
exists in the United States, it will no longer exist anywhere . . . or
perhaps in England?*

MARCUSE: Yes. England may turn out to be one of the last liberal
countries. The democracy of the masses is not favorable to noncon-
formist intellectuals. . . .

*This is the crux of the matter. You have often been criticized for
wanting to establish a Platonic dictatorship of the élite. Is this correct?*

MARCUSE: There is a very interesting passage in John Stuart Mill,
who was not exactly an advocate of dictatorship. He says that in a
civilized society educated people must have political prerogatives
to oppose the emotions, attitudes and ideas of the uneducated
masses.

I have never said that it was necessary to establish a Platonic
dictatorship because there is no philosopher who is capable of
doing this. But to be perfectly frank, I don't know which is worse: a
dictatorship of politicians, managers and generals, or a dictatorship
of intellectuals.

Personally, if this is the choice, I would prefer the dictatorship of
the intellectuals, if there is no possibility of a genuine free democracy. Unfortunately this alternative does not exist at present.

*The dictatorship of the intellectuals must first be established to
educate and reform the masses, after which, in a remote future,*

when people have changed, democracy and freedom will reign. Is that it?

MARCUSE: Not a true dictatorship, but a more important role for intellectuals, yes. I think that the resentment of the worker movement against the intellectuals is one of the reasons why this movement has stopped today.

The dictatorship of the intellectuals is rather disturbing, to the extent that intellectuals often become cruel because they are afraid of action.

MARCUSE: Is that really so? There is only one example in history of a cruel intellectual: Robespierre.

And Saint-Just.

MARCUSE: We must compare the cruelty of Robespierre and Saint-Just with the cruelty and the bureaucratized violence of an Eichmann. Or even with the institutionalized violence of modern societies. Nazi cruelty is cruelty as a technique of administration. The Nazis were not intellectuals. With intellectuals, cruelty and violence are always much more immediate, shorter, less cruel. Robespierre did not use torture. Torture is not an essential aspect of the French Revolution.

You know intellectuals: they are not, or are only slightly, in touch with reality. Can you imagine a society functioning under their direct government? What effect would this have on trains running on time, for example? Or on organizing production?

MARCUSE: If you identify reality with established reality you are right. But intellectuals do not or should not identify reality with established reality. Given the imagination and rationality of true intellectuals, we can expect great things. In any case, the famous dictatorship of the intellectuals has never existed.

Perhaps because an intellectual is by his very nature an individualist. Lenin said this, too. What form of dictatorship do you prefer? One that operates directly as is the case in the Soviet Union, for example, or one that adopts the mask of democracy?

MARCUSE: It is absolutely necessary not to isolate a given situation from its tendencies for development. There is a social and political repression which can foster human progress, which can lead toward a true democracy and a true freedom. And there is a repression which does the opposite. I have always said that I utterly reject Stalinian repression and the repressive policy of Communism, although I recognize that the Socialist base of these countries contains the possibility of development toward liberalization and ultimately toward a free society.

It is a question of not being too skeptical about the end. . . .

MARCUSE: I am very skeptical about the end, in both cases.

Do you think that man can be free and at the same time believe in the existence of God?

MARCUSE: The liberation of man depends neither on God nor on the nonexistence of God. It is not the idea of God which has been an obstacle to human liberation, but the use that has been made of the idea of God.

But why has this use been made of it?

MARCUSE: From the beginning, religion has been allied with the ruling strata of society. In the case of Christianity, not from the very beginning, but still, rather early on.

In short, one must belong to the ruling strata of society! That is the sad conclusion that one could cynically draw from what you say. All the rest is adventure, more or less doomed to failure. Of course, one can prefer adventure, need adventure, and dream of being Guevara, in Paris or Berlin.

MARCUSE: Guevara was not adventure; it was the alliance between adventure and revolutionary politics. If revolution does not contain an element of adventurism, it is worthless. All the rest is organization, labor unions, social democracy, the establishment. Adventure is always beyond. . . .

What you call adventurism, others call romanticism. . . .

MARCUSE: Call it what you will. Adventure is transcendence of the given reality. Those who no longer wish to contain the revolution within the framework of the given reality. Call it what you will—adventurism, romanticism, imagination—it is an element necessary to all revolution.

No doubt. But it would seem that a concrete analysis of the situation in the countries in which one wants to make a revolution is also not an entirely negligible element. Provided, of course, that one wants to bring it off, and not merely to dream. One more question. You denounce as a painful form of oppression and one from which we suffer the deprivation of solitude and silence inflicted on us by modern society. Isn't this a plague that is just as characteristic of collectivist societies?

MARCUSE: First of all, we must eliminate the concept of collectivist societies. There are many modes of collectivization. There is a collectivism that is based on true human solidarity. There is a collectivism that is based on an authoritarian regime that is imposed on people. The destruction of autonomy, silence and solitude occurs in the so-called free societies as well as in the so-called collectivist societies. The decisive problem is to determine whether the limitations imposed on the individual are imposed in order to further domination and indoctrination of the masses, or, on the contrary, in the interest of human progress.

It would be interesting to learn which noises are the progressive ones, if only so as to bear them with a smile. Sorry . . . we were being facetious.

MARCUSE: So was I. There is no free society without silence, without the internal and external space of solitude in which individual freedom can develop. If there is neither private life, nor autonomy, nor silence, nor solitude in a Socialist society—well, it is very simple: it is not a Socialist society! Not yet.

26 / Black Power

STOKELY CARMICHAEL AND CHARLES V. HAMILTON

. . . The advocates of Black Power reject the old slogans and meaningless rhetoric of previous years in the civil rights struggle. The language of yesterday is indeed irrelevant: progress, non-violence, integration, fear of "white backlash," coalition. Let us look at the rhetoric and see why these terms must be set aside or redefined.

One of the tragedies of the struggle against racism is that up to this point there has been no national organization which could speak to the growing militancy of young black people in the urban ghettos and the black-belt South. There has been only a "civil rights" movement, whose tone of voice was adapted to an audience of middle-class whites. It served as a sort of buffer zone between that audience and angry young blacks. It claimed to speak for the needs of a community, but it did not speak in the tone of that community. None of its so-called leaders could go into a rioting community and be listened to. In a sense, the blame must be shared—along with the mass media—by those leaders for what happened in Watts, Harlem, Chicago, Cleveland and other places. Each time the black people in those cities saw Dr. Martin Luther King get slapped, they became angry. When they saw little black girls bombed to death *in a church* and civil rights workers ambushed and murdered, they were angrier; and when nothing happened, they were steaming mad. We had nothing to offer that they could see, except to go out and be beaten again. We helped to build their frustration.

We had only the old language of love and suffering. And in most places—that is, from the liberals and middle class—we got back the

SOURCE: *Black Power* by Stokely Carmichael and Charles V. Hamilton. Copyright 1967 by Stokely Carmichael and Charles Hamilton. Reprinted by permission of Random House, Inc.

old language of patience and progress. The civil rights leaders were saying to the country: "Look, you guys are supposed to be nice guys, and we are only going to do what we are supposed to do. Why do you beat us up? Why don't you give us what we ask? Why don't you straighten yourselves out?" For the masses of black people, this language resulted in virtually nothing. In fact, their objective day-to-day condition worsened. The unemployment rate among black people increased while that among whites declined. Housing conditions in the black communities deteriorated. Schools in the black ghettos continued to plod along on outmoded techniques, inadequate curricula, and with all too many tired and indifferent teachers. Meanwhile, the President picked up the refrain of "We Shall Overcome" while the Congress passed civil rights law after civil rights law, only to have them effectively nullified by deliberately weak enforcement. "Progress is being made," we were told.

Such language, along with admonitions to remain non-violent and fear the white backlash, convinced some that that course was the *only* course to follow. It misled some into believing that a black minority could bow its head and get whipped into a meaningful position of power. The very notion is absurd. The white society devised the language, adopted the rules and had the black community narcotized into believing that that language and those rules were, in fact, relevant. The black community was told time and again how *other* immigrants finally won *acceptance:* that is, by following the Protestant Ethic of Work and Achievement. They worked hard; therefore, they achieved. We were not told that it was by building Irish Power, Italian Power, Polish Power or Jewish Power that these groups got themselves together and operated from positions of strength. We were not told that "the American dream" wasn't designed for black people. That while today, to whites, the dream may *seem* to include black people, it cannot do so by the very nature of this nation's political and economic system, which imposes institutional racism on the black masses if not upon every individual black. A notable comment on that "dream" was made by Dr. Percy Julian, the black scientist and director of the Julian Research Institute in Chicago, a man for whom the dream seems to have come true. While not subscribing to "black power" as he understood it, Dr. Julian clearly understood the basis for it: "The false concept of basic Negro inferiority is one of the curses that still lingers. It is a problem created by the white man. Our children just no longer are going to accept the patience we were taught by our generation. We were taught a pretty little lie—excel and the whole world lies open before you. *I obeyed the injunction and found it to be wishful thinking.*" (Authors' italics) [1]

[1] *The New York Times* (April 30, 1967), p. 30.

A key phrase in our buffer-zone days was non-violence. For years it has been thought that black people would not literally fight for their lives. Why this has been so is not entirely clear; neither the larger society nor black people are noted for passivity. The notion apparently stems from the years of marches and demonstrations and sit-ins where black people did not strike back and the violence always came from white mobs. There are many who still sincerely believe in that approach. From our viewpoint, rampaging white mobs and white night-riders must be made to understand that their days of free head-whipping are over. Black people should and must fight back. Nothing more quickly repels someone bent on destroying you than the unequivocal message: "O.K., fool, make your move, and run the same risk I run—of dying."

When the concept of Black Power is set forth, many people immediately conjure up notions of violence. The country's reaction to the Deacons for Defense and Justice, which originated in Louisiana, is instructive. Here is a group which realized that the "law" and law enforcement agencies would not protect people, so they had to do it themselves. If a nation fails to protect its citizens, then that nation cannot condemn those who take up the task themselves. The Deacons and all other blacks who resort to self-defense represent a simple answer to a simple question: what man would not defend his family and home from attack?

But this frightened some white people, because they knew that black people would now fight back. They knew that this was precisely what *they* would have long since done if *they* were subjected to the injustices and oppression heaped on blacks. Those of us who advocate Black Power are quite clear in our own minds that a "non-violent" approach to civil rights is an approach black people cannot afford and a luxury white people do not deserve. It is crystal clear to us—and it must become so with the white society—*that there can be no social order without social justice*. White people must be made to understand that they must stop messing with black people, or the blacks *will* fight back! . . .

. . . And when there are explosions—explosions of frustration, despair and hopelessness—the larger society becomes indignant and utters irrelevant clichés about maintaining law and order. Blue ribbon committees of "experts" and "consultants" are appointed to investigate the "causes of the riot." They then spend hundreds of thousands of dollars on preparing "authoritative" reports. Some token money from the Office of Economic Opportunity may be promised and then everybody either prays for rain to cool off tempers and vacate the streets or for an early autumn.

This country, with its pervasive institutional racism, has itself created socially undesirable conditions; it merely perpetuates those conditions when it lays the blame on people who, through whatever means at their disposal, seek to strike out at the conditions. What has to be understood is that thus far there have been virtually no *legitimate* programs to deal with the alienation and the oppressive conditions in the ghettos. On April 9, 1967, a few days after Mayor Daley won an overwhelming, unprecedented fourth-term victory (receiving, incidentally, approximately 85 percent of Chicago's black vote), *The New York Times* editorialized: "Like other big-city mayors, Mr. Daley has no long-range plans for coping with the social dislocation caused by the steady growth of the Negro population. He tries to manage the effects of that dislocation and hopes for the best."

Herein lies the match that will continue to ignite the dynamite in the ghettos: the ineptness of decision-makers, the anachronistic institutions, the inability to think boldly and above all the unwillingness to innovate. The makeshift plans put together every summer by city administrations to avoid rebellions in the ghettos are merely buying time. White America can continue to appropriate millions of dollars to take ghetto teen-agers off the streets and onto nice, green farms during the hot summer months. They can continue to provide mobile swimming pools and hastily built play areas, but there is a point beyond which the steaming ghettos will not be cooled off. It is ludicrous for the society to believe that these temporary measures can long contain the tempers of an oppressed people. And when the dynamite does go off, pious pronouncements of patience should not go forth. Blame should not be placed on "outside agitators" or on "Communist influence" or on advocates of Black Power. That dynamite was placed there by white racism and it was ignited by white racist indifference and unwillingness to act justly.

27 / On Not Prosecuting Civil Disobedience

RONALD DWORKIN

How should the government deal with those who disobey the draft laws out of conscience? Many people think the answer is obvious: The government must prosecute

SOURCE: *The New York Review of Books*, X (June 6, 1968), 14–21. Reprinted by permission of the author.

the dissenters, and if they are convicted it must punish them. Some people reach this conclusion easily, because they hold the mindless view that conscientious disobedience is the same as lawlessness. They think that the dissenters are anarchists who must be punished before their corruption spreads. Many lawyers and intellectuals come to the same conclusion, however, on what looks like a more sophisticated argument. They recognize that disobedience to law may be *morally* justified, but they insist that it cannot be *legally* justified, and they think that it follows from this truism that the law must be enforced. Erwin Griswold, the Solicitor General of the United States, and the former Dean of the Harvard Law School, appears to have adopted this view in a recent statement. "[It] is of the essence of law," he said, "that it is equally applied to all, that it binds all alike, irrespective of personal motive. For this reason, one who contemplates civil disobedience out of moral conviction should not be surprised and must not be bitter if a criminal conviction ensues. And he must accept the fact that organized society cannot endure on any other basis."

The New York Times applauded that statement. A thousand faculty members of several universities had signed a *Times* advertisement calling on the Justice Department to quash the indictments of the Rev. William Sloane Coffin, Dr. Benjamin Spock, Marcus Raskin, Mitchell Goodman, and Michael Ferber, for conspiring to counsel various draft offenses. The *Times* said that the request to quash the indictments "confused moral rights with legal responsibilities."

But the argument that, because the government believes a man has committed a crime, it must prosecute him is much weaker than it seems. Society "cannot endure" if it tolerates all disobedience; it does not follow, however, nor is there evidence, that it will collapse if it tolerates some. In the United States prosecutors have discretion whether to enforce criminal laws in particular cases. A prosecutor may properly decide not to press charges if the lawbreaker is young, or inexperienced, or the sole support of a family, or is repentant, or turns state's evidence, or if the law is unpopular or unworkable or generally disobeyed, or if the courts are clogged with more important cases, or for dozens of other reasons. This discretion is not license— we expect prosecutors to have good reasons for exercising it—but there are, at least *prima facie,* some good reasons for not prosecuting those who disobey the draft laws out of conscience. One is the obvious reason that they act out of better motives than those who break the law out of greed or a desire to subvert government. If motive can count in distinguishing between thieves, then why not in distinguishing between draft offenders? Another is the practical reason that our society suffers a loss if it punishes a group that includes—as the group of draft dissenters does—some of its most loyal and law-re-

specting citizens. Jailing such men solidifies their alienation from society, and alienates many like them who are deterred by the threat. If
practical consequences like these argued for not enforcing prohibition, why do they not argue for tolerating offenses of conscience?

Those who think that conscientious draft offenders should always
be punished must show that these are not good reasons for exercising
discretion, or they must find contrary reasons that outweigh them.
What arguments might they produce? There are practical reasons for
enforcing draft laws, and I shall consider some of these later. But
Dean Griswold and those who agree with him seem to rely on a fundamental moral argument that it would be unfair, not merely impractical, to let the dissenters go unpunished. They think it would be
unfair, I gather, because society could not function if everyone disobeyed laws he disapproved of or found disadvantageous. If the government tolerates those few who will not "play the game," it allows
them to secure the benefits of everyone else's deference to law, without shouldering the burdens, such as the burden of the draft.

This argument is a serious one. It cannot be answered simply by
saying that the dissenters would allow everyone else the privilege of
disobeying a law he believed immoral. In fact, few draft dissenters
would accept a changed society in which sincere segregationists were
free to break civil rights laws they hated. The majority want no such
change, in any event, because they think that society would be worse
off for it; until they are shown this is wrong, they will expect their officials to punish anyone who assumes a privilege which they, for the
general benefit, do not assume.

There is, however, a flaw in the argument. The reasoning contains
a hidden assumption that makes it almost entirely irrelevant to the
draft cases, and indeed to any serious case of civil disobedience in
the United States. The argument assumes that the dissenters know
that they are breaking a valid law, and that the privilege they assert
is the privilege to do that. Of course, almost everyone who discusses
civil disobedience recognizes that in America a law may be invalid
because it is unconstitutional. But the critics handle this complexity
by arguing on separate hypotheses: If the law is invalid, then no
crime is committed, and society may not punish. If the law is valid,
then a crime has been committed, and society must punish. This reasoning hides the crucial fact that the validity of the law may be
doubtful. The officials and judges may believe that the law is valid,
the dissenters may disagree, and both sides may have plausible arguments for their positions. If so, then the issues are different from what
they would be if the law were clearly valid or clearly invalid, and the
argument of fairness, designed for these alternatives, is irrelevant.

Doubtful law is by no means special or exotic in cases of civil disobedience. On the contrary. In the United States, at least, almost any law which a significant number of people would be tempted to disobey on moral grounds would be doubtful—if not clearly invalid—on constitutional grounds as well. The constitution makes our conventional political morality relevant to the question of validity; any statute that appears to compromise that morality raises constitutional questions, and if the compromise is serious, the constitutional doubts are serious also.

The connection between moral and legal issues is especially clear in the current draft cases. Dissent has largely been based on the following moral objections: (a) The United States is using immoral weapons and tactics in Vietnam. (b) The war has never been endorsed by deliberate, considered, and open vote of the people's representatives. (c) The United States has no interest at stake in Vietnam remotely strong enough to justify forcing a segment of its citizens to risk death there. (d) If an army is to be raised to fight that war, it is immoral to raise it by a draft that defers or exempts college students, and thus discriminates against the economically underprivileged. (e) The draft exempts those who object to all wars on religious grounds, but not those who object to particular wars on moral grounds; there is no relevant difference between these positions, and so the draft, by making the distinction, implies that the second group is less worthy of the nation's respect than the first. (f) The law that makes it a crime to counsel draft resistance stifles those who oppose the war, because it is morally impossible to argue that the war is profoundly immoral, without encouraging and assisting those who refuse to fight it.

Lawyers will recognize that these moral positions, if we accept them, provide the basis for the following constitutional arguments: (a) The constitution makes treaties part of the law of the land, and the United States is a party to international conventions and covenants that make illegal the acts of war the dissenters charge the nation with committing. (b) The constitution provides that Congress must declare war; the legal issue of whether our action in Vietnam is a "war" and whether the Tonkin Bay Resolution was a "declaration" is the heart of the moral issue of whether the government has made a deliberate and open decision. (c) Both the due process clause of the Fifth and Fourteenth Amendments and equal protection clause of the Fourteenth Amendment condemn special burdens placed on a selected class of citizens when the burden or the classification is not reasonable; the burden is unreasonable when it patently does not serve the public interest, or when it is vastly disproportionate to the interest served. If our military action in Vietnam is frivolous or perverse, as the dissenters claim, then the burden we place on men of draft age is unreasonable and unconstitutional. (d) In any event, the discrimination in favor of college students denies to the poor the equal protection of the law that is guaranteed by the constitution. (e) If there is no pertinent difference between religious objection to all wars and moral objection to some wars, then the classification the draft makes is arbitrary and unreasonable, and unconstitutional on that ground. The "establishment of religion" clause of the First Amendment forbids governmental pressure in favor of organized religion; if the draft's distinction coerces men in this direction, it is invalid on that count also. (f) The First Amendment also condemns invasions of freedom of speech. If the draft law's prohibition on counseling does inhibit expression of a range of views on the war, it abridges free speech.

The principal counterargument, supporting the view that the courts ought not to hold the draft unconstitutional, also involves moral issues. Under the so-called "political question" doctrine, the courts deny their own jurisdiction to pass on matters—such as foreign or military policy—whose resolution is best assigned to other branches of the government. The Boston court trying the Coffin, Spock case has already declared, on the basis of this doctrine, that it will not hear arguments about the legality of the war. But the Supreme Court has shown itself (in the reapportionment cases, for example) reluctant to refuse jurisdiction when it believed that the gravest issues of political morality were at stake and that no remedy was available through the political process. If the dissenters are right, and the war and the draft are state crimes of profound injustice to a group of citizens, then the argument that the courts must refuse jurisdiction is considerably weakened.

We cannot conclude from these arguments that the draft (or any part of it) is unconstitutional. If the Supreme Court is called upon to rule on the question, it will probably reject some of them, and refuse to consider the others on grounds that they are political. The majority of lawyers would probably agree with this result. But the arguments of unconstitutionality are at least plausible, and a reasonable and competent lawyer might well think that they present a stronger case, on balance, than the counterarguments. If he does, he will consider that the draft is not constitutional, and there will be no way of proving that he is wrong.

Therefore we cannot assume, in judging what to do with the draft dissenters, that they are asserting a privilege to disobey valid laws. We cannot decide that fairness demands their punishment until we try to answer the further question: What should a citizen do when the law is unclear, and when he thinks it allows what others think it does not? I do not mean to ask, of course, what it is *legally* proper for him to do, or what his *legal* rights are—that would be begging the question, because it depends upon whether he is right or they are right. I mean to ask what his proper course is as a citizen, what, in other words, we would consider to be "playing the game." That is a crucial question, because it cannot be unfair not to punish him if he is acting as, given his opinions, we think he should.[1]

There is no obvious answer on which most citizens would readily agree, and that is itself significant. If we examine our legal institutions and practices, however, we shall discover some relevant underlying principles and policies. I shall set out three possible answers to the question, and then try to show which of these best fits our practices and expectations. The three possibilities I want to consider are these:

(1) If the law is doubtful, and it is therefore unclear whether it permits someone to do what he wants, he should assume the worst, and act on the assumption that it does not. He should obey the executive authorities who command him, even though he thinks they are wrong, while using the political process, if he can, to change the law.

(2) If the law is doubtful, he may follow his own judgment, that is, he may do what he wants if he believes that the case that the law permits this is stronger than the case that it does not. But he may follow his own judgment only until an authoritative institution, like a court, decides the other way in a case involving him or someone else. Once an institutional decision has been reached, he must abide by that decision, even though he thinks that it was wrong. (There are, in theory, many subdivisions of this second possibility. We may say that the individual's choice is foreclosed by the contrary decision of any court, including the lowest court in the system if the case is not appealed. Or we may require a decision of some particular court or institution. I shall discuss this second possibility in its most liberal form, namely that the individual may properly follow his own judgment until a contrary decision of the highest court competent to pass on the issue, which, in the case of the draft, is the United States Supreme Court.)

(3) If the law is doubtful, he may follow his own judgment, even after a contrary decision by the highest competent court. Of course, he must take the contrary decision of any court into account in making his judgment of what the law requires. Otherwise the judgment

---

[1] I do not mean to imply that the government should always punish a man who deliberately breaks a law he knows is valid. There may be reasons of fairness or practicality, like those I listed in the third paragraph, for not prosecuting such men. But cases like the draft cases present special arguments for tolerance; I want to concentrate on these arguments and therefore have isolated these cases.

would not be an honest or reasonable one, because the doctrine of precedent, which is an established part of our legal system, has the effect of allowing the decision of the courts to *change* the law. Suppose, for example, that a taxpayer believes that he is not required to pay tax on certain forms of income. If the Supreme Court decides to the contrary, he should, taking into account the practice of according great weight to the decisions of the Supreme Court on tax matters, decide that the Court's decision has itself tipped the balance, and that the law now requires him to pay the tax.

Someone might think that this qualification erases the difference between the third and the second models, but it does not. The doctrine of precedent gives different weights to the decisions of different courts, and greatest weight to the decisions of the Supreme Court, but it does not make the decision of any court conclusive. Sometimes, even after a contrary Supreme Court decision, an individual may still reasonably believe that the law is on his side; such cases are rare, but they are most likely to occur in disputes over constitutional law when civil disobedience is involved. The Court has shown itself more likely to overrule its past decisions if these have limited important personal or political rights, and it is just these decisions that a dissenter might want to challenge.

We cannot assume, in other words, that the Constitution is always what the Supreme Court says it is. Oliver Wendell Holmes, for example, did not follow such a rule in his famous dissent in the *Gitlow* case. A few years before, in *Abrams,* he had lost his battle to persuade the court that the First Amendment protected an anarchist who had been urging general strikes against the government. A similar issue was presented in *Gitlow,* and Holmes once again dissented. "It is true," he said, "that in my opinion this criterion was departed from [in *Abrams*] but the convictions that I expressed in that case are too deep for it to be possible for me as yet to believe that it . . . settled the law." Holmes voted for acquitting Gitlow, on the ground that what Gitlow had done was no crime, even though the Supreme Court had recently held that it was.

Here then are three possible models for the behavior of dissenters who disagree with the executive authorities when the law is doubtful. Which of them best fits our legal and social practices?

I think it plain that we do not follow the first of these models, that is, that we do not expect citizens to assume the worst. If no court has decided the issue, and a man thinks, on balance, that the law is on his side, most of our lawyers and critics think it perfectly proper for him to follow his own judgment. Even when many disapprove of what he does—such as peddling pornography—they do not think he must desist just because the legality of his conduct is subject to doubt.

It is worth pausing a moment to consider what society would lose if it did follow the first model or, to put the matter the other way, what society gains when people follow their own judgment in cases like this. When the law is uncertain, in the sense that lawyers can reasonably disagree on what a court ought to decide, the reason usually is that different legal principles and policies have collided, and it is unclear how best to accommodate these conflicting principles and policies.

Our practice, in which different parties are encouraged to pursue their own understanding, provides a means of testing relevant hypotheses. If the question is whether a particular rule would have certain undesirable consequences, or whether these consequences would have limited or broad ramifications, then, before the issue is decided, it is useful to know what does in fact take place when some people proceed on that rule. (Much anti-trust and business regulation law has developed through this kind of testing.) If the question is whether and to what degree a particular solution would offend principles of justice or fair play deeply respected by the community, it is useful, again, to experiment by testing the community's response. The extent of community indifference to anti-contraception laws, for example, would never have become established had not some organizations deliberately flouted those laws.

If the first model were followed, we would lose the advantages of these tests. The law would suffer, particularly if this model were applied to constitutional issues. When the validity of a criminal statute is in doubt, the statute will almost always strike some people as being unfair or unjust, because it will infringe some principle of liberty or justice or fairness which they take to be built into the Constitution. If our practice were that whenever a law is doubtful on these grounds, one must act as if it were valid, then the chief vehicle we have for challenging the law on moral grounds would be lost, and over time the law we obeyed would certainly become less fair and just, and the liberty of our citizens would certainly be diminished.

We would lose almost as much if we used a variation of the first model, that a citizen must assume the worst unless he can anticipate that the courts will agree with his view of the law. If everyone deferred to his guess of what the courts would do, society and its law would be poorer. Our assumption in rejecting the first model was that the record a citizen makes in following his own judgment, together with the arguments he makes supporting that judgment when he has the opportunity, are helpful in creating the best judicial decision possible. This remains true even when, at the time the citizen acts, the odds are against his success in court. We must remember, too, that the value of the citizen's example is not exhausted once the decision has been made. Our practices require that the decision be criticized, by the legal profession and the law schools, and the record of dissent may be invaluable here.

Of course a man must consider what the courts will do when he decides whether it would be *prudent* to follow his own judgment. He may have to face jail, bankruptcy, or opprobrium if he does. But it is essential that we separate the calculation of prudence from the question of what, as a good citizen, he may properly do. We are investigating how society ought to treat him when its courts believe that he judged wrong; therefore we must ask what he is justified in doing when his judgment differs from others. We beg the question if we assume that what he may properly do depends on his guess as to how society will treat him.

We must also reject the second model, that if the law is unclear a citizen may properly follow his own judgment until the highest court has ruled that he is wrong. This fails to take into account the fact that any court, including the Supreme Court, may overrule itself. In 1940 the Court decided that a West Virginia law requiring students to salute the Flag was constitutional. In 1943 it reversed itself, and decided that such a statute was unconstitutional after all. What was the duty, as citizens, of those people who in 1941 and 1942 objected to saluting the Flag on grounds of conscience, and thought that the Court's 1940 decision was wrong? We can hardly say that their duty was to follow the first decision. They believed that saluting the Flag was unconscionable, and they believed, reasonably, that no valid law required them to do so. The Supreme Court later decided that in this they were right. The Court did not simply hold that after the second decision failing to salute would not be a crime; it held (as in a case like this it almost always would) that it was no crime after the first decision either.

Some will say that the flag-salute dissenters should have obeyed the Court's first decision, while they worked in the legislatures to have the law repealed, and tried in the courts to find some way to challenge the law again without actually violating it. That would be, perhaps, a plausible recommendation if conscience were not involved, because it would then be arguable that the gain in orderly procedure was worth the personal sacrifice of patience. But conscience was involved, and if the dissenters had obeyed the law while biding their time, they would have suffered the irreparable injury of having done what their conscience forbade them to do. It is one thing to say that an individual must sometimes violate his conscience when he knows that the law commands him to do it. It is quite another to say that he must violate his conscience even when he reasonably believes that the law does not require it, because it would inconvenience his fellow citizens if he took the most direct, and perhaps the only, method of attempting to show that he is right and they are wrong.

Since a court may overrule itself, the same reasons we listed for rejecting the first model count against the second as well. If we did not have the pressure of dissent, we would not have a dramatic statement of the degree to which a court decision against the dissenter is felt to be wrong, a demonstration that is surely pertinent to the question of whether it was right. We would increase the chance of being governed by rules that offend the principles we claim to serve.

These considerations force us, I think, from the second model, but some will want to substitute a variation of it. They will argue that once the Supreme Court has decided that a criminal law is valid, then citizens have a duty to abide by that decision until they have a reasonable belief, not merely that the decision is a bad law, but that the Supreme Court is likely to overrule it. Under this view the West Virginia dissenters who refused to salute the Flag in 1942 were acting properly, because they might reasonably have anticipated that the Court would change its mind. But if the Court were to hold the draft laws constitutional, it would be improper to continue to challenge these laws, because there would be no great likelihood that the Court would soon change its mind. This suggestion must also be rejected, however. For once we say that a citizen may properly follow his own judgment of the law, in spite of his judgment that the courts will probably find against him, there is no plausible reason why he should act differently because a contrary decision is already on the books.

Thus the third model, or something close to it, seems to be the fairest statement of a man's social duty in our community. A citizen's allegiance is to the law, not to any particular person's view of what the law is, and he does not behave unfairly so long as he proceeds on his own considered and reasonable view of what the law requires. Let me repeat (because it is crucial) that this is not the same as saying that an individual may disregard what the courts have said. The doctrine of precedent lies near the core of our legal system, and no one can make a reasonable effort to follow the law unless he grants the courts the general power to alter it by their decisions. But if the issue is one touching fundamental personal or political rights, and it is arguable that the Supreme Court has made a mistake, a man is within his social rights in refusing to accept that decision as conclusive.

One large question remains before we can apply these observations to the problems of draft resistance. I have been talking about the case of a man who believes that the law is not what other people think, or what the courts have held. This description may fit some of those who disobey the draft laws out of conscience, but it does not fit most of them. Most of the dissenters are not lawyers or political philosophers; they believe that the laws on the books are immoral, and inconsistent with their country's legal ideals, but they have not considered the question of whether they may be invalid as well. Of what relevance to their situation, then, is the proposition that one may properly follow one's own view of the law?

To answer this, I shall have to return to the point I made earlier. The Constitution, through the due process clause, the equal protection clause, the First Amendment, and the other provisions I mentioned, injects an extraordinary amount of our political morality into the issue of whether a law is valid. The statement that most draft dissenters are unaware that the law is invalid therefore needs qualification. They hold beliefs that, if true, strongly support the view that the law is on their side; the fact that they have not reached that further conclusion can be traced, in at least most cases, to their lack of legal sophistication. If we believe that when the law is doubtful people who follow their own judgment of the law may be acting properly, it would seem wrong not to extend that view to those dissenters whose judgments come to the same thing. No part of the case that I made for the third model would entitle us to distinguish them from their more knowledgeable colleagues.

We can draw several tentative conclusions from the argument so far: When the law is uncertain, in the sense that a plausible case can be made on both sides, then a citizen who follows his own judgment is not behaving unfairly. Our practices permit and encourage him to follow his own judgment in such cases. For that reason, our government has a special responsibility to try to protect him, and soften his predicament, whenever it can do so without great damage to other policies. It does not follow that the government can guarantee him immunity—it cannot adopt the rule that it will prosecute no one who acts out of conscience, or convict no one who reasonably disagrees with the courts. That would paralyze the government's ability to carry out its policies; it would, moreover, throw away the most important benefit of following the third model. If the state never prosecuted, then the courts could not act on the experience and the arguments the dissent has generated. But it does follow that when the practical reasons for prosecuting are relatively weak in a particular case, or can be met in other ways, the path of fairness lies in tolerance. The popular view that the law is the law and must always be enforced refuses to distinguish the man who acts on his own judgment of a doubtful law, and thus behaves as our practices provide, from the common criminal. I know of no reason, short of moral blindness, for not drawing a distinction in principle between the two cases.

I anticipate a philosophical objection to these conclusions: that I am treating law as a "brooding omnipresence in the sky." I have spoken of people making judgments about what the law requires, even in cases in which the law is unclear and undemonstrable. I have spoken of cases in which a man might think that the law requires one thing, even though the Supreme Court has said that it requires another, and even when it was not likely that the Supreme Court would soon change its mind. I will therefore be charged with the view that there is always a "right answer" to a legal problem to be found in natural law or locked up in some transcendental strongbox.

The strongbox theory of law is, of course, nonsense. When I say that people hold views on the law when the law is doubtful, and that these views are not merely predictions of what the courts will hold, I intend no such metaphysics. I mean only to summarize as accurately as I can many of the practices that are part of our legal process.

Lawyers and judges make statements of legal right and duty, even when they know these are not demonstrable, and support them with arguments even when they know that these arguments will not appeal to everyone. They make these arguments to one another, in the professional journals, in the classroom, and in the courts. They respond to these arguments, when others make them, by judging them good or bad or mediocre. In so doing they assume that some arguments for a given doubtful position are better than others. They also assume that the case on one side of a doubtful proposition may be stronger than the case on the other, which is what I take a claim of law in a doubtful case to mean. They distinguish, without too much difficulty, these arguments from predictions of what the courts will decide.

These practices are poorly represented by the theory that judgments of law on doubtful issues are nonsense, or are merely predictions of what the courts will do. Those who hold such theories cannot deny the fact of these practices; perhaps these theorists mean that the practices are not sensible, because they are based on suppositions that do not hold, or for some other reason. But this makes their objection mysterious, because they never specify what they take the purposes underlying these practices to be; and unless these goals are specified, one cannot decide whether the practices are sensible. I understand these underlying purposes to be those I described earlier: the development and testing of the law through experimentation by citizens and through the adversary process.

Our legal system pursues these goals by inviting citizens to decide the strengths and weaknesses of legal arguments for themselves, or through their own counsel, and to act on these judgments, although that permission is qualified by the limited threat that they may suffer if the courts do not agree. Success in this strategy depends on whether there is sufficient agreement within the community on what counts as a good or bad argument, so that, although different people will reach different judgments, these differences will be neither so profound nor so frequent as to make the system unworkable, or dangerous for those who act by their own lights. I believe there is sufficient agreement on the criteria of the argument to avoid these traps, although one of the main tasks of legal philosophy is to exhibit and clarify these criteria. In any event, the practices I have described have not yet been shown to be misguided; they therefore must count in determining whether it is just and fair to be lenient to those who break what others think is the law.

I have said that the government has a special responsibility to those who act on a reasonable judgment that a law is invalid. It should make accommodation for them as far as possible, when this is consistent with other policies. It may be difficult to decide what the government ought to do, in the name of that responsibility, in particular cases. The decision will be a matter of balance, and flat rules will not help. Still, some principles can be set out.

I shall start with the prosecutor's decision whether to press charges. He must balance both his responsibility to be lenient and the risk that convictions will rend the society, against the damage to the law's policy that may follow if he leaves the dissenters alone. In making his calculation he must consider not only the extent to which others will be harmed, but also how the law evaluates that harm; and he must therefore make the following distinction. Every rule of law is supported, and presumably justified, by a set of policies it is supposed to advance and principles it is supposed to respect. Some rules (the laws prohibiting murder and theft, for example) are supported by the proposition that the individuals protected have a moral right to be free from the harm proscribed. Other rules (the more technical antitrust rules, for example) are not supported by any supposition of an underlying right; their support comes chiefly from the alleged utility of the economic and social policies they promote. These may be supplemented with moral principles (like the view that it is a harsh business practice to undercut a weak competitor's prices) but these fall short of recognizing a moral right against the harm in question.

The point of the distinction here is this: if a particular rule of law represents an official decision that individuals have a moral right to be free from some harm, then that is a powerful argument against tolerating violations that inflict those injuries. Laws protecting people from personal injury or the destruction of their property, for example, do represent that sort of decision, and this is a very strong argument against tolerating civil disobedience that involves violence.

It may be controversial, of course, whether a law does rest on the assumption of a moral right. The question is whether it is reasonable to suppose, from the background and administration of the law, that its authors recognized such a right. There are cases, in addition to rules against violence, where it is plain that they did; the civil rights laws are examples. Many sincere and ardent segregationists believe that the civil rights laws and decisions are unconstitutional, because they compromise principles of local government and of freedom of association. This is an arguable, though not a persuasive, view. But these laws and decisions clearly embody the view that Negroes, as individuals, have a right not to be segregated. They do not rest simply on the judgment that other national policies are best pursued by preventing racial segregation. If we take no action against the man who blocks the school house door, therefore, we violate the moral rights, confirmed by law, of the schoolgirl he blocks. The responsibility of leniency cannot go this far.

The schoolgirl's position is different, however, from that of the draftee who may be called up sooner or given a more dangerous post if draft offenders are not punished. The draft laws, taken as a whole and with an eye to their administration, cannot be said to reflect the judgment that a man has a moral right to be drafted only after certain other men or groups have been called. The draft classifications, and the order-of-call within classifications, are arranged for social and administrative convenience. They also reflect considerations of fairness, like the proposition that a mother who has lost one of two sons in war ought not to be made to risk losing the other. But they presuppose no fixed rights. The draft boards are given considerable discretion in the classification process, and the army, of course, has almost complete discretion in assigning dangerous posts. If the prosecutor tolerates draft offenders, he makes small shifts in the law's calculations of fairness and utility. These may cause disadvantage to others in the pool of draftees but that is a different matter from contradicting their moral rights.

This difference between segregation and the draft is not an accident of how the laws happen to have been written. It would run counter to a century of practice to suppose that citizens have moral rights with respect to the order in which they are called to serve; the lottery system of selection, for example, would be abhorrent under that supposition. If our history had been different, and if the community had recognized such a moral right, it seems fair to suppose that some of the draft dissenters, at least, would have modified their acts so as to try to respect these rights. So it is wrong to analyze draft cases in the same way as cases of violence or civil rights cases, as many critics do when considering whether tolerance is justified. I do not mean that fairness to others is irrelevant in draft cases; it must be taken into account, and balanced against fairness to dissenters and the long-term benefit to society. But it does not play the commanding role here that it does when rights are at stake.

Where, then, does the balance of fairness and utility lie in the case

of those who counsel draft resistance? If these men had encouraged
violence or otherwise trespassed on the rights of others, then there
would be a strong case for prosecution. But in the absence of such actions, the balance of fairness and utility seems to me to lie the other
way, and I therefore think that the decision to prosecute Coffin,
Spock, Raskin, Goodman, and Ferber was wrong. It may be argued
that if those who counsel draft resistance are free from prosecution,
the number who resist induction will increase; but it will not, I think,
increase much beyond the number of those who would resist in any
event.

If I am wrong, and there is much greater resistance, then a sense of
this residual discontent is of importance to policy makers, and it
ought not to be hidden under a ban on speech. Conscience is deeply
involved—it is hard to believe that many who counsel resistance do
so on any other grounds. The case is strong that the laws making
counseling a crime are unconstitutional; even those who do not find
the case persuasive will admit that its arguments have substance. The
harm to potential draftees, both those who may be persuaded to resist
and those who may be called earlier because others have been persuaded, is remote and speculative.

The cases of men who refuse induction when drafted are more complicated. The crucial question is whether a failure to prosecute will
lead to wholesale refusals to serve. It may not—there are social pressures, including the threat of career disadvantages, that would force
many young Americans to serve if drafted, even if they knew they
would not go to jail if they refused. If the number would not much
increase, then the state should leave the dissenters alone, and I see no
great harm in delaying any prosecution until the effect of that policy
becomes clearer. If the number of those who refuse induction turns
out to be large, this would argue for prosecution. But it would also
make the problem academic, because if there were sufficient dissent
to bring us to that pass, it would be most difficult to pursue the war
in any event, except under a near-totalitarian regime.

There may seem to be a paradox in these conclusions. I argued earlier that when the law is unclear citizens have the right to follow
their own judgment, partly on the grounds that this practice helps to
shape issues for adjudication; now I propose a course that eliminates
or postpones adjudication. But the contradiction is only apparent. It
does not follow from the fact that our practice facilitates adjudication, and renders it more useful in developing the law, that a trial
should follow whenever citizens do act by their own lights. The question arises in each case whether the issues are ripe for adjudication,
and whether adjudication would settle these issues in a manner that

would decrease the chance of, or remove the grounds for, further dissent.

In the draft cases, the answer to both these questions is negative: There is much ambivalence about the war just now, and uncertainty and ignorance about the scope of the moral issues involved in the draft. It is far from the best time for a court to pass on these issues, and tolerating dissent for a time is one way of allowing the debate to continue until it has produced something clearer. Moreover, it is plain that an adjudication of the constitutional issues now will not settle the law. Those who have doubts whether the draft is constitutional will have the same doubts even if the Supreme Court says that it is. This is one of those cases, touching fundamental rights, in which our practices of precedent will encourage these doubts. Certainly this will be so if, as seems likely, the Supreme Court appeals to the political question doctrine, and refuses to pass on the more serious constitutional issues.

Even if the prosecutor does not act, however, the underlying problem will be only temporarily relieved. So long as the law appears to make acts of dissent criminal, a man of conscience will face danger. What can Congress, which shares the responsibility of leniency, do to lessen this danger?

Congress can review the laws in question to see how much accommodation can be given the dissenters. Every program a legislature adopts is a mixture of policies and restraining principles. We accept loss of efficiency in crime detection and urban renewal, for example, so that we can respect the rights of accused criminals and compensate property owners for their damages. Congress may properly defer to its responsibility toward the dissenters by adjusting or compromising other policies. The relevant questions are these: What means can be found for allowing the greatest possible tolerance of conscientious dissent while minimizing its impact on policy? How strong is the government's responsibility for leniency in this case—how deeply is conscience involved, and how strong is the case that the law is invalid after all? How important is the policy in question—is interference with that policy too great a price to pay? These questions are no doubt too simple, but they suggest the heart of the choices that must be made.

For the same reasons that those who counsel resistance should not be prosecuted, I think that the law that makes this a crime should be repealed. The case is strong that this law abridges free speech. It certainly coerces conscience, and it probably serves no beneficial effect. If counseling would persuade only a few to resist who otherwise would not, the value of the restraint is small; if counseling would persuade many, that is an important political fact that should be known.

The issues are more complex, again, in the case of draft resistance itself. Those who believe that the war in Vietnam is itself a grotesque blunder will favor any change in the law that makes peace more likely. But if we take the position of those who think the war is necessary, then we must admit that a policy that continues the draft but wholly exempts dissenters would be unwise. Two less drastic alternatives might be considered, however: a volunteer army, and an expanded conscientious objector category that includes those who find this war immoral. There is much to be said against both proposals, but once the requirement of respect for dissent is recognized, the balance of principle may be tipped in their favor.

So the case for not prosecuting conscientious draft offenders, and for changing the laws in their favor, is a strong one. It would be unrealistic to expect this policy to prevail, however, for political pressures now oppose it. Relatively few of those who have refused induction have been indicted so far, but the pace of prosecution is quickening, and many more indictments are expected if the resistance many college seniors have pledged does in fact develop. The Coffin, Spock trial continues, although when the present steps toward peace negotiation were announced, many lawyers had hoped it would be dropped or delayed. There is no sign of any movement to amend the draft laws in the way I have suggested.

We must consider, therefore, what the courts can and should now do. A court might, of course, uphold the arguments that the draft laws are in some way unconstitutional, in general or as applied to the defendants in the case at hand. Or it may acquit the defendants because the facts necessary for conviction are not proved. I shall not argue the constitutional issues, or the facts of any particular case. I want instead to suggest that a court ought not to convict, at least in some circumstances, even if it sustains the statutes and finds the facts as charged. The Supreme Court has not ruled on the chief arguments that the present draft is unconstitutional, nor has it held that these arguments raise political questions that are not relevant to its jurisdiction. If the alleged violations take place before the Supreme Court has decided these issues, and the case reaches that Court, there are strong reasons why the Court should acquit even if it does then sustain the draft. It ought to acquit on the ground that before its decision the validity of the draft was doubtful, and it is unfair to punish men for disobeying a doubtful law.

There would be precedent for a decision along these lines. The Court has several times reversed criminal convictions, on due process grounds, because the law in question was too vague. (It has overturned convictions, for example, under laws that made it a crime to charge "unreasonable prices" or to be a member of a "gang.") Conviction under a vague criminal law offends the moral and political ideals of due process in two ways. First, it places a citizen in the unfair position of either acting at his peril or accepting a more stringent restriction on his life than the legislature may have authorized: As I argued earlier, it is not acceptable, as a model of social behavior, that in such cases he ought to assume the worst. Second, it gives power to the prosecutor and the courts to make criminal law, by opting for one or the other possible interpretations after the event. This would be a delegation of authority by the legislature that is inconsistent with our scheme of separation of powers.

Conviction under a criminal law whose terms are not vague, but whose constitutional validity is doubtful, offends due process in the first of these ways. It forces a citizen to assume the worst, or act at his peril. It offends due process in something like the second way as well. Most citizens would be deterred by a doubtful statute if they were to risk jail by violating it. Congress, and not the courts, would then be the effective voice in deciding the constitutionality of criminal enactments, and this also violates the separation of powers.

If acts of dissent continue to occur after the Supreme Court has ruled that the laws are valid, or that the political question doctrine applies, then acquittal on the grounds I have described is no longer appropriate. The Court's decision will not have finally settled the law, for the reasons given earlier, but the Court will have done all that can be done to settle it. The courts may still exercise their sentencing discretion, however, and impose minimal or suspended sentences as a mark of respect for the dissenters' position.

Some lawyers will be shocked by my general conclusion that we have a responsibility toward those who disobey the draft laws out of conscience, and that we may be required not to prosecute them, but rather to change our laws or adjust our sentencing procedures to accommodate them. The simple Draconian propositions, that crime must be punished, and that he who misjudges the law must take the consequences, have an extraordinary hold on the professional as well as the popular imagination. But the rule of law is more complex and more intelligent than that and it is important that it survive.

June 6, 1968

Postscript

The Nixon Administration, according to *The New York Times*, has sharply increased the number of prosecutions for draft offenses. The current rate of prosecution is well above the rate of prosecution when this article was written. The administration has not increased prosecutions in response to practical dangers of the sort I said might justify prosecution, for the draft call reductions and troop withdrawals it has announced would, if anything, reduce these dangers. On the contrary, it seems to have acted in the name of that maxim which I argued is too simple for an intelligent and fair legal policy, the maxim that the law is the law and must always be enforced.

28/ Group Theory and Political Obligation[1]

HARMON ZEIGLER

This essay is an analysis of two efforts to provide a framework for the study of public policy. The purpose is a consideration of the distinction between interest-group activity and individual perceptive and response mechanisms as frames of reference. It is hypothesized that the individual's perception of his political environment will contribute to an understanding of obligation, defined here as rationalization for obedience. This simply means that "if men define situations as real, they are real in their consequences." This approach to obligation differs from Tussman's arguments in that it posits a theory of political obligation as a set of "descriptive and predictive hypotheses" and does not ask questions answerable by value judgments.[2] However, it should be understood that the question of political obligation is one toward which the efforts of normative theorists have been addressed since the beginnings of systematic explorations of political philosophies. This question can hardly be examined without crossing the bridge between fact and value. Therefore, it is hoped that descriptive statements can contribute to the understanding of political evaluation.[3]

Attempts to interpret the political process as a conflict among groups have developed a degree of sophistication sufficient to stimu-

[1] Revised version of a paper presented at the 1962 annual meeting of the Southern Political Science Association.
[2] Joseph Tussman, *Obligation and the Body Politic* (New York: Oxford University Press, 1960), p. 15.
[3] Robert A. Dahl notes that modern logical positivism, in contrast to the extremism of earlier years, does not regard statements of value as meaningless merely because there is no universal hierarchy. See *Modern Political Analysis* (Englewood Cliffs: Prentice-Hall, Inc., 1963), pp. 100–101.

SOURCE: *Southwestern Social Science Quarterly* (September 1964), 156–166. Reprinted by permission of the author and the publisher.

late precise and knowledgeable criticism. Indeed, the criticism has become so intense that one scholar has predicted that Arthur Bentley's *The Process of Government,* the intellectual cornerstone of the group interpretation, is "headed for disciplinary oblivion." [4] While some of the criticism is based on normative objections to the implications of group theory for democratic society and other on the limits of group theory as a methodological device, there is a common denominator which prevails. If one examines the objections to group theory he will be quick to realize that a large part of the objections are based on Bentley's inability to solve the problem of providing an adequate concept of the individual as a causal factor in the political process.

It is not the intention of this essay to offer a refutation of this criticism but rather to attempt a re-phrasing of the political process incorporating some aspects of the group approach while recognizing its limitations. The essential limitation, as noted above, is the failure to take into account the psychological properties inherent in the individual's reaction to his political environment. In this analysis primary reliance will be placed upon political research which, although accepting the general framework of politics as a process by which disputes between competing values are reconciled, is unwilling to infer the nature of such values solely from group activity. First, however, it will be useful to inquire into the process whereby Bentley and his followers are able to discount the individual as an actor in the political process.

The stated goal of the scholars subscribing to Bentley's theories, as they attempt to devise a useful tool for political analysis, is the reduction of the problems of political science to their "simplest terms and smallest number of explanatory principles." To achieve this goal they have suggested that all political activity is group activity with the individual existing only as the "intersection" of groups. That is to say, each person is the sum total of a particular combination of group affiliations which intersect in a unique way to form an individual personality. Hence, when we describe someone as being an old, southern, Democratic, Methodist banker we have provided an adequate profile of his personality. Since "group" and "activity" are not distinguishable the legitimate focus of political research can only be observable, purposive activity, never perceptions of this activity. We must only ask "how" and never "why." However a theory of obligation must ask: why do men obey laws, or (as Tussman says) we must delineate the "demands of the political role and . . . propriety in response to these demands, obligations, or duties." [5]

[4] Robert T. Golembiewski, "The Group Basis of Politics," *American Political Science Review,* LIV (December 1960), 962.
[5] Tussman, *op. cit.,* p. 15.

Bentley arrived at his group theory by building upon the writings of the conflict school of sociology which, under the dominant influence of Social Darwinism, was flourishing at the end of the nineteenth century. He acknowledges his indebtedness to Marx and then proceeds to abstract what he regards as useful from the writings of Spencer, Von Jhering, Ratzenhofer, Gumplowicz, and Simmel. Each of these sociologists contribute to Bentley's synthesis but each of these, considered singly, is found to be wanting. The fundamental insufficiency, according to Bentley, is the introduction of "extraneous" explanatory devices (devices beyond group activity). To Bentley, any satisfactory explanatory system must identify "causes." The most commonly advanced "cause" among the conflict sociologists was an individual's psychological state. Spencer's sociology, for example, described the instinct of the individual as the basic motive factor in social progress. While individual instinct is admittedly not a rational cognitive process in the Spencerian scheme, Spencer's followers such as Franklin Giddings and, to a lesser extent Albion Small, built a structure of causation upon the foundation of mental states. They argued that there is a measurable correlation between "cultural advancement" and inherent psychological attributes, the character of the individual thus forming the character of the society.

In Germany, Ratzenhofer and Simmel, while still relying on the Spencer-Giddings-Small scheme, were more satisfactory to Bentley because of their more extensive reliance upon "interests" (goals) as opposed to "instincts" (desires). Although not abandoning the individual, they conceptualized the social process as a means whereby competing groups sought to enforce their values. Consider, for example, this statement by Ratzenhofer: "The social process is a continual formation of groups around interests and the continual exertion of reciprocal influence by means of group action." [6] We see in this approach much similarity to David Truman's definition of an interest group as "a shared-attitude group that makes certain claims upon other groups in the society." [7] In both cases the individual is the possessor of attitudes which define the group. To Bentley, such attitudes are "ghosts" since the individual is to be treated only as the combination of a certain patterning of group activity but never as the basis for such activity. The same criticism can be brought to bear against Simmel who, although defining the individual as "spiritual" and not describing individual psychic states, nevertheless did not believe group activity to be the primary causal factor.

[6] Quoted in Harry Elmer Barnes and Howard Becker, *Social Thought From Lore to Science* (New York: D. C. Heath and Co., 1938), p. 717.

[7] David Truman, *The Governmental Process* (New York: Alfred A. Knopf, 1951), p. 33.

There were, among the advocates of the conflict school of sociological theory, those who explicitly rejected the individual as a viable unit for study. This was the case with Von Jhering and Gumplowicz, upon whom Bentley places firm reliance. However they committed an equally serious error in Bentley's eyes by beginning from the opposite assumption of a social whole, or structure of society. In language which sounds much like the theoretical model of Talcott Parsons, they spoke of the capacity of a social system to get things done in its collective interest; of the integration of the system by means of a binding of its component units. Nevertheless, their rejection of the individual held much fascination for Bentley and he was particularly impressed with Von Jhering's idea that all interests in a society are forces originating beyond the individual. The individual thus became a product, not an initiator, of action. The Spencerian biological man had been removed. Gumplowicz, in addition to the positing of the social whole, had an essentially Marxian type of group conflict in mind. The group was a reified physical mass, not a cross-section of activity.

Bentley, here seen against the backdrop of his intellectual environment, attempted to abstract from these writings the factors which could be used in a study of politics. In rejecting on the one hand the individual and on the other hand the social whole, he distilled the social process down to purposive, goal-oriented activity. He argued that the conflict model, as it then existed, could not explain certain aspects of observable behavior patterns without the addition of new explanatory devices. Bentley perceived dimensions of experience that could not be handled by the existing conflict theories. Some of the conflict theorists, he believed, were guided by normative considerations which led them to be repelled by the possible ethical implications of unrestrained conflict. Thus Ratzenhofer introduced a "civilization phase" as part of the progress of society in order to modify the consequences of the social struggle. Many of the earlier Social Darwinists faced a similar problem. For example, T. H. Huxley was unable to accept a brutal "struggle for existence" and wrote of the "ethical process" in organized society as opposed to the "cosmic process" in nature. Bentley, however, dismissed this type of normative hesitation to accept the possible consequences of conflict theory without serious consideration and concentrated his rebuttal against causal theories of an inadequate stature. Thus he noticed that Gumplowicz, in describing conflict in terms of concrete groups, found that some types of social phenomena could not be attributed to such physical masses and fell back on the concept of "psycho-social" behavior, or behavior only peripheral to group structure.

By treating only activity as data for study, Bentley believed he indeed had avoided the problem of explanation. Gumplowicz had reified the group and had thus presented an inadequate theory. In treating only the operational group Bentley had, he thought, reduced the problems of politics to their smallest number of explanatory elements. But is it not possible that the quest for an all-inclusive theory of politics might, because of over-simplification, cast aside some potentially useful tools of analysis? A rigid adhering to the Bentleyan scheme will result in an implicit model recognizing only the existence of tangible values. Since inquiry into cognitive processes is not allowed, the only method of ascertaining group goals is by means of the activity of the group. Odegard correctly indicated that Bentley denies the role of reason in the political process.[8] However, it is equally correct to state that he also denies the role of nonrational processes since he does not deal with response mechanisms in any form. By eliminating mental processes the Bentleyan method assumes that all group activity can be traced ultimately to an interest in the re-allocation of tangible resources such as economic advantage or to other such easily identified palpable rewards. Therefore, obligation exists only because of the expectation of rewards, or perhaps because of the fear of the consequences of disobedience. A leading follower of Bentley, Charles B. Hagan, states: "Values are authoritatively allocated in society by the conflict of groups." [9] Professor Hagan does not inquire into the nature of the values thus allocated because there is no need. The nature of the value can be inferred from the activity undertaken. However, given the assumption that politics is the process whereby values are allocated, experience tells us that there may be a wide range in the types of values for which group competition is instituted. We can observe parallel development in sociology. Durkheim's work in suicide, for example, seeks to explain self destruction by disregarding the individual and looking only at the environment in which suicides occur. Presumably, in this most final act of withdrawal, the motives of the individual are of no importance. Durkheim, like Bentley, wanted to stem the tide of psychologism and create an awareness of the uniquely social aspects of many forms of individual behavior, a goal not without merit.

II

In opposition to the Bentleyan model there is a school of thought, finding a major exponent in Harold Lasswell, which argues that many

[8] Peter H. Odegard, "A Group Basis of Politics: A New Name for an Old Myth," *Western Political Quarterly*, XI (September, 1955), 689–702.

[9] Charles B. Hagan, "The Group in a Political Science," in Roland Young, ed., *Approaches to the Study of Politics* (Evanston: Northwestern University Press, 1958), p. 40.

values are essentially nontangible or symbolic. The inquiry into the nature of values requires that the individual's perception of his environment be taken into account. Lasswell, while resembling Bentley in his emphasis on power relations, posits a theory in which symbolic manipulation and satisfaction play a vital role. He states that disturbing changes in the status of individuals produce adjustment attempts that are resolved through symbolizations. Symbolic perception and symbolic satisfaction "resist the discipline of external events." [10] Individual perception of political events may exist in a set of such rigid categories that alternations in the "real" world will result not in a shift in group activity to meet the threat of dis-equilibrium but in an intensification of the reiteration of symbols. This indicates, in contrast to Bentley, that individual feelings and ideas are indeed part of the political process and are "causes" of certain types of political events. This type of psychological explanation does not necessarily see group activity as an attempt to solve specific problems through collective activity. Although the activity of a social movement may appear as the explanatory element, the movement provides a mechanism through which the individual satisfies personal motives. From this standpoint goals may be understood in terms of their impact on the participants and this necessitates inquiry into perception.[11]

In the process whereby the individual views his political environment the importance of symbols may be easily ascertained. Logicians and psychologists distinguish a symbol from other representative devices on the basis of multiple significance. Anything that stands for something else is a sign, but a symbol must express a multiple, undifferentiated significance. Symbols contain "hidden values" and are imprecise. Words, as symbols, may generate responses which manifest themselves in the form of political activity. This indicates that certain forms of activity are undertaken because of the desire of individuals for symbolic satisfaction.

Although, as Murray Edelman points out, the political process has been only cursorily studied as a purveyor of symbols there is a growing body of literature which investigates symbolic values. Most important for our purposes, social scientists who accept the fundamental assumptions of group theory are nevertheless attempting to differentiate between the types of values being sought. One of Odegard's major criticisms of Bentley is that there is no way of understanding what was indicated by the term "value." Let us examine some efforts which may help to remedy this deficiency.

---

[10] Harold Lasswell, *Psychopathology and Politics* (New York: The Viking Press, 1961), p. 341.
[11] Kenneth Boulding, *The Image* (Ann Arbor: The University of Michigan Press, 1961).

Seymour Lipset has dealt with the problem of the "radical right" as a symbolic conflict. According to Lipset the key to this behavior, which he designates as extreme, is to be found in status frustrations. Status frustrations or anxieties, as manifested in political consequences, have no clear-cut solution. Unlike economic conflict in which the goals are reasonably clear, political activity precipitated by status anxieties does not result in interest in the reallocation of tangible resources. Political movements based on status resentments are irrational and seek out scapegoats which symbolize a threat.[12]

Lipset's analysis, in addition to suggesting that politics is often a process in which persons and groups seek symbolic satisfaction, suggests the circumstances in which such a symbolic conflict is most likely to occur: when the status aspirations of a societal group are frustrated. Edelman has undertaken an exhaustive study of political symbols; and Bernard C. Cohen's study of the Japanese peace settlement has classified group activity according to whether interest is oriented toward tangible or intangible goals.[13] These two studies suggest that interest in symbolic threats will be greatest when the homogeneity of the potential membership in the group is lowest. Edelman has developed an explicit statement of the components of symbol-motivated behavior. He states that the following characteristics describe the pattern of activity usually associated with symbolic satisfaction: relatively large numbers, shared interest in the improvement of status through protest activity, unfavorably perceived status position with respect to reference groups, stereotyped and inexact information and perception, relative ineffectiveness in securing tangible resources through political activity, and little organization for purposive activity.[14]

Notice that Edelman's pattern of activity, as does Lipset's, involves as a basic component the perception of political events by participants. If these theoretical models of symbol-motivated activity are employed, many facets of political behavior become more easily understood. Many legislative acts, for instance, indicate that groups can achieve the symbolic importance of victory without affecting an alteration in the distribution of tangible values. For example, the activity surrounding the creation of the Small Business Administration in 1953

---

[12] Seymour Martin Lipset, "The Sources of the 'Radical Right'," in Daniel Bell, ed., *The New American Right* (New York: Criterion Books, 1955), pp. 192–195.

[13] Murray Edelman, "Symbols and Political Quiescence," *American Political Science Review*, LIV (September, 1960), 695–704.

[14] *Ibid.*, p. 701. See Harmon Zeigler, *The Politics of Small Business* (Washington: Public Affairs Press, 1961), for an elaboration of this thesis.

contains many of the elements of Edelman's scheme. Small businessmen are a large and heterogeneous group. There is little that they
have "in common" with respect to tangible goals.[15] Organizationally,
small business is weak and almost mercurial in longevity. Also, there
is substantial evidence indicating that the federal government has
been able to accomplish very little toward improving the economic
position of small business. This is especially true in the area of defense contracts which, in spite of frequent legislative and executive
statements to the contrary, are being concentrated among a few large
firms. Nevertheless, the creation of a special agency whose sole function was to help small business seemed to do much toward the alleviation of anxiety. The government was "doing something" and the
fact that the Small Business Administration did not materially advance the economic position of small firms, while not irrelevant, did
not reduce the intensity of its support. This seems to suggest that,
within contexts defined by group membership, individuals are given
rewards of a symbolic nature which are sufficient to insure continuous
participation in a social system (participation implying an acknowledgment of obligation) even though such individuals are not getting a
tangible pay-off.

It is essential to understand that the relief of anxieties by symboli-
zation need have no logical relation to tangibly identified goals.
Gussfield remarks that the lynching of Negroes in the South, although
this action correlated with a decline in cotton prices, did not lead to
higher prices.[16] Similarly, the evidence indicates that the Small Business Administration was actually intended to reduce the amount of
money that had formerly been loaned to business by Reconstruction
Finance Corporation. If we conceptualize the political system as
roughly comparable to a voluntary association, we can use Herbert
Simon's equilibrium theory to advantage. Individuals contribute in relation to inducements. In the larger system, inducements are given
meaning through subgroup identification and, varying with the structural characteristics of the subgroup, acquire symbolic connotations.

If it is true that symbolic satisfaction occurs most frequently in response to status frustrations, one of the most logical areas in which to
expect this type of activity is the current conflict over race relations.
Negroes as a social group are certainly heterogeneous as are their
white opponents in the South. Also, it is difficult to argue that school
segregation is rational from the purely economic point of view. As
Allport indicates, the states in which segregation is most rigidly en-

[15] Zeigler, op. cit., Ch. 3.
[16] Joseph Gussfield, "A Dramaturgical Approach to Status Politics" (unpublished),
    p. 4.

forced are the states which can least afford the expense of separate facilities.[17] Actually, few students are involved and the ability of whites
to maintain segregation through less formal patterns has been demonstrated. However, the symbolic impact of the conflict is considerable.
To use Allport's phrase, the words "segregation" and "integration" are
"emotionally toned labels." [18] Although logically these words should
apply to specific attributes or goals, the words come in for much more
extensive uses. Operating as symbols the words connote an array of
undifferentiated feelings and impulses which do not reach the cognitive level. Much the same can be said for the word "communist"
which certainly does not designate merely members of the Communist Party.

In a survey research project undertaken in a southern urban area
prior to a campaign against segregated lunch counters, Charles Grigg
and Lewis Killian asked a group of Negro respondents to rank the
goals which they were most anxious to achieve. The goals were
ranked in this manner: (1) equal job opportunities, (2) equal treatment by police and courts, (3) the end of segregation in public transportation and at sports events, (4) the end of segregation in public
schools, (5) the chance to vote without restriction or fear, (6) freedom
to visit in white homes, to swim in the same place with whites, and to
eat in the same restaurants.[19] One readily notices that the issues
around which the greatest amount of protest activity has been cen-
tered, school and lunch counter segregation, rank low on the list of
goals. If one assumes that organizations act as catalysts to transmit
dissatisfaction into action, as Truman does, the selection of issues becomes crucial. Why is not the organized protest activity directed at
the area in which dissatisfaction is greatest, the matter of equal employment opportunities? Before immediately attributing this variance
to symbolic factors, let us concede the role of pressure-group strategy.
Obviously the improvement of employment opportunities is a slower
and more arduous task than a court suit to gain admittance to a
white school. On the other hand, sit-ins and other protest demonstrations symbolize and dramatize the Negro's dissatisfaction with an inferior status. These quick and decisive actions provide a rallying
point. Segregation, no matter how insignificant its form, is a symbol
of inferiority. Destroying segregation serves to reduce the psychic
anxieties associated with inferior status, even if the number of actual
Negroes who will benefit tangibly is small. Killian states: "Breaking

[17] Gordon W. Allport, *The Nature of Prejudice* (Garden City: Doubleday and
Co., 1954), pp. 50–56.
[18] *Ibid.*
[19] Charles M. Grigg and Lewis M. Killian, "What the Negro Wants: Negro and
White Conceptions" (unpublished), pp. 4–5.

down segregation in relatively inconsequential areas while the living conditions of most of the Negro population remain almost unchanged is like capturing the enemy's colors while the ground which he occupies remains to be won." [20] This analysis suggests that politics is often an arena in which persons or groups seek the symbolic importance of victory, as well as some more tangible goal. Edelman, echoed by Gussfield, states that, although power is often a means to a concrete end, it is also a source of prestige as well.[21] While Lipset maintains that the government can do little to alleviate status anxieties, in terms of symbolic satisfaction there is much that can be achieved. Gussfield remarks that "the politics of ethnic minorities has often demonstrated the political efficacy of appointments to judgeships and other offices of hitherto unrecognized minorities." [22] The economic plight of the minorities thus recognized will not be improved by a few appointments, such as the appointment of a Negro to a position in the Kennedy administration; nor will the position of Negroes be improved by "capturing the enemy's colors" in relatively insignificant areas. However, these acts can serve to symbolize an equalitarian relation.

III

The point of this discussion is that, while politics may be understood as the result of the interplay among groups, the socio-psychological problems encountered by an examination of group values must lead one to account for individual perception. The "ghosts" of Bentley's system will have to be given a role. Once we discover that political activity supports goals logically unrelated to tangible benefit we can inquire into the manner in which the competing groups perceive the threat. This lends more credence to Truman than to Bentley. Since Truman's group is formed as a result of shared attitudes one may inquire into the nature of these attitudes and conclude, with Lasswell, that symbolic perception or stereotyping are functions of certain types of environmental circumstance.

Politics is indeed the process whereby values are allocated by group conflict; but the values which accrue to the competing groups vary considerably, and the activity surrounding the allocation displays variations which correlate with the nature of the value. This is not intended to convey the impression that political activity must be

[20] Lewis M. Killian, "Community Satisfaction and Race Relations in a Florida City," *Research Reports in Social Science,* III (August 1960), 27.
[21] Edelman, "Concepts of Power," *University of Illinois Bulletin* (October 1958), p. 623.
[22] Gussfield, *op. cit.,* p. 4.

either symbolic or tangible. Rather it is intended to suggest that "every instance of policy formulation involves a 'mix' of symbolic effect and rational reflection of interest in resources, though one or the other phenomenon may be dominant in a particular case." [23] Certainly the labor movement is an example of both an interest in tangible resources and the arousal of intense emotional reactions which are symbol oriented. The recognition that symbolic satisfaction may be a key element in understanding obligations can do much to enable group theory to provide adequate tools for the study of political reality. Tacit acceptance of the way the game of politics is played, as manifested in apathy or quiescence, keeps many groups "in their place." David Easton's concept of the political system places considerable reliance on "feedback" of the consequences of the outputs (decisions) in the system. Outputs vary in reality according to perceptions which in turn vary with group affiliations. Thus people obey even though you or I might think it is "irrational" for them to do so. While it is has been standard to assume that every act has two aspects, namely: the act as it exists is reality (objective) and the act as perceived (subjective); the approach adopted in this paper suggests that *all* acts are subjective. It is true that rational action is best defined as action contributing to a stated goal and thus the lynching of Negroes or sacrifices to Poseidon by Greek sailors prior to a voyage are irrational. However the consequences of such acts to the individual might be rational for the society if they contribute to the acknowledgment of obligation.[24]

This brief outline of a group theory of obligation operates on the premise that the individual's willingness to submit to the authority of government depends upon the rewards he receives. The political system is thus seen to be functioning on the familiar input-output basis. In many cases the input (obedience) does not seem related to tangible rewards and hence we speak of a sense of moral compulsion which is presumably disassociated with the expectation of rewards. Sample surveys of attitudes have shown that, among certain subgroups of the population, there is indeed a sense of obligation which is often expressed in terms of community identification.[25] However, it is plausible to suggest that such a sense of obligation is not an attitude which exists beyond the general theory outlined above, for the identification itself is a form of reward. Normative theorists should there-

---

[23] Edelman, "Symbols and Political Quiescence," p. 703.

[24] The "objective"—"subjective" categorization is best explained in Wilfredo Pareto's *The Mind and Society*, Vol. I (New York: Harcourt, Brace and Co., 1935). The best statement in refutation is Robert Merton, *Social Theory and Social Structure* (Glencoe: The Free Press, 1957), pp. 421–436.

[25] See James S. Coleman, *Community Conflict* (Glencoe: The Free Press, 1957).

fore not assume that behavioral research necessarily disregards values, for at least one of its aims is to probe the source of political obligation and to estimate the conditions under which sense of obligation can be expected to continue to provide the consensus necessary for the survival of stability in the political system.

29 / Superior Orders, Nuclear Warfare, and the Dictates of Conscience: The Dilemma of Military Obedience in the Atomic Age

GUENTER LEWY

When Francis Gary Powers was asked by the presiding judge of the Soviet military tribunal trying him for espionage whether he had not considered the possibility that his U-2 flight might provoke armed conflict, the captured pilot answered, "The people who sent me should think of these things. My job was to carry out orders. I do not think it was my responsibility to make such decisions."[1] This article deals with a similar problem, a predicament which to this day, fortunately, has remained hypothetical, but which may become distressingly real at some time in the future. It concerns the unenviable position of the military subordinate commanded to use nuclear weapons, who may be punished today if he disobeys and prosecuted tomorrow if he obeys. The discussion initially evolves around three issues in international law: (1) the validity of the plea of superior orders as a defense in war crimes trials; (2) the question of the legality of using nuclear weapons; (3) the present status and future of the law of war. That these problem areas are intimately related should become clear as we proceed.

The disregard for humanitarian and moral considerations which has increasingly characterized the conduct of war in the twentieth century, and, more recently, the development of nuclear weapons—

---

[1] *New York Times,* August 19, 1960, p. 8.

SOURCE: *American Political Science Review,* LV (March 1961), 3–23. Reprinted by permission.

the tools of mass extermination *par excellence*—have led many students of international law to conclude that the laws of war are dead. Grotius' doctrine of the *temperamenta belli,* requiring belligerents to conduct hostilities with regard for the principles of humanity and chivalry, as well as the many conventions drawn up prior to World War I in order to regulate the use of violence, are said to have become largely obsolete. A committee of the American Society of International Law concluded in 1952 that the laws of war were in a "chaotic" state and that "few distinguishable rules of the law of war" were still in existence.[2] Only regulations which do not really hamper the conduct of total war, like those concerning the treatment of prisoners of war and hostages, are still seen to be of some limited value. As to the rest of the body of the law of war, it cannot and ought not "restrict the effective employment of militarily advantageous techniques so long as war itself is the ultimate sanction behind [international] law."[3] Should mankind have the misfortune to be involved once more in a war of global proportions, writes H. A. Smith, "it is not likely that the belligerent powers will pay much attention to anything which the lawyers may have to say. On all sides it will be agreed that the law of self-preservation over-rides all other law."[4] The prediction of Douhet, the prophet of total war, that in the face of "self-interest, of national survival, every convention loses its value, every humanitarian sentiment loses its weight"[5] has seemingly been borne out.

And yet, this trend toward the indulgence of international lawlessness and the unfettered use of force has not gone completely unchallenged. The defeated camp at least, at the end of World War II, was brought into the dock of justice and was judged quite severely for persistent violations of the law of war. The majority of the Nazi war crimes, "attended by every conceivable circumstance of cruelty and horror," declared the Nuremberg tribunal in its judgment, had arisen from the hideous German National Socialist conception of total war. In "this conception of 'total war' the moral ideas underlying the conventions which seek to make war more humane are no longer regarded as having force and validity. Everything is made subordinate to the overmastering dictates of war. Rules, regulations, assurances,

---

[2] *Proceedings of the American Society of International Law,* Vol. 46 (1952), p. 218.

[3] C. P. Phillips, "Air Warfare and Law," *George Washington Law Review,* Vol. 21 (1952–53), p. 442.

[4] H. A. Smith, *The Crisis in the Law of Nations* (London, 1947), p. 66.

[5] Giulio Douhet, *The Command of the Air,* trans. Dino Ferrari (New York, 1942), p. 309, quoted in Edward M. Earle, ed., *Makers of Modern Strategy: Military Thought from Machiavelli to Hitler* (Princeton, 1943), p. 492.

and treaties, all alike, are of no moment." [6] In the *High Command Case* another panel of judges explicitly rejected the notion "that military necessity includes the right to do anything that contributes to the winning of a war . . . such a view would eliminate all humanity and decency and law from the conduct of war and it is a contention which this Tribunal repudiates as contrary to the accepted usages of civilized nations." [7] The same court also affirmed the supremacy of international law over municipal law and declared that in certain circumstances individuals may have to break the latter in order to obey the dictates of the former:

> International law operates as a restriction and limitation on the sovereignty of nations. It may also limit the obligations which individuals owe to their states, and create for them international obligations which are binding upon them to an extent that they must be carried out even if to do so violates a positive law or directive of state. [8]

Following the same logic is the provision of the Charter of the International Military Tribunal which lays down that orders of a government or of a superior do not free a defendant from responsibility for crimes committed in violation of international law, though a court may consider this fact in mitigation of punishment. [9]

The continued validity of the laws of war is similarly affirmed in the military codes of the principal nations. The American *Law of Land Warfare*, for example, stresses that hostilities must be conducted "with regard for the principles of humanity and chivalry" [10] and that the means of injuring the enemy "are definitely restricted by international declarations and conventions and by the laws and usages of war." [11] The manual reaffirms the so-called Martens Clause, the preamble to the Hague Convention No. IV Respecting the Laws and Customs of War on Land (Oct. 18, 1907), according to which "until a more complete code of laws has been issued, . . ., the inhabi-

---

[6] International Military Tribunal, *Nazi Conspiracy and Aggression: Opinion and Judgment* (Washington, D. C., 1947), p. 56, hereafter cited as *I.M.T. Judgment.*

[7] *Trials of War Criminals Before the Nuremberg Military Tribunals Under Control Council Law No. 10, October 1946 to April 1949* (Washington, D. C., 1950), XI, 541, hereafter cited as *Trials of War Criminals.*

[8] *Ibid.*, p. 489.

[9] Art. 8, quoted in Robert H. Jackson, *The Case Against the Nazi War Criminals* (New York, 1946), p. 101.

[10] U. S. Department of the Army, *The Law of Land Warfare*, Field Manual 27–10 (Washington, D. C., 1956), Art. 3, p. 3, hereafter cited as *U. S. Law of Land Warfare* (1956).

[11] *Ibid.*, Art. 33, p. 17.

tants and the belligerents remain under the protection and the rule of the principles of the law of nations, as they result from the usages established among civilized peoples, from the laws of humanity, and the dictates of the public conscience." [12] The same homage to the international law of war is to be found in the comparable British manual which emphasizes that the laws of war "are binding not only upon States as such but also upon their nationals and, in particular, upon the individual members of their armed forces." [13] Both manuals insist that members of the armed forces are bound to obey lawful orders only and, subject to a few minor qualifications, reject the plea of superior orders as a valid defense in the trial of an accused person for violation of the laws of war and the commisson of a war crime.[14]

The paradoxical situation has thus been created in which, according to one highly influential school of thought at least, the new weapons of mass destruction and the announced determination to use them have made the whole basis of the law of war obsolete, while, on the other hand, military codes of law continue to espouse high-sounding affirmations of the laws of humanity, and individual members of the armed forces are made explicitly and directly responsible for violating international law and flouting the dictates of the public conscience. The new weapons, if ever to be used in all their frightful destructiveness, seem to demand the complete suppression of all moral scruples. They put a premium upon blind obedience to orders issued by superiors far from the scene of action and insulated from the horrors committed by the subordinate in a plane or at a missile launcher. At the same time, the citizen in uniform is burdened with the duty to disobey commands and orders in violation of the laws of humanity and is held accountable for the commission of war crimes even if acting under superior orders.

The possible conflict of loyalties and duties which this state of affairs has brought about was the subject of several interesting debates in the British House of Lords in 1950 and 1952. What should an airman do, it was asked, when ordered to drop an atomic bomb? Should he obey the order or refuse on the ground that using this weapon violates the international law of war? He may end up between the Charybdis of being shot for insubordination in war-time and the Scylla of being hanged, if a military tribunal organized by the victor decides that his act shocked the conscience of civilized peoples.

---

[12] *Ibid.*, Art. 6, p. 6.

[13] Great Britain, War Office, *Manual of Military Law*, 9th ed., Part III: *The Law of War on Land* (London, 1958), Art. 1, p. 1, hereafter cited as *British Law of War* (1958).

[14] *Ibid.*, Part I, sec. 34(1); Part III, par. 627; *U. S. Law of Land Warfare* (1956), Art. 509.

Some of the participants in the discussion questioned the ability of the military subordinate to decide whether an order he was commanded to execute violated "the unchallenged rules of warfare" and outraged "the general sentiments of humanity." "What are to-day the unchallenged rules of warfare?" inquired Lord Chatfield. "Are there any at all? . . . What are the general sentiments of humanity today? Are there any?" [15] Two years later, in a renewal of the debate, Lord Winster asked, "Do we tell the air crews who carry and deliver an atomic bomb not to outrage the general sentiments of humanity? Do we hold that one of the air crew, if captured, ought not to be treated by the enemy as a war criminal?" Would not every airman who takes part in what the victors eventually describe as a "war of aggression" be a war criminal? [16] Lord Cook was afraid that the rule about superior orders would undermine military discipline. Soldiers, he argued, must be able to execute orders without delay and misgivings about their legality under international law. "There should be no risk of any one being troubled, subconsciously or otherwise, by doubts as to whether, by so doing, he is laying himself open to future charges of being a war criminal if he should fall into the hands of the enemy." [17]

An attempt to answer the question so raised open up a number of problem areas. There is the question how far the war crimes trials held after World War II and contemporary military codes have resolved the problem of superior orders in accordance with international law, and what may be the implications for military obedience as well as for modern total war. There is next the issue of the legality of using nuclear weapons under international law, for the duty of disobedience comes into play only if the illegality of an order is clearly established. This leads into the much argued point of whether international law is indeed still able to concern itself with such a strictly legal issue, a controversy that involves the broader problem whether the law of war is really dead, as some say, or has only been breached without thereby losing its legal status. Whether an airman who under orders dropped an atomic or hydrogen bomb could be considered a war criminal, whether he should challenge such orders and risk being punished by his superiors for breach of discipline or mutiny, whether international law can effectively protect individuals against a domestic law which is illegal from the point of view of international law—these are questions which today may seem rather theoretical and removed from reality; they involve fine technical points. And yet it is perhaps no exaggeration to say that upon the answers given to these questions may some day depend the future of the human race.

---

[15] *House of Lords Debates*, 168 (July 19, 1950), col. 460.
[16] *Ibid.*, 176 (May 14, 1952), cols. 998–999.   [17] *Ibid.*, col. 965.

I. THE PLEA OF SUPERIOR ORDERS

Prior to the end of World War II there was no settled rule of international law on the validity of the defense of *respondeat superior*. The military laws of the major powers varied, Great Britain and the U.S.A., for example, allowing the plea, and Germany rejecting it. Article 3 of the Washington Treaty of 1922—binding only the major powers possessed of capital ships—found submarine attacks on merchant ships to be a violation of the laws of war irrespective of whether the attacker was "under orders of a governmental superior." [18] The London Convention of 1930, on the other hand, which embodied very similar substantive principles of maritime warfare, did not include this repudiation of the defense of superior orders, an omission which informed students of the subject consider deliberate and indicative of the controversial nature of the problem.[19]

Early English law had posited the absolutely binding character of military orders. The military code of 1749 made obedience extend to *lawful* orders only, but this provision was withdrawn again in the 1914 edition of the *Manual of Military Law*. Article 443 returned to the doctrine of unconditional obedience and of absolute non-liability for violations of international law when under superior orders. It read: "Members of armed forces who commit such violations of the recognized rules of warfare as are ordered by their government or by their commander are not war criminals and cannot therefore be punished by the enemy." [20] The source of the provision was L. Oppenheim's *International Law*, first published in 1906, and a pamphlet authored by Oppenheim and Colonel James E. Edmonds entitled *British Land Warfare: An Exposition of the Laws and Usages of War on Land* and published in 1913.

Article 443 of the British *Manual* remained unchanged from 1914 till 1944. In April of that year the War Office in a complete about-face changed the article on superior orders to read: "The fact that a rule of warfare has been violated in pursuance of an order of the belligerent Government or of an individual belligerent commander does not deprive the act in question of its character as a war crime; . . .

---

[18] *Cf.* Sheldon Glueck, *War Criminals: Their Prosecution and Punishment* (New York, 1944), p. 155.

[19] *Cf.* N. C. H. Dunbar, "Some Aspects of the Problem of Superior Orders in the Law of War," *Juridical Review*, Vol. 63 (1951), p. 247; J. M. Spaight, *Air Power and War Rights* (3d ed.; London, 1947), p. 57, hereafter cited as Spaight, *Air Power* (1947).

[20] Quoted in Glueck, *op. cit.*, p. 150.

members of the armed forces are bound to obey lawful orders only and . . . cannot therefore escape liability if, in obedience to a command, they commit acts which both violate unchallenged rules of warfare and outrage the general sentiment of humanity." [21] The change had been foreshadowed in the sixth edition of Oppenheim's classic, brought out in 1940 by H. Lauterpacht. But this has not stifled the misgivings of many who see the shift of position as a poorly disguised and self-serving way of preparing the ground for the trials of the German and Japanese war criminals who were sure to invoke the plea of superior orders.

Until 1914 the American military code did not contain any reference to superior orders, though in several judicial decisions that doctrine had been rejected as an unqualified defense. [22] In these judgments soldiers were held civilly as well as criminally liable when the orders they had obeyed were later found to be illegal. The basic principle followed was that obedience was due only to a lawful order, although in practice the test of legality apparently did not involve a possible conflict with the international law of war. An order was seen to be legal as long as it emanated from an officer authorized to give it, did not extend beyond the superior's power or discretion, and did not involve a manifest violation of the law of the land. Most of the cases on record pertain to rather trivial offenses like being upheld in the refusal to obey an order to assist in the building of a private stable for an officer. [23]

The first explicit linking of the problem of superior orders and the laws and customs of warfare is to be found in the 1914 edition of the *Rules of Land Warfare*. Paragraph 347 of that manual, clearly inspired by the British formulation, laid down that "individuals of the armed forces will not be punished for these offenses [against the law of war] in case they are committed under the orders or sanction of their government or commanders." [24] This provision remained in force until November 1944, one year before the Nuremberg trials. Worried experts had pointed out that the earlier formulation "would give almost the entire band of Axis war criminals a valid defense." [25] It was superseded by the following new Section 345.1:

---

21 Full text of Art. 443 in United Nations War Crimes Commission, *History of the United Nations War Crimes Commission and the Development of the Laws of War* (London, 1948), p. 282.

22 For a discussion of these cases see Glueck, *op. cit.*, pp. 144–149.

23 See William Winthrop, *Military Law and Precedents* (2d ed.; Washington, D.C., 1920), pp. 296–297, 575, 887.

24 Quoted in Glueck, *op. cit.*, p. 140.

25 *Loc. cit.* "In view of Nazi excesses," writes Julius Stone, "a conference of Allied jurists were instructed to review their respective national laws on 'superior orders,' then ranging from the Norwegian which excluded the plea, to the

Individuals and organizations who violate the accepted laws and customs of war may be punished therefor. However, the fact that the acts complained of were done pursuant to order of a superior or government sanction may be taken into consideration in determining culpability. . . .[26]

The reference to organizations probably adumbrates the declaration of criminality against certain Nazi organizations like the SS and SD by the Nuremberg International Military Tribunal.

While British and American law, as we have seen, accepted the plea of superior orders until 1944, German law rejected it from the very beginning. The Military Penal Code adopted by the Reichstag in 1872 laid down that in case a penal law was violated through the execution of the order of a superior, "the obeying subordinate shall be punished as accomplice (1) if he went beyond the order given to him, or (2) if he knew that the order of the superior concerned an act which aimed at a civil or military crime or offense." [27] In 1921 the German Supreme Court relied on this law in the case of *The Llandovery Castle,* a Canadian hospital ship sunk by a German submarine without prior warning in 1918 and with a loss of 234 persons. Two officers of the submarine were on trial for assisting in the machine-gunning to death of helpless life-boat survivors of the ship. They pleaded superior orders, but the court rejected the plea. While military subordinates, according to the court, ordinarily can count on the legality of orders given by their superior officers, "no such confidence can be held to exist if such an order is universally known to everybody, including the accused, to be without any doubt whatever against the law. . . . They should, therefore, have refused to obey. As they did not do so, they must be punished." [28] Germany continued to reject the plea during World War II, notably in the cases of captured allied airmen accused of terror bombing. Summarizing the German attitude, Goebbels wrote in the *Völkischer Beobachter:* "The pilots cannot say that they as soldiers acted upon orders. It is not provided in any military law that a soldier in the case of a despicable crime is exempt from punishment because he blames his superior, especially if

---

French and British and American which admitted it. The United States Rules of Land Warfare were subsequently amended along with the British and French." *Legal Controls of International Conflict: A Treatise on the Dynamics of Disputes- and War-Law* (New York, 1954), p. 362, n. 75.

[26] U. S. War Department, General Staff, *Rules of Land Warfare,* Field Manual 27-10 (Washington, D. C., 1947), loose leaf insert.

[27] Sec. 47, quoted in *Trials of War Criminals,* IV, 471–472.

[28] Quoted in Glueck, *op. cit.,* p. 152. The full opinion can be found in Georg Schwarzenberger, *International Law and Totalitarian Lawlessness* (London, 1943), Appendix 2, pp. 128–147.

the orders of the latter are in evident contradiction to all human morality and every international usage of warfare." [29] Goebbels may not have realized that soon the victorious Allies would quote his words and use them to convict the surviving leaders of the Nazi military machine.

After considerable debate the United Nations War Crimes Commission agreed upon the following rule regarding the problem of superior orders: "The fact that the Defendant acted pursuant to order of his Government or of a superior shall not free him from responsibility but may be considered in mitigation of punishment if the Tribunal determines that justice so requires." [30] All of the trials held pursuant to the Charter and Control Council Law No. 10 essentially conformed to this principle. It is due to the disingenuous use of the plea of superior orders by the Nazi war criminals and the vigorous repudiation of this defense by the various military tribunals that the doctrine of the duty of absolute obedience to superior orders today stands largely discredited. The rulings have also shown, however, that the opposite view, according to which superior orders can never constitute a defense, is equally untenable. Despite the restrictive wording of Article 8 of the London Charter, the Nuremberg courts recognized that in cases of duress and error, for example, the plea of superior orders could afford a defense.[31]

The plea of superior orders was raised by the defense more frequently than any other. It was couched in various forms, of which the appeal to the legal nature of the acts committed as judged according to German law, got the most uncharitable reception. It is of the very essence of the Charter, declared the tribunal judging the so-called major war criminals, "that individuals have international duties which transcend the national obligations of obedience imposed by the individual State. He who violates the laws of war cannot obtain immunity while acting in pursuance of the authority of the State, if the State in authorizing action moves outside its competence under international law." [32] The contention that the defendants had acted pursuant to the direct orders of Hitler, the head of State and supreme military commander, was likewise rejected. "That a soldier was ordered to kill or torture in violation of the international law of war has

---

[29] "A Word on the Enemy Air Terror," *Völkischer Beobachter*, May 28 and 29, 1944, quoted in *Trials of War Criminals*, XI, 168.

[30] Charter of the International Military Tribunal, Art. 8, quoted in Jackson, *op. cit.*, p. 101. Art. 6 of the Tokyo Charter for the International Military Tribunal for the Far East uses almost identical language.

[31] *Cf.* Dunbar, *op. cit.*, p. 251; Günter Stratenwerth, *Verantwortung und Gehorsam: Zur strafrechtlichen Wertung hoheitlich gebotenen Handelns* (Tübingen, 1958), p. 41.

[32] *I.M.T. Judgment*, p. 53.

never been recognized as a defense to such acts of brutality, though, as the Charter here provides, the order may be urged in mitigation of the punishment. The true test, which is found in varying degrees in the criminal law of most nations, is not the existence of the order, but whether moral choice was in fact possible." [33]

The rule here suggested is somewhat ambiguous, for even the soldier faced with death, if he disobeys a criminal order, has a moral choice, *i.e.*, between accepting his own punishment or harming an innocent party.[34] But an examination of the full record of the proceedings leaves no doubt as to what was intended. The real purpose, as Telford Taylor explained in the *High Command Case*, was to protect those "whose opportunity for reflection, choice, and the exercise of responsibility is non-existent or limited." [35] In a modern military organization everyone is subject to orders. Yet whereas one can hardly expect a private soldier, drafted into the armed forces and ignorant of the law of war, to screen the orders of superiors for questionable points of legality, the same excuse is not available to those in responsible positions, whose duty it is to ensure the preservation of honorable military traditions. Moreover, most of the defendants, part of the hard core of the Nazi party or SS, could not claim in good faith that they had been unaware of Hitler's criminal plans. As the judgment in *The Einsatzgruppen Case* put it: "The sailor who voluntarily ships on a pirate craft may not be heard to answer that he was ignorant of the probability he would be called upon to help in the robbing and sinking of other vessels." [36] The defendants, far from acting under duress, had shared the ideological goals of the *Führer*. They could and had opposed orders when they did not agree with them, but they were unable to produce any evidence of an attempt to disengage themselves from the catastrophic assignments for which they were being judged at Nuremberg. Quite the contrary, many of the most hideous crimes had been committed on the accuseds' own initiative.

The tribunals recognized that a defendant might legitimately claim ignorance of the illegality of an order not criminal upon its face. "We are of the view," declared the tribunal in *The Hostage Case*, "that if the illegality of the order was not known to the inferior, and he could not reasonably have been expected to know its illegality, no wrongful intent necessary to the commission of a crime exists and the inferior will be protected." [37] But this was not the situation of most of the accused Nazis. Otto Ohlendorf, for example, commanding officer of one of the notorious *Einsatzgruppen*, admitted that, on the basis of an

---

[33] *Ibid.*, pp. 53–54.

[34] For a good discussion of this point see Morris Greenspan, *The Modern Law of Land Warfare* (Berkeley and Los Angeles, 1959), pp. 493–495.

[35] *Trials of War Criminals*, XI, 373.   [36] *Ibid.*, IV, 473.   [37] *Ibid.*, XI, 1236.

order, he and his troop had executed more than 90,000 "undesirable elements composed of Russians, Gypsies, and Jews and others." [38] He stated further: "The order, as such, even now I consider to have been wrong, but there is no question for me whether it was moral or immoral, because a leader who has to deal with such serious questions decides from his own responsibility and this is his responsibility and I cannot examine and [can] not judge. I am not entitled to do so." [39] The court concluded that in view of this acknowledged unwillingness to exercise moral judgment the plea of superior orders was unavailable. "The obedience of a soldier is not the obedience of an automaton. A soldier is a reasoning agent. He does not respond, and is not expected to respond, like a piece of machinery. . . . To plead superior orders one must show an excusable ignorance of their illegality." [40] This might be the case, for example, when an officer executes an order in the belief that it constitutes a justifiable reprisal against unlawful methods of warfare employed by the enemy.[41]

The legal principles established by the war crimes trials have come in for a good deal of criticism, and this has included their basic thesis that international law imposes duties and obligations upon individuals and that these therefore can be punished for war crimes committed under orders of a sovereign state or their military superiors. The law of warfare, like all international law, is held to be addressed to states and not individuals. So one critic writes:

> International law is not in position to protect individuals, wherever they may be, against a domestic law which is illegal from the point of view of international law. According to general legal principles, it therefore cannot expect the individuals to expose themselves to such a risk. For the individual, always and everywhere, national law precedes international law. He has to obey the national law even where it compels him to violate international law. [42]

According to this view, no soldier has an unqualified duty to disobey as long as states exist with a sovereignty of their own and the community of nations is unable to shield a citizen who wants to obey international law rather than the law or orders of his own government. Given this strong current of criticism—which is not limited to Ger-

---

[38] *Ibid.*, IV, 134.   [39] *Ibid.*, IV, 303.   [40] *Ibid.*, IV, 470, 473.

[41] *Cf.* United Nations War Crimes Commission, *Law Reports of Trials of War Criminals* (London, 1947), XI, 25–27.

[42] August von Knieriem, *The Nuremberg Trials*, trans. Elizabeth D. Schmitt (Chicago, 1959), p. 47. The same point is stressed by Hellmuth von Weber, "Die strafrechtliche Verantwortlichkeit für Handeln auf Befehl," *Monatsschrift für Deutsches Recht*, Vol. 2 (1948), pp. 34–42.

man scholars [43]—the question whether the law of the war crimes trials is international law would seem to be still open. The action of the General Assembly of the United Nations on December 11, 1946, affirming the principles of international law recognized by the Charter of the Nuremberg Tribunal, certainly does not establish the identity of these principles with international law.[44] The International Law Commission, cognizant of this fact, in its 1950 report merely *formulated* the principles of international law recognized in the Charter and judgment of the Nuremberg Tribunal. It did not evaluate them, realizing that their legal validity has yet to be proven by general acceptance and consent evidenced by conduct.

The need for common agreement on the status of the plea of superior orders is clear: "The cause of humanity and of the development of international law demands that license to commit atrocities shall not indirectly be conferred upon members of the armed forces by permitting the latter to take shelter under the canopy of superior orders." [45] While army regulations are not competent sources of international law, the fact that practically all military codes today follow the Nuremberg doctrine on this matter is to be welcomed as a step in this direction and is of evidential value in determining the existence of usage and practice, an important stage in the crystallization of the customary law of war. The rulings of the Nuremberg trials on the plea of superior orders, in view of the hurried changes introduced in the military codes of the United Nations in 1944, were open to the objection of retroactivity. Given the consensus existing today, it will be difficult to make this same charge in the future.

The most recent edition of the American *Law of Land Warfare* reads as follows:

> The fact that the law of war has been violated pursuant to an order of a superior authority, whether military or civil, does not deprive the act in question of its character as a war crime, nor does it constitute a defense in the trial of an accused individual, unless he did not know

[43] Percy E. Corbett, for example, in his *Law and Society in the Relations of States* (New York, 1951), p. 232, argues that the Nuremberg tribunal has ignored "the long and undecided doctrinal debate on the question whether, and how far, the individual is subject to rights and duties under the law of nations. It was also ignoring the negative trend of practice, in which recognition of the international personality of the individual hitherto has certainly been exceptional." See also Hans Kelsen's article "Will the Judgment of the Nuremberg Trial Constitute a Precedent in International Law?" *International Law Quarterly*, Vol. 1 (1947), pp. 153–171.

[44] *Cf.* Hans-Heinrich Jescheck, "Die Entwicklung des Völkerstrafrechts nach Nürnberg," *Schweizerische Zeitschrift für Strafrecht*, Vol. 72 (1957), pp. 217–248.

[45] Dunbar, *op. cit.*, p. 261.

and could not reasonably have been expected to know that the act ordered was unlawful. In all cases where the order is held not to constitute a defense to an allegation of war crime, the fact that the individual was acting pursuant to orders may be considered in mitigation of punishment.[46]

The 1958 edition of the British *Laws of War on Land* is even more far-reaching and entirely rules out acceptance of the plea of superior orders as a defense. Art. 627 provides that "obedience to the order of a government or of a superior, whether military or civil, or to a national law or regulation, affords no defense to a charge of committing a war crime but may be considered in mitigation of punishment." [47] An attached note points out that no mitigating factor will be recognized in the case of military commanders at the highest level of the military hierarchy. "Far from being irresistibly compelled to obey unlawful orders they are in a position, by a refusal to obey them, to arrest or prevent their operation." [48] Following Bacon's maxim that "urgent necessity no matter how grave is no excuse for the killing of another," the *Manual* provides that even peril of death does not remove criminal responsibility for the taking of innocent life.[49]

The relevant provisions of the new military code of the German Federal Republic are based upon Article 25 of the Basic Law (*Grundgesetz*), according to which "the general rules of international law shall form part of federal law. They shall take precedence over the laws and create rights and duties directly for the inhabitants of the federal territory." [50] Military superiors must make sure that their orders conform to international law,[51] and the subordinate is not guilty of insubordination if an order violates human dignity. "An order may not be executed if obedience to it would constitute a crime or transgression." [52] A subordinate who fails to obey an order because of

---

[46] *U. S. Law of Land Warfare* (1956), Art. 509(a), p. 182. Art. 330b (1) of the *Law of Naval Warfare* (1955) uses practically identical language. *Cf.* Robert W. Tucker, *The Law of War and Neutrality at Sea* (Washington, D. C., 1957), pp. 374–375.

[47] *British Law of War* (1958), Art. 627, p. 176.   [48] *Ibid.*, Art. 627, n. 2(f), p. 177.

[49] *Ibid.*, Art. 629, p. 177. The English law on the question of duress is more stringent than the Nuremberg trials. The judgment in *The Einsatzgruppen Case*, handed down by a panel of American judges, had asserted that "there is no law which requires that an innocent man must forfeit his life or suffer serious harm in order to avoid committing a crime." *Trials of War Criminals*, IV, 480.

[50] Quoted in Herbert W. Briggs, *The Law of Nations* (2d ed.; New York, 1952), p. 58.

[51] *Soldatengesetz und Verordnungen über die Regelung des militärischen Vorgesetztenverhältnisses* (erläutert von Werner Scherer) (Berlin, 1956), Art. 10(4), p. 4.

[52] *Ibid.*, Art. 11, pp. 4–5.

the mistaken belief that its execution would bring about a crime or transgression is not liable to punishment, if he cannot be blamed for the error.[53] The military code of the new West German army, one can readily see, leans over backward in order to accommodate the individual soldier and to prevent a return to the Nazi dogma of unquestioning obedience to orders.

The military law of the Soviet Union stresses the duty of instant obedience to orders but grants servicemen "the right to make complaints about illegal actions and orders of commanders." [54] A soldier carrying out the unlawful order of a superior "incurs no responsibility for the crime, which is that of the officer, except where the soldier fulfills an order which is clearly criminal, in which case the soldier is responsible with the officer who issued the order." [55] After surveying the relevant provisions of many other national military codes one student of the subject comes to the conclusion that the principle of unconditional obedience and of complete freedom from responsibility for superior orders has all but disappeared today.[56]

International lawyers speak of a custom "when a clear and continuous habit of doing certain actions has grown up under the aegis of the conviction that these actions are, according to International Law, obligatory or right." [57] Since the teachings of the most highly qualified jurists of the various nations can be regarded as a subsidiary source of international law,[58] we may turn to them in order to ascertain the existence of such a conviction. Such an examination reveals that practically all writers do indeed approve of the recent formulations which deny that the plea of superior orders constitutes an absolute defense to a clearly criminal act. Even authors critical of the way the Nuremberg Courts handled this issue and sceptical about the principle of individual responsibility agree that in cases of certain atrocious orders obviously incompatible with the laws of war the duty of obedience ceases and the subordinate will commit a crime if

---

[53] *Wehrstrafgesetz* (mit Erläuterungen von Gotthard Frhr. von Richthofen) (Cologne-Berlin, 1957), Art. 22, p. 44.

[54] Disciplinary Code of the Armed Forces of the USSR (1946), Art. 96, quoted in Harold J. Berman and Miroslav Kerner, eds. and trans., *Documents on Soviet Military Law and Administration* (Cambridge, Mass., 1955), p. 70.

[55] V. M. Chkhikvadze, *Sovetskoe Voenno-Ugolovmoe Prava* [Soviet Military Criminal Law] (Moscow, 1948), pp. 198–199, quoted in Greenspan, *op. cit.*, p. 491.

[56] Stratenwerth, *op. cit.*, pp. 28–40.

[57] L. Oppenheim, *International Law: A Treatise*, vol. I (8th ed. by H. Lauterpacht; London, 1955), p. 26, hereafter cited as Oppenheim-Lauterpacht, I (8th ed., 1955).

[58] The statute of the International Court of Justice speaks of the writings of eminent publicists in this sense. *Cf. ibid.*, 33.

he carries out the order.[59] The same view is held by Lauterpacht, the most recent editor of Oppenheim, on whose teaching, as we have seen, the contemporary British *Manual* is based.[60] And Dunbar maintains flatly that this rule today "may properly be regarded as forming part of international law." [61]

All authorities stress that the plea of superior orders can be rejected only when the illegality of the act is manifest or if the subordinate could and should reasonably have known that the act ordered was unlawful. This means that the disputed character of some of the laws of war has a direct bearing on the question of superior orders. "If it is true," writes Lauterpacht, that "the obviousness and the indisputability of the crime tend to eliminate one of the possible justifications of the plea of superior orders, then the controversial character of a particular rule of war adds weight to any appeal to superior orders." [62] Does the legality of nuclear weapons, then, fall into this category of controversial precepts of the international law of war?

II. THE LEGALITY OF NUCLEAR WEAPONS

The question of the legality of nuclear weapons has received surprisingly scant attention from international lawyers. This may be due to a feeling of futility on the part of men who know that the employment of new and decisive weapons or methods of warfare has never yet yielded to considerations of humanity and that the decision whether to use or not to use nuclear weapons most probably will be made on military or political (including moral), but not on legal grounds. There is also the disappointing status of fifteen years of negotiations designed to bring about an end to the nuclear arms race, an attempt which, as Lauterpacht points out, "is not likely to receive a notable accession of strength from controversial assertions as to the present illegality of the use of the atomic weapon either in general or against the civilian population." [63]

---

[59] So von Knieriem, for example: "If in a territory behind the front line, a local commander orders a Massacre of the Innocents, or if he orders all Jewish civilians of the district of occupation to be shot for the exclusive reason that they are Jews, nobody will believe that such acts could be justified by the laws of war, even though the harshest necessities of war be taken into account. If a subordinate ever receives such an order, he knows that it aims at a crime and nothing but a crime and all conditions of the duty of obedience are removed" (*op. cit.*, p. 244).

[60] *Cf.* Oppenheim-Lauterpacht, II (7th ed., 1952), pp. 568–572.

[61] Dunbar, *op. cit.*, p. 252.

[62] H. Lauterpacht, "The Law of Nations and the Punishment of War Crimes," *British Year Book of International Law*, XXI (1944), 58–95.

[63] "The Problem of the Revision of the Law of War," *ibid.*, XXIX (1952), 370.

Since nuclear bombs had not as yet been invented when most of the existing conventions regulating the methods of warfare were drawn up, no explicit conventional law presently exists regarding the legality of these weapons. The American *Law of Land Warfare* concludes, therefore, that nuclear weapons are legal or at least not illegal. "The use of explosive 'atomic weapons,' whether by air, sea or land forces, cannot as such be regarded as violative of international law in the absence of any customary rule of international law or international convention restricting their employment." [64] Yet it is doubtful that the absence of an express international agreement or customary rule is as decisive as this formulation would make it appear. This is recognized by the British *Manual* which declares that, lacking a rule of international law dealing specifically with nuclear weapons, "their use . . . is governed by the general principles laid down in this chapter [on the means of carrying on war]." [65] These include the principle that the means employed in weakening the enemy's power of resistance are not unlimited and that "there are compelling dictates of humanity, morality, civilization and chivalry, which must not be disregarded." [66] For a more detailed discussion the reader of the *Manual* is referred to the 7th edition of Oppenheim's treatise edited by Lauterpacht. The latter, in turn, suggests that the question be judged by reference "(a) to existing international instruments relating to the limits of the use of violence in war; (b) to the distinction, which many believe is fundamental, between combatants and non-combatants; and (c) to the principles of humanity, which, to some degree, must be regarded as forming part of the law of war." [67] We will follow Lauterpacht's suggestion and build our discussion around these three criteria.

International Agreements Limiting the Use of Violence. Article 23 (e) of the Hague Convention No. IV regulating land warfare (Oct. 18, 1907) prohibits resort to "arms, projectiles, or material calculated to cause unnecessary suffering." [68] All the major powers, including the United States, are a party to this convention. Given the horrible character of nuclear heat and radiation injuries, it may be thought that nuclear weapons violate the rule against the infliction of "unnecessary suffering." In practice, however, the line between necessary and unnecessary suffering has been drawn in a way hardly suggested by the humanitarian spirit of the Hague Convention. The criterion has nor-

[64] *U. S. Law of Land Warfare* (1956), Art. 35, p. 18.
[65] *British Law of War* (1958), Art. 113, p. 42.   [66] *Ibid.*, Art. 107, p. 40.
[67] Oppenheim-Lauterpacht, II (7th ed., 1952), pp. 347–348.
[68] U. S. Department of the Air Force, *Treaties Governing Land Warfare* (Washington, D. C., 1958), p. 12, hereafter cited as *U. S. Treaties on Land Warfare* (1958).

mally been whether a weapon inflicts suffering disproportionate to the military advantage to be gained by its use,[69] and this has meant that no militarily decisive weapon has ever been regarded as causing superfluous injury, no matter how painful the suffering resulting from its use. "The legality of hand grenades, flamethrowers, napalm and incendiary bombs in contemporary warfare," notes Schwarzenberger, "is a vivid reminder that suffering caused by weapons with sufficiently large destructive potentialities is not 'unnecessary' in the meaning of this rule." [70] Since nuclear weapons are notoriously potent and destructive, their use would seem unaffected by the prohibition of "unnecessary suffering."

That the law is interpreted in this way is brought out by the American *Law of Land Warfare* which accepts the illegality of "lances with barbed heads, irregular-shaped bullets, and projectiles filled with glass," [71] but sees nothing wrong with atomic bombs. Indeed, carrying the argument several steps further, it has been suggested that atomic warfare may be more humane than a prolonged conflict fought with inefficient weapons, for it will shorten the war and therefore bring about a return to peace with the least amount of general suffering.[72] This doctrine, originally developed by German military leaders like Moltke and von Hindenburg, is one which Western writers rejected until the use of the atomic bomb against Japan in World War II gave it some respectability. It is clear that, quite apart from the possibility that an all-out nuclear war may not leave any humanity to enjoy the restoration of peace,[73] the acceptance of this line of reasoning would mean the formal end of the entire international law of war.

---

[69] *Cf.* Richard R. Baxter, "The Role of Law in Modern War," *Proceedings of the American Society of International Law*, Vol. 47 (1953), p. 91.

[70] Georg Schwarzenberger, *The Legality of Nuclear Weapons* (London, 1958), p. 44, hereafter cited as Schwarzenberger, *Legality*. My discussion of the legal aspects of nuclear warfare leans extensively upon Schwarzenberger's succinct analysis.

[71] *U. S. Law of Land Warfare* (1956), Art. 34, p. 18.

[72] *Cf.* Phillips, *op. cit.*, note 3 above, p. 409.

[73] Edward Teller wrote in 1947 that an atomic war fought with greatly perfected weapons might "endanger the survival of man," "How Dangerous Are Atomic Weapons?" *Bulletin of the Atomic Scientists*, Vol. 3 (1947), p. 36. This was written before the coming of the hydrogen bomb. The Nobel Prize-winning nuclear physicist Otto Hahn has stated since that 10 powerful H-bombs, surrounded with a heavy coat of cobalt, could jeopardize the continued existence of the human race, no matter where dropped. "Cobalt 60: Gefahr oder Segen für die Menschheit?" *Frankfurter Allgemeine Zeitung*, February 19, 1955, and this estimate has been accepted by other scientists. For the view that human life on earth can not *as yet* be terminated see Ralph E. Lapp, *The New Force: The Story of Atoms and People* (New York, 1953), p. 97.

412 CONTEMPORARY APPLICATIONS

The argument that nuclear weapons violate the prohibition of the use of poison seems considerably stronger. Article 23 (a) of Hague Convention No. IV forbids the employment of poison or poisoned weapons, and this rule today is regarded as so basic to the practice of civilized nations as to be part of international customary law. This means that the resort to poison would not be legal even in a war in which not all of the belligerents were parties to the Hague Convention, thus overcoming the *si omnes* or "all-participation clause" of the agreement. Poison, in contemporary usage, means any substance which "when introduced into, or absorbed by, a living organism destroys life or injures health." [74] Since all nuclear devices, including the so-called "clean bomb," result in some radioactive fall-out which when introduced into the human body in sufficiently large doses, is harmful if not fatal, Schwarzenberger concludes that "a *prima facie* case appears to exist for regarding the use of nuclear weapons as incompatible with the prohibition of the use of poison." [75] There is also the fact that the explosion of bombs yielding large amounts of fission energy causes radioactive contamination over very wide areas and thus would poison the water supply as well as crops. Such measures are expressly forbidden by the military codes of all nations.[76]

It can also be argued that nuclear weapons are unlawful because they are an analogue of gas and bacteriological warfare and thus in violation of still another species of the genus "poison." That high fission content bombs are, in effect, weapons of radiological warfare is undisputed.[77] But even "cleaner" bombs release atomic clouds and gas bubbles which would seem to bring them within the prohibitions of the Geneva Gas Protocol of 1925, which forbids "the use in war of asphyxiating, poisonous or other gases and all analogous liquids, materials or devices." This agreement binds over forty states, including Great Britain and the Soviet Union. The U.S.A., after signing the Protocol, did not ratify it, and, according to the *Law of Land Warfare*, the United States expressly reserves the right to resort to gases, chemicals and bacteriological warfare.[78] It is generally accepted, however, that the prohibitions of the Geneva Gas Protocol, one agreement in a

---

[74] *Shorter Oxford Dictionary*, quoted in Schwarzenberger, *Legality*, p. 27.

[75] *Ibid.*, p. 28. See also the detailed analysis in Nagendra Singh, *Nuclear Weapons and International Law* (New York, 1959), pp. 155–162, which leads to the same conclusion. For an authoritative discussion of radiation injuries see U. S. Armed Forces Special Weapons Project, *The Effects of Nuclear Weapons* (Washington, D. C., 1957), chap. xi, hereafter cited as *Effects of Nuclear Weapons* (1957).

[76] *Cf. U. S. Law of Land Warfare* (1956), Art. 37(b); *British Laws of War* (1958), Art. 112.

[77] *Cf. Effects of Nuclear Weapons* (1957), p. 428.

[78] *U. S. Law of Land Warfare* (1956), Art. 38.

succession of conventions outlawing deleterious gases, today are declaratory of international customary law and thus binding on all states.[79] This, then, is another link in the chain of legal provisions which seems to spell the illegality of nuclear warfare even if directed against undoubted military objectives. If we add the long-range somatic and genetic effects which these weapons produce in their victims, it may also be considered within the orbit of biological warfare "which has been condemned by the conscience of mankind" [80] no less emphatically than poison gas and chemical warfare.

The Distinction Between Combatants and Non-Combatants. The distinction between combatants and non-combatants is generally regarded "as being of the essence of the law of war" [81] and as perhaps the greatest triumph of international law. It is here, in respect to one of the most fundamental aspects of the traditional law of war, that modern total war has scored its most far-reaching victory. Indeed, as Lauterpacht states, "there are many who believe that the advent of aircraft and aerial bombing has . . . obliterated the distinction between combatants and non-combatants." [82] The same result, others maintain, may have been achieved by the mechanization of warfare which requires the mobilization and productive effort of virtually the total working population, thus undermining the principle of civilian immunity. The advent of nuclear warfare, in this respect, has merely continued a trend the beginning of which can be traced to World War I and which reached an apex in the aerial bombardments of World War II.

Prior to the outbreak of World War II a number of attempts were

[79] Oppenheim-Lauterpacht, II (7th ed., 1952), p. 344; Stone, *op. cit.*, p. 556. F. D. Roosevelt, speaking of "poisonous or noxious gases or other inhumane devices of warfare," stated in 1943 that "the use of such weapons has been outlawed by the general opinion of civilized mankind" and that the United States would never resort to these weapons unless in retaliation for prior use by the enemy; quoted in Alexander N. Sack, "ABC—Atomic, Biological, Chemical Warfare in International Law," *Lawyers' Guild Review*, Vol. 10 (1950), p. 167. This statement raises the interesting but unanswerable question whether F. D. R. would have authorized the use of the atomic bomb on two densely populated Japanese cities. He had ordered its development to forestall a German effort and might have kept it in reserve, as gas was. *Cf.* J. M. Spaight, *The Atomic Problem* (London, 1948), p. 41.

[80] Oppenheim-Lauterpacht, II (7th ed., 1952), p. 348. See also Spaight, *Atomic Problem*, pp. 23–25; Greenspan, *op. cit.*, pp. 374–375.

[81] Oppenheim-Lauterpacht, II (7th ed., 1952), p. 350.

[82] *Loc. cit.* See also Lester Nurick, "The Distinction between Combatants and Noncombatants in the Law of War," *American Journal of International Law*, Vol. 39 (1945), p. 680, and Charles G. Fenwick's comments on William G. Downey's paper "Revision of the Rules of Warfare" in *Proceedings of the American Society of International Law*, Vol. 43 (1949), p. 110.

made to establish an authoritative code of air warfare. The most important of these was the draft drawn up by a conference of jurists, convoked by the governments participating in the Washington Conference, that met at The Hague from December 1922 to February 1923. This commission embodied its findings in a convention which allowed the bombing of military forces, military establishments and factories engaged in war production (Art. 24/2) but forbade aerial bombardment for the purpose of terrorizing the civilian population (Art. 22). The general principle followed was that air attacks are "legitimate only when directed at a military objective—that is to say, an object of which the destruction or injury would constitute a distinct military advantage to the belligerent" (Art. 24/1).[83] The draft convention was never officially accepted by the great powers, but even its ratification would probably have done little to change the nature of air warfare. For in World War II the destruction of the enemy's capacity to make war came to include the breaking of the morale of his labor force. Civilians thus became a military objective and the bombing of their cities came to constitute an allegedly legitimate military purpose.

In the absence of a conventional instrument regulating the conduct of hostilities in and from the air, although not necessarily causally related to it, air warfare in World War II soon outran all considerations of humanity. The savage German air attacks on Warsaw, Rotterdam and Belgrade could still be rationalized as siege bombardments in support of the operations of ground forces. But both sides soon went over to the strategic offensive, which clearly violated the commitment made prior to the outbreak of hostilities to refrain from the bombardment "of any except strictly military objectives in the narrowest sense of the word." [84] As the war dragged on the notion of "military objective" was enlarged to such an extent that it largely lost its original purpose.

In a speech before the House of Commons on June 21, 1938, Prime Minister Chamberlain had condemned as "absolutely contrary to international law" the policy of trying "to win a war by demoralizing the civilian population through a process of bombing from the air." [85] In practice it soon became almost impossible to distinguish the effects of the bombing of cities aiming at the destruction of factories and centers of communication from those of bombing for purposes of ter-

---

[83] Quoted in Arthur L. Goodhardt, *What Acts of War Are Justifiable?* (Oxford, 1940), p. 16. The complete draft convention is reproduced in Spaight, *Air Power* (1947), pp. 498–508.

[84] This promise was made by Britain and France in response to an appeal by Roosevelt on September 1, 1939. Hitler had agreed to abide by the same commitment. *Cf.* Georg Schwarzenberger, *Power Politics: A Study of International Society* (2d ed.; London, 1951), p. 548.

[85] Quoted in Spaight, *Air Power* (1947), p. 257.

ror.[86] The distinction became further obscured by the switch, necessitated by the intensification of defensive measures, from day-time precision to night-time area bombing, which both camps made as early as 1940. At the beginning of 1942, the British Bomber Command was given the explicit directive of attacking the principal industrial cities of the Ruhr, the operations to be "focussed on the morale of the enemy civil population and in particular of the industrial workers." [87] And in January 1943 the combined Chiefs of Staff at the Casablanca Conference authorized an enlarged scale of air attacks against Germany, with its primary objective "the destruction and dislocation of the German military, industrial and economic system and the undermining of the morale of the German people." [88] The shattering of morale, according to this policy statement, was to be a by-product of crippling the enemy's war machinery. In reality, when entire cities were attacked with high explosives and incendiary bombs the destruction of armament factories and communication networks was achieved almost incidentally to the wholesale destruction of civilian life and the spreading of terror.[89] Indeed, German war production was not seriously impaired by these attacks until the Allies, especially the Americans, began precision bombing of the German transportation system and the production centers of oil.[90]

The belated realization by the military experts that morale bombing is a very slow and inefficient method of breaking the enemy's

---

[86] *Cf.* Myres S. McDougal and Florentino P. Feliciano, "International Coercion and World Public Order: The General Principles of the Law of War," *Yale Law Journal*, Vol. 67 (1957–58), p. 833.

[87] Lord Tedder, *Air Power in War* (London, n.d. [1948]), p. 98. Sir Arthur Harris related that when he became Commander-in-Chief of Bomber Command in February 1942, "the main and almost only purpose of bombing was to attack the morale of the industrial workers." *Bomber Offensive* (New York, 1947), p. 76.

[88] Quoted in U. S. Strategic Bombing Survey, *Over-all Report (European War)* (n.p., 1945), p. 3.

[89] The British raids on Hamburg in July and August 1943, for example, destroyed seventy-five per cent of the city and killed between 70,000 and 100,000 people, most of them being burnt to death. The Allied attack on Dresden in February 1945 is supposed to have caused more than 100,000 fatal casualties, many of them refugees from the Russian advance in the East. There is room for the view that many German and Japanese cities suffered as grievously and on as great a scale as Hiroshima and Nagasaki. The number killed by the German bombing of Great Britain throughout the war is given as 60,585. Spaight, *Air Power* (1947), p. 29. Needless to say, this discrepancy is not due to the greater sense of humanity on the part of the German military leaders but mainly to the weakness of the Luftwaffe.

[90] That morale bombing failed to achieve the expected results is admitted by the U.S. Strategic Bombing Survey. See also the discussion of P. M. S. Blackett, *Fear, War and the Bomb: Military and Political Consequences of Atomic Energy* (New York, 1948), p. 22.

ability and will to resist is, of course, not likely to help matters in a future war, for even a small atomic bomb will do an immensely more thorough job of destruction than ordinary explosives.[91] This was demonstrated by the use of two such bombs against Japan in 1945, which achieved the Japanese surrender in a few days. The terror effect, according to all accounts, was no less important than the actual devastation caused. The fact that the combined result of the American blockade and bombing offensive had already seriously undermined Japan's willingness to stay in the war and might have led to a surrender even without an invasion [92] is important in assessing the wisdom, moral justification and legality of using the first atomic bomb, but does not affect the point we are making here.

The important truth is that nuclear weapons have a destructive action many thousands of times more powerful than the largest TNT bombs and therefore have proven highly effective as a morale buster where old explosives failed. Aerial bombing with conventional bombs, as the precision bombing of Germany in the last stage of the Allied air offensive demonstrated, could still make some distinction between combatants and non-combatants, if the will to do so was present and the opposition weak. Nuclear explosives delivered from the air on urban centers are probably inherently incapable of being used in this selective manner. If so they would violate one of the basic premises of the international law of war.[93]

In order to disprove this conclusion one would have to deny that there are any non-combatants left in modern total war—a rather dif-

[91] According to one American student of Soviet strategy, the primary objective of Soviet "military operations is the destruction of hostile military forces, and not the annihilation of the economic and population resources of the enemy." Cf. Raymond L. Garthoff, *Soviet Strategy in the Nuclear Age* (New York, 1958), p. 71. Since the dominant view in the United States, however, seems to be that a future war can be won by disrupting the enemy's capacity and will to fight, *i.e.*, by concentrating on attacking his economic and population centers, Soviet strategy is unlikely to remain as planned and undoubtedly will become one of retaliation in kind.

[92] Based on a detailed investigation of all the facts, the U. S. Strategic Bombing Survey expresses the opinion "that certainly prior to 31 December 1945, and in all probability prior to 1 November 1945, Japan would have surrendered even if Russia had not entered the war, and even if no invasion had been planned or contemplated." *Summary Report, Pacific War* (Washington, D. C., 1946), p. 26. See also Paul Kecskemeti, *Strategic Surrender: The Politics of Victory and Defeat* (Stanford, 1958), ch. 6, and Robert J. C. Butow, *Japan's Decision to Surrender* (Stanford, 1954).

[93] Cf. Singh, *op. cit.*, p. 193; Oppenheim-Lauterpacht, II (7th ed., 1952), p. 349. The same would probably hold true for target area saturation bombing with conventional explosives. Cf. Eberhard Spetzler, *Luftkrieg und Menschlichkeit: Die völkerrechtliche Stellung der Zivilpersonen im Luftkrieg* (Göttingen, 1956), p. 290. For the opposite view see J. M. Spaight, *Bombing Vindicated* (London, 1944), p. 98.

ficult task. While it may be possible to argue that in a modern war civilian laborers employed in armament production are no longer genuine civilians but quasi-combatants,[94] the same can hardly be said for infants, the old and sick, or those employed in outright civilian work and living outside important target areas. Even in today's total war, countries still have non-combatants like piano tuners, insurance agents, bookkeepers, hospital and prison inmates. And if it be maintained that even these serve the war effort, however indirectly, one will have to deny non-combatant status also to children, for they too have "war potential," write letters of encouragement to their brothers and fathers and in a long war will eventually bear arms.[95]

The most powerful bombs of World War II took out city blocks, the atomic bomb of the Hiroshima type destroys cities, the big hydrogen superbomb can devastate a metropolitan area and, if "dirty," make much of the surrounding countryside uninhabitable for a considerable time. A 10 megaton bomb packs an explosive energy more than three times as great as that of all the bombs used in World War II.[96] Whatever legal objections arise against aerial bombardment with atomic bombs are therefore all the more pertinent with regard to hydrogen bombs. Such a bomb not only could not discriminate between combatants and non-combatants, but might spread radioactive effects over neutral countries. The area of devastation and contamination resulting from several thermo-nuclear weapons would be so large that it would probably be impossible to protect the wounded and captured members of the armed forces, whose humane treatment and safety is reaffirmed in the Geneva Convention of 1949.[97] If a weapon is powerful enough to obliterate completely the distinction between civilians and combatants and to injure neutral states, Nagendra Singh concludes, its use "must be considered a violation of international law and, if it involves the killing of innocent neutrals, a clear war crime." [98]

---

[94] Stone, op. cit., p. 631.

[95] This point is well made by John C. Ford, S. J., "The Morality of Obliteration Bombing," Theological Studies, Vol. 5 (1944), pp. 276–285.

[96] "If a 10-meg. H-bomb 'clean' or 'dirty' should be dropped," writes Noel-Baker, "everything would be destroyed by blast or burnt, and few human beings would survive, within a circle of more than twenty miles across." The Arms Race: A Programme for World Disarmament (London, 1958), p. 135. "A 30-megaton bomb," according to Jack Shubert and Ralph E. Lapp, "could spread its lethal dose over 14,000 square miles—an area equal to that of Massachusetts, Rhode Island, and Connecticut." Radiation: What It Is and How It Affects You (New York, 1957), p. 239.

[97] Cf. Singh, op. cit., p. 202. For the text of the conventions see U. S. Treaties on Land Warfare (1958), pp. 24–194.

[98] Singh, op. cit., p. 106. Robert W. Tucker, consultant to the U. S. Naval War College, writes: "There should be little doubt that, as judged by the traditional

There remains the possibility that nuclear weapons will be employed in a tactical sense, *e.g.*, against enemy combatants and military objectives like ships, airfields or fortified places. Such use, from the point of view of the protection of non-combatants at least, would not be illegal. This reasoning is accepted by the draft code for the protection of the civilian population in time of war, drawn up by the International Committee of the Red Cross in 1956. Pending the achievement of a complete ban on weapons disseminating incendiary, chemical, bacteriological and radioactive agents, the Committee proposed that the resort to these weapons be prohibited if and when their harmful effects "could spread to an unforeseen degree or escape, either in space or in time, from the control of those who employ them, thus endangering the civilian population." [99] The emphasis here is on the protection of the civilian population against uncontrollable consequences, leaving open the use of nuclear weapons when their effects can be strictly limited, *e.g.*, when attacking a warship on the high seas. Whether the distinction between the tactical and strategic use of nuclear weapons could be maintained in an actual war situation is an unresolved question outside the scope and competence of this discussion, crucial though it may prove to be.

The Principles of Humanity. Criminality under international law, the judgment in the *High Command Case* declared, may arise not only because an act is forbidden by international agreements, but also when it "is inherently criminal and contrary to accepted principles of humanity as recognized and accepted by civilized nations." [100] This finding was based on Article 6 (c) of the Charter of the International Military Tribunal and the corresponding clause in Control Council Law No. 10 which made crimes against humanity, along with crimes against peace and war crimes in the narrow sense, punishable acts within the jurisdiction of the military tribunals. The phrase "accepted principles of humanity," in turn, was derived from the preamble of Hague Convention No. IV, the Martens Clause. This preamble, asserted the tribunal in the *Krupp Case*, was "much more than a pious declaration"; it was "the legal yardstick to be applied if and when the specific conventional provisions of the Convention and the regulations annexed to it do not cover specific cases occurring in war-

---

meaning given to the principles distinguishing combatants and noncombatants, the use of nuclear weapons against cities containing military objectives must be deemed illegal." *Op. cit.*, p. 55, n. 21.

[99] International Committee of the Red Cross, *Draft Rules for the Limitation of the Dangers Incurred by the Civilian Population in Time of War* (2d ed.; Geneva, 1958), Art. 14, p. 12, hereafter cited as *ICRC Draft Rules* (1958). The same conclusion is reached by Tucker, *op. cit.*, p. 55.

[100] *Trials of War Criminals*, XI, 543.

fare. . . ." [101] Our question here is whether the destruction and suffering inflicted on the civilian population by nuclear weapons pass, in the terminology of Justice Jackson, "in magnitude or savagery any limits of what is tolerable by modern civilizations," and thus make resort to these weapons a crime against humanity.

The military codes of the Western nations today accept the principle of individual responsibility for crimes against humanity.[102] Nevertheless it has been criticized as being too imprecise and elastic and an invitation to abuse. According to the critics, the principle has a resemblance to Hitler's doctrine of acts contrary to sound public opinion and violates the maxim *nulla poena sine lege*.[103] The term "principles of humanity," writes Dunbar, "stands for a vague and subjective criterion liable to alter with the passing years." [104] Given the fact that wide differences exist between the moral standards and humanitarian principles adhered to by the nations of the world and in view of the lack of a single authority able to lay down and enforce authoritative and uniform interpretations of these standards, the "principles of humanity," like the notion of "justice," are held to conceal "an unchartable area of discretion." [105] It has furthermore been argued that the Martens Clause merely reaffirmed the illegality of weapons already prohibited by existing customary law, but could not be used as a source of new rules of warfare.[106]

---

[101] *Ibid.*, IX, 1341. For a good discussion of the problems raised by this finding see Egon Schwelb, "Crimes Against Humanity," *British Year Book of International Law*, XXIII (1946), 178–226.

[102] *Cf. U. S. Law of Land Warfare* (1956), Art. 498(b); the *British Law of War* (1958), while not specifically mentioning crimes against humanity, speaks of "the compelling dictates of humanity, morality, civilization and chivalry" which must not be disregarded. Art. 107, p. 40.

[103] *Cf.* John Hartman Morgan, *The Great Assize: An Examination of the Law of the Nuremberg Trials* (London, 1948), p. 21. After World War I, a dissenting minority of the League of Nations "Commission of Fifteen" inquiring into the causes and conduct of the war concluded similarly that "a judicial tribunal only deals with existing law and only administers existing law, leaving to another forum infractions of the moral law and actions contrary to the laws and principles of humanity." Quoted in Schwelb, *British Year Book of International Law*, XXIII (1946), 182.

[104] "The Legal Regulation of Modern Warfare," *Transactions of the Grotius Society*, Vol. 40 (1954), p. 83.

[105] *Cf.* Corbett, *op. cit.*, p. 268. The authorization granted the two World Courts to apply "the general principles of law recognized by civilized nations" has so far been used sparingly. *Cf.* Max Sørensen, *Les sources du Droit International: Etude sur la jurisprudence de la Cour Permanente de Justice Internationale* (Copenhagen, 1946). A currently conducted research project on this topic, reported by Rudolf B. Schlesinger in the *American Journal of International Law*, Vol. 51 (1957), pp. 734–753, apparently does not include the law of war.

[106] *Cf.* Schwarzenberger, *Legality*, pp. 7–11.

The case for the "principles of humanity" today would be stronger if the United Nations after World War II had applied these standards not only to the crimes of the losing side, the Axis, but to all belligerents, for brutality, inhumanity and illegality were not absent in the conduct of the winners as well. The statement made by Goering upon receiving the indictment that "the victor will always be the judge, and the vanquished the accused" [107] thus has a modicum of justification. Moreover, the victorious Allies not only limited the jurisdiction of the International Military Tribunal at Nuremberg to crimes committed by persons "acting in the interests of the European Axis countries" (Art. 6 of the Charter), but they refrained from pressing charges which involved acts also committed by the military forces of the United Nations. For example, the tribunal in sentencing Admiral Doenitz expressly excluded from consideration his orders for unrestricted submarine warfare, since both sides had resorted to this illegal practice. Similarly, the Germans were not convicted of terror bombing and other illegal methods of air warfare, even though the indictment had accused the Nazi leaders of waging war "in violation of the rules and customs of war, including . . . the indiscriminate destruction of cities, towns, and villages, and devastation not justified by military necessity." [108] The fact that both sides had waged aerial warfare with complete disregard for "the principles of humanity," which should have controlled these hostilities in the absence of more specific rules, apparently was sufficient to absolve the accused loser of these crimes. This procedure, according to one vigorous critic of the Nuremberg trials, enthroned "the novel principle that, whether a particular act was a crime or not, depended on whether the victors could be shown to have committed it." [109]

Two wrongs, Stone correctly notes, do not make one right. "The fact that guilty men on the side of the victors may have escaped does

[107] G. M. Gilbert, *Nuremberg Diary* (New York, 1947), p. 4.

[108] Quoted in Jackson, *op. cit.*, p. 101. During the war, the Nazis had allowed and encouraged the lynching of Allied "terror fliers." In 1952 a German court ruled that since the Allied "bomb attacks against the civil population violated the Hague convention and possibly were crimes against humanity," the killing of a captured U. S. airman by storm troopers in 1944 had not been murder but manslaughter. *New York Times*, November 16, 1952, p. 30. The Japanese formally tried and executed a considerable number of Allied airmen for bombing the civilian population. See Charles Cheney Hyde, "Japanese Executions of American Aviators," *American Journal of International Law*, Vol. 37 (1943), pp. 480–482, and R. B. Pal, *International Military Tribunal for the Far East: Dissentient Judgement* (Calcutta, 1953), pp. 675–693. Judge Pal holds these trials to have been legal under international law.

[109] F. J. P. Veale, *Advance to Barbarism: How the Reversion to Barbarism in Warfare and War-Trials Menace Our Future* (2d ed.; Appleton, Wis., 1953), p. 169.

not in itself render illegitimate the punishment of the guilty on the side of the defeated." [110] But it does point up the precarious status of the "principles of humanity" which all too often become associated with what the strong desire most at any given moment. Schwarzenberger argues that the employment of "nuclear weapons of a size which precluded the protection of the civilian population in the most limited sense of the term" or their use "against the civilian population for purposes of terrorization" would be a crime against humanity.[111] The contention would have more weight if the military tribunals of the victorious Allies had not so blatantly ignored the inhumanity of these very tactics. And by an ironic and sad coincidence the news accounts of the Charter of the International Military Tribunal, which laid down the law against violations of the law recognized by civilized nations, shared the front pages of the world press with accounts of the dropping of the first atomic bomb on Hiroshima. Here were the Western Allies trying to defend civilization through means of warfare more ruthless and uncivilized than anything the world has seen since the Middle Ages.

Lauterpacht seems to go back to rationalizations produced about Hiroshima and Nagasaki when he entertains the possibility that the use of nuclear weapons might be legal against "an aggressor intent upon dominating the world" and imperiling the "ultimate values of society." In such a case the threatened nations "might consider themselves bound to assume the responsibility of exercising the supreme right of self-preservation in a manner which, while contrary to a specific prohibition of International Law, they alone deem to be decisive for the ultimate vindication of the law of nations." [112]

Schwarzenberger deems this argument so obviously mistaken as hardly to require refutation. He has on his side the firmly established principle that the laws of war bind all parties to a conflict, irrespective of the justice of their cause, and are not to be violated even in self-defense. "It is an essence of war," declared the military tribunal in the *Milch Case*, decided in 1947, "that one or the other side must lose and the experienced generals or statesmen knew this when they drafted the rules and customs of land warfare." [113] Military necessity or the necessities of war ordinarily do not excuse a violation of these rules.[114] Even if one were to grant that states have the highly controversial right of violating otherwise undeniable duties under international law in title of self-preservation,[115] this would not necessarily le-

---

[110] Stone, *op. cit.*, p. 326.   [111] Schwarzenberger, *Legality*, p. 45.
[112] Oppenheim-Lauterpacht, II (7th ed., 1952), p. 351, n. 2.
[113] Quoted *ibid.*, p. 233, n. 2.   [114] *Cf. U. S. Law of Land Warfare* (1956), Art. 3.
[115] The existence of this right is asserted by Stone, *op. cit.*, pp. 352–353. For the opposite view see N. C. H. Dunbar, "Military Necessity in War Crimes Trials,"

gitimize the use of illegal weapons against an aggressor if alternative ways of repelling the attack were available. As long as the major powers still have military forces equipped with conventional armaments, the resort to these weapons, unless in a strike-back after receiving a nuclear attack, probably could not be considered legitimate since it would not be the only possible method of defending their existence.[116] The plea of acting for the purpose of self-preservation under these circumstances should be disallowed for it would be a cloak for military expediency or advantage. Finally, since each side, as Schwarzenberger points out, undoubtedly would claim to act in defense of the "ultimate values of society" against the other's design of world domination, this asserted right to be the self-appointed guardian of humanity merely functions "to provide in advance, and indiscriminately, both sides with semi-legal justification for the 'ultimate deterrent.' " [117]

Our first conclusion that nuclear weapons violate the rules of international customary law with regard to poison and poisoned weapons is derived by analogy. The second conclusion that their strategic use against urban centers would obliterate the distinction between combatants and non-combatants is similarly based on principles established in conditions fundamentally different from those obtaining in modern war. In the absence of an express prohibition of the use of nuclear weapons in either conventional or customary law, any finding of illegality is therefore open to the objection that it is derived "from prescriptions created with respect to very different weapons in a very different world." [118] As we have seen, such a determination would also have to brand as illegal and criminal much of recent usage. Given the importance of nuclear weapons in the military planning of the major powers today, it would be obviously hazardous to expect too much from controversial analogies and principles flying in the

---

British Year Book of International Law, XXIX (1952), 443. Schwarzenberger calls the principle of self-preservation "a psychological, but not a legal principle" (*Legality,* p. 42).

[116] According to the U. S. memorandum attached to the report of the League of Nations Commission on Responsibilities, "the assertion by the perpetrator of an act that it is necessary for military reasons does not exonerate him from guilt if the facts and circumstances present reasonable grounds for establishing the needlessness of the act. . . ." Quoted by Dunbar, *British Year Book of International Law,* XXIX, 444. There can be little doubt that in the unlikely event of a Japanese victory in World War II the Japanese would have been on solid ground in rejecting the plea that the use of the atomic bomb was justified by military necessity.

[117] Schwarzenberger, *Legality,* p. 42.

[118] Myres S. McDougal and Norbert A. Schlei, "The Hydrogen Bomb Tests in Perspective: Lawful Measures for Security," *Yale Law Journal,* Vol. 64 (1955), p. 689.

face of generally followed practice. Moreover, and irrespective of the question of legality as such, the use of nuclear weapons remains of course legal as an act of reprisal, *i.e.*, to force the enemy to stop their use.

The difficulty of ascertaining the legality of nuclear weapons underlies the basic question of the current status of the international law of war. If it should turn out that the annihilation of millions of men, women and children in one city by one hydrogen bomb is perfectly legal, this would clearly call into question the relevance of the international law of war, which came into being to diminish the evils of war and to prevent such indiscriminate slaughter.

The uncertainty whether any of these rules are left intact is also of importance in assessing the validity of the plea of superior orders. For irrespective of the development of the theory of international law, there is a good chance that the victor in any future war fought with nuclear weapons—assuming that there will be a victor in any meaningful sense of that term—will put the political and military leaders of the defeated side on trial as war criminals. Both the United States and the Soviet Union have for years charged each other with planning aggression; the Soviet Union, at one time, branded nuclear weapons as "incompatible with the generally accepted rules, and the ideas reinforced by the common sense of humanity" and this view could be resurrected in case of need.[119] In these circumstances the Nuremberg judgment might serve as a ready-made gallows for the leaders of the vanquished; such a tribunal may not share the scruples of the United Nations after World War II, which refrained from accusing the Axis of using methods of warfare also resorted to by the Allies. In such a case, the plea of superior orders would gain added strength if it could be shown that the written and unwritten law of war, whereby the legality of orders would have to be tested, was really no longer meaningful or ascertainable. "The *mens rea* which bases criminal responsibility," writes Stone, "presupposes the accused's access to criteria of moral judgment transcending the nationalized truth of his State." [120] The moral sentiments which alone enable the individual effectively to criticize the actions of his own government and the commands of his superiors today are in a most precarious state.

---

[119] The quoted words are those of Gromyko, speaking to the United Nations Atomic Energy Commission in 1946, quoted in Phillips, *op. cit.*, p. 413.

[120] Stone, *op. cit.*, p. 329. Whether the victor will be willing to entertain this excuse remains, of course, an open question.

III. THE CRISIS IN THE LAW OF WAR

During the war of 1914–18 conventional and customary restrictions on the methods and scope of violence were put under severe strain. The Hague Conventions, generously sprinkled with expressions like "so far as possible" or "except when absolutely necessary," proved unable to stem the progress of science and technology and failed to prevent the use of new weapons like planes and flamethrowers. "Their vagueness," one writer notes appropriately, "furnished belligerents with justification at the same time that it afforded ample grounds for mutual recrimination." [121] The imposition of the Allied blockade, designed to undermine the will of the German civilian population to resist, violated at least the spirit of the Hague Conventions, which had wanted to restrict the conflict to the armed forces. Many of the more explicit prohibitions, as those relating to poison gas, were openly flouted. [122]

We have seen that in World War II the laws of war were violated on a grand scale. While some international lawyers maintain that violations as such cannot impair the validity of the law of war and lack any law-creating faculty even in the case of analogous conduct by both belligerents, [123] others speak of new law made by way of practice. Usages of war, it is conceded, have a tendency to harden into legal rules, and reprisals and counterreprisals often fulfill the function of adapting the law to changed conditions of warfare. The "sink at sight" practice of submarine warfare in World War II is a case in point. [124] Similarly, airmen were at first considered and treated as war criminals, while during World War II tactical and strategic bombardment from the air, including the bombing of centers of civilian population containing war industries, came to be accepted as legal. Indeed, the fact that the war crimes tribunals so completely failed to raise the issue of terror-bombing may amount to ratification of the practice and its absorption into the legal mode of warfare.

The invention of nuclear weapons in the context of these developments has led to the forementioned view that the law of war is now finally obsolete. The Hague Conventions are seen to be outmoded on the basis of *rebus sic stantibus,* for war no longer is waged in two dimensions only. [125] The laws of war are held to be unable to rule out

---

[121] Phillips, *op. cit.,* p. 323.

[122] *Cf.* J. W. Garner, *International Law and the World War* (London, 1920).

[123] See, *e.g.,* the discussion of aerial warfare by Alfred Verdross, *Völkerrecht* (3d ed.; Vienna, 1955), p. 397.

[124] *Cf.* Lauterpacht, *British Year Book of International Law,* XXI (1944), 76.

[125] Smith, *op. cit.,* pp. 68–69.

useful weapons decisive in securing the ends of war. The free world's lawyers, writes one observer, "must not fetter its defensive strength with restrictive doctrines which advance no goals but those of the enemy. They must recognize that if war comes, no militarily effective technique can be unilaterally abandoned without inviting suicide."[126] Indeed, in view of the decisive nature of the first blow dealt with strategic nuclear weapons, the idea of preventive or pre-emptive war has reappeared in some quarters. "There is urgent need," suggests a well-known theologian, "for a thorough moral re-examination of the basic American policy that 'we will never shoot first.' " [127]

The chaotic status of the laws of war at the present time, according to another view, calls for their revision in the form of international treaties so as to constitute legally binding rules overcoming total war. "While the statement of the law actually in force must closely follow the practice of states objectively determined, the proposals *de lege ferenda* must, as in the time of Grotius, be made in opposition to the recent practice of states." [128] This revision should aim not only at banning nuclear weapons but also other weapons of mass destruction of the so-called ABC family (atomic, bacteriological and chemical). Until the possibility of entirely banishing the scourge of war is clearly in sight, these men stress, it is of the greatest importance to make all possible efforts to reduce the sufferings, in the event of war, of both combatants and non-combatants. Even the development of the United Nations into a world government with its own police force, it is argued, would not eliminate the need for rules of war regulating the conduct of such an international instrument of peace enforcement.[129] The International Red Cross admits that many provisions of the Hague Conventions are no longer adapted to the new situations created by revolutionary developments in the methods of warfare. At the same time the Red Cross emphasizes that these regulations merely express principles of humanity, "which, in the absence of any more suitable code of rules, *are and remain valid at all times.*" [130] These principles ought to be reaffirmed and applied to the new methods of violence.

[126] Phillips, *op. cit.*, p. 397 (italics omitted).
[127] John Courtney Murray, S.J., *Morality and Modern War* (New York, 1959), p. 21, n. 2.
[128] Josef L. Kunz, "The Laws of War," *American Journal of International Law*, Vol. 50 (1956), p. 337. See also his earlier article "The Chaotic Status of the Laws of War and the Urgent Necessity of Their Revision," *ibid.*, Vol. 45 (1951), pp. 37–61.
[129] Philip C. Jessup, *A Modern Law of Nations* (New York, 1958), p. 221. See also his "Political and Humanitarian Approaches to Limitation of Warfare," *American Journal of International Law*, Vol. 51 (1957), pp. 757–761.
[130] *ICRC Draft Rules* (1958), p. 54.

The proposed revision and restatement of the laws of war met with the objection that any legal regulation of warfare on a humanitarian basis requires generally accepted criteria or standards of conduct and that these universally approved principles of humanity are today no longer clearly ascertainable. "It is essential," writes Dunbar, "not only to fix the limits at which the necessities of war ought to yield to the requirements of humanity but first of all to establish what are in fact those principles of humanity." [131] This was also the conclusion arrived at by the "Committee of Three" appointed by the Institute of International Law at its Siena session in 1951 and charged with exploring the problem of the revision of the international law of war. The Committee reported back that in its view the existing rules of warfare were largely obsolete and that, in the absence of guiding principles, any restatement of *lex lata* would be a sheer waste of time. [132]

The real problem, then, is the gulf which has opened up between the existing law of warfare, to the extent that any agreed law can be found, and what at one time were thought to be the considerations of humanity. The conscience of humanity has been confronted with saturation bombing with TNT and incendiaries, the atomic bomb, napalm. It is now in the throes of accepting the hydrogen bomb. The question which waits for an answer is: where does legal warfare end and humanity begin? When the victorious powers of World War II condemned and punished the leaders of the Axis, it was hoped that this act of retribution would create a new standard of international morality. "We are here to define a standard of conduct, of responsibility," declared the tribunal in the *Ministries Case*, "not only with regard to past and present events, but those which in the future can be reasonably and properly applied to men and officials of every state and nation, those of the victors as well as those of the vanquished." [133] This noble attempt has so far failed. Future historians, reading the Allied tribunals' eloquent denunciations of total war and German *Kriegs-raison*, may find in the subsequent record a mockery.

IV. THE DICTATES OF CONSCIENCE

Granting that most of the international law of war lies in shambles and the "dictates of the public conscience" have seemingly surren-

---

[131] Review of *U. S. Law of Land Warfare* (1956) in *British Year Book of International Law*, XXXIII (1957), 365.

[132] "La révision du Droit de la Guerre," *Annuaire de l'institut de Droit International*, XLV (1954), vol. I, pp. 555–558. The Committee was composed of Frederick R. Coudert, J. P. A. François and H. Lauterpacht.

[133] *Trials of War Criminals*, XIV, p. 527.

dered to military expediency, in his dilemma the individual will find little guidance on the level of legality. Even if he could be sure—which he cannot be—that after a nuclear war nobody will be in a position to institute war crimes proceedings against anyone, he may still be troubled by the moral question. The incertitude of the collective conscience will force him back on his own personal judgment and sense of right.

It may well be, of course, that the dilemma "to press or not to press the button" will not be felt by very many. Indeed, one of the most distressing results of the degeneration of warfare in World War II has been the loss of appreciation, on the part of many otherwise honorable people, of the distinction between right and wrong in matters of warfare.[134] Aerial warfare and, *a fortiori*, long distance missiles, have depersonalized the activity of killing and maiming. "Weapons with which the enemy can be attacked while he is at a distance," Clausewitz wrote in his treatise *On War*, "allow the feelings, the 'instinct for fighting' properly called, to remain almost at rest, and this so much the more according as the range of their effects is greater. With a sling we can imagine to ourselves a certain degree of anger accompanying the throw, there is less of this feeling in discharging a musket, and still less in firing a cannon shot." [135] Today the distance between the soldier and the horror perpetrated on his victims is even greater and the amount of feeling accompanying the infliction of death and injury correspondingly smaller. In previous ages, notes a German atomic scientist, war was dreadful because man could become a wild animal. Today's wars are dreadful because man can exterminate his fellows as easily as vermin. "Not anger but the lack of feeling is our problem." [136] The depersonalization of the destructive process, warns Stone, "may yet render the principle of humanity as archaic as the principle of chivalry may already have become." [137]

This condition of declining moral sensitivity is all the more striking in view of the impressive regard paid today to the alleviation of suffering in our domestic life, in the treatment of the sick, the poor, criminals and even animals. Here the abhorrence of cruelty and respect for the sanctity of life have increased, while the clash of ideologies in the context of revolutionary developments in the art of killing has all but done away with any sense of common humanity in relation to the "enemy." That even the enemy is composed of human

[134] *Cf.* Sack, *Lawyers' Guild Review*, Vol. 5, p. 168.
[135] Quoted in John U. Nef, *War and Human Progress: An Essay on the Rise of Industrial Civilization* (Cambridge, Mass., 1950), p. 372.
[136] Carl Friedrich von Weizsäcker, "Ethische und politische Probleme des Atomzeitalters," *Aussenpolitik*, Vol. 9 (1958), p. 305.
[137] Stone, *op. cit.*, p. 339.

beings—men, women, and children—seems to have been forgotten; today, as C. Wright Mills notes correctly, "if men are acting in the name of 'their nation' they do not know moral limits but only expedient calculations." [138] Leading statesmen have agreed that war no longer is an acceptable "instrument of policy" in the adjustment of differences between nations, that it threatens to become a horror of slaughter and destruction intolerable to any decent mind. Yet public opinion accepts the need to use the weapons of annihilation. Secretary Forrestal, during the crisis created by the Berlin blockade in 1948, was worried whether the American public, should the need arise, would permit resort to the atomic bomb. It was the unanimous agreement of a score of prominent newspaper publishers and editors, questioned by Forrestal, "that in the event of war the American people would not only have no question as to the propriety of the use of the atomic bomb but would in fact expect it to be used." [139] This acceptance of savagery as unavoidable is probably unchanged today. The equanimity with which in discussions of nuclear attacks entire metropolitan areas, if not countries, are written off is symptomatic of the same moral insensibility, of the turning of horror into morally condoned conventions of thinking.

And yet, there may be men for whom the moral dilemma will be real, who will not be content with doing their duty and imputing moral responsibility for their actions to their superiors. There may be men who, if and when faced with the consequences of the deeds they are asked to commit in the name of their nation, will want to follow the counsel of Thoreau to "be men first, and subjects afterwards." [140] Given the possibility that blind obedience to orders may lead not only to the killing of millions on the side of the enemy but may also spell the doom of one's own nation, and perhaps of mankind as such, a case could be made for the choice of disobedience even on grounds of prudence. Such loyalty to humanity might turn out to be the only meaningful national allegiance while at the same time preserving the moral integrity of the individual.

It is simple enough to point out that blind obedience is a relic of primitive man, that soldiers do not cease to be human beings, and that the best soldier is not necessarily the one who fights like a ma-

---

[138] *The Causes of World War Three* (New York, 1958), pp. 79–80.

[139] Walter Millis (ed.), *The Forrestal Diaries* (New York, 1951), p. 487, quoted in Millis, *Arms and Men: A Study in American Military History* (New York, 1958), p. 289. By 1951, Millis adds, the American public "would probably have had little hesitation in incinerating any number of Communist troops—or Communist women and babies—in the nuclear fires" (p. 299).

[140] Henry David Thoreau, "Civil Disobedience," *Walden and Other Writings* (New York, 1950), p. 637.

chine, regardless of the means and unaware of the moral meaning of victory. It is also true that no army could exist or operate if every man's personal standards of duty and morality were to prevail. The Nuremberg war criminal Jodl was right in saying "that the prosecution could thank its own obedient soldiers for being in a position to prosecute." [141] At the same time, one can find a powerful justification of the criticism of military policies on ethical grounds in the proved fallibility of the calculations of competent soldiers and statesmen. The decision to use the atomic bomb against Japan, for example, judged by the knowledge we have today of Japan's military potential in the summer of 1945, was probably a mistake. But even if the employment of the bomb spared the Allies an invasion and a bloody campaign in the main islands of Japan, a country claiming to defend the cause of freedom and the ultimate dignity of the individual human being cannot justify such a step on grounds of military strategy only. One cannot accept the argument that the shortening of a war is the supreme end without at the same time abandoning all moral restraints on the conduct of hostilities. This line of reasoning would justify not only the use of nuclear weapons but also the resort to poison gas, the dissemination of deadly germs, the torturing of prisoners, and mass killings of innocents by any other conceivable invention as long as strategists suppose they will be able to avoid the enemy's retaliation in kind. It may well be that the floodgates are already open to any atrocity that proves militarily effective. Yet who will be morally obtuse enough to deny the protest of an individual who refuses to be a party to what seems to him barbarism? Can one easily reject the eloquent plea of Sir Hartley Shawcross at the Nuremberg trials that "there comes a point where a man must refuse to answer to his leader, if he is also to answer to his conscience"? [142]

A number of religious leaders, men of diverse faiths, have argued that all-out nuclear war is not only suicidal as well as self-destructive in the sense of undermining the values we are seeking to preserve, but that it also violates absolute moral imperatives and therefore is morally wrong even if we could protect ourselves against nuclear attack. Speaking to the World Medical Congress in 1954, Pope Pius XII declared that the employment of ABC weapons, escaping from the control of man, is to be rejected as immoral: "Here it is no longer a question of defense against injustice and of the necessary safeguard of legitimate possessions, but of the annihilation, pure and simple, of all human beings within its radius of action. This is not permitted on any

---

[141] Related by Gilbert, *op. cit.*, p. 365.
[142] *Trial of the Major War Criminals Before the International Military Tribunal,* Nuremberg 14 November 1945–1 October 1946, vol. III (Nuremberg, 1948), p. 144.

account." [143] A committee set up by the World Council of Churches has concluded similarly that a military strategy contemplating the use of hydrogen bombs against urban centers violates "every element of Christian faith, hope and ethics." Christians should openly declare that such weapons should never be resorted to, and "if all out war should occur, Christians should urge a cease fire, if necessary on the enemy's terms, and resort to non-violent resistance." [144] Others have counselled against retaliation with nuclear weapons against nuclear aggression on the ground that a nuclear war of defense today is a contradiction in terms. "The truth is that this would double the enormous evil physically and morally." [145] According to George F. Kennan, "the weapon of indiscriminate mass destruction.goes farther than anything the Christian ethic can properly accept." [146]

It is clear that any unilateral renunciation of strategic nuclear weapons destroys the efficacy of the policy of deterrence and does away with the so-called "balance of terror." If one declares openly and in advance that these weapons will never be used, there is no conceivable reason for stockpiling them. The other side, then, could act as it saw fit and this might well lead to "nuclear blackmail" and ultimately defeat. Even merely to argue that, once the deterrent has failed to preserve peace, surrender is better than all-out nuclear war, weakens the effect of the deterrent, the strength of which depends on one's resolution to use it in retaliation. Yet it is probably true, as von Weizsäcker puts it, that "these bombs can protect peace and freedom only on condition that they never fall, for if they should ever fall there would remain nothing worth protecting." [147] If so, the balance of terror amounts to a gigantic game of bluff, each side threatening the other side with weapons the use of which could not serve any sane purpose. Unless the absurd immorality of a world nuclear con-

---

[143] Quoted in John Courtney Murray, S.J., "Remarks on the Moral Problem of War," *Theological Studies*, Vol. 20 (1959), p. 51.

[144] World Council of Churches, Division of Studies, *Christians and the Prevention of War in an Atomic Age—A Theological Discussion* (n.p., 1958), p. 30.

[145] Francis P. Stratmann, O.P., *War and Christianity Today*, trans. John Doebele (London, 1956), p. 57. That retaliation will not serve any positive end is fairly clear. "Rationally, of course," writes John H. Herz in his excellent study *International Politics in the Atomic Age* (New York, 1959), p. 189, "there is no 'reason' for the attacked, once his threat of retaliation has proved futile, actually to make good on his threat and retaliate; he will do so only to satisfy his 'irrational' urge for revenge." Instead of achieving the prevention of a take-over by the enemy, retaliation may well lead to counter-retaliation or even a series of desperate nuclear exchanges, which eventually may threaten human life everywhere.

[146] "Foreign Policy and Christian Conscience," *Atlantic Monthly*, May 1959, p. 47.

[147] *Aussenpolitik*, IX, 306.

flict is kept in mind and reaffirmed constantly, nations may lose the sense of restraint which today still makes nuclear arsenals a deterrent threat rather than weapons readily used. That such moral affirmations may weaken the restraints upon would-be aggressors and, therefore, encourage aggression, tyranny and immorality is another of the paradoxes inherent in the situation of mutual deterrence.

The subordinate in front of the button may have neither time nor inclination to think of all these complexities. Yet these considerations must not be ignored. The remarks of Karl Jaspers, speaking of the declaration made in 1957 by eighteen outstanding German physicists not to participate in the making of atomic weapons, are pertinent: "The personal 'No' is unassailable as long as it represents an act of conscience and therefore becomes a visible event only when others bring it before the public. It is unassailable only then when one also accepts personal responsibility for all consequences." [148] Whether all possible consequences of pressing or not pressing the button can be foreseen is doubtful. It is obvious that an individual can not restrict the effects of such a choice to his own personal life. The conscientious objector in wars past could remain faithful to the dictates of his conscience without thereby significantly influencing the outcome of the armed conflict. Today, given the potency of the new weapons, the refusal to obey on the part of a single important individual could spell a nation's defeat, though it might save the world from ruin, and so would make his decision all the more fateful. He would have to weigh the claims of the present generation against those of the future, the possibility of the adversary's world triumph against the danger of race suicide. He would have to answer the question whether any single individual should make the fateful choice for all humanity. And he might wonder what could be the justification of choosing non-existence for those who, in the years ahead, would have been born into life.

[148] *Die Atombombe und die Zukunft des Menschens: Politisches Bewusstsein in unserer Zeit* (3d. ed.; Munich, 1958), p. 274.